# A STRANGE

# A STRANGE CELESTIAL ROAD

My Time in the Sun Ra Arkestra

Ahmed Abdullah
with Louis Reyes Rivera

Blank Forms Editions
Brooklyn, New York

I have capitalized the word *Jazz* in this book for the same reason we capitalize *African American* or any other proper noun. The oppression of Africans within this country is systemic. It has been developed into an art wherein the oppressed don't even understand the nature of their oppression; in fact, oftentimes they use the words of the oppressor to gleefully define themselves. Jazz, a Music of the Spirit, is an art form where that is not allowed, because we have determined that our art form is one of liberation, and therefore we define the principles of what determines this expression of liberation culture.

    —Ahmed Abdullah

# FOREWORD

Ahmed Abdullah is an exceptionally lyrical trumpeter and musician. His is a natural approach to improvising and musical world-building. A self-avowed disciple of both Booker Little and John Coltrane, Abdullah makes music that is rich with grace and spiritual power. His legacy is built upon neither the heroic legacies of change running nor neoclassical musical idolatry, but rather on his heartfelt ability to create within a post-bop musical universe.

My own introduction to his artistry occurred in my hometown, at the 1998 Montreux-Detroit Jazz Festival. He was leading one of the Sun Ra legacy ensembles and I was playing with Henry Cook's band, which featured Cecil Brooks, the last trumpeter added to the Arkestra under Sun Ra's leadership. Once I moved to New York, I would go on to collaborate with Ahmed, both as an arranger and a performer, in his band Dispersions of the Spirit of Ra (aka Diaspora).

This memoir explains how he began playing, and traces his apprenticeship and long-term association with Sun Ra and his innovative Arkestra: We follow Ahmed's journey from his days as Leroy Bland, a kid in late-1950s Harlem acquiring his first trumpet and making forays into the mysteries of Jazz, up through his career as Abdullah, an independent bandleader and international performing and recording artist. Much like his playing itself, *A Strange Celestial Road* is free of the many clichés of Jazz biography and is the antithesis of the artist's bildungsroman.

While it is indeed a story of Mr. Abdullah's spiritual education, the book is centered around the greatness and importance of Sun Ra, to whom he is a musical disciple, and therein lies its originality. Appearing in his earthly guise as Herman Blount from Alabama, Sun Ra (officially LeSony'r Ra after 1952, following his migration to Chicago) is in fact an extraterrestrial musician who creates for the enjoyment of the Creator of the multiverse. More prosaically, Sun Ra had the distinction of forming a big band that became an institution, inviting comparison to those of Duke Ellington and Count Basie, in part because of the extraordinary longevity of the group under his direction. But Ra's importance truly lies in the vitality and originality of his music. If Ellington's band was the epitome of modern orchestration, and Basie's was the apex of modern 4/4 swing, then the Sun Ra Intergalactic Arkestra represents the zenith of postmodern experimentalism in the big-band format.

It is the special charm of this music that held the Arkestra together for decades and inspired the loyalty of world-class musicians such as Marshall Allen, Pat Patrick, and, especially, John Gilmore, whose fame as a top-tier improviser would surely have grown had he focused on his own career rather than submitting to the leadership of his guru.

I truly feel a sense of loss for those musicians who are too young to have experienced Sun Ra in person. There are no words to adequately describe his ritual multidisciplinary musical affairs, encompassing costume, dance, poetry, light shows, and more as the band whipped through the modern history of Jazz, from the stomps Sunny played with Fletcher Henderson to the intricacies of the Ellington big band, all the way to the space chords of Ra, which were products of the Black Arts movement's avant-garde expressions, radical experimentalism, and musical crying out for political and social emancipation.

○

*A Strange Celestial Road* makes an additional contribution to the Jazz bibliography, as it documents one of the most radical and least-known periods in the music: His disc- and sessionographies reveal that Abdullah was playing with a who's who of the Jazz world. In addition to Sun Ra we learn of Sam Rivers, Sirone, Billy Bang, Charles Moffett, Ed Blackwell, Vincent Chancey, and others. We now have enough evidence and perspective to know how important these musicians are to a complete understanding of the continuum of Jazz, which Abdullah calls "the Music of the

Spirit." While critics and aficionados will debate the political and perhaps even the social meanings of the music, no serious listener will disavow that its genesis is spiritual.

In a sense, this music answers existential questions. It sustains the souls of Black folk and indeed of all humanity. Both a part of modernity and a critique of its classical formulation, this music was decidedly left of center and initially, like most forms of Jazz, an underground movement—underground metaphorically, that is, as we now refer to this era's music as loft Jazz. The term refers to the independent musician-owned spaces that presented au courant performances of the new post-bop music.

Jazz historiography would now admit the loft artists into the canon: the likes of Betty Carter, Pharoah Sanders, Elvin Jones, Henry Threadgill, and many others. Then there are the musicians who ran the lofts themselves: Rivers, Hakim Jami, Rashied Ali, and Joe Lee Wilson. Ahmed Abdullah was completely in the mix both as sideman and as leader. His meticulous notes about personnel, dates, and clubs are a treasure trove for all scholars of the music.

In some ways, loft Jazz is of all forms of Jazz the least beholden to Eurocentric notions of the music—it decentered the piano, reveled in non-tempered tunings and "impure" timbres, and adopted other formal devices that changed the way we think about harmonic progression and melodic development. Thus, it was by turns ignored and maligned.

This book is a contribution toward our collective mission of getting it right. The music represents the times that produced it, embracing its young devotees' healthy skepticism toward mainstream ways of thinking and acting. These rebels of the 1970s have since produced multiple generations of artists, giving testament that the movement itself was more than a fad. Its concerns went beyond rebellion and represent an authentic artistic rendering of the complexities and breadth of human life. Just as there is pre-Bird and post-Bird, pre-Trane and post-Trane, the innovators of the loft era changed the tradition. These musical mavericks created art that was controversial, but which continues to feed and inform us to this day.

There are at least two book-length studies to be written one day on subjects that no one currently wants to touch: Jazz musicians and drug use is one, and the other is Black Jazz musicians and white women. The misperception that Jazz is immoral and the related notion that Black culture is spiritually bereft are prejudices so hurtful and so painful that insiders are reluctant to speak about the first topic. I submit that if a few people fall prey to substance abuse, there might be an argument to be made about moral failings, but if a generation succumbs, a social explanation is needed, not a moral one.

Abdullah casually discusses cocaine use in the 1980s among certain members of the Arkestra, himself included, against a social backdrop in which the federal government was complicit in the nationwide distribution of powdered and crack cocaine to Black neighborhoods.

Similarly, the question of the propensity of Black Jazz musicians to partner with white women is also a social question, and not reducible to any individual's purported rejection of Blackness or Black women. Ahmed describes both of these volatile situations without moralizing and with minimal explanation. The Ahmed of this memoir is a polyamorous musician who had no compunctions about exploring the erotic dimension of his life as a peripatetic performer, often resulting in his having multiple sexual partners at any given time. The careful reader may notice that these erotics are also related to the *economy* of the itinerant musician. Another insight is that the prevalence of white partners had also to do with the removal of the music's primary residence from Black communities to "white" commercial spaces. Perhaps this memoir will be read by that brave soul who decides to research these phenomena in depth.

Black readers will no doubt either laugh or grimace as we read of Ahmed's dalliances with white women (who were financially and administratively involved in his career) while he was in loving relationships with Black women who were politically progressive at a time when racial solidarity was a political desideratum. His past behavior is certainly not unusual for musicians; what *is* unusual in this narrative is that he makes no attempt to sanitize the unsavory aspects of his behavior. Tellingly, there is also no recourse to the mythos of the "pimp" found in the Jazz brotherhood, and even in canonical biographies of such prominent Jazzmen as Miles Davis and Charles Mingus.

The feminist perspectives he learned as he matured guide Ahmed's discussion of his interactions with women, especially with those with whom he had children. Coming of age at a time when Black women were launching a profound critique of gender oppression and its intersections with racist practices, Abdullah had the benefit of Black feminist literature's insights at a time when these ideas were first being widely discussed.

His education in feminism was cemented at the steadfast insistence of his wife, Monique Ngozi Nri. It was his marriage and his commitment to Buddhism that provided the spiritual space for him to combat the masculinist tendencies that inundate the Jazz world, from dating to improvisational styles. And it's his spiritual practice and family life that guide Abdullah's present musical activity, in the group NAM, composed of Buddhist musicians, and his group Diaspora, which features Monique as poet and vocalist.

I remember one instance of his Music of the Spirit most keenly: While I was playing with Diaspora, along with baritone saxophonist Alex Harding, trombonist Craig Harris, bassist RaDu ben Judah, drummer Codaryl Moffett, guitarist Masujaa, Bang on violin, and Monique and Louis Reyes Rivera as poets, the spirit was so high during one of Harris's solos that Craig pulled his instrument from his mouth and began shouting as he slammed his hand into a wall. It was a moment of musical intensity and spiritual ecstasy. Surely this is art, music, to accompany a celestial journey.

Salim Washington
Durban, South Africa
2022

# INTRODUCTION

Aarburg, Switzerland, March 29, 1992: A train depot of a town. We have just arrived from Germany, where we performed in Dresden, Jena, and Leipzig. "The hotel is right across the street," someone says. "If you look straight ahead, you can't miss it."

The town is in a valley surrounded by mountains. "Are these the Alps?" I ask, of no one in particular. Most of the fellows in the band are preoccupied with moving their equipment from the train station to the hotel lobby. As I walk to the hotel, I turn right and look up to the mountains and notice the castle built into them. Its majesty reminds me of a castle I'd seen before in Edinburgh, while traveling with the Sun Ra Arkestra. A man-made structure etched into the fiber of rock and crevice, making it appear as if mountain and castle were one. Nature and man forging a common image.

The hotel lobby's wooden decor makes you feel at home immediately. For me, it's a rare pleasure to be in a comfortable dwelling while on the road. We're to wait in the lobby until all the rooms are ready. While in the relaxed and laid-back setting of this area, I receive a page for a long-distance call from London, where the new love in my life, Monique Ngozi Nri, is living. It's her birthday today. I intended to call her as soon as I had settled into my room. It's great to hear her voice, a blend of the Nigerian, Barbadian, and British backgrounds from which she'd been raised. I notice a hesitancy in her voice as I wish her happy birthday. While on the phone I am given my room key, and she suggests I might want to go to my room, as she has something important to tell me. What she was to say would weaken me at the knees, deliver a punch against which I had no defense.

"Are you sitting down?" she asks.

"Why do I need to sit down?"

"I couldn't reach you for the last couple of days. There was no way to contact you in East Germany. I don't know how to tell you this but . . . Ahmed, your mother passed away."

I say nothing. Then, "Oh, no!" Twelve days before, on St. Patrick's Day, just as the Arkestra was to leave from New York, I made a special trip at Monique's insistence to visit my parents. On my way to the airport, I stopped by to say hello and to give them some photos Monique had taken when she last visited New York during the Christmas holidays. It was the last time I would see my mother alive.

After hanging up the phone, I somehow manage to find Sun Ra's room to tell him I want to cut the tour short due to these unexpected circumstances. Sitting in his wheelchair, he says little these days in comparison to years gone by. His condition now is one that makes me deeply anxious, as it has created a profound new relationship between us. My mentor, my musical and sometimes spiritual teacher, the person who could talk to me for hours on any subject known and unknown to man, woman, or angel, is now someone I only play music with. His illness has given me an overwhelming sense of impending loss. Sun Ra had taught us for many years that we had to do the impossible, which, he said, was to give up death, our ownership of it, our submission to it. His philosophy was about expanding possibilities, of envisioning cities without cemeteries. It was a philosophy of eternal things and immeasurable equations.

Now, faced with the reality of my own dilemma, I realize that philosophy means little to me, and the person who could have best explained it and walked me through this moment of extreme personal tragedy is unavailable. He has nothing to say, about death or about my early departure from the tour.

I leave his room and walk outside to be in the open air. I need sunlight and nature's beauty. I turn left, walking toward the castle in the mountains. I can't hold back the tears streaming down my face amid the pathways and beautiful flowers. I walk across a footbridge heading to the castle, wondering how such a structure could be built into a mountain. It's peaceful here, yet I'm lost and abandoned. In some ways, I knew I should be in control, but I had no full understanding of what was transpiring and its impact on my life. We were to record on this night, and it would be Sun Ra's last recording, appropriately called *Destination Unknown*.

The part of me that trained to play music tells me I must somehow get a grip. I convince myself I can do it. After a mile along this road I look right up at this castle. I stand before it for a few minutes and take in its ancient beauty, then head back to the hotel. One of my good buddies, Jothan Callins, trumpeter and bassist with the Arkestra, is heading in my direction. He has heard and tries to say something comforting. I feel no comfort. His well-intentioned sympathy only makes the waterfall of tears spill again.

Later that evening, I find my way to the bandstand and perform. I can concentrate on the music, but once the show is over, I leave my newly purchased Besson trumpet right where I was sitting onstage. After the gig, I find myself hanging out with brass-section mates Michael Ray and Tyrone Hill and drinking myself into a state of unconsciousness.

In the morning, I get up, pack, and get on the band bus, never even realizing I'm leaving my horn. I consider myself fortunate to be among friends in this Sun Ra Arkestra. Someone has seen to it that my instrument was packed and placed on the bus. I sit on the bus, put my face in my hat, and cry for what seems like several hours. In two days, I will return to New York on the first available flight from Munich, after the gig we were to do at a club called the Allotria. Monique will fly to New York from London to be at my side. She's the one who tells me to deal with this pain and go view my mother in her coffin. She helps me realize what true friendship is. Two weeks later, I marry my friend.

The pain of my mother's death, the joy of my twin sons' birth, the meeting of my wife, and my adoption of Buddhism as a way of life all specifically connect to my tenure with the Arkestra. I had gradually begun to understand the profundity of my relationship to Sun Ra.

During the last European tour with the Arkestra and before my mother's departure, I had started a campaign designed to make my fellow band members more aware of the need to assume responsibility in view of Sun Ra's debilitating condition. Out of that campaign came the concept for Satellites of the Sun, a concert series designed to show the leadership potential in the Arkestra. Sun Ra was still in human form when this concept was being worked on. His last years on the planet were just as purposeful and instructive as his earlier years, but the lessons now required more than our passive attention. To "give up one's death," to overcome it, was to achieve greatness by rising above pain and fear with courage.

Sunny had demonstrated this by defying earthly medical opinions, making his last tours in a wheelchair. Was he attempting to inspire the Arkestra members out of our condition of Earthritis?

The Satellites of the Sun concept finally did inspire an ill John Gilmore to take on the leadership of the Arkestra once Sun Ra had made his departure. Gilmore was somehow able to hold on as leader of the Arkestra until May 1995, at which point he was too weak to continue and passed the baton to Marshall Allen. During Gilmore's tenure as leader, the Arkestra was less active, almost to the point of invisibility. Monique and I would attempt once more, in November 1995, to jump-start the Arkestra to do more work while the band was under Marshall Allen's leadership. We produced fifteen concerts at a place called Context on Manhattan's Lower East Side. These concerts drew the loyal fans, and the Arkestra was presented as a viable entity even without Sun Ra's corporeal presence.

The concerts ended in June 1996, when the Arkestra failed to show for a monthlong series of scheduled concerts. It took a year of healing before I was ready to work again with the band. The opportunity came in May 1997, at the Moers Festival in Germany. I had learned from past mistakes that, although my help was needed, it would not be appreciated. I worked behind the scenes to help ensure the success of our first European tour since 1992. One of the things I did was bring the brilliant baritone saxophonist

Alex Harding into the fold. His sound was in the tradition of the greats like Pat Patrick and Charles Davis, neither of whom was available for this mini-tour. I was given every indication by the results of this performance that the teachings of Sun Ra, if understood and adhered to by the surviving members of the Arkestra, could make as serious an impact on the rest of the world as it did on the audience at Moers.

Before we made our entrance, we formed a circle, held hands, and invoked the name of Ra. The audience's reaction, after the encore, was completely without precedent. For three hours after we finished playing, people were singing our closing number. When one of the musicians went out to retrieve his horn, he almost caused a riot.

The Arkestra had been built on the fundamental principle of brotherhood. Sun Ra was an advanced spiritual being who created a family of musicians who were supposed to work together to encourage spiritual growth and development. His music was intended to prepare us for the coming millennium. To grow spiritually means to empower one's self in order to work through pain and fear, to take on personal responsibility.

July 29, 1997: I had gone to John F. Kennedy Airport to meet Monique, who was just coming back from a trip to England visiting family. While waiting for her plane to land, I felt like having an ice-cream sandwich. I decided I had too many quarters in my pocket, so I put eight of them in the machine. The ice-cream sandwich came out along with every quarter in the vending machine. Swarms of people came around and helped me collect the quarters rolling around the floor of the waiting area. I filled my pockets and left the rest to the delight of all concerned. While waiting for Monique, I counted the quarters and pondered the significance of this unusual event. I had forty-three quarters ($10.75) in my pockets, a sure sign from the Creator, though I didn't quite understand it at the time. The events of the next two weeks would clarify this message.

At a picnic in Brooklyn's Prospect Park sponsored by Sisters and Allies, Be Present, an organization Monique belonged to, I engaged in an intense conversation with Robert Roth, writer and copublisher of a unique literary magazine *And Then*. I expressed my feelings about the John Szwed Sun Ra biography, *Space Is the Place*, which I had recently read. I also spoke about the connection I had seen between the Szwed book and two others, *Troubles I've Seen* on the life of Bayard Rustin by Jervis Anderson, and *Lush Life* on the life of Billy Strayhorn by David Hajdu. Robert convinced me to write an article for his magazine. The essay is a comparative study of the three books. I was already aware of much of Szwed's information on Sun Ra, but the process of writing it helped me see the larger mission. The next day, August 3, 1997, while on another picnic, I began writing the article "Sun Ra, Bayard Rustin and Billy Strayhorn."

The Szwed book made good reading, but I was especially troubled by its last chapter, which seemed to disregard the importance of the final quarter of Sun Ra's life. The mid-1970s happens to have been when I joined the Arkestra and coincides with the beginning of Ra's most successful period. Also, the Loft Movement of the 1970s, one of the most misrepresented and oft-neglected eras of Jazz, was once again being left out of a book dealing with the music.

The message I got from the incident at JFK a few days before began to make sense: 10 + 7 + 5 = 22, exactly the number of years I was involved with Sun Ra and the Arkestra. From that experience, there was abundance in my life. The ease with which I was able to recall events and the writing of the article took me deep into my being, where other clues and connections began to manifest. These clues were metaphysical in nature and indicated that a circle was about to be completed. It was time for me to share the wealth I had been given.

Sun Ra has been called the prophet of the planet, a master of the Music of the Spirit. He said he was sent here by the Creator.

It makes sense to me that if the Creator would send anyone here, it would be a person who had mastered music, the planet's universal language. Sound is the beginning of all creation, the Nommo, the Om, and the Nam that direct our lives, the basis for what Sun Ra called a Sound Government.

# I
# THE CALL

> It's not easy to play in this band because there's certain stuff you have to have. You have to belong, you have to be rated by Superior Beings as suitable, and if you're not rated . . . I be telling everybody, it's not my band. It's the Creator's band, and if they're not suitable for the future, they won't be fit for the present.
> —Sun Ra

The call never seems to come when I expect, but it always comes when it's supposed to. This one came on a Sunday morning in April 1975. I was in bed with Iyabode, who was pregnant with what would turn out to be our twin sons. She answered the phone. I'll never forget the incredulous way she handed it to me, as if the Creator Him/Herself were on the other end.

She whispered, while cupping the phone with one hand, "Ahmed, it's Sun Ra!" This was pretty amazing to me as well. I tried to calm myself enough to say hello. The voice on the other end was deliberate, matter-of-fact, and very Southern. Somehow, I knew that in the years to come, I would become quite familiar with it.

"This is Sun Ra. I been trying to get ahold of you."

I could feel an intense sense of excitement running through me. Sun Ra has been trying to find me? In 1975, in New York City, and especially in Brooklyn, where we lived, Sun Ra was *it.* They didn't come any bigger. At least not in the music known as Jazz. In the more than ten years since Sun Ra had migrated to New York from Chicago, he had made his presence thoroughly known.

He had become a folk hero in the Black community, especially among people who considered themselves aware of African American culture. Iyabode and I were among those people. I had met Iyabode, born Cheryl Taylor, about three years before, when our destinies literally collided on Sixth Avenue and Eighth Street in Greenwich Village. She was working for a jeweler on Third Street known as Dar El-Sudan and I was coming from a rehearsal with my horn in its case. The handle on my case snapped just as I bumped into her. She was the most attractive woman I had ever seen! She had her head completely shaved in an East African style and she wore beautiful silver hoop earrings. We began a conversation that resulted in our going on a date that evening, December 9, 1972, to hear the Freddie Hubbard band at the Beacon Theatre on the Upper West Side. Our two children were the result of that fateful meeting.

Sun Ra had rendered himself a unique artist by owning his own record label and publishing company, as he did. His independence was both an asset and a hindrance. The asset was that he played where he wanted, how he wanted, with and for whom he wanted; the hindrance was a lack of recognition. So in the early 1970s, when Sunny (as he was called) and his business partner Alton Abraham had licensed ABC-Paramount's Impulse! Records to distribute several of their 1950s recordings (which up to that point had been modestly available), things began to change. Sun Ra was well on his way to becoming a major international star. By 1975, when I received the call, he was already there.

When I hung up the phone on that Sunday in April, I immediately turned to face a person whose bright eyes revealed the same mixture of surprise and joy I was experiencing. The potential birth of our sons, moreover, endowed Iyabode's ebonic skin with a radiance reserved for those who bring forth the young. She had been favored by the Creator, who appeared not to want any to be unaware of this fact. She had been blessed with full lips and a nose just flat enough, along with almond-shaped eyes and an elongated neck that gave her an aura of royalty (I had written a song for her called "Ebony Queen"). The pregnancy had affected her in another interesting way: She had lost weight everywhere except in her stomach. Her shoulders had become so thin she looked almost undernourished. It was as if all of her food went to the babies while making her stomach seem incredibly huge. A moment ago, she had been trying to hear my conversation with Sun Ra by putting her chin on my shoulder. Now she wanted a report.

"Ahmed, was that really Sun Ra? What'd he want?"

"Yes, it was really him," I said.

"Well, what'd he want?" she repeated excitedly.

"He wants me to play with him."

"Where?" she asked.

"Here in Brooklyn, at the East."

"At the East! When?"

"He didn't say exactly when, but it seems like it's gonna be sometime this month. He said he wants me to come to Philadelphia to rehearse with him."

"To Philadelphia?" I could feel her enthusiasm dimming. "I thought you promised that you wouldn't go out of town until the babies were born."

"I know I did, sugar, but it's only going to be for a day and the babies aren't due until next month. And besides, this means I can earn a little extra money. I could probably earn more in a night than I do in a week working at that copying job." This seemed to reanimate her and bring back some of her initial joy.

"Ahmed," she said, as if she were thinking out loud, "you know, I never really thought that Sun Ra called people. I always thought he'd simply transport himself into somebody's living room."

"Yeah, Yabo, I can dig it. But you know, I'm just happy he called me."

I was so happy about the call, in fact, that I hadn't been completely honest with Iyabode about it. I happened to have noticed a few weeks back that Sun Ra and the Arkestra were going to play in Brooklyn. Sun Ra, however, had not mentioned the gig. I didn't even know whether he actually wanted me to play with the band. All he said on the phone was how he had gone about getting my number from someone in Brooklyn, and that he wanted me to come to Philadelphia to rehearse. Philadelphia is ninety miles from New York. Iyabode and I had two children on the way. I had a job copying documents at night in an office building in downtown Manhattan, yet I didn't think that what I was being asked to do was crazy.

A few days later, I received another call from Sun Ra. This time I was told that money would be sent to me through Western Union, and with that money I could purchase a round-trip ticket to Philadelphia. I was told that, upon arrival, I would be met at the train. Early Friday morning, I set out for Philadelphia with horn in hand.

I was met at the North Philly station by Pico, aka Danny Thompson. Pico had one of those 1960s Fleetwood Cadillacs; it was a funky limo with a different kind of style.

The Cadillac is the people's luxury car. There appeared to be lots of room in the front. The back of the car was laden with records. I stood looking at Pico before getting in.

He was my height, about six feet, a light cream-colored complexion, with glasses and a head full of hair. He was neatly dressed in black turtleneck and dark-colored slacks with some hip-looking Italian boots to match. I pulled the door and noticed it was locked. As he walked around to the passenger side and unlocked the door, I noticed that his tongue was hanging from the corner of his mouth, giving him the appearance of someone preoccupied in thought. We had met a couple of times before; in fact, I'm sure it was Pico whom Sun Ra had alluded to in his mysterious way when he claimed he got my number from someone in Brooklyn.

"Damn, man, I forgot to open it. But the lock's been giving me some trouble lately, anyway. How was your trip?"

"It was cool, man."

"I got to remember to pick up some graphite."

"Graphite?"

"Yeah, for the lock. You been down here before, right?"

"Yeah, but I never really spent any time here."

"Oh yeah, that's right. I remember when you worked in Vernon Park, here in Germantown. You're lucky; at least you *were* lucky, because they got you now."

We were now riding away from the North Philadelphia station and I was seeing a little more of the city that had initially appeared to me from the train as some huge industrial plant.

"What do you mean by *they*?" I asked.

"The Forces, man. Ain't you hip to the Forces? It's the Forces that got us down here from New York. Sunny wouldn't have left New York if it wasn't for the Forces. But once they get hold of you, man, you can just forget it."

"I guess you're not from Philly then," I said.

"No, man. I'm from California. That's how I got the name Pico, because I come from Pico Boulevard. Marshall gave me that name, and when Marshall names you, that's it!" He was referring to Marshall Allen, the multi-instrumentalist and longtime member of the Arkestra. Pico's statement implied an appreciation that seemed to convey more than one would normally associate with a nickname.

"Is Marshall going to be at the rehearsal today?" I noticed Pico doing the thing again with his tongue out of the corner of his mouth.

"Yeah, man. Everybody's supposed to be there."

"Who's everybody?" I asked, thinking of John Gilmore, while hoping not to give away my boyish idolization.

"Well, let's start with the boss. Sunny's definitely going to be there." It was Sun Ra's house that we were rehearsing at. "John lives at the house as well as Jacson and Eloe, so they're going to be there."

I got my answer without directly asking the question. John Gilmore would be at the rehearsal! As we were talking, I noticed that we had come to a street with a row of greenish-gray brick houses on the passenger side.

"This is it, man. This is Morton Street." Just as he said this, we pulled up to another light-cream-complexioned man with a beard and straight hair tied in a ponytail that extended past his leather cap. He too was neatly dressed, but with a frown on his face as he saw the car approaching the curb. Pico asked me to pull the window down.

"Hey, Dep, what's going on? I was going to stop by to pick you up," Pico yelled across me.

"Man, you know I got all these instruments and things. But I can't be waiting for you all day. You be slowing around, and I'll be the one to get the fire. Sunny said the rehearsal was at twelve, and it's already one, and I ain't had nothing to eat yet. I'm hungry!" All this was said as if in one sentence, with a rhythm that exposed the speaker's musicality and a twang that gave away his Kentucky roots.

"Yeah, man, I was going to pick you up, but Sunny told me I had to go down to the station to pick up the new trumpet man. Dep, this is Ahmed. You remember when he played over in the park last year with Ronnie, Roger, and them?"

"Hey, what's happenin'? I'm Marshall." The frown suddenly disappeared and warmth and beauty of déjà vu began to characterize this meeting, as it would the rest of the day. Marshall Allen (nicknamed Dep, an abbreviation for deputy) was the oldest member of the Arkestra. He had become a member of the band after John Gilmore and Pat Patrick. These three saxophonists had been around since Sun Ra had begun his space concept in the mid-1950s and were most closely identified with him. Neither Marshall nor Pat lived at 5626 Morton Street, as some of the other band members did. The house on Morton Street had been given to Sun Ra by Marshall's father.

Pico turned to Marshall and said, "Look here, Dep, if you wait, I'll come back and take you to get something to eat, because I need to get something myself. You know once we start rehearsing, that's it."

We walked into the house, with Pico leading the way through a small entrance and then turning left to enter the living room.

"Sunny, I was looking all over the train station, but I couldn't find that cat nowhere. Did he call?" Pico asked.

Sun Ra was seated at the piano, playing and writing, facing the entrance to the living room. I was standing directly behind Pico, whose frame prevented Sun Ra from seeing me immediately but allowed me a view of the space, which resembled a museum. There was music manuscript paper, music stands, paintings, instruments strewn all over.

"Danny, I keep telling you: You got to get with the Space Age. Now you supposed to be my right-hand man. But you keep on, and you are going to be left out. This ain't no time for you to be acting like no earthling. And furthermore . . ."

Pico moved out of the way with a body language that said, "Surprise," which stopped Sun Ra mid-sentence. The chastising mode he was about to get into turned into a smile of recognition and a warm Space Age greeting. I had not seen him for a while.

Sunny was a round dark-brown being with eyes that were small but looked as if they missed nothing. His face was one that would draw you to it in a crowd for no known reason, but you would definitely be comforted after seeing it. He always gave me the impression that he knew even more than I gave him credit for knowing, and that was already a lot.

"How're you doing, Sun Ra?" I asked.

"I'm trying. What's the latest news from New York?" he asked.

"I don't know about New York in general, but in my household, we're about to have twin boys."

Pico had pulled his prank and was off to some other duty or mischief. I was left alone in the room with Sun Ra. "When are they due?"

"Well, they're supposed to come in May."

"If they come in May, then they'll be May sons. That's what I am, you see, a Son of May, because my arrival day is May 22."

"Oh yeah. I dig. Then I'm a Son of May, too."

"When is your arrival day?"

"I was born May 10."

"See, now I got to get you over into an understanding of Space, because when you know about Space, you won't be talking about being born and dying and all that sort of Earth stuff. You'll understand about arrivals and departures."

The colors in the room, like the colors of his clothes and conversation, were too much to take in at one time. I had once visited his house on New York's Lower East Side many years ago and was well aware that entering his presence was not an ordinary act. He had an artist's sensitivity to color schemes that would look totally out of place on the average person, but that fit him perfectly.

I took out my horn and began to warm up. I had been practicing for hours every day since his call. Sun Ra, John Gilmore, Pat Patrick, and Marshall Allen had reputations for being consummate musicians.

"Do you know any standards?"

"Sure, I know some."

"Do you know this one?" He handed me the sheet music for a composition called "At Sundown."

"No. I never heard it before."

"Can you read it?"

"Sure. Do I play it as written?"

"No, you got to transpose. Ready? About like this." He counted it off. It was a melody that sounded like one I had heard before, just as this scene felt like one I had experienced before. In its Tin Pan Alley form, the obscure song was recognizable. I would find out that Sun Ra had a storehouse of songs like this, standards of another era, tunes like "I Dream Too Much," "I Struck a Match on the Moon," or "Cocktails for Two."

After Sun Ra had ascertained that I could transpose and read fairly well, he seemed to choose more difficult compositions and much faster tempos. Then we started working on his original compositions. One, called "October," had a haunting melody, as did "Halloween in Harlem." The songs "Velvet" and "El Is a Sound of Joy" were others we rehearsed. Both of them were familiar to me from Sun Ra albums I had heard.

"Okay, you got an idea of that?" We went over a composition a few times and then went to another one. We rehearsed by ourselves for maybe an hour or more. It was an intense exercise in focus and concentration. Sun Ra would often be playing different harmonies underneath whatever melodic line I was given.

"I'm trying to catch you up to the others," he said. "You got to be ready when you play with this band. Sometimes, the harmony might have to be real odd and strange and totally different from the melody. It might have to be, if that's the message. If the harmony is what it is according to what they teach in schools and things, then it wouldn't be any other message than what they've been hearing all along. But when the harmonies move in a direction that they *seemingly* are not supposed to move in and still fit, you got another message from another realm from somebody else, and Superior Beings would definitely speak in other harmonic ways because they're talking to something different. You have to have chord against chord, melody against melody, and rhythm against rhythm. When you have that, you're expressing something else."

Out of all he said, the part that had the most resonance was about my having to catch up to the rest of them. To me, that indicated I had passed the test and was being groomed to play in the Arkestra.

As I was thinking this, the powerful and yet unobtrusive form of John Gilmore appeared from somewhere in the house. John came over to me and said, "What's happening, Ahk?"

I had never formally met John before, but I had listened to him for years. The fact that he not only knew my name but had given me a nickname upon our first meeting left me even more in awe of him. John Gilmore had played or recorded with some of my favorite trumpet players: Thad Jones, Lee Morgan, and Freddie Hubbard. The great John Coltrane had said in print that he listened to Gilmore before he recorded *Chasin' the Trane*.

John was as thin and tall as Sun Ra was round. Their eyes gave away the fact that they were kindred spirits. John's face was elongated and brown. He had a head, if you could ever see it, shaped like an enlarged pecan. He usually wore a hat.

"Sunny, I think this one's going to work. The cat I bought it from said he'd give me my money back if it didn't."

"John, when are you going to stop giving these people your money?" Sunny asked. "It's like they see you coming."

"But look, Sunny, it's already growing back." John said this while raising his hat and pointing to the spot to show that the hair tonic had miraculously done its job. What I saw when he took off his hat was a head, with hair only around the rim. John, however, was insistent that he had received the desired result.

"We've got to catch Abdullah up on some of the stomps and things, John." That seemed to end the hair discussion. John took out a bag of music that easily had a couple of hundred songs in it and began leafing through them.

"Let's go over 'Images,'" Sunny said, as he pointed to one of the lead sheets in front of me. "You can read it off of there. Ready. One!" With Sunny you rarely got to hear *two*. The sound of John's tenor playing in a speechlike interpretation of the melody was moving. The melody was simple. It was in 4/4 time. I read along as John played. It started with a quarter-note concert C down to a B-flat eighth note and then an eighth-note G tied to a quarter-note G, and then rest one beat. The next measure started on concert G, an eighth note tied to a dotted quarter note followed by a G eighth note on the upbeat of three on to a concert E and D, eighth notes on the fourth beat of that measure. If you looked at the manuscript, you might have thought the song was in E-flat concert, but the way Sun Ra played, tonal centers weren't really important.

Sunny was laying down the harmonic cushion on his old upright piano. The phrasing was the thing. John had an ability to get inside a song and make it completely his own. I paid close attention to his phrasing, which I finally thought I'd heard well enough to match my sound with. So I joined in. This was a moment of absolute delight. John Gilmore, the great John Gilmore who had even impressed the great John Coltrane, is rehearsing alongside of *me*! And Sun Ra is on the piano! These legends played with such hypnotic beauty that their solos can sometimes leave your mouth open in amazement. They did mine.

When John picked up his horn, it was as if a clarion call had sounded throughout the house and neighborhood. Slowly, others began (as if by some mystical communication) to appear. James "Jack" Jacson walked in, bassoon and flute in hand. Jack, dark complexioned and bearded, exuded his military background. He came in promptly as if ordered and quickly found his spot. He was about six feet tall, hair cut short, and rarely smiled.

"Y'all got to get yourselves together," Sunny stated firmly. "You know I represent the Creator of the Universe. And the Creator is always on time. I called rehearsal for twelve, and here it is almost three and some of y'all ain't got it together yet."

"I'm sorry, Sunny. I had to go and get some reeds," Jacson explained.

"Where's Marshall and that Eloe and Ebah? Y'all always be talking about you ain't got this and you ain't got that. And when it's time to rehearse so we can get something, I can't find you. Now Danny, he knows he supposed to be back here by now. He done picked Abdullah here up at the station and gone off somewhere. And that Ebah, he's going to keep on missing my rehearsals until he finds himself right out of this band. It don't matter that he's got the trumpet music. I'll write all new arrangements. I'm tired of waiting on folks."

It was hard to tell at this point whether it was John's sound or Sun Ra's reprimand that brought people into the room. But into the room they came. Marshall walked in; this time the frown had gone. Marshall, like Sun Ra, was a Gemini, and the other side of his personality, the Trickster, was on display.

"You got to play some of them paradiddles and ratamacues on your ax?" Marshall asked me, and without waiting for an answer, he turned to Gilmore. "Did you sweeten him up, John?"

It was at this moment that Eloe Omoe walked into the room. He had apparently just come in from outside and he did not have his instrument. Marshall turned toward the entrance and heralded his presence. "Oooh, look out now! Here's Eloe! What's happening, Eee-loe?"

"Dep, you got another square?" Jacson asked, pointing to the cigarette dangling from the corner of Marshall's mouth.

"I bet you didn't even know we got us a new trumpet man," Marshall said to Eloe as he reached for his pack of Shermans, handing one to Jacson. Eloe left the room as quickly as he'd come in.

"Hey, Dep, let me get one too," John said.

Sun Ra was observing all that was going on in the room. He then spoke, seemingly to no one in particular, but everyone listened.

"The one thing that the people of planet Earth don't have is discipline. Now, I know I was sent here to demonstrate what has never been done before, and that is to show that a group of Black people could actually stick together and create something of beauty for the Creator. It's a difficult job, and the only way it can be done is if folks begin to respect leaders. Y'all got to learn how to play follow-the-leader. Now we got a job to do; we are going to play for some Black folks in Brooklyn. We played there before. They respect what we do. We may not make no whole lot of money and things playing there, but they respect what we do and that means, fellows, that we got to rehearse this music."

Eloe walked back into the room, this time with his bass clarinet. He looked as if he could be Jack Jacson's brother. They were the same complexion and height, and they also shared an expertise in martial arts. Eloe smiled more easily than Jacson, revealing gorgeous white teeth and a deep dimple in both cheeks. "What's happening, Sunny?" Eloe greeted, as he placed his bass clarinet on its stand and found his spot. Marshall handed a cigarette to John and started fingering the pads of his horn.

"Just waiting on Eloe to get himself together," Sun Ra said while making notations on the lead sheet in front of him. He then looked up at Eloe to make the point. "We got a guest who came all the way from New York, and we got a job to do, and y'all just be slowin' around."

"Ain't nobody told me about no job," Eloe retorted with a sharpness that implied more than what was stated. "As usual, I get blamed for everything, but don't nobody tell me nothin'." Eloe's voice had a real deep resonance. He spoke with a different kind of Southern accent. It was the kind one often hears up south in Detroit or Chicago. He was from the latter. He had belonged to a gang and had been sent to Sun Ra by Alton Abraham, obviously for some sort of reform. He didn't seem to have complete reverence for Sun Ra.

"Hey, what's happening, man?" Eloe said, turning to me. Just as quickly, he asked, "You from New York, right? Yeah, I remember when you played over in the park. They were pretty mean, weren't they, John?" Eloe's tone had changed dramatically in addressing John and myself.

"Yeah, y'all were really taking care of business. What's that tenor player doing? He was playing some different shit, man," John said.

"You mean Charles Brackeen? He *is* really bad. I haven't seen him in a while. Because, you know, the band broke up."

It was all making a little more sense to me. The gig I had played in Philadelphia almost a year ago with a group called the Melodic Art-Tet had obviously affected this band of rugged individuals. Most of the guys in the Arkestra, including Sun Ra, had come out to hear us. Half of our group on that occasion had been former members of the Arkestra.

"How about Blank? You seen him lately?" Jacson asked. Musicians are primarily concerned about instrumentalists of like kind. Jacson played the big log drum as well as the bassoon and flute and was alluding to drummer Roger Blank.

"I see Roger every now and then," I answered.

"I knew that Ronnie Boykins wasn't going to make it when we came from Chicago," Sun Ra added. "When you be playing music for the Creator, you can't be messing with all them drugs and white women and things. It slows you down. Keeps you playing this Earth music. You see, I'm talking about eternal things."

Sunny said this apropos of nothing, as if he were speaking to himself. Ronnie Boykins was a bassist and longtime member of the Arkestra who had gone to New York with Sun Ra in the early 1960s. He was also a member of the Melodic Art-Tet.

By now, Pico had come back from whatever he had been doing and was pulling out his baritone sax. We were about to have a fuller band rehearsal. We had arranged ourselves in a circle facing Sun Ra. On his left was Marshall Allen; next to Marshall was Jack Jacson. Pico had moved into the area between Eloe and Jack. John had set up to the left of the living room entrance on the opposite side of Marshall and Sunny. I was sitting right next to Sun Ra.

Once again, "Images" was called by Sunny. Now I was playing this melody with John, and I could hear how rich the inner voices were as played by the other horns. There was a velvet tapestry of sounds. It was exciting to hear my horn in this ensemble. Sun Ra motioned me to play by moving his fingers the way I would on the trumpet. And, charged with the duty of improvising for this group of seasoned veterans, I tried to play everything I knew in one solo. Gilmore played a brief solo after me that wiped me out completely.

We went over "El Is a Sound of Joy." The melody's first eight measures alternated between whole tones and half notes. The fact that Sun Ra was eclectic as an arranger and composer allowed me to recognize his style from the recordings I had heard. Now I was in the midst of it. The baritone, bassoon, and bass clarinet combination was a rare one, providing depth and a powerful anchor to the celestial. Once again, Sunny motioned me to play. Now I was given a bluesy rhythmic vamp to improvise on. After a much briefer solo this time (I learned quickly), the melody was taken out as it came in, almost rubato, robbed of tempo.

Sun Ra called his musicians "tone scientists." He was obviously looking for and found something unique in orchestral voicing. Whether it was John or Marshall playing a lead line, the individualism of their sounds mixed with the strange and beautiful compositions of Sun Ra left my head reeling. We went on rehearsing for several hours, going over many compositions. Pico reminded Sun Ra that he had to take me back to the train station. Sunny nodded yes, but found another hour's worth of music to go over.

Somehow, the rehearsal ended. Sun Ra sat back on the piano stool and I began to pack up my horn. The other players started getting their music together and putting their horns back in their cases. It was a good first rehearsal. I said my goodbyes to the band as Pico and I went out the door, headed for the train station. We got in Pico's car. "El Is a Sound of Joy" was still going on in my head, and I felt as if something had profoundly changed in my life as a result of this experience.

"I'm going to take you down to Thirtieth Street Station, because I don't really know the schedule for trains going back to New York," he said.

"You know what time it is?" I asked.

"Yeah, let's see. It's twenty after nine."

"Damn, man, I didn't realize it was that late. It didn't seem like the rehearsal was so long."

"It wasn't. That was a quickie, man. Sometimes we be rehearsing until three or four in the morning," Pico replied, and then asked with a smile, "Hey, man, you hip to a coolie?"

"Naw. What's a coolie?"

"A coolie is a quickie in the snow." The two of us laughed even beyond the humor of the joke. We laughed so hard that Pico had to pull over. Tears welled up in my eyes and I was holding my stomach. I felt like I was going to wet my pants. This wasn't about the joke. It was about how good I was feeling. About how good this music and this day had made me feel. Finally, the emotion subsided and I suddenly felt a real closeness to this person named Danny Thompson.

"Pico, I heard Sun Ra talk about a gig in Brooklyn. You think I'm going to be doing it with y'all?"

"Man, shit, you think Sunny would spend a whole day going over music with you and pay your way down here cause he *didn't* want you to play with the band? Look here, man, like they used to say, 'You in like Flynn.'"

"I heard Sun Ra mention something about Ebah. He plays trumpet too?"

"Yeah, man, but Ebah is a *space* cadet in a *space* band. You see he didn't show up for rehearsal, and he's got all the trumpet music. This is a strange cat, man. He's got these long dreads down to his ass. Sunny said it's messing with his brain to have all that hair like that. And then, man, this cat don't eat nothing but falafels. Sunny says if he keeps on, he's going to turn into one."

"I like falafels, man. What's wrong with eating them?"

"Oh, shit. You better watch out them dreaded falafels don't get your ass, too!" We both burst out laughing again. I felt as if I had smoked a joint but I had played music for eight hours.

When we arrived at 30th Street Station it was ten minutes to ten. I had left Brooklyn and Iyabode at a quarter to ten that morning. I would probably arrive back in New York at eleven thirty and possibly get home by midnight. Pico and I said our goodbyes at the station.

"Well, I guess I'll hear from you and find out what's happening."

"Definitely, man. We'll be calling you."

"So you say it's at the East, huh?"

"Yeah, man, it's going to be at the East."

○

The East, at 10 Claver Place in Brooklyn, was a school envisioned by Jitu Weusi—then Les Campbell—and named Uhuru Sasa Shule (Freedom Now School). Jitu was a teacher in the New York City public school system and had become frustrated at the failure of the Board of Education to deal with issues of quality education and community control. He went the way of independent schools with an Afrocentric agenda.

Sun Ra was the perfect artist for the East, having made a similar assessment of the music industry and a similar move toward independence. The East was housed in a three-story rectangular brick building. The façade's primary liberation colors of red, black, and green jumped out at you; on the building's front was the Wall of Respect, painted with images of African American cultural heroes. The imagery of the Wall of Respect was universal during the Second Reconstruction, aka the post–civil rights movement—also known as the Black Power era. These were deliberate efforts to demonstrate that Black lives matter.

The most dominant images were those of Malik El Hajj Shabazz, or Malcolm X (you know, the one that shows him pointing his finger), and Marcus Garvey, who was easily recognizable owing to the Napoleonic bicorne one usually saw him in. Claver

Place was intersected by Jefferson Avenue right in the middle, and bookended by Putnam Avenue to the north and Fulton Street to the south. The beginning of summer in Brooklyn was signaled by an event known as the African Street Carnival (later the International African Arts Festival), which in 1975 was in its fourth year. The street festival was then held on Claver Place. The sponsor for the event was the East. Back then, a stage would be set up across from a Catholic church and right in front of the East, facing out into the crowds that thronged the street. The church was on the corner of Jefferson. Its priests would, in years to come, create enough of a hassle over the festival that it would have to be moved to the much larger football field of Boys and Girls High, farther east along Fulton Street and deeper into Bed-Stuy, to accommodate the ever increasing crowds.

For several days around the Fourth of July, cultural giants such as Pharoah Sanders, Leon Thomas, Carlos Garnett, Roy Brooks, and Babatunde Olatunji would interact with audiences in a symbiotic high. Every year Sun Ra would be featured on the bill, and every year his would be the designated closing act. Hundreds of culturally aware people would hear and marvel at Sun Ra and his amazing Arkestra from Outer Space. Sun Ra preached discipline but he made people feel free.

The East remained a mecca for innovative music in Brooklyn for years. I had played there before, but as it turned out, my first gig with the Arkestra there was one of the last concerts on those premises.

The East had a strict policy on limiting its audience only to people of African descent. It was as rare a thing in the 1970s for people of any other cultural group to venture into Bed-Stuy. This policy, however, created a great deal of conflict with musicians who had cross-cultural relationships, as they were forbidden to bring their mates with them. I recall playing there once in a band called the Master Brotherhood, opposite a group led by drummer Sunny Murray, whose bass player was involved in such a relationship. I happened to be coming to the entrance just as the commotion was taking place. As I got nearer, I could hear the exchange.

"Brother, you are welcome to come in but she can't!"

"What're you talking about, she can't? Man, she's with me!"

"Yes, my brother, I can see she's with you."

"So what are you telling me? That I can come and play in this place, but I got to leave my woman outside?"

"My brother, I am in no way telling you what to do. I am only informing you of the policy of this African American institution."

"Don't give me this double-talk bullshit. I'm as Black as you and every other motherfucker up in here. And I ain't got to wear no dashiki or no motherfucking kufi to prove it!"

Things were boiling. The bass player was holding his bass as if it were an upright lance positioned parallel to his body. He was wearing a brown leather bombardier jacket with a red silk scarf tied around his neck. His black bell-bottoms and black McCreedy and Schreiber boots suggested he was hip in at least one section of this city. The white woman with him looked befuddled and nervous. Her hair, which showed past the tam she was wearing, was dark and curly. She was much shorter than her mate but as hiply dressed in bell-bottoms. She had on a trench coat with the collar turned up, and low black heels. The young man at the door was wearing an African suit with alternating patterns of pyramids in red and green against a black background. He had on socks and sandals that strapped from his toes to his ankles, and he wore a green kufi. His horn-rimmed glasses and full beard gave him a scholarly appearance of calm demeanor.

"Listen, this is a community cultural institution. Would you mind lowering your voice and refraining from the use of profanity?"

"Oh, now you are going to tell me how to talk, too. Right?"

"Listen, my brother." The young man took a long breath in a seeming effort to calm himself down. "I said to you before, the— —"

Sunny Murray, the leader of the group, came from inside the East.

"Sunny! What is this shit? You didn't tell me nothing about this!" The bass player gave Sunny the details of the confrontation.

"Every leader who works at the East is informed of our policy," insisted the brother at the door, "which has been in existence for quite a while now."

"Listen, brother, can't we work something out?" Sunny asked. "I mean, when I call a cat for a gig, man, I don't ask him what color his woman is. Or who he's going to bring to the gig. Or who he's sleeping with. No disrespect meant," he said to the woman. He turned again to the doorman. Murray intoned as if he were trying out for an ambassadorial post, "Suppose it was your wife who had to go through this, man," he says. "Think about the shoe being on the other foot for a minute."

"My wife, my brother, if I had one, wouldn't have to be concerned about getting into this or any other African American cultural institution," said the gatekeeper. "As far as the shoe being on the other foot, the shoe, my brother, is on the other foot in most other places in this country except here."

"Ah, man, I don't want hear this cat give me this soapbox shit again!" the bass player interjected.

"Here we try to present our culture in the most supportive of atmospheres," the doorman continued. "Our goal, brother—in fact, our mission—is to educate, agitate, and organize among and with African people."

The woman, visibly shaken by this incident, could no longer keep silent. "For God's sake! What are you trying to do here? Take us back to the 1950s? This is 1970. This is New York. You have no right to treat me like this."

"We don't feel we have to defend our position, nor do we feel any enmity toward this brother's wife." The brother went on addressing Sunny Murray. "He made his choice and we've made ours."

"Listen, I heard enough! I'm getting the fuck out of here! You can find another bass player!" the bassist said angrily. "Sunny Murray, don't call me no more for no dumb-ass gigs!" he shouted and made an about-face. With one arm around his woman, he walked to his car.

Prior to the April 1975 concert with Sun Ra, I had worked at
the East several times with different groups. Besides working with
the Master Brotherhood, I had performed in 1970 with baritone
saxophonist Hamiet Bluiett in his New York debut as a bandleader. The concert with Sun Ra and the Arkestra was going to
be something of special significance to me. One could feel the
electricity in the room. Iyabode, who was just one month away
from delivery (we were told she was due in May), seemed to know
everyone in Brooklyn, and Sun Ra was Brooklyn's folk hero. The
stage was set for fireworks. I was ready.

Sun Ra had me sit next to him, as he was still figuring out
where I would fit in as far as my solo capabilities were concerned.
The horn players were arranged in a row at the front of the
stage. The song we started with was "Discipline 27." I was hearing
it for the first time. The trumpeter, Ebah, did show up for this gig,
as did about ten other people I had not rehearsed with: Danny
Davis and Pat Patrick on reeds, Brother Ah (Robert Northern) on
French horn, Charles Stephens playing brass, John Ore on bass,
Jimmy Johnson playing drums, three dancers, and a singer. Ebah
knew the music, but he and I were separated from each other by
the sax section, which made it difficult to pick up the trumpet
parts from my position.

The next song was the 6/8 African-flavored "Watusi," and Sun
Ra pulled out all the stops. This song brought on four dancers:
Judith Holton, who went by the name Wisteria el Moondew;
Cheryl Banks; Ted Thomas; and June Tyson (who doubled as the
band's singer). The audience was totally with the band. Jacson
put down his flute, picked up two long curved sticks, stood on
a chair and played the Ancient Infinity Drum. Soon everyone
onstage was playing a drum. People in the audience were playing
drums. I looked at Sun Ra as he rocked from side to side, smiling,
listening, engrossed, shaking his head to the rhythms. The dancers
leaped across the stage to the polyrhythms of the drums. This was

no longer a concert. It was some kind of sacred ritual, akin to a Yoruban bembé.

On the wall behind the band, another person had set up a slide projector and was showing pictures of the Sun Ra Arkestra in Egypt. You could feel the audience and performers together lifting the energy of the room. Sun Ra let this go on for quite a while and then abruptly shifted gears. He played a melody on piano and suddenly the band broke out into a song led by the tall, graceful June Tyson: "This song . . . is dedicated to . . . dedicated to Nature's God . . . to Nature's God." The audience went wild. Next, I could hear the melody of "Images" being played on piano. My palms started sweating as I gripped my trumpet. John Gilmore kicked off the melody for the band. This was my moment. I stood up to take my first solo with the Sun Ra Arkestra!

When I finished, the applause was deafening. For the rest of the gig I played on every song that called for improvisation, at Sunny's command. He had a way of signaling you so that you knew he was talking to you and no one else. It wasn't rehearsed, but it was something you comprehended quickly. It was a form of telepathy. Suddenly I understood why he didn't count off tunes in rehearsal. Onstage he just played the piano to introduce the song and the band would come in. When he played "El Is a Sound of Joy" on piano it sent chills through me. This was my song and this was my audience.

The East was our Carnegie Hall; it was our Lincoln Center. The people were with the band from the moment we arrived. Applauding and encouraging with "Go ahead brother!" "Right on!" The audience was educated to appreciate the importance of the culture we represented. I always played beyond what I thought was possible in this environment.

While onstage with Sun Ra, I felt as if I had been transported to a magic land where everything seemed right. When I improvised on a song, with Sun Ra and the band accompanying me, I felt there really was no such thing as a wrong note or mistake. I confidently felt that Sun Ra was there, supporting and leading me all the way. I began to think there was something about my ability as a soloist that he had found attractive. We played for at least three hours. After several encores, the band was allowed to leave.

Late that night, when we were home in bed recounting the amazing event that had transpired, Iyabode told me how Sun Ra was rocking back and forth when I played, as I had seen him do during "Watusi." This inflated my self-importance to no end. In the years ahead, however, as I saw him doing this with a number of different players on their initial gigs with the Arkestra, I would come to understand that there was a profound methodology at work. Sun Ra was a genius who allowed a person to exhibit the full breadth of his capabilities before he decided where that person would fit best for maximum impact. This was real leadership.

Even though we had been told that the twins would arrive in May, the month came and went and Iyabode continued to get larger. The next time I was called to Philly for a rehearsal was right around the time my sons were about to be born. It was on the morning of June 6, 1975. I was feeling a little anxious, as I had taken a few Lamaze classes with Iyabode, but I had a real fear of hospitals and of watching childbirth in general.

It would take years of introspection and therapy for me to see how this fear was related to my oldest sister dying of a botched abortion and practically bleeding to death in the house for days before my sister Lorraine took her to the hospital, where she died shortly thereafter. Consciously, I was not able to explain to Iyabode why I was ready to provoke an argument with her around whether I should go to Philly or stay in New York, even while understanding full well that she was due any minute. Unconsciously, I knew I had to go, and right then.

I had to run as far away from a hospital as I could. My sister's death at the age of twenty-four was the point in my life when I turned to music to transform the pain. But because I never truly dealt with the grief her death left me with at the age of thirteen, the wound hadn't healed. But then, it had never been treated.

One of the great attractions of the Sun Ra Arkestra was that one could avoid all responsibilities, if one were so inclined, and just make music. Sun Ra, in fact, encouraged this. I am sure it was also a part of the mystical charm that the band had on audiences wherever we went.

If a musician does nothing but work on his music four to five hours every day, that person will become really good after a while, if he or she has any talent. The Arkestra rehearsals were sometimes ten to twelve hours daily. That, of course, did not leave a lot of time for relationships or anything else in one's life. But this is what made the Arkestra great.

On the morning of June 6, after an argument with Iyabode, who probably intuitively knew that she would be giving birth in a couple of hours, I set off for Philadelphia to rehearse with Sun Ra. At that time, the philosophy of Sun Ra was one that was totally meant for me. The two things I was most confused about and feared, birth and death, were completely covered by Sun Ra's philosophy, in that I could admirably avoid both of them without worry.

I followed the routine of picking up money from Western Union and purchasing the round-trip Amtrak ticket. Pico once again met me at the station and took me to the house. Once inside, we started rehearsing. We'd barely gotten through one song before the phone rang.

Pico answered the phone. "Hey, Pops, it's for you." He handed me the phone.

"Oh man!" I jumped up and did a little dance. "I've got two sons who are four pounds and eight ounces!"

"Look out now! Ahmed and the boyz!" This, said by Marshall, as if by proclamation, was, of course, a name that would stick.

"All right, Ahk," John said.

"Well, they didn't become May sons, but they are Geminis. Now you know us Geminis are a little different." Sun Ra made the understatement of the moment.

We rehearsed all day into the late afternoon. After that, I had to get back to New York to work with dancer Dianne McIntyre's group Sounds in Motion. This forced me to arrive at the hospital at midnight, a full twelve hours after my sons were born. I was able to see them, even though there was a bit of opposition to a father showing up so long after his children were born. This was going to be something difficult for me to live with and would create many problems and much tension in my relationship with Iyabode. It was nevertheless a choice I had made that I would have to deal with.

The rehearsal in Philly was for a two-week stint at the Five Spot Café in New York. The Five Spot, still a major venue for Jazz in 1975, had a reputation for featuring cutting-edge music. Sun Ra was cutting edge at that time, as he was throughout his career. The Five Spot was owned and operated by Joe and Iggy Termini and had been in existence for a number of years. This was Sun Ra's first performance at this hallowed Jazz club, which said something about his status in the music world at the time.

When I was a teenager in the 1960s, coming to the Lower East Side from Harlem, as I walked home from school along St. Marks Place, I would take note of the names of the musicians on the marquee of the Five Spot. People like Charlie Mingus, Max Roach and Abbey Lincoln, Randy Weston, Thelonious Monk— they spent months working there during the 1950s and 1960s. Now groups were booked for shorter periods. In the 1970s, the vanguard groups who played there included Sun Ra, Sam Rivers, the Art Ensemble of Chicago, Betty Carter, and Don Cherry. It had been the home of a couple of important events in Jazz history. John Coltrane played there with Thelonious Monk. Ornette Coleman and Don Cherry made their New York debut there. Eric Dolphy had one of the important engagements of his life recorded there with Booker Little, Mal Waldron, Richard Davis, and Ed Blackwell in his live *At the Five Spot*.

In June 1975, I had my first extended engagement with Sun Ra at the Five Spot. My sons, Rashid and Shahid, and their mother had just come home from the hospital and I was on another planet. Things were coming together in a crazy way. Here I was, the father of twins, and working at a major New York nightclub with the great Sun Ra.

I arrived at the club a little before showtime. The audience hadn't started showing up, and some of the Arkestra members were relaxing at the bar.

"Ahmed and the boyz! What's happening, Ahkto? I bet you got your hands full now!" I was greeted by Marshall Allen, who was seated at the bar, which was to the right as one entered the club. He seemed particularly animated— perhaps *inebriated* was a better term.

"Hey Marshall, how're your feelings?"

"My feelings are fine. How's yo' feelings?"

Before I could answer, bassist Ronnie Boykins came up to me, "Congratulations, young man. I heard you had twins."

Ronnie always called me *young man*. It was his way, I suppose, of defining our relationship, which in the Melodic Art-Tet had been that of teacher and student, even though it was a cooperative group.

"Thanks, R and B. I'm surprised to see you here. You playing tonight?" I asked. Given what Sun Ra had said about him at my first rehearsal with the band, I'd thought Ronnie would be persona non grata as far as the Arkestra was concerned. There was a lesson to be learned here.

The inside of the Five Spot was dimly lit as the night's performance was being prepared for. The room was set up with circular tables covered with maroon tablecloths arranged in rows throughout. It was larger than most Jazz clubs, but there were several rectangular pillars that were mirrored, which seemed to enlarge the space and obscure the view of the stage from certain seats. Off to the left of the stage, as viewed from the audience, was a room with fluorescent lighting that would interrupt the mood as the doors opened and shut. That area, an unused kitchen, was our dressing room.

"I just came down here to fire this reed section up. You know, if I don't come on the scene every now and then, the guys get lazy and start playing yesterday's licks," Ronnie said.

"Well, if you gonna fire us up, I hope you brought some kerosene and a match, because I know you ain't gonna do nothin' with that old little bitty bass of yours." Marshall, always quick with the repartee, took his cigarette and held it at an angle, looking at Ronnie sideways as if to say, *Come on with it.*

Pico came over to the bar. "Hey, Ahmed, how you making out in the nursery department?"

"Everything's cool, man, though things are a little hectic."

"You better go get you something to wear, man, 'cause it's a bunch of cats on the scene tonight."

"Yeah, man, thanks."

"You know where to go, don't you? Sunny's in his office."

Part of the uniqueness of Sun Ra's vision entailed the use of costumes. Sunny himself often made them, sometimes assisted by members of the band. Those worn across the upper torso were called space plates. There were also some that covered your entire body, as well as some kind of head covering. Sun Ra's office was the kitchen turned dressing room turned Ra's temporary shrine. When we'd played at the East, I had somehow missed the dressing ritual. At that time, I'd just been given a costume and been seated next to Sun Ra.

When I entered the dressing room at the Five Spot, I saw several suitcases of materials of different colors and designs opened and laid out across the floor. Cheryl and Wisteria, two dancers whom I had seen for the first time at the East, seemed to be aiding in the administration of these costumes.

"Give me that one over there," Sun Ra said.

"This one, Sun Ra, the red one?" Wisteria said.

"Yes, and give me that gold halo over there too. He looks like he could be a member of the angel race."

"You think so, Sunny?" Brother Ah, the French hornist, was being outfitted as I walked in. Sun Ra sat back in a chair with the suitcases open in front of him while making a meticulous appraisal of Bob in his outfit. "Either that or I got to put you over into the demon category. Of course, it's more than enough demons to go around on this planet. Sometimes I just ask the Creator. Of all the planets in the universe and the multiplicity of universes, why with all the infinite possibilities known and unknown, was I sent to this planet?

"Greetings, Sun Ra, how you doing?" I had been standing there for a minute listening.

"Oh, I'm trying."

Bob modeled his costume for Sunny. Sun Ra looked pleased by the costume fit and signaled by nodding his head that it was all right. "Well, now I guess we got to find something for Abdullah to wear."

Bob spoke as he was leaving, "Hey man, I didn't get to tell you how much I liked your playing at the East."

"Oh yeah, thanks." The mention of playing brought me back to the realization of what I was here to do. I needed to warm up my chops. With the babies asleep before I had left, I hadn't had much of an opportunity for fear of waking them. I was suddenly eager to get a costume, put it on, be done with it, and get to my ax.

Sun Ra seem to take an interminably long time deciding what he thought I would look best in. I thought to myself, *What an odd thing for a Jazz band to go through this whole procedure before playing music.* I could think of only one other group in the music (the Art Ensemble of Chicago) that did a comparable thing, and they had probably been influenced by Sunny.

"I think Abdullah would look good in the red; then we can have all the brass in red.

That one over there looks like it might fit him, Cheryl."

She silently followed Sun Ra's pointing finger and found a piece of red polyester that had been cut so that there was an opening for a head. I thanked her for the costume and put it on quickly.

"No, Abdullah, that's the wrong way!"

I started to adjust the material hurriedly, more concerned with getting to my ax than with trying to figure out which end of this costume was up.

"You see, if you put it on the other way, then it'll look like you got wings. You got to start using your intuition. The problem with the people on this planet is they be forgetting they got other senses." I took the costume off and turned it around, and it actually did look as if I had wings in that position.

"Now, see? That's the way it's supposed to look. That's better. Now we got to find something for your head."

After being given a headpiece I was free to get my horn and warm up. I opened my trumpet case, only to find that with all the excitement of the past few days, I had no mouthpieces with me. This was a horrible discovery for a trumpet player. Pico walked in just as I had realized my error.

"Damn, man, you look like you just saw Casper. What's wrong?"

"I left all my mouthpieces at home."

He shook his head, thought for a moment, and then said, "You know, it's supposed to be a couple of other trumpet players here tonight. Maybe you can borrow one of theirs."

"Naw, man, I got a mouthpiece that was made especially for my chops. I gotta go home!"

"I don't know, man. You better ask Sunny."

I could see that he was as serious about my getting Sunny's approval as I was in knowing that I had to go home and get back. I didn't bother contesting the issue. I knew what I was going to do, and that entailed getting out of this club as quickly as possible and getting back as quickly as possible. I did, however, make note of the fact that I was slowly getting involved in a different culture, and it was one created by Sun Ra.

# PREPARATION

Q:    Do you think of yourself as a preacher, a teacher, or just a musician?
A:    I'm a destiny-maker. I change the destiny of planets, change the destiny of countries. Everybody can't do it, you have to have the authority. You get it from the Creator, the one who this planet belongs to.
—Sun Ra

One interesting thing about our destiny is how we are prepared through seemingly random encounters to meet our fate. In spite of, or perhaps because of, the fact that my parents didn't have much of a formal education, they had a good understanding of what it took to motivate a person to learn. My father would always ask me to teach him the lessons I learned in school, knowing that having to teach what I learned would make me a much more attentive student. On a given evening I would be working on my homework when he came in.

"Hey, Daddy!" I was always excited when he came home from work, anxious to share my latest bit of information with him.

"How you doin', Leroy? It sure was a lot of traffic tonight. Did you finish your homework yet?"

"Uh-huh. I just finished it when I heard you coming up the stairs."

"You heard me comin' up the stairs, huh?"

"Uh-huh. I mean Trixie really heard you. I could tell from the way she was wagging her tail that it was you." Trixie was my dog. In Harlem we used to call dogs like her summer dogs, short for "some of this and some of that."

"How'd Trixie do today?"

"She was okay." Trixie had a bad habit of eating our shoes while we were out of the house. My father and mother didn't particularly care for their shoes getting covered with dog dribble, so Trixie was often in trouble in the evenings when my parents came home.

"What did you learn today?" he asked, as he sat in his favorite chair and glanced at the headlines of the *Daily News*.

"We were learning about these people who were explorers: Magellan, Balboa, and Ponce de León."

"How did you say that first name, Leroy? *Ma-who?*"

"Magellan, Daddy. He was an explorer and he went around discovering places like Columbus did."

"I see. Now you said a couple more names too."

"Well this other man was named Ponce de León. . . ."

"Leroy, gimme me a hand with my shoes, will you please?"

I had been standing over my father eagerly and excitedly regurgitating the information that had been given to me. I had almost forgotten about the other part of our ritual, where I helped him out of his brogan shoes.

"He was searching for someplace called the Fountain of Youth and that's how he discovered Florida," I said, while loosening my father's shoelaces.

"What you mean? Florida down south?"

"Yeah, Daddy, all of them were Spanish explorers. That's what we were learning about. Spanish explorers," I said, pulling one shoe and then the other off his feet.

"Well, what's Spanish got to do with Florida? They don't speak Spanish down there." "The teacher was sayin' this happened a long time ago."

"Well, that was real good. You keep on learning your lessons and you gonna be all right. Boy, I sure am hungry. Go in the kitchen and tell your mama to make ase with supper, will you?"

The phrase *make ase* was one my father often used when we were growing up. Intuitively, we knew it meant to hurry up. Years later, I would learn he'd been saying *make haste*.

These conversations we had before dinner were very important to me. They helped me to focus on the material we had learned in school that day and prepared me for the next day. As a result, I was an A student right up until high school.

When my parents moved to the Lower East Side in 1963, I was placed in one of the most fertile creative areas in the world. Giants from many different disciplines and cultures walked the streets of the Lower East Side. People like William White, Marion Brown, Bennie Maupin, LeRoi Jones (later known as Amiri Baraka), Hettie Jones, Archie Shepp, Bill Dixon, Judith Dunn, Pony Poindexter, Charles Greenlee, Vertamae Smart-Grosvenor, Ellsworth Ausby, Sunny Murray, Pharoah Sanders, A. B. Spellman, Nan and Walter Bowe, Albert Ayler, Jackie McLean, Charles Moffett, Sun Ra, and many of the luminaries from the Arkestra.

From our Harlem apartment on East 131st Street we moved into the Jacob Riis Houses at 118 Avenue D near East Eighth Street. We were my mother, Anna Townes Bland; my father, Lubia Bland; my sister, Helen Bland; and me, Leroy Bland. We had left one sister, Lorraine Bland Logan, at our old Harlem apartment.

My father, Lubia, was the oldest male of eight brothers and sisters who lived to adulthood in a family in which eighteen children had been born. The Bland family was from Vanceboro, North Carolina, about twenty miles from the coastal town of New Bern. My mother was from Franklin, Virginia, but her family background was a secret not talked about too much. My grandparents on my father's side were farmers, working mainly in tobacco and cotton. They had a generous amount of land to be farmed, and for a people one generation removed from slavery, a combination of instinct, agricultural environment, and lack of medical facilities dictated the need for a large family. My father, unappreciative of farm work as a youngster, often told me that he left home at the first opportunity.

*Lubia* means "string bean" in Arabic. I don't know if my grandparents knew Arabic any more than my mother and father knew French well enough to name my sister and me Lorraine and Leroy. I was told recently that Lubia is a name known in the

African country of the Cameroon, which was a French colony. Our family lore had it that the people on my grandmother's side came from the area of Africa referred to as Guinea, which before European divisions were imposed encompassed most of West Africa. So the Cameroonian origin story could be true. Of interest to me also was the implication of my parents' giving us (including my sister Helen) names that signified royalty. We might come to the understanding that, unfettered by a Western education (neither of them went past the sixth grade), they held onto the fundamental African concept of giving children meaningful names.

Being the oldest male gave my father a strong sense of family, something my parents instilled in me and my sisters. For the first fourteen years of my life, I thought that we celebrated the best Christmas, Thanksgiving, and Easter holidays in the world.

My mother came from a much smaller family (she had three sisters), and she seemed to adopt my father's much larger family as he did her smaller one. Both my parents were born in 1902. Three generations of us (my father, my sons, and I) share the same brown complexion. We also have eyebrows that peak in the center and make a boomerang shape. I am now almost a head taller than my father, which would probably make him about five-foot seven. He was one of the coolest people you would ever want to meet. Even-tempered as he was, he rarely raised his voice or said much. My mother was about the same height as my father and of a much darker complexion. She was a buxom woman who compensated for my father's lack of verbal dominance with a sharp tongue. My two sisters each took on the characteristics of a different parent.

Helen looks more like my mother, though she is taller; Lorraine looks more like my father, though she is of lighter complexion. I was the youngest in my family and the only male child, which meant, I was told, that I was given a lot of attention as a much-desired new addition. I was born May 10, 1947, just a month after Jackie Robinson had become the hero of the African American people and the Brooklyn Dodgers had become the Black folks' team.

My father took me everywhere with him. I loved to go to Ebbets Field, where I could watch the Dodgers. I knew the names of the players on the 1955 World Championship Dodgers team backward and forward. But what I liked most of all was the Macy's Thanksgiving Day parade. We would always somehow be right at the front, where I could get a good view of the marching bands. My father also took me to work with him at Mitchel Field, which was an air force base on Long Island. Our family environment was a loving one, but not the kissy-huggy-lovey kind. It was more like there was an understanding of love.

My interest in music started while we lived in Harlem. In our family, we attended three different churches. My sisters and I went to Sunday school at Grace Gospel Chapel, on 133rd Street between Lenox and Seventh Avenues. My mother went to Greater Central Baptist Church on Fifth Avenue at 132rd Street. My father attended Metropolitan Baptist Church on 128th Street at Seventh Avenue. As far as I was concerned, the churches in Harlem had some of the best singers you could hear. I had a distinct advantage over many of my friends in being able to commune at any of these institutions. I was always fascinated by the singers, especially during that moment when the spirit of the Holy Ghost would possess them. The excitement generated in the room on those occasions would sweep me up, but I would be fully observant as the congregation flailed their arms and jumped up and shouted, *Hallelujah!* The folks—inspired by the choir with vigorous shouts of *Amen!* and *Yes Lawd!* with a few *Well*s thrown in, flinging hats and pocketbooks and sometimes kicking off shoes—were a treasure and a delight to observe.

In my family, there was no separation between the profane and the profound. My father loved the blues. On occasion, he would put on a record by his favorite bluesman, Jimmy Reed. I was only mildly interested in the blues, but I remember Reed's "Left-Handed Woman" very well.

Mornings, I would awaken to the rhythm and blues of *Jocko's Rocket Ship Show*: "*Ooo tillee op this is the Jock and I'm back on the scene with my record machine singing ooo papa doo and how do*

A STRANGE
CELESTIAL ROAD

Ahmed Abdullah
with Louis Reyes Rivera

*you do?"* I would often hear Joe Bostic's *Gospel Train*: *"Wu wup waa wu wup, yeah the train will be here soon."* This was the music my mother enjoyed. Sometimes she would take me to shows at the Apollo Theater. One show I recall featured heavyweight champ Joe Louis and comedian Slappy White. The matinee shows were reasonably priced and were complete with a band.

The band music I most remember was from a record my sister Marilyn frequently played called *Dinah Jams*, and featured Dinah Washington in a session with trumpeters Clifford Brown, Maynard Ferguson, and Clark Terry (playing in top form), with Max Roach on drums. I was listening to those trumpet solos even before I knew they were Jazz.

In Harlem we lived at 49 East 131st Street between Park and Madison. These were distinctly different Park and Madison Avenues from the ones most other New Yorkers knew. Park Avenue has a train that takes suburbanites to and from work in Midtown Manhattan. The train becomes elevated as it goes through Harlem, giving these people an opportunity to look down on us while passing.

Underneath the El, on either side of Park Avenue, were factories. On our block, a large gray building that took up a quarter of the street housed a company run by the father of one of the originators of the Living Theatre, Julian Beck. The firm was called Beck Distributing Corporation. Marilyn worked for them as a clerk. Next to Beck's were a series of apartment buildings, then several brownstones and two large buildings that are best described as tenements. All these buildings ran together in a row until they reached Madison at the west end of the street.

We lived on the other side of the street, where there was only a row of tenements. The buildings on our side were numbered from 55, closest to Park, to 43, at the corner of Madison. Number 49, where we lived, was just about in the center of the block, slightly closer to Park than to Madison. Despite the fact that there were no trees on 131st Street, I would never think of the area I grew up in as being impoverished, because spiritually we were wealthy. I had a wonderful time in the streets of Harlem. It didn't matter whether my friends and I were creating games that involved rolling car tires down the block; playing stickball, stoopball, or skully; turning on fire hydrants in the summer; or racing Popsicle sticks in the gutter after the hydrant had been turned on. It was all big fun!

On the same side of the street we lived on, closer to Madison Avenue, there was a candy store with a jukebox that had lots of different music on it. My favorite tune was one by trumpeter Donald Byrd, "Fuego," with Jackie McLean on alto sax. There was also a record by the great swing drummer Cozy Cole, "Topsy," parts one and two.

One of the kids I grew up with was named Frankie. He was like a magician to me because he could scat Donald Byrd's solo on "Fuego" note for note. I was so impressed that I would put nickels in the jukebox just to listen to him do his thing. He would make believe he had a trumpet in his hands, fingers moving and all, as he scatted the solo along with the record. Once my father heard me whistling passionately in the hallway as I was coming up the stairs — no doubt trying to imitate Frankie. I recall him saying to my mother later on that evening, "I think Leroy's gonna be a musician."

The two Harlem schools I attended were PS 24 on 128th Street between Madison and Fifth, and JHS 139, Frederick Douglass Junior High School, spanning 139th and 140th between Lenox and Seventh. These were schools that author James Baldwin also attended. Poet Langston Hughes had a house on 127th Street (which is now a landmark building), and he was a frequent guest at my school's graduations. I didn't know what a great writer he was until much later in life.

JHS 139 was a school in transition when I went there from 1959 to 1961. There were young men going to school who had been left back so many times that they no longer went to class. They were made monitors, probably until they would be old enough to legally sign themselves out of school. These guys with their processed hair looked like men to me as they towered over our freshmen class.

The first week of school at Douglass was known as "rookie week." As a welcome, the upperclassmen tried to beat the living daylights out of the freshmen. This barbaric tradition had apparently been handed down without challenge for several generations. Every day for the first week I had to run like hell after school to avoid getting a good ass-whipping. I saw a fellow freshman get tied to a fence while these so-called upperclassmen beat him so hard that he could barely walk. In truth, we seventh graders were a pretty wild bunch too, with teenage hormones wreaking havoc on our psyches. We had a teacher, Ms. Pittman, a nice gentle woman in the wrong class at the wrong school. Her method of disciplining young men in her care was a bit bizarre. She had us pull up our pants legs and hit ourselves with a ruler. Many of us laughed openly as we "punished" ourselves with this method.

Academically, we were next to the Special Progress class, which admitted the smartest of the seventh graders, but we had a real discipline problem as a group. And no wonder, considering that the school monitors we had as role models were obviously preparing themselves for criminal careers.

About three weeks into the school year, Mr. Brindel, one of my most influential teachers, took over our class. H. W. Brindel looked and carried himself as if he had just come out of a branch of the military. Standing about six-foot two, with light brown skin, and curly hair parted and combed to the side, he had a no-nonsense look about him from the day he walked into our class. Always immaculately dressed, with shoes shined so that your reflection could be seen in them, Mr. Brindel probably saved many of our lives.

At Douglass, there was such a thing as class sheets, which were taken by students from class to class so that each teacher could report on our classroom behavior. The group that was able to bring class sheets unblemished with behavioral reports was awarded a commendation card by the school principal.

Brindel's first order of business, which immediately changed the way we thought and acted, was to make us our brother's keepers. If one of us marred the class sheet, all of us would suffer.

After a couple times messing up, we understood that he too would use the ruler as a tool of discipline. Deviating slightly from the theme established by Ms. Pittman, Mr. Brindel would ask us to hold out the palms of our hands while he himself administered blows that would sometimes leave welts and would always sting.

One of our classmates, Maurice "Bun Bun" Washington, could be counted on for comic relief during these proceedings. Maurice was called "Bun Bun" not only because he liked the pastry of the same name (sold at the shop around the corner from school), but also because he had a large future behind him. When Brindel would ask him to hold out his hands, he would dance and shake his rather large posterior singing, "*Please, Mr. Brindel, ah ah no mo'. Please, Mr. Brindel, ah ah no mo',*" in a rhythmic way that almost got a smile out of our stern teacher. After we all had our turn with the ruler, we understood we were indeed our brothers' keepers.

Brindel, however, was not about discipline as an end in itself. He had real information to pass on that demanded an environment of respect. For some reason, he seemed to be fond of British poets. It was in his class that I developed an interest in Rudyard Kipling, Samuel Taylor Coleridge, William Wordsworth, and Percy Bysshe Shelley—as well as in American poets like Edgar Allan Poe, Robert Frost, Walt Whitman, and Henry Longfellow. He had us commit "Invictus," William Ernest Henley's poem, to memory. I can still recite this poem at a moment's notice:

Out of the night that covers me,
   Black as a pit from pole to pole,
I thank whatever gods may be
   For my unconquerable soul.

In the fell clutch of circumstance
   I have not winced nor cried aloud.
Under the bludgeonings of chance,
   My head is bloody, but unbowed.

This encouraging poem has remained a great comfort to me during moments of difficulty. Mr. Brindel also insisted on developing our vocabulary by asking us to decipher phrases like, "Simians indigenous to Zamboanga are destitute of caudal appendages." He expected no less than the best from his students. I had him as a teacher for two years. It was partly due to his efforts that I passed exams in English and math that guaranteed my admission into one of New York's special high schools.

After school, I sometimes walked through the Harlem streets enjoying the life, sights, and sounds of that neighborhood. If I walked on Lenox, I might stop at the Countee Cullen Library (named for the Harlem Renaissance poet) at 136th Street right off Lenox. Around the corner was the Schomburg Library (named for the Afro Rican researcher Arturo Alfonso Schomburg), which housed African American historical books and artifacts. Usually I would walk east on 135th Street, passing the place of my birth, Harlem Hospital. One day, when I was coming home from school, there were picketers at the site of the construction of a new hospital wing. Apparently the company undertaking this construction in Black Harlem had no intention of employing Black workers. On the south side of the street stood a tall man in a suit.

As I walked toward him, I noticed that his penetrating gaze was focused on the activities taking place across the street. I stopped, struck by his regality and seeming importance. Other people had stopped to observe him, too, with some of them murmuring, "That's Malcolm X!"

It was indeed the powerful Muslim minister I had seen on television giving reporters hell and making me feel so proud. I walked closer to him and stood around for a long time. Even at that age I could feel he possessed something unique.

I continued my journey homeward, buoyed by having stood near greatness. The building we lived in was a five-story tenement, and we were on the fourth floor. To get to our apartment we had to enter the building and walk down a long corridor. There were apartments on either side of the corridor and one at the end as well. If you looked to the left of the staircase you could see a compartment door that housed a dumbwaiter. This tool was really an elevator for garbage, which was a convenience to tenants who lived on the upper floors. The dumbwaiter would come to your floor at a prearranged time: tenants, notified by a bell, would set their garbage onto the platform of the dumbwaiter, and then our super, Mr. Wallace, would pull on the chain to lower it. The mechanics of the dumbwaiter were always a source of fascination to me.

Our apartment was number eleven. It was what people called a railroad flat, meaning that from the kitchen at one end one could see right into the large living room on the other. There were no separate rooms. I slept in the living room with my two older sisters on a convertible couch that became a bed for the three of us. My parents slept in the room next to us. I can still recall the security I felt whenever I had occasion to sleep in the bed with them. Marilyn slept in the room on the other side of my parents, next to the kitchen.

The two big living-room windows afforded a great view of the sky and stars at night. The private homes across the street didn't obstruct the view. I would always sit and stare at the star formations, dreaming of what it would be like to be on one of those planets and wondering if anyone really did live in outer space.

Jocko's morning show was programming my subconscious with thoughts of outer space. At thirteen, the idea of being somewhere else really occupied my mind. I was in Mr. Brindel's class a few weeks before Easter vacation when I received news of my acceptance to Brooklyn Technical High School.

Marilyn was one of the first people I shared the news with. After school, I went to her job across the street, and she showed me off to all of her friends at work, bragging about her baby brother's accomplishment. Two weeks later, Marilyn was in the hospital suffering from the effects of a botched abortion.

Abortions were illegal back then, and she had apparently sought to hide her pregnancy from our parents, even at the age of twenty-four. The butchery that was done on her left her bleeding for days. The smell of what in later years I knew to be discharged tissue was unavoidable as I walked past her room to the living room. When she was finally taken to the doctor by my sister Lorraine and eventually ended up at Harlem Hospital, it was too late. She died during Easter vacation. No holiday would be much fun for many years after.

Her funeral was at a parlor on Lenox Avenue right around the corner from our Sunday school. I faintly recognized people who had come to the service. The feelings I had throughout it were difficult to express. I didn't understand why one moment I wanted to laugh and the next instance I was trying not to cry. It was a weird experience of dammed-up emotions.

That September, I began four years at Tech, from 1961 to 1965, but it seemed like an empty victory with Marilyn gone and our family life broken. Academically, I had never done as poorly as during those years at Tech.

It turned out that my sister Lorraine, then eighteen, was pregnant at the same time. Fortunately she did not attempt to abort. Her boyfriend and the father of her soon-to-be child was Harold "Junny" Logan.

Junny took over the ownership of the local candy store on the block. He was really into music, with an extraordinary Jazz collection, and he played the clarinet as well. He married my sister soon after my nephew "Peppy" (Harold Jr.) was born, and I spent some time around them. They were living with Junny's parents in the Lincoln projects right around the corner from where we lived.

Shortly after Marilyn had died, I'd come home to a surreal scene. My mother was really upset and the house was in complete chaos. I couldn't immediately distinguish the cause of it all. What else could possibly happen to this family? I heard my mother repeatedly saying: "Oh, no, Lubia, how could you?" She sounded as if she were in a state of shock. She was crying softly, yet the sound of her pain through sobs seemed magnified. I was distressed that she was troubled but couldn't find the words to ask what the matter was. I didn't want to hear any more bad news so I went into the living room. I was in for a greater shock, as I saw my father standing there with a young man whom I had never seen before.

"Leroy, this is your brother, Harry," my father said.

"Hey, Leroy," Harry said, and came toward me with his hand outstretched.

"Huh?" is all I could manage to get out of my mouth. From as early as I could remember, I had wanted a brother. I could hear my mother's voice in the kitchen and I knew this was not right. Harry was standing next to me now, taller and much darker than me, with an expectant grin on his face.

"I heard all about you, Lee. I heard you really good at those books."

"I never heard about you."

"Oh, no? Daddy didn't tell you about me? I guess he wanted to surprise y'all."

"Yeah, I guess so," I murmured. It was unbelievable that he was calling my father "Daddy" in our house.

I saw Harry one more time in my entire life. That first time was enough to drive a wedge right through the place where I had felt the most security, with my family. There were so many questions I wanted answers to, but I didn't know whom to ask. The silence around Harry replaced any explanation of his presence that day and left me with a feeling of disappointment. This in turn led to a distancing from my family that would take years for me to understand and heal from.

I had already felt a sense of shame and noticed finger-pointing going on around my sister's death. What could my father have been thinking of by bringing Harry to us at this time? Marilyn's death, now this guy claiming to be my brother and further upsetting everything. I had to leave. I needed space to express the emotions I was experiencing. Music became the way.

The trumpet had been an instrument I was very attracted to for as long as I could remember. I would think back to Frankie imitating Donald Byrd's solo on "Fuego," or those trumpets on *Dinah Jams*. Louis Armstrong was the trumpet personified, and he was often on television while I was growing up. Symphony Sid had a show on the radio at night and he featured a track from an Oliver Nelson recording, *The Blues and the Abstract Truth*, featuring a young trumpeter named Freddie Hubbard. Most recently, Mr. Brindel had brought a trumpeter into our classroom. I heard and saw that instrument close up. One day, I said, I will play the trumpet too.

Harlem was a transplanted African village, and the concept that it takes a village to raise a child was a reality during my last two years there. Fortunately, I had a few places to go to try to deal with some of the stuff that was happening. Sometimes I would spend time with Lorraine and Junny. Just before I made the decision to purchase a trumpet, I had a conversation with them.

"When I go to Tech," I said, "I think I'll play an instrument."

"Oh, yeah, Killer, what are you gonna play?" Junny asked.

"You should get a saxophone," suggested Lorraine. "Don't you like the sound of the sax?" she added. "I was just listening to this great album called *Sonny's Crib*. It's got John Coltrane on it."

"Yeah, that's before he started getting out there with that Eastern music, playing 'My Favorite Things,'" Junny added.

"I don't know about the sax. It's got all those things on it. I bet it's too hard to play."

"Well, Killer, ain't nothing harder than the clarinet, Jack. I can testify to dat."

"I been thinking more about the trumpet."

"Oh, yeah. Now that will be slick," Junny said. "You can't let the trumpet fool you though, even if it looks simple because it only has three valves. It ain't that easy. Otherwise everybody would be playing it."

"Are you going to join the school band when you get to Tech?" Lorraine asked.

"Yeah, I was thinking about it. But since I don't know how to play yet, I'm gonna try to get one before I get to Tech. In fact, I think I have enough money saved to buy one now."

"Look out, Jack! You got some loot, huh?"

"Where'd you get enough money to buy a horn?" my sister asked with concern.

"Well, you know I've been sweeping the hallway in Mr. Slide's building and I've been saving the money. They got trumpets at the pawnshop on one-two-five for $35. I already saw one."

"Okay, but now, after you get it, how will you learn to play it?" Junny asked.

"Well, right down from the pawnshop there's this place called Bastian's School of Music. I was going to see if I could get some lessons."

"All right, Killer. Looks like you got it all mapped out."

Among the first people I showed my trumpet to was a family living in the building next door. The Brown family—parents Bertha and Jessie, and sons James (known as Butch) and Bobby—became really important to me during this time of crisis within my own family. I spent many a day and evening in their apartment and had in a way adopted them as a family to compensate for my own. Butch was a few years younger than me, and Bobby was younger than him. James had the same teacher I had at PS 24, Willis A. Williams. I had been asked to tutor James in math, one of my better subjects, and for the two years we remained in Harlem after my sister's death, this was one of the places that was an oasis and a healing zone for me. It was a household where I felt a recovering sense of security that my own grieving family could not provide.

The Clark family was another I had adopted during this period. Alice Diane Clark was my first girlfriend. She had eight other brothers and sisters. I had met her on the 135th Street handball courts of the Lincoln projects right around the time my sister had died. I used to play handball for hours in those days. Sometimes I would just practice by myself into the late evening.

"Hey, you! You wanna play a game?" Diane had walked into the park and come up behind me without my noticing. She was accompanied by Donna Gibson, a slim, dark-skinned girl I had often played handball with.

"Naw, I don't feel like playing right now."

"What's the matter? You don't want to play with girls?"

"I didn't say that," I answered, and continued hitting the ball against the wall, running after it as it ricocheted to different parts of the court.

"My name is Diane. Donna said you're pretty good. Didn't you, Donna?"

"Girl, don't get me involved in this. Hey, Leroy."

"Hi, Donna. Who's your friend?"

"Umm, her friend can speak for herself."

"Yeah, I can see you can."

"So how come you can't ask me my own name? Besides, I already told you, so you must be hard of hearing or something." She sucked her teeth while moving her head and neck with that attitude only Black females seem to know how to express.

"I guess I didn't hear you."

"Well, my name is Alice Diane Clark. Some people call me Alice and some people call me Diane. I might let you call me Miss Clark." Diane and Donna laughed and gave each other five.

"Well, Miss Clark, did I hear you say you wanted to play handball?"

"Oh, so you're not hard of hearing, after all. Me and Donna have to play together though, 'cause I can't get all sweaty. And we get to serve first,"

"Wait a minute! I ain't going for all that."

"What's the matter, you scared we'll win? I thought you could play real good?"

"Go 'head and serve! I am good!"

Diane served first. She didn't get either of her serves past the short line. Donna was a handball wiz and could probably have played the game by herself. She served and we volleyed until Diane missed the ball. The game went on for a few more minutes.

"Diane! Diane!" A high-pitched male voice was getting louder and louder. As the voice got closer I noticed it was actually two voices. Soon I was able to see a boy younger than us calling Diane's name. With him was an even younger child echoing the same thing the older boy was saying. The way they pronounced her name it became, "*Die-n.*"

"Diane! Mommy said you need to get your fresh self out of this park, playing around with all these worldly people, and come on home, because it's time for Bible study and you know it."

"Oh, Tommy, stop exaggerating. You know Mommy didn't say all that."

"Well, she did say to tell you it was time for Bible study, and everybody's waiting on you. I said I knew where to find you."

"I'm going to have to go, y'all."

"When do you come to the park? Maybe I can give you some handball lessons," I said. "You live here in the Lincoln?" she asked.

"No, I live on 131st."

"Oh. Well, you have to walk past where I live to come over here. I live at 1980 Park Avenue. You can give me a call when you're going to be here. Can you remember my number? It's Foundation 8-4949."

"I got a good memory."

Our handball lessons turned into a teenage love affair. Diane and her family were Jehovah's Witnesses. Tommy, however, was joking about their mother's depiction of people outside of that faith as being worldly. It was the general premise of people of the faith, but it was not one shared by the Clark family, who welcomed me into their midst with open arms.

When I got to know Diane, I found out that she played bass in the All-City Orchestra, as well as piano, and most of her family played the piano and read music. Her father worked as a pianist and photographer, and his sister, Diane's aunt Bebe, was one of those great singers I spoke about who graced my mother's church on Sundays.

I found a lot of comfort in this family environment. It kept me from being out on the streets in a state of despair and open to negative influences. Many of my friends had already started using marijuana and drinking cheap wine and hanging out late at night. Though I would join them on occasion in an effort to belong, my tendency was to spend long periods of time with my adopted families.

I'm pretty sure Diane was a virgin when I met her, and she was one when our young love affair ended. But, man, there were moments when we started kissing and making out that we got close to doing it. Her oldest sister, Henrietta, who we called Retta, was probably about twenty-one at the time. She was into Jazz, and she had a friend, Arlene, who was into Freddie Hubbard. At the time, this was a good place for me to be.

Marilyn's death and the introduction of Harry to our family was too much for all of us. We did mention Marilyn from time to time, but we never talked about our feelings in regards to her passing. Harry never was mentioned again, and the silence around him was deafening. Our apartment, like our family, was no longer what it once was. Internally, I could feel myself distancing from my family just as externally we were preparing to leave Harlem.

We needed to move. My parents had long before applied for public housing, and the offer was just now coming through. The first offer was in Brooklyn's Red Hook Houses, which my parents rejected. The next one was for the Jacob Riis Houses on the Lower East Side, which they accepted. The new friends I found on the Lower East Side—Arturo Algarin, an Afro Rican, and Donald Tilner, a Jew—were essential in my adjustment to the culture shock I was experiencing. Life in Harlem had been one in which the primary cultural group was African American. There was the odd Jewish merchant, and I did have a few teachers from various European cultures. But, generally speaking, life in Harlem for my first sixteen years was a "Black thing." At Brooklyn Tech, I was usually the only Black person in most of my classes. The one African American teacher I had, probably the only one in the school, had such an unwelcoming attitude that I dared not establish a relationship with him. He appeared too busy dealing with his own survival in that environment. Having little support in my school and home situation during these years, I searched for the meaning of life through the study of existential writers like

Camus, Sartre, Dostoyevsky, and Nietzsche. There was, however, much to learn from my new Lower East Side neighborhood.

Arturo and Donald were guides into my new cultural, political, social, and artistic worlds. Both Arturo and Donald lived in the Lillian Wald Houses, which ran along Avenue D south of Sixth Street. Arturo had an older brother, Miguel, a poet who would become a cofounder of the Nuyorican Poets Cafe. On Fridays, Arturo, Donald, and I would go to a folk dance class conducted by a hip and progressive social studies teacher from Seward Park, the high school that Diane and my sister Helen attended. Marty Koenig, the teacher, would give us instruction in dances that had originated in Greece, Bulgaria, Turkey, and Russia. The students embodied a mixture of cultures from around the world, reflecting the population of the Lower East Side. On some occasions after the classes, large groups of us would hang out together and find silly things to do in the Village. There were also times when excellent programs would be presented at the Great Hall at Cooper Union. This school, situated on Astor Place, at the edge of New York's Greenwich Village, frequently presented concerts that were free, entertaining, and informative.

Gus Dinizulu had an African dance and drum group that performed at Cooper Union annually. To watch one of his performances was to get an education in African political, social, and musical history. He would feature dances and music from all over the continent, and he always closed with my favorite, the South African boot dance. For several years he used the articulate Baba Oseijeman, of Harlem's Yoruba Temple, as his host. Oseijeman's precise presentation deeply impressed my young mind.

Donald Tilner was a little eccentric and had a real love of Jazz; we got along fine. He had a hawk as a pet, which many thought was strange but no one dared to comment on. Donald knew the McLean family, who lived in the same housing development. Jackie McLean was then a popular alto saxophonist with an international reputation. He lived with his wife, Dollie, and sons Rene and Vernon. Donald took me to meet them. Jackie, however, was not at home; I met only Dollie and Vernon.

By then I did own a trumpet and was into music, but I was hardly considered a trumpet player. Jackie McLean was the alto saxophonist on "Fuego." My interest in music was developing rapidly, and my first "serious" job would move me along at a fast pace.

Mr. Willis A. Williams, who taught Lorraine, Butch, and me at PS 24, had taken a liking to my family. Like Mr. Brindel, he was the kind of teacher who understood the true meaning of the vocation. He made an extra effort to get employment for me at the Donnell Library Center, even though I was no longer his student. He had even come to Marilyn's funeral and later connected me with a friend of his, Ms. Hutson, head librarian at the education division at the Donnell, a branch of the New York Public Library on Fifty-Third Street between Fifth and Sixth Avenues. My job was to work as a page, putting books back on the shelves. It was a great job for me, as I had already begun my love affair with books.

Among the people who frequented the particular division I worked in was the brother of the great and short-lived alto saxophonist Ernie Henry. I would always see Mr. Henry (who was both a teacher and a musician himself) writing out music. To my teenage mind it was fascinating that one could actually write music down on paper.

Working in the education division allowed me access to the library's record division, which had many interesting recordings available. My favorites were *The Essential Charlie Parker*, his compilation disc on Verve; Thelonious Monk's live *At the Blackhawk*; Sonny Rollins's *Brass/Trio*; *Music for Brass*, written by J. J. Johnson featuring Miles Davis; and John Coltrane's *Coltrane*, the album on Prestige on which he plays "Violets for My Furs," "Straight Street," and "Bakai." I spent my lunchtime and breaks listening to these recordings, and my consciousness was expanding so that I got turned on to many other artists just by reading the liner notes. I had an enormous appetite for the music and at one time had a large portion of the record division's music in my house.

I'll never forget the day I first met a fellow I knew only as Mr. Murphy. I was asked to go into Ms. Hutson's office one afternoon when I came to work. Murphy was waiting for me in the office. In Harlem, we called detectives "bulls," and growing up in Harlem, you could always spot a cop. Mr. Murphy apparently wanted to be recognized as one because, with his wrinkled beige trench coat and Dick Tracy–like square face, he looked as if he had come straight out of central casting.

"Are you Leroy Bland?" he asked.

"Yes, I am," I said.

"Do you work here at the library?"

"Yes, I work as a page."

"Leroy, do you own a New York Public Library card?"

"Yes, I do."

"Well, Leroy, I am a special investigator for the NYPL. Do you know why I'm here?"

"Whew! I thought you were going to say the NYPD. Anybody ever tell you that you look like a cop?"

Having said this, I really didn't know whether I should have been relieved or not, so thoughtfully, I added, "No, no, I don't know why you're here."

"Is there any reason for your concern about my being a policeman?"

I suddenly thought about the records at home and I knew I was caught! How do I get out of this? Run? But there was no place to go. Suddenly, I had to go to the bathroom. "Uh—what did you say your name was?"

"I didn't say. I'm Mr. Murphy."

"Mr. Murphy, I'm a really good student, and I just came from school and I really need to go to the bathroom for a few minutes, if that's okay with you?"

"Leroy, I have some files that suggest you have quite a few records from this library that have not been returned," he said, ignoring my bathroom request.

A STRANGE
CELESTIAL ROAD

Ahmed Abdullah
with Louis Reyes Rivera

"Uh, y-yes, but I didn't mean to keep 'em. I just kept on listening to them and I really forgot to bring them back. I'm gonna return them," I blurted out, almost in tears.

"We've also noticed that some of the records you've borrowed have been returned by means, we suspect, of this elevator shaft," he said pointing to a device outside of Ms. Hutson's office that was used to carry books and records internally from one division to another.

I was beginning to feel like I wanted to be invisible. They were going to put me in the youth house or worse, maybe jail. No, I was too young to go to jail. But they were probably going to fire me from my job and tell my mother and father and Mr. Williams. I wasn't going to say any more. I once saw on *Perry Mason* that if you told people you were taking the Fifth, then you didn't have to say anything.

"Now, Leroy, before you came in today, Ms. Hutson and I had a long talk. We decided that if you return all the records you have at home and promise never to do what you have done again, we'd be willing to forget that any of this ever happened. We can't have someone on staff who doesn't respect the principles of the public lending library. So we do have to have a promise from you, if you are to continue in your job."

They weren't going to put me in the youth house or in jail! I was going to be able to keep my job, too. I could feel the tears coming now. "I p-p-promise I w-will return th-th-th-the records I have at home and I won't ever do this again." This was a promise I was going to keep. I had almost the entire Jazz collection in my house, and I must have thought that the library existed solely for my own musical education.

There was a librarian named Frank Wessells who was also into Jazz. We often talked about the music we shared a passion for.

"Hey, Lee, I just picked up this great Dizzy side, *The Ebullient Mr. Gillespie*. I heard it at the store, man. Diz jokes around and does some real great blowing. I especially like this track called 'The Umbrella Man.'" Wessells had just come back from lunch and shared this information with me like he did every day. We had these Jazz discussions around the checkout desk when the library wasn't busy.

"Yeah, you keep on telling me about Dizzy, man, but you know you better get hip to Freddie Hubbard. He's playing the music I want to hear," I replied.

"Yes, Freddie Hubbard's quite good. I grant you that. I guess I'm just a moldy fig because I can't get enough of that bebop music. But you know, Dizzy is playing at Birdland this week on a triple bill that includes someone you might like."

"Oh yeah? Who's that?"

"John Coltrane."

"Wow! John Coltrane!" I said, and my mouth stayed open for a few minutes while I pondered this revelation. "You think I could get in there to hear that?" I had never been or considered going to a Jazz club in my short life.

"I don't know. How old are you?"

"I'm sixteen, but everyone says I look older."

"You think your parents will let you go? They do serve alcohol at Birdland and you're still a minor."

"I don't know whether they will or not." I had no intention of asking to find out, either. Better to go and have the experience and face the repercussions later. Besides, my parents had given me a lot of room since Marilyn had died and Lorraine had moved out. I almost felt as if I were on my own, anyway.

Birdland was not far from Donnell's midtown location. One night, I decided to work a late shift so I could remain in the area and try my luck at New York's premier Jazz club. Birdland was on Broadway close to Fifty-Second Street, about four blocks from the library.

I left the library and walked west to the Avenue of the Americas. The building that is now CBS headquarters was then under construction. I liked to walk along Sixth Avenue by the construction site because there were samples of some of the latest Columbia gems conveniently placed for advertising purposes. One record I loved to sample was Miles Davis's *Seven Steps to Heaven*. The title track, complete with Tony Williams's drum solo, could be heard here. Since I had a little time, I indulged myself and listened to the track twice.

Dressed in a red Viking outfit, helmet and all, Moondog stood deathly still at the corner of Fifty-Second and Sixth. He held a spear at attention and looked straight ahead. He was actually a composer and had been a fixture on that corner for the whole time I'd worked at the library. One could only suppose that his presence was some form of silent protest and that he chose the corner of Fifty-Second Street because of its relevance to the bygone bebop era. Walking past Moondog, I headed west on Fifty-Second, passing one of the last remaining clubs on the Street, the Hickory House, a piano bar, on my way toward Broadway to Birdland.

I walked down the stairs of Birdland with feelings of excitement and fear. A man stood like a sentry by the door. I asked, in what I imagined was my most adult voice, "Excuse me, but who's playing here tonight?"

"We are proud to have a triple bill tonight, sir. Dizzy Gillespie, Irene Reid, and John Coltrane," the doorman stiffly informed me.

"Do you have an admission price?"

"Yes, sir. Our price is five dollars and we like our customers to buy one drink."

I handed over the money, surprised and relieved that I wasn't asked to produce proof of my age. I thought the five-dollar admission cost was steep, but I had nothing to compare it with. I walked as close to the bandstand as I could. The bar was on the left as you entered the club. Irene Reid was just finishing her set and John Coltrane was on next. Now that I had found a spot in the club and had overcome my initial fear, I felt a growing sense of excitement.

The drummer with the Coltrane group appeared, looked the audience over, and went to the drums to make adjustments. He had a cymbal bag and began taking the other drummer's cymbals down, replacing them with his own. Once his cymbals were in place, he sat at the drums, positioning himself on his stool, sticks in hand. The bass player brought his ax onto the stand next. He set up onstage to the right of the drummer, where he'd be closer to the audience at the bar. There were seats and tables to the right of the bar that afforded a better view of the bandstand. As the rest of the band was setting up, the seats were filling. The piano was right next to the bass, which meant the pianist was looking out toward the bar. Onto the stage walked a heavyset man in a gray suit, shirt open a little at the collar and saxophone in hand. A little man walked up to the microphone to announce the proceedings.

"Welcome to Birdland, ladies and gentleman. My name is Pee Wee Marquette. For your listening enjoyment, we are proud to bring you our second set this evening. We have the John Coltrane Quartet: Elvin Jones on the drums, Jimmy Garrison on the bass, McCoy Tyner on the piano, and John Coltrane on the sax. Ladies and gentlemen, put your hands together and give a warm welcome to the John Coltrane Quartet! Thank you!"

Nothing I had heard at the library or in my brother-in-law's collection or anywhere in the world prepared me for what I heard from this group of musicians. The sound lifted me to a place I somehow believed in but never knew when and where I would find it.

The first song was "I Want to Talk About You." John Coltrane played like a Baptist preacher turned saxophonist. His sound was startlingly familiar, mesmerizing, and powerful. It was sound that came from deep within the ancient part and touched the core of one's heart. It was the Holy Ghost experience in the Harlem churches transformed and crystallized into a magnificence beyond my understanding. But I could feel it. And I could see and hear that John Coltrane was possessed of something incredible. He played sometimes doubled over as if he were extracting the last possible bit of music from that saxophone.

Elvin Jones had more hands and rhythms going than seemed humanly possible. He was as much the drum as he was the sweat that rained profusely from his brow. Those were African sounds he made with that instrument! Once Jimmy Garrison got started, he seemed never to look up again. He, too, was on a mission to merge with his ax. Even when Elvin Jones was playing at his most intense volume, Jimmy Garrison was there, cutting right through. McCoy Tyner played in that hypnotic-repetitive way I had heard on records but here stretching out way beyond the boundaries of what I would have imagined a pianist capable of. His playing set you up for Coltrane to return to deliver his final invocation: an unaccompanied cadenza. The force of John Coltrane's playing and the completeness of the four of them as an ensemble seemed to drive the saxophonist and me to the brink of both the stage and ecstasy.

I stayed to see Dizzy Gillespie, and as great a musician as he was, I cannot remember anything about his set. I was so opened up by that Coltrane music that it took all of Dizzy's set to return me to Earth.

The next day I was back to work at the library, and Wessells and I were in conversation about our favorite topic. "So, Lee, did you go to Birdland last night?"

"Mr. Wessells, I got to thank you for telling me about that. Man! That music was great! I couldn't believe what I heard."

"Shhh! Keep it down, please!" Ms. Hutson had just walked into the room. I really had to be on my best behavior considering the hot water I was in.

"Sorry, Ms. Hutson," I said quickly, but I continued excitedly in a low voice telling Mr. Wessells about my first Jazz club experience. After I told him all about my impressions of the quartet, he asked the predictable question.

"So, what did you think of Diz?"

"He was really good, man, but I'm so into Coltrane's music, I could hardly hear where Dizzy Gillespie was coming from."

"But Lee, I thought you wanted to play the trumpet? Diz, man, is the greatest!"

Our conversations continued through the next couple of years. New developments were occurring within the music. There was a movement taking place in the country on a social and artistic level. Freedom Riders. Sit-ins. The SCLC. SNCC. Martin Luther King. Malcolm X. The March on Washington. Fannie Lou Hamer. The

Mississippi Freedom Democratic Party. CORE. The NAACP. Desegregation opposing American apartheid. Literally a Second Reconstruction. Another opportunity to make this country a true democracy.

Mr. Wessells and I were not only from different cultural backgrounds but there was a significant difference in our ages. He had been informed from the privileged position he held in society as a white male, and tended to champion the status quo. I, on the other hand, was moved by the emotional content of the music as well as by the intellectual understanding that a change was needed in our society.

"So, you like this new stuff, huh? That music's a little militant, though, isn't it? I was reading something in *DownBeat* the other day by LeRoi Jones. It seemed a little political to me. They shouldn't mix politics with music. They've got something they call the October Revolution. Now what are these guys, communists or something? I was reading about them, Bill Dixon, Archie Shepp, Cecil Taylor, Sun Ra, Paul Bley, Mike Mantler, Carla Bley."

"Some of those names are new to me; I'm gonna have to check 'em out."

"Well, you won't have to go far. I hear they're going to be starting a concert series of this music across the street at the Museum of Modern Art in a few months."

In the spring of 1965 I was supposed to graduate from Brooklyn Tech. I had long lost interest in school and by now was much more absorbed in music. I started playing my trumpet more, practicing along with records, learning the Donald Byrd, Freddie Hubbard, Miles Davis, and Clifford Brown solos as best I could by ear. I had already been accepted to Queens College School of General Studies. I was so glad to be done with Brooklyn Tech that I decided not to go to my high school graduation. That summer before starting college was going to be one musical adventure.

There was a summer concert series in the garden at MoMA, but none of the musicians who had been identified as leaders of the new movement were asked to participate. I did see a few great gigs that were pretty way out. One concert was with a group called the New York Art Quartet, which featured the great drummer Milford Graves and the alto saxophonist John Tchicai. Milford was an original with a totally personal approach to drumming. He had even created his own drum set and didn't play on a traditional drum stool but used a common chair instead.

Another concert featured Alan Shorter (saxophonist Wayne's brother), who played some really amazing music. He had a garbage can set up on a table with both ends opened. Man, the notes he blew through that can were sweet!

In the fall of 1965, I enrolled at Queens College as a freshman. There I came in contact with other young musicians who were similarly curious about this new music. We all increased our information base by hanging out with each other. I had begun to take Wessells' advice and became an avid reader of *DownBeat* magazine. I was most impressed by LeRoi Jones's Apple Cores column, which focused almost exclusively on happenings around the new music by then referred to as avant-garde, and considered the next evolutionary step in Jazz's unfolding. The two musicians most popular with my college buddies were Miles Davis and John Coltrane. Nineteen sixty-five was the year of *A Love Supreme*. Trane had won every award possible in *DownBeat* for that great album and for his amazing group. Among my college friends, we all agreed that one should just simply purchase a Miles Davis album when it came out with no questions asked. *Seven Steps to Heaven* and *Miles Davis in Europe* had come out in the past two years. The recording *E.S.P.* had us foaming at the mouth. Four of us were trumpeters: Jack Harris (now photographer Ptah Hotep), Arthur Williams, Lamon Fenner (aka Faruq), and myself. The other male member of the group was a drummer, Charles Downs (now Rashid Bakr). We also included two female members, Helen Toppins and Lynette Harris. We were armchair revolutionaries who came together with a growing understanding of our relationship to culture and social awareness.

The 1964 October Revolution in Jazz and the subsequent though sadly short-lived Jazz Composers Guild, conceived by Bill Dixon, as well as the writings of LeRoi Jones, Archie Shepp,

Frank Kofsky, and Ralph J. Gleason gave us a framework, a reference point, a means to make an intelligent connection between art and the social conditions that existed within the country.

My preparation for the social upheaval of the 1960s had come a few years earlier as a result of going to a fifty-cent movie in Harlem on my own. The movie was *Hannibal* and it was playing at the RKO Alhambra (now a Masonic Temple), on 126th Street and Seventh Avenue. There was a picket line in front of the theater. The picketers were chanting, "Hannibal was a Black man! A Black man!"

I stopped in utter thirteen-year-old delight. All this attention around a movie I was going to see. One of the picketers came up to me.

"Young brother, I know you're not going to go in to see that movie. That man on the screen can't portray Hannibal because Hannibal was a Black man!" The man on the screen was Victor Mature.

I really wanted to see this movie, so I went in. When I came out, the demonstration was even larger. The same person came up to me once again.

"Well, young brother, you went in anyway, huh? You didn't heed my advice. But maybe there's still hope for you. I want you to look over there across the street. You see that sign that says the House of Common Sense? You go over there and you might get some. Now read the next line for me. What does it say?"

"It says: And Home of Proper Propaganda, World History Book Outlet on Two Billion Africans and Non-White Peoples," I said, feeling a little embarrassed.

"See. Now that's real good. You can read real good. Now you ought to find yourself in that bookstore so you can learn about who you are."

He was referring to Lewis Michaux's National Memorial African Book Store. I was informed that it was a place where I could get my brainwashed head screwed on properly. That advice I did take to heart. Many a Saturday afternoon I would find myself in Mr. Michaux's bookstore, looking at books and listening to the spirited conversations that informed me about African history and the history of the American African.

The area surrounding the bookstore was known as Harlem Square, a focal point for rallies back then. The speakers at any given demonstration might include Malcolm X, James Farmer, Bayard Rustin, Dick Gregory, or Adam Clayton Powell Jr. They would speak on a podium set up right in front of Michaux's bookstore.

Malcolm was by far the most impressive orator of any of the speakers. The things he said were an inspiration and a source of awakening:

"The revolution we need is a revolution of the mind. . . ."

"That's what we are—Africans who are in America. You're nothing but Africans. . . . In fact, you'd get farther calling yourself African instead of Negro. Africans don't catch hell. . . . They don't have to pass civil rights bills for Africans."

"The only revolution in which the goal is loving your enemy is the Negro revolution. It's the only revolution in which the goal is a desegregated lunch counter, a desegregated theater, a desegregated park and a desegregated public toilet. . . . There is nothing in our book, the Quran, that teaches us to suffer peacefully. Our religion teaches us to be intelligent."

It was statements like these and many more that would leave me with a sense of pride and dignity.

On February 21, 1965, Malcolm was shockingly assassinated at the Audubon Ballroom at Broadway and West 165th Street in Washington Heights. I heard the report on the radio that Sunday at my parents' apartment. I was really upset by the news. It was because of Malcolm's powerful influence that I was motivated in the latter part of 1965 to change my name to Ahmed Abdullah and to adopt the Islamic faith. It was, in fact, one of the new friends I met on the Lower East Side, who was both Muslim and musician, who became my guide into the Sunni Muslim religion. He had recently changed his given name, John Owens, to Yayah Salih Abdullah. Yayah was my age but lived in a home for boys on St. Marks Place between First and Second Avenues. He never talked about his parents so I assumed he was an orphan. My parents, with typical Southern/African hospitality, always welcomed him and offered him meals. He played all the saxophones plus flute and we spent lots of time listening to music. We would analyze, critique, and enjoy the music of Yusef Lateef's *Jazz 'Round the World* and *The Centaur and the Phoenix*. Charles Lloyd, Mingus, and Eric Dolphy were also big with us. Yayah himself was already a really good musician.

He was as passionate about music and Islam as he was tall. His six-foot-four frame made the tenor saxophone look like a toy in his hands. He would often demonstrate his knowledge of the Quran by reciting passages in Arabic. He also made a serious distinction between the religion he practiced and that of Elijah Muhammad's Nation of Islam. It was clear to me, however, that I was drawn to Islam not by his sales pitch but by a much more powerful role model in the spirit of Malcolm. In the late fall of 1965, I left my parents' apartment and moved a few blocks away to 377 East Tenth Street, between Avenues B and C. There I shared an apartment with my first real lady, Pat Mallory. She was a graduate of Seward Park High School and had attended the Friday folk dance classes (which was where we had met). She was, however, an infrequent attendee. She had much more serious stuff on her mind.

Mae Mallory, Pat's mother, was a real freedom fighter who had been involved in aiding Robert F. Williams, author of *Negroes with Guns*, from Monroe, North Carolina. Williams was head of a local chapter of the NAACP. When, in 1958, a white man attempted to rape a young Black woman and was subsequently set free by an all-white jury, Williams called for Black people to defend themselves. Needless to say, this did not endear him to the hood-wearing, crossburning locals. Klansmen who had decided that they were going to prevent meetings of the NAACP in Monroe would take people's lives to show their serious intent.

They had not counted on a liberated person such as Williams, who was ready to pick up a gun for what he believed to be a just cause: the protection of his own life. In addition, he had helped organize a protective group in Monroe called the Black Guard, which later became the Deacons for Defense and Justice. Mae

Mallory and other freedom fighters put their own lives on the line to aid Williams in his battle against the Klan by forming a committee in the north that raised money and people's consciousness regarding the details of that travesty. Robert Williams eventually had to flee the state and the country for sanctuary in a newly independent Cuba under Fidel Castro.

In comparison to me, Pat was politically astute in most areas; she was also Afrocentric. Her apartment was full of literature that contained in-depth information about the worldwide struggle for human rights. One evening while I was looking through some of the pamphlets in the apartment, our conversation turned to a discussion about the Fulgencio Batista regime in Cuba and its subsequent toppling by Fidel Castro.

"Did you ever read Fidel's speech at the United Nations?" Pat asked.

"No, I never even heard about it."

She began looking through another pile of pamphlets that she had stacked in the corner of her living room. She found the one she was searching for and handed it to me. "Here! You should check this out. After you read that, I've got some material on Che Guevara that you should read, too.

"Who's Che Guevara?"

"Oh boy, I see we've got a lot of work to do here. Che is a brilliant Argentinean freedom fighter and Fidel Castro's right-hand man. He was important to the Cuban Revolution and is still important, but no one has heard anything from him for a few months now. He just disappeared. People suspect he's either in the Congo or in Bolivia doing what he does best.

"What is it that he does best?" I asked, suspecting the answer.

"Come on, Leroy. . . ."

"Ahmed. I changed my name, remember?"

"So you did. You know it's going to take me some time getting used to this change, because you still look, act, and think like Leroy. What did you say Ahmed means?"

"'The chosen one,'" I said proudly.

"And what's your other name mean?"

"*Abdullah* means 'the servant of Allah.' Together they mean I was chosen to serve God," I expounded, even more full of myself.

"So I guess you going to be running around here like some of the brothers uptown at the Truth coffee shop talkin' about peace, huh? Yeah, everything is peace. They shot Malcolm and people got the nerve going around here talkin' about peace."

That greeting, "Peace," had become a popular one. Pat was a couple of years older than me and a serious freedom fighter. To her, the greeting indicated people had sold out and implied a contradiction.

Patricia Mallory was the first in what for me would be a long series of relationships with women who would become my lovers and my mentors. Aware of world politics, Pat informed me of the changes taking place on the African continent. The countries of Benin, Burkina Faso (then Upper Volta), Chad, Congo, Gabon, Ghana, Ivory Coast, Mali, Nigeria, Senegal, and Somalia all had won their independence by the early 1960s. There was a new and wonderful feeling of identification with these newly emerging nations that I gradually learned to appreciate.

The music of Miriam Makeba, even though she was from South Africa—a country that would not come close to being truly independent for decades—was symbolic of the spirit of the times. Pat owned all of her albums. Like Makeba and a handful of other Black women at the time, Pat wore her hair natural. This was a political statement that connected the African in America to the newly independent countries back home.

Pat also turned me on to a recording known as *Missa Luba*, by a Congolese group called Les Troubadours du Roi Baudouin, singing their own traditional music on one side and interpreting a Catholic Mass from an African-centered perspective on the other. This record was my initiation into the Music of the Spirit. Though I could not understand the words, I was extremely moved by the feelings expressed and by my connection to that music.

After Pat and I started living together, we didn't go to the folk dance classes any more. Pat and I spent more time at political rallies than at any other functions. About the time we met, she had just finished an affair with one of the three men arrested for conspiring to blow up the Statue of Liberty and other sacred monuments. This symbolic effort by Walter Bowe, Robert Collier, and Khaleel Sayeed (her former boyfriend) placed them among the first group of people (considered by some to be revolutionaries) to become political prisoners in the 1960s, as the government of the United States sent out a message that it would tolerate no opposition.

Walter Bowe's wife and daughter, Nan and Nandi Bowe, lived across the street from us. Pat and Nan were close and committed to the struggle for human liberation. I was like a child in their company, soaking up all the information I could from their books and conversations.

Through Pat, I met the intellectual crème de la crème of the Lower East Side. Through my relationship with Cornelius Starkley, I was introduced to its artistic equivalent. Corky (or Corny, as Amiri Baraka calls him in his autobiography) grew up in Harlem's Lincoln Houses and was my sister Helen's former boyfriend. With his charm and wonderfully quick wit, he knew many of the creative folks on the Lower East Side. Through Corky I was able to get firsthand information and meet many of the artists involved in the Black Arts Repertory Theatre/School.

The BART/S, a mission directed by LeRoi Jones and dedicated to bringing the arts back to Harlem, was situated in a brownstone at 109 West 130th Street, between Lenox Avenue (now Malcolm X Boulevard) and Seventh Avenue, four blocks from where I grew up.

The effort made to raise the seed money for this ambitious project came through the relationship that LeRoi Jones had with Bob Thiele at Impulse! Records. A benefit for the BART/S was held and recorded March 28, 1965, at the Village Gate. Some of the participating artists were John Coltrane, Archie Shepp, Albert Ayler, Charles Tolliver, Grachan Moncur III, James Spaulding, Sunny Murray, Marion Brown, Elvin Jones, McCoy Tyner, Jimmy Garrison, Billy Higgins, and Bobby Hutcherson. Sun Ra and the Arkestra also played, but for some unexplained reason their performance did not show up on the recording. Sun Ra, however, would play a key role in BART/S.

Malcolm's death served to catalyze the formation of this organization. The theater and school became effective in Harlem through the use of government-sponsored anti-poverty funding.

Adam Clayton Powell Jr., Harlem's congressional representative for two decades now and chairman of the House Committee on Education and Labor, was skillful in proposing legislation that became known as Lyndon Johnson's Great Society programs. These programs funneled millions of dollars into inner cities throughout the land in one of the few efforts by government to address centuries of neglect characterized most recently by costly urban rebellions, aka "riots."

Haryou-Act was one of the community organizations that benefited from the skill of its congressman and the resultant generosity of government funding. It was with funds from Haryou-Act that LeRoi Jones was able to finance a summer concert series the likes of which few Black communities would ever see. The innovative music of Sun Ra, Archie Shepp, Milford Graves, Albert Ayler, and others was brought to the people in their local domain. These artists demonstrated that the music some were calling "avant-garde" or "way out" was in fact a folk art. It told the story of a people, and thus enjoyed a resonance in the community of its artists' origin. The concerts provided a rare opportunity for groundbreaking artists to be appreciated and to give back to Harlem's historically tough audience.

After a successful summer, BART/S went downhill. Word on the street was that though BART/S recieved government funding, the organization would not allow officials hoping to show off the prize program to visiting dignitaries into its building.

LeRoi Jones abandoned the project in December. In March 1966, the New York *Daily News* reported that guns alleged to have been purchased with money allotted for poverty programs were found on the premises of the Black Arts School. People were arrested and BART/S was officially cut off from further funding.

Corky worked at BART/S as a carpenter and had some knowledge of lighting. After BART/S closed, I met many of the participants on the Lower East Side. Through Corky, I was introduced to visual artists like William White and Joe Overstreet; playwright Charles "Charmy" Patterson; actor Walter Jones; musicians Sun Ra, Sunny Murray, and Albert and Don Ayler; poet John Farris; social commentator Johnny Moore; and a person in a class by himself, William Patterson, who I thought was a certified mental case.

Sun Ra was quite visible on the Lower East Side during this period. When BART/S folded, Sunny was able to secure a regular working situation at Slugs', then a newly opened Jazz club in the area. We would often see Sun Ra or musicians from the Arkestra walking the streets. Manny Smith, one of the trumpeters in the Arkestra, lived in a flat across Tenth Street from the apartment I shared with Pat. He happened to have been sharing a room with saxophonist Gary Bartz and pianist John Hicks, who were then working with Art Blakey in a group that included tenor player John Gilmore (on leave from the Arkestra) and trumpeter Lee Morgan.

Slugs' in the Far East, as it was billed, was the site of real innovative Jazz from the mid-1960s, when it opened its doors, until Lee Morgan was murdered there in 1972. Promoted and sometimes booked by the legendary Jim Harrison, Slugs' East Third Street location was less than half a mile from both my parents' and my current address. For many years I thought I had been there on the first night they began their Jazz program, with local hero Jackie McLean the featured performer on that occasion. Years later, while performing with Sun Ra at the Artists Collective—the art school Jackie founded with his wife, Dollie, in Hartford, Connecticut—I was informed that it was drummer Charles "Mack" Moffett who received the honor of inaugurating the series. So I must have missed that one.

In any event, I was getting a thorough firsthand Jazz education at Slugs' by observing and listening. My musical taste was broadening even if my emphasis was on the avant-garde. I had for instance recently learned who trumpeter Booker Little was. I had made a point of getting all three volumes of *At the Five Spot* recorded under reedman Eric Dolphy's name. Besides Dolphy and Little, pianist Mal Waldron, bassist Richard Davis, and drummer Ed Blackwell were also on those great recordings done back in 1961.

*Ascension* by John Coltrane and *Complete Communion* by Don Cherry were both released in 1966. I was really amazed by both of these efforts, which, though characterized as free music, were quite different. Don Cherry played his pocket trumpet melodies in a quartet setting. A new suite form. Rhythm master Ed Blackwell kept things swinging with his African/New Orleans beat. Trane's was a big-band polyphonic approach to improvisation—another concept that was new to me. I was already hooked on John Coltrane as leader of his quartet. A. B. Spellman's brilliant liner notes to *Ascension* delineated its historical precedents: the music of New Orleans, Sun Ra, Ornette Coleman's *Free Jazz*. The titles, *Ascension* and *Complete Communion*, were an indication of the spiritual direction I was being drawn to without really knowing it.

At some point in 1966, Sun Ra began doing a series of Monday nights at Slugs'. One night I stepped into his celestial sound when the entire band was playing stringed instruments. The strange and captivating sounds were shocking and enchanting. Suddenly there was silence and Sun Ra spoke with his Southern space voice. "Sometimes the Universe speaks and all is silent!" The Arkestra members repeated Sun Ra's statement.

"Haven't you heard how loud the silence is lately?" The Arkestra repeated.

Sun Ra then led a chant: "We take a trip through Space; the next stop Mars. We take a trip through Space; the next stop Mars."

Sun Ra led his band through the planets. "Mercury is the first Heaven. Venus is the second Heaven. Planet Earth is the third Heaven." They did this until they got to Uranus and then they stopped. Together they said "Uranus! You ain't us! Is you?"

This was wild stuff! Along with the cosmos drama there were costumes and headpieces arranged in ways that signified originality, flair, and style. The guys in the band were some of the hippest-looking and baddest-dressing dudes I had ever seen at Slugs', and I had been checking out all the groups. The Sun Ra Arkestra was in its own class.

I made quite a few of those Monday sets while living downtown. When and if the band did take a break (sometimes Sun Ra would play three hours without stopping), I would position myself outside the club for closer observation. I made contact on one occasion with Nimrod Hunt, aka Carl Malone, a percussionist and flutist who acted more like he was Sun Ra's personal representative, even to the point of selling Sun Ra records. That's how I got to purchase a copy of *We Travel the Spaceways*, a newly released record with his Myth Science Orchestra, or so I was told.

I took the record home and listened to it. I was disappointed, as I was expecting what I had been hearing at last year's concerts, on Trane's *Ascension* record, or at Ra's Monday night sessions at Slugs'. I wanted to hear the more wildly adventurous music that his contemporary band was playing. Sun Ra's album, although just released, was about ten years old. The music was well arranged and was obviously advanced, but it wasn't what I was expecting. The changes in music that had gone on in the past couple of years were much influenced by Sun Ra, and if I could have heard *We Travel the Spaceways* when it was created (1956–57) it too would have been influential to me.

In the mid-1960s, it was well known throughout the Lower East Side that Sun Ra and a number of the band members lived in a house on East Third Street between First and Second Avenues. I asked Corky to take me around to the house with the intention of registering my complaint in person and possibly exchanging the record. Corky agreed.

Sun Ra appropriately handled me with kid gloves. He listened to my criticism, such as it was. His response to my desire to hear more avant-garde music was the most terse I would ever get from him. He dismissed me by saying simply, "It's in there!"

Listening to it today, the first track alone, "Interplanetary Music"—with its space harp, cosmic-tone organ, cosmic bells, and Ronnie Boykins's ostinato line setting up an otherworldly sound against vocalists chanting "interplanetary music"—makes me wonder how Sun Ra could have conceived these ideas at that time. There was no one he could have drawn from, who created in that way. Indeed it *was* in there. Much more was in there than I could have known at the time.

There is something about the transformative nature of this music people call Jazz that puts it into a separate realm and makes it a spiritual endeavor. This occurs whether or not the musician understands it that way. When there is both a recognition of the spiritual nature of the music and an effort is made on the part of the musician to develop spiritually, we get a music like those made by Sun Ra, John Coltrane, or Duke Ellington.

Sun Ra was clear about the source of his inspiration and often spoke of it. On one occasion he said, "Leading a large band is an impossible job, and I would have given up some time ago, but I'm under the jurisdiction of other forces that want to help the planet, and they keep certain musicians with me."

# III
# THE SUN RA
# CULTURE

In a sense, *Sun Ra* means "Solar" and *Sol* means "Sun." You got it over in the Solar System. Solar = Sun Ra. It's about the Solar System. It's about the Universe. It's about things that are not of this planet. It's about a great test for humanity. It's not Judgment Day. It's Examination Day, as to whether man has a brain.
—Sun Ra

After the initial gig at the Five Spot in June 1975, the band was asked to come back for two weeks at the end of August. We were billed as Sun Ra and His Humanitarian Arkestra.

During my first few months with the band, we didn't travel much. There was a memorable performance that took place in Pittsburgh right after our second Five Spot gig. It was the first time I had actually traveled with the band by bus to an engagement.

Sun Ra usually sat at the front of any bus, whether it was a sleeper or a passenger vehicle. This may have been the Creator's band but he was definitely the leader. There was no other fixed seating arrangement, except that whatever seat you took going you were expected to take returning. I enjoyed positioning myself close to John Gilmore, because I idolized him and because of a new discovery. John was a chess player and I was into the game. I had a magnetic set that was good for road travel. Saxophonist Pat Patrick and drummer Thomas "Bugs" Hunter were also chess players and would participate when they were around. John's chess playing was as incisive as his tenor sax and clarinet playing. I didn't really mind losing to him because he was so humble in victory. With Pat, Marshall, Danny Thompson, or Bugs, one could also expect a good card game on board.

Sun Ra never took part in any of these games: He would be busy writing music, listening to music, reading from one of his philosophical texts, lecturing anyone who cared to listen, or catnapping (he was a master at that as well).

Loading up a bus before and after a gig was an experience. The main responsibility for packing equipment seemed to fall to bassoonist and percussionist Jack Jacson. This was not only because he was good at it, but because no one else dared touch his instrument, the Ancient Infinity Drum (really a tree trunk). You couldn't properly pack a vehicle before the drum was in place. Horn players like myself, carrying little, were expected to help with the loading and unloading of instruments. This was one of the unstated laws of the Arkestra. Since seats on the bus were never assigned, we had to quickly secure seats for ourselves because we never knew how many people might be on any engagement.

Sun Ra was known for getting a job that might have been a really good-paying gig for fifteen performers and then having twenty-five players on stage. He was making music for the Creator and couldn't be bothered with such earthly things as salaries or group size. This philosophy was facilitated by having a core group of musicians who lived with him and therefore bore the brunt of his spontaneous creative urges. From the beginning, I, too, marched in step with his philosophy, in that I rarely asked Sunny what a gig paid before I performed with him. This, of course, was not a good business practice. I never did it in any other context. Intuitively, I knew that my relationship with Sun Ra was not merely gig-related, even though there were times when I balked at the paltry payment received.

There was a correlation between the lack of financial demands placed on Sun Ra by a willingly exploitable core group and his actual public earnings, in spite of his rising star status. For a musician like myself, being with Sun Ra, life was not easy in the finance department. In associating with the ensemble, I had an opportunity that I didn't have elsewhere. But I also had bills to pay and people to feed. With Sun Ra you just never knew. And most folks didn't bother to ask.

For the performance in Pittsburgh, Sun Ra had found a dancer who thought like he did. Bob Johnson was a fabulous dancer and the leader of a dance company in Pittsburgh. The first time I saw BJ was at the second Five Spot gig. The song that made me take notice of him was a Sun Ra original, "Discipline 27-II." At the time, this song was played in an incredibly sensuous way, and Bob found the hook in the dance. It was all about a shoulder movement that was so suggestive of bump and grind that we couldn't tell if Bob was trying to turn on the men or the women. The Pittsburgh gig was at a Masonic Temple that looked like the Blue Mosque of Istanbul. It had a circular dome and was wonderfully spacious inside. When we entered the temple, we met Bob with at least fifty dancers who had been hip enough to Sun Ra to have come prepared complete in space gear. The gig was two months before Halloween, but that didn't seem to matter to the dancers who came to the event costumed.

During the performance a particularly excited dancer found a moment of silence in the middle of the concert an opportune time to yell out, "I'm catching stars y'all. I'm catching stars!" The trumpeter Akh Tal Ebah made this gig. During the first couple of gigs he had apparently seen me as a threat (probably with Sun Ra's coaxing) and attempted to set up his music stand on the other side of the room. Now that he had decided I was not out to take his gig, we actually became a brass section, sitting side by side.

Charles Davis, the great baritone saxophonist, was on this gig, too, adding a second baritone to the traditional Sun Ra section of two alto saxes, one tenor, a bass clarinet, and one baritone. Davis's inclusion here was an echo of Ra's innovative Chicago Arkestra recording dates back in the 1950s. Charles had made the Five Spot performance and stayed on for Pittsburgh. The band was really playing together after two weeks' work. The heightened inspiration transmitted by BJ's dancers made this one of the many legendary performances I would experience with the Arkestra over twenty-two years.

The show started with whomever Sun Ra deemed appro-priate to warm up the audience, be it June Tyson doing Sunny's space lyrics, Cheryl or Wisteria doing their space dance, Jacson on percussion, one of the horn players, or any combination of individuals Sunny might imagine at the moment. Master musical painter that he was, he would choose the instrument he wanted for whatever particular color he desired. When Sun Ra appeared onstage there would invariably be applause. He told us that we would know when we became masters because people would applaud just because we appeared onstage.

Sunny had an innovative musical concept he called the Space Chord, a collection of extraterrestrial sounds designed to jar a person's sensibilities and jolt him or her out of complacency. The Space Chord was always directed by Sunny. Sound, he would explain, could change things because sound was used to run things. Accordingly, sound was, in fact, the origin of all creation, as in Om, Nam, I Am, or as in, "In the beginning was the word."

Sun Ra, like any great bandleader able to stay on top, had a special gift for choosing talent. On the Pittsburgh gig, he had invited a couple of rhythm-and-blues crooners from Philadelphia to be part of his space world. Philly has a reputation for its R&B singers, and these fellows didn't disappoint. I taped the show, and it is interesting to hear the Arkestra sing, *"There's only twenty-five years before the century of twenty-one twenty-first century,"* in 1975. We served up a pretty funky rendition of that song, "Greetings from the 21st Century," as well as "Face the Music," *"What do you do when you know that you know that you know that you're wrong?"* By the end of this gig, I had become much more familiar with the repertoire, as varied as it was.

◖◗

During this period, Sunny was into his historical pageantry. At different gigs, we were doing pieces like Duke Ellington's "Lightnin'" and "Slippery Horn," Fletcher Henderson's version of "Yeah Man," and Jelly Roll Morton's "King Porter Stomp." When I joined the Arkestra I knew nothing of these compositions and didn't necessarily feel it was important to learn about the swing era. One day, Sun Ra suggested I spend some time listening to Henry "Red" Allen Jr., the trumpeter from Algiers, Louisiana, who Sunny said was probably as great as Louis Armstrong. In my effort to learn this great music, I had already started to investigate bebop. Sun Ra suggested I had to go back further and study some more. Ra had a unique way of looking at things. While he was from an older generation, and was influenced accordingly, he was quite adventurous.

While I was growing up, I had many opportunities (which I missed) to hear Red Allen. He was popular from the 1950s into the 1960s, working regularly at the Metropole, a club on Broadway down the street from Birdland. I could easily have heard him live if I had been aware of his importance. He had also worked for a period (as did Sun Ra) in the band of swing master Fletcher Henderson. A little known fact about Henderson is that he had written over five hundred arrangements for Benny Goodman. That—along with clever management, good clarinet technique, and the right complexion—insured Benny Goodman a place in Jazz history as the King of Swing, at the expense of Henderson, who would remain a footnote.

Sun Ra would arrange a composition from a past master, such as Fletcher Henderson, and write out the solo from that composition to give to his musicians. We were expected to play these solos as they had been played on record. Sunny would instruct his musicians to get inside of the original soloist's sense of nuance and the attitude that might have prevailed at the moment the solo had been executed.

He would say, "You got to bend notes a certain way, and then you got to rest just the right number of microseconds, not too long, not too short, and that's meticulous, you see." This kind of spiritual projection was part of the concept he identified as precision-discipline.

Trumpeter Akh Tal Ebah did a great job of getting inside the music of the "stomps," as Sunny used to describe the swing songs. Sun Ra would say Ebah was "from back there somewhere," and that was why he could do it so well. He seemed to want me to develop this ability as well. Under Sun Ra's guidance I was beginning to understand a few broader musical possibilities, as his approach to music was indeed spiritual and not categorical. I was beginning to understand music without bars. A Music of the Spirit, if you will.

He always spoke of the musicians with him as being in the "Ra Jail." He would explain that it was one of the best jails in the world because the prisoners, rather than having thoughts of escape, loved to languish where they could learn. Of course, he said, only those who were pure of heart would be allowed in the band anyway.

The Ra Jail was without bars. Because the jailer dealt with developing one's spirituality, a sense of timelessness was easily a byproduct of this imprisonment.

"Musicians have to activate their spirits," Sunny would say. "I'm not talking about righteousness; I'm talking about something else. I write with my spirit, you see. Musicians can play, and sometimes I tell 'em, 'I can't hear you,' and they play louder. And I say, 'I still can't hear you because my spirit can't hear you.' Now, when my spirit hears them, it's all right. But they can play their very best, and still it wouldn't be right because my spirit would say no.

"If I was dealing with my ears, I would say, 'It's all right.' But when you start dealing with spirit things like I am, you rise up above religion, philosophies, and everything else man is talking about. That makes it quite difficult to get to a person, because they are not used to that. They're used to measuring everything.

"I'm dealing with the spirit and it's not measurable. That's why I talk about immeasurable equations. It's quite a problem, particularly in America, which is more materialistic than any other country in the world. I suppose because most people came here to make money. So that's why I haven't really been successful here, because the materialists are so busy making money they can't hear me and they can't see me. Therefore, when I go to other countries that don't have too much money and are trying to do something in a social way for everybody, they can hear me."

Sun Ra offered great learning possibilities in music and philosophy, as well as lessons in life. Oftentimes, his teaching would
occur at rehearsals. During my first couple of years with him,
the band was as much a rehearsal band as a performing unit. Sun
Ra would speak of "tailor-making" compositions. In rehearsal, he
would write out parts or give people notes from the piano, and
then we would put it all together. If there was a mistake, it would
give Sunny the opportunity to lecture on anything that came to his
mind. It might be on the music at hand or anything in the universe
or, as he called it, the omniverse.

He probably would have been content with rehearsing and
never performing. Basically, he saw himself as playing music for
the Creator, which meant that every day he had to create something new. It didn't matter whether he did it in a club, at a festival,
or in the house on Morton Street. The Arkestra was basically his
means of realizing this ultimate goal. To have musicians at one's
beck and call who are able to read whatever is put in front of them
is a composer's dream.

One of the fascinating observations I made when I joined the
band was how Sun Ra could sit at the piano for hours without
needing to relieve himself in any way. He was like an Indian yogi
doing *tapas* while instructing us in this Music of the Spirit.

In my later years with the band, I once brought a trumpet player
to a rehearsal. This fellow had played with the band before in a live
performance, but he hadn't gone through the rehearsal process,
which was a form of initiation into the inner understanding of
the Arkestra. He was given music to play and had some problem
with its legibility. Being an outspoken individual, he mentioned
this several times and even suggested that John Gilmore wasn't
playing it accurately. It was at this point that he ventured a suggestion to Sun Ra about how things could be better organized. Sunny
did something I had never seen him do before. He got up from the
piano and said, pointing to my friend, "Either he goes or I go!"
He then walked out of the living room and up to his room. The

rehearsal ended on that note and my friend and I left. This band was not meant for everyone.

During that first year, the Arkestra did the odd Midwest tour as well as several points along the eastern seaboard. In the Midwest we would work a tour that included the Jazz Showcase on North Rush in Chicago, Gilly's in Dayton, and the Smiling Dog Saloon in Cleveland. This happened at least twice a year, once in the spring and once in late fall.

I remember my first tour with the band. We stopped in Cleveland. I was wearing one of a couple of lumber jackets my father had given to me. It was of blue-and-black checkered design and more like a heavy shirt. It had a kind of ruggedness about it that I liked. I had not previously done any extensive touring in the Midwest during winter. We were going to stay in Cleveland for a week. I was completely unprepared for the change in temperature that was about to occur.

What I was prepared for was to supply the guys in the band with nickel bags of marijuana. I had been smoking pot since my last two years in Harlem. Most of my friends did it, and at the time it seemed hip and harmless. When I moved into my own apartment next door to the one that Pat Mallory and I had shared, it occurred to me that I should sell marijuana. If I bought it in large enough quantities, I could smoke for free and make my money back from the five-dollar bags I sold. In America, one learns all these ingenious capitalist tricks. I would buy an ounce of marijuana from a friend, purchase a few small manila packets from the local Woolworth's, and be ready to take care of business. My customers were found at the two local hangout bars for artists, the Annex and Pee Wee's. My "career" as a marijuana salesman, in truth a half-hearted attempt, was interrupted when I had an encounter with one of the bona fide nuts that LeRoi Jones (now Amiri Baraka) had left at BART/S.

This brother, Hackensack (Tong in Baraka's autobiography), ten years my senior, had bought a bag from me and came back the next day to return it; I heard a pounding on my door at midnight.

"Who is it?"

"It's me. Hackensack. Open the door!"

"What do you want, man? I'm sleeping."

"That shit you sold me had sugar in it!" he said, loud enough for the whole building to hear.

I pulled open the door to quiet him down and looked into his snarling face and that deranged look in his eyes. Even at nineteen, I knew this brother was not well.

"You got the bag with you?" I asked. Being a good capitalist, I was ready to make a reasonable exchange to satisfy my customer.

"No. I smoked it! But I want another bag 'cause that one had sugar in it," he growled.

I had heard this cat was a little off. Even with that, he had to be kidding. I didn't want to ask the obvious question, because maybe he really was crazy.

"Oh, man," I said, thinking quickly, "I just ran out. I gotta re-up."

"I'll be coming back tomorrow. You better have some then," he threatened.

He did come the next night and every night thereafter for at least a week. I could tell it was him because he would bang on my door at all kinds of odd hours. And I mean bang. He would hammer away for five or ten minutes and then leave. Generally, I try to be a peaceful person, but I was born under a sign that does not take well to bullies, and I do have a bit of a temper. This guy apparently thought he was a gangster hustling a young kid, but my sister Helen had a boyfriend who was the real deal in the world of tough guys. I gave him a call.

"Hey Udo, what's happenin'?"

"What's going on, kid?"

"Udo, you remember when you said if I ever had any problem with anyone to just give you a call?"

"Yeah, man. What's happening? Somebody stole your marbles? Ha!"

"Naw, man. I'm serious, man."

"What you want from me, Jim? You ain't said nothing yet."

"Udo, I need a piece, man."

"A what? See—I was right! Somebody did steal your marbles or you lost them or some shit. What are you talking about, a piece, man?

"Udo, man, this guy keeps coming 'round banging on my door at night."

"So call the police. That's what they get paid for. What you gonna do, shoot somebody for bangin' on your door?" he shot back.

"No, man, you don't understand."

"What'd I miss? A guy's buggin' you, knockin' on your door. You want him to stop. You say you want a piece. I say call the man. You say I don't understand."

"I sold the guy a bag of smoke and he claimed it had sugar in it."

"Oh, so you trying to be a hustler and shit down there, huh?"

Udo Salters was still living in Harlem. He paused for a long time on the other end. Then he asked, "Well, did it?"

"Did what?" I asked.

"Man, did the goddamn bag have sugar in it?"

"No, man, I wouldn't do nothing like that," I said. "Udo, this guy is really crazy. He comes every night and bangs on the door and says, 'I know you're in there,' and then he goes away. He's been doing this every night for the last week. Udo, I need a piece, man. Can you get one for me?"

"Boy, you must be crazy! Your sister would probably never speak to me again if she knew I gave you a gun. Besides, you'd probably shoot yourself in the foot, or worse, shoot this nut and we'd all be up shit's creek without a paddle. But I'm thinking while I'm talking. So listen carefully: Get yourself a lead pipe. You can get one at any junkyard. You take that thing and wrap it up real good with a rag or some newspaper, you dig? When this cat comes banging on your door next time, wait till he's finished banging. Tiptoe down the stairs after him. Run up on him outside. You say he comes late at night, right?"

"Yeah, right."

"Well, there shouldn't be nobody on the street too tough. Be sure you check anyway. Run up on him and hit him right on the knees. You hit him on the knees with that lead pipe, and he ain't gonna be knocking on your door no time too soon. Now, after he's on the ground, that's on you to size up the situation."

So the next night when Hackensack came back and pounded on my door again, I followed Udo's instructions. I went downstairs looking for him. He had walked too swiftly for me to catch right away. When I got to the corner of Tenth Street and Avenue B, I met up with the brilliant artist William White. It happens that a few doors down on Avenue B was the Annex. William asked me what was happening, probably noticing my agitation. Word must have spread about Hackensack's harangue. I was protected by benevolent forces, because William talked me into giving up the pipe by saying he would have a word with the guy. William was a much older person I had come to trust. That night he took on the role of guardian angel. Sure enough, I never got another visit from my harasser. That also suspended my brief career as a pot salesman until ten years later.

When I joined the Arkestra, I was still smoking marijuana. Being a social person and desiring to make friends in the band, I would readily share my supply with other members. This became a rather costly exercise, as word seemed to spread that whenever I came to Philly it was Christmas. After getting hit enough times, I decided it was better to bring a couple of extra bags to sell, and that way, instead of losing money, I could at least smoke for free again and be generous if I so desired. This arrangement didn't last long, but it was still in effect during this Midwest tour. So, in Cleveland, on that cold fall day, I had only my checkered lumber shirt, a family heirloom of sentimental value, completely ineffective against the Midwest hawk. I was about to freeze my tail off. One of the guys in the band had an extra overcoat that he exchanged for a bag of marijuana. Once again, it looked as if I was being protected by a friendly force.

Sun Ra had a pretty strict no-drug policy, but I never remember him catching or berating anyone for smoking, as no one dared smoke anywhere near him. Every now and then, an overly enthusiastic fan would turn on some of the guys in the band and then get the brilliant idea that the "Captain of the Spaceship" might want a couple of drags. Needless to say, this person would be met with a resounding, "We don't think so!"

Being on the road with Sun Ra was a lot like traveling with your parents. He was as much a protective and nurturing mother as he was a disciplining and lecturing father. Often, we could forget about getting high at one of those marathon rehearsals we had. But if, in between sets of a gig or before we went onstage, we got high, someone would be sure to have oil incense. This would be rubbed on your outfit or your person to eliminate the pungent aroma that marijuana was sure to leave.

The other thing Sun Ra did not approve of was band members fraternizing with white women. As far as Sunny was concerned, it was a real no-no. This too posed a dilemma for the Arkestra's rank-and-file members who were so inclined. At most venues we performed at during my first year (with the exception of the East in Brooklyn), the clientele was 95 percent white. In the same manner that we acknowledged Sun Ra's lectures on drugs, some members heeded what he said while others made sure Sunny didn't see them with white women.

I'm sure his feelings about white women ran deep. Sun Ra, born Herman "Sonny" Blount, had spent the first thirty-two years of his life in the South. He had developed a reputation as a bandleader in what he called the "Capital of the Confederacy"—Birmingham, Alabama, where a Black man could be lynched just for looking at a white woman. He left the South in 1946, leaving his orchestra and music, to re-create himself in Chicago during the 1950s.

As recently as 1955, the murder of Emmett Till—a native of Chicago's Bronzeville visiting his relatives in Mississippi—had let people know what a serious problem America had. Fourteen-year-old Emmett was said to have whistled at a white woman. As a result of that indiscretion, his disfigured body was found so horribly mutilated that his mother could not recognize him. I remember that incident as an eight-year-old in Harlem. The impact had to have been powerful in Chicago, where Sun Ra was at the time. Much closer to home, tenor saxophonist Albert Ayler's body was found in 1970 floating in the East River, reportedly with his testicles in his mouth. Sun Ra would say this was the result of unwelcomed fraternization with a white woman.

We had seen that even in liberal Europe, mixed couples were looked upon disapprovingly. We played a concert once in Pescara, Italy, and we saw no women in the audience. It was like the parking sign: DON'T EVEN THINK ABOUT PARKING HERE. You could also see this attitude in the way promoters dealt with you if you were with one of their women. What I understood was that the music business was essentially a plantation system, whether in Europe or America. If we were dealing with someone in the big house, the information we might accrue could jeopardize the delicate balance of control that seemed implicit in the relationship between artist and producer/promoter/agent. Sun Ra, however, just warned us to leave white women alone.

In 1976, just before we embarked on a two-month tour of Europe, this warning was especially pronounced. I was not completely innocent of encounters with white women at that time, but I wasn't quite ready to acknowledge this fact publicly. It was through a former white female friend of mine that I had introduced French hornist Vincent Chancey to Sun Ra. She had suggested that Vincent was a really good musician and could probably use a gig with the Arkestra.

I was hanging out at the Five Spot during a Don Cherry gig when this French horn player decided to sit in. There were only two French horn players in New York that I knew who played Jazz: Richard Dunbar and Julius Watkins. Brother Ah was up in Rhode Island at Brown University. This fellow was Vincent Chancey, who I had heard about from our mutual friend Celia Seligson. When I'm told someone can play, I make a mental note: *plausibility, pending further information.* So when I hear the person, it all comes together. Or it doesn't. In Vincent's case, it did. I gave Sun Ra a call, and thanks to Celia, Vincent became part of the Arkestra. That was our secret.

The way the Ra Jail concept worked in social matters, such as drugs and white women, was that we would be put on notice. Sunny had done his job as Representative of the Creator. We then had to deal with the consequences of our actions and of Sun Ra finding out. We had the choice of listening to a being who had chosen Alabama in 1914 as the site and time of his earthly incarnation, and totally understood the ramifications involved. Or we could, through personal experience, come to the same or a different conclusion. In some cases, he allowed us to individually choose, and in others he did what he called "babysitting." It would be hard to understand through whom, how, why, or where Sun Ra might enact this babysitting concept. I couldn't believe he would try it on me years later in 1990, when I was not twenty-nine, but actually forty-three years of age.

The Arkestra made six trips to Europe in 1990. During June, we played at the Jazz and Blues Festival in Stockholm, where I met Tara Ollia, a young woman from Finland whom I was attracted to. She had short blond hair, full red lips, and a body with more curves than the Coney Island Cyclone. She obviously had eyes for me as well. When we traveled to Freiberg, Germany, and took a week off, she came to visit me. Sun Ra, "the eagle-eyed one," took notice, because there was discussion about my hotel room. I had been doubling with an Arkestra member, and when Tara arrived, I changed rooms with other band members to accommodate this new situation. I had long had a reputation in the Sun Ra Arkestra for hawking women. Sun Ra had in fact tagged me, Danny "Pico" Thompson, and a couple of other guys in the band as "the romance boys." Up until this event, he had never really said anything to me about my philandering. As I advanced further along the path, I realized that the objective of my incarnation is to learn through women. It would, however, take a little more time before I got this together and became at ease with this fact. Sun Ra would be a catalyst in this transformative process.

The next week, when we played the North Sea Jazz Festival, I invited Tara. She was going to stay with me once more. Sun Ra had other plans, however. He was going to room next door to me and check on my goings and comings. This was totally out of character. I thought it amusing until one morning, in order to avoid him, I had to resort to my own intrigue. I got my mate up real early and got down to the restaurant before Sunny could knock on my door. He came into the restaurant about a half an hour later and spotted me. He walked over and told me he wanted to speak to me privately.

Sun Ra always chose his words carefully. In fact, he was a master wordsmith. He began with "I'm not trying to run your life or anything, but I just want to tell you that if you don't stop messing around with all these white women, you gonna end up having a baby by one of them, and that would be just like me having a baby, and I don't sleep with none of 'em."

What? Where'd he get that from? What was he talking about? What he said left my mouth open for a couple of minutes. It also left me with something to think about for a couple of years.

One could never guess what would elicit a response from Sun Ra. Some people, like me, he gave a lot of leeway to; others he would come down on immediately. He was in no way an equal opportunity employer. But that was part of the Sun Ra culture.

◖◗

My first European tour with the Arkestra occurred in July 1976, the month the American bicentennial was being celebrated and President Jimmy Carter, former peanut farmer, invited Max Roach and Dizzy Gillespie to the White House on the Fourth of July to sing Gillespie's "Salt Peanuts." Cecil Taylor was also invited; later that month he and Sun Ra were going to headline a couple of the European concerts.

The Sun Ra Arkestra, some twenty-eight people, left for Europe a few days after the big bash at the White House. I was leaving Iyabode and my two sons, Rashid and Shahid, who were now a year old. One of the musicians who was extremely important to the Arkestra decided to bring his daughter on this tour. She had all the guys in the band tripping over their feet and stumbling and mumbling, trying to get her attention. She was twenty-one and a fully grown woman in every physical sense of the phrase. With a woman back home and two kids, even I couldn't stop looking.

Of all the guys in the band, she decided to choose me. For the next couple of weeks, we developed a pretty steamy relationship. Whenever we could, we'd sneak off together to release our pent-up passion. It wasn't easy to find opportunities or places, considering the number of eyes on us and the fact that both of us had roommates.

One afternoon in Paris, we were talking on the phone in our respective rooms. As our conversation heated up, she told me she was alone. Horniness won out. It took less than a minute for me to run out of my room, barefoot, along the carpeted hall, down the carpeted stairs, two at a time, out of breath and into her waiting arms. We didn't have time to lock the door. Fifteen minutes of ecstasy and the door opened: "What the fuck?"

We were both buck naked and it wasn't room service. It was her father. I thought I would drop dead right there. We hadn't even considered that he might return. I was totally embarrassed. This man was one of my heroes, and if anything I was hoping . . .

Hoping what Ahmed? That by sleeping with his daughter in his room while your lady was back home with two children, this man was going to become your friend for life?

The ripple had begun. News spread through the Sun Ra band quicker than Western Union (and the story changed from person to person). Her father probably wanted to kill me but he took his anger out on Sun Ra and on his daughter, instead. She was sent back to Chicago. Nothing else came of our relationship. We had a couple more passionate encounters in Chicago, and that was it. The unfortunate thing was that from that day on, her father, whom I deeply admired, would play in the band only when I was not there. Sun Ra, however, never said a word about this to me.

This 1976 tour was interesting in another way. I was really able to see the esteem in which Sun Ra was held in Europe. At Nîmes and Arles in France and at Ravenna in Italy the double bill was Sun Ra and Cecil Taylor. The two leaders of the progressive music of the 1960s were treated like visiting royalty.

We lived in Paris for two months, at a hotel on the boulevard de Magenta. A really nice man named Michel Salou booked the tour. We would stay at this hotel in between gigs, if there was time off. The hotel, our second one in Paris, was one that musicians frequented, so we could practice and rehearse there. Our first hotel was close to our first gig in Europe at Paris's Mutualité theater. I had started practicing with my mute in the early evening and incurred the wrath of half the hotel guests who were not musicians. People started cursing at me in French to stop the noise. It made me question two of the myths regarding Europeans: One had to do with how liberal they were to musicians, and the other with their sense of social equality.

During this period, I wore an Islamic skullcap known as a kufi. There were many Africans from the continent in Paris at this time, and our hotel wasn't far from Barbès, the Harlem of Paris. There, one could eat inexpensively and be well fed. My favorite was rice with chicken cooked in peanut sauce. One day, I took the Métro with the intention of getting something to eat. I was grabbed by two gendarmes who pushed me up against the wall. I thought they were going to bash my head in. First these guys scared the shit out of me, then they made me very angry. And just like back home, I was asked to produce ID. Upon giving the two cops my American passport, a miracle happened. Their complete attitude and body language changed, and all of a sudden I was a respected, worthy human being. I'd never known the power vested in an American passport before. But now I also learned through this personal experience that lack of respect for an individual based on skin color is not confined to North America.

Being on the road with Sun Ra was in and of itself a major event. It would sometimes take hours before we checked into a hotel. Sun Ra had a ritual that was consistent, regardless of what time we arrived at a hotel or how long we had to travel. Like everything else about Sunny, this, too, was unique. He would get the names of all the people in the band, and would personally go to each separate room and check out the vibrations therein; then he would decide which room would be most appropriate for which individual or couple. This was similar to the "tailor making" he performed with musical compositions and costumes.

To new band members like myself, this was an especially annoying procedure. The only thing I really desired after being on the road was a bed. You would hear grumbling, but nobody dared say anything. Confronting Sun Ra with this would guarantee you a lecture on the fact the he was "representing the Creator of the Universe," and that, as he would say, he wasn't "over into no consideration of time."

Some guys who were really slick decided they would accompany Sun Ra on this room-to-room expedition with the idea of getting their keys first. You can only imagine how irritated we could become sitting in the bus or hotel lobby an extra hour or so while room assignments were being doled out. Sunny seemed completely oblivious to how this might somehow be problematic. What I did not understand then was Sun Ra's relationship to a purely African sensibility.

It was a reality that existed outside of Western constructs, wherein everything that surrounds it is as important and as connected as the event itself. He lived by the concept that Space is the Place. The Space he spoke of had many more spiritual ramifications. Being in his presence required the suspension of any presupposed realities such as *time* and *tired*.

When you came into the band you inherited this way of doing things. What helped perpetuate it was the fact that John Gilmore seemed so perfectly cool in accepting these concepts. As far as I was concerned, Gilmore was third only to Sun Ra and Coltrane in their proximity to God. So if he went for it, who was I to do otherwise?

There was yet another hook into the Ra culture. Sunny would give information generously on matters pertaining to music and spirituality. There wasn't a question in either of these areas that he didn't have a reasonable answer for. In fact, he made me so aware of what I didn't know that later, in 1978, when I took my first hiatus from the Arkestra, I went back to school to study both music and spiritual culture.

Sun Ra's generosity with information wasn't limited to Arkestra members. He would often be questioned by audience members after a gig. A fan might come and literally sit at Sun Ra's feet, totally opened up by the set we had just played. Sunny would patiently answer any question even if it took hours, and even while the guys in the band would be waiting to get paid for their night's work. It was known throughout the world, wherever we played, by whomever operated the facility, that they would have to wait several hours after the music before the band would leave.

As far as the guys in the band getting paid, nothing was done without Sun Ra's approval. The night's money wasn't distributed until it was determined how many extra persons had made a particular gig. It didn't matter if Sun Ra had quoted you a particular price before the show, because it was going to be a different story afterward. Oftentimes, the guys who lived on Morton Street would be paid less than the members outside of the house. They had their rent and food taken care of for them anyway. The point here is that no one was going to get rich playing in the Sun Ra Arkestra, whether he lived in Philly in the house or elsewhere. It was truly a labor of love.

One really bizarre financial debacle happened at the Montreux Jazz Festival in July 1976. Montreux is one of a couple of dreamlike places I have been to. The Swiss Alps surround this immaculate, rich-smelling town. The hotel we stayed at was fabulous. I had a huge room with a bathroom large enough to have been mistaken for a bedroom. I even used the tub as if it *were* a bed, especially after that long trip from Paris. Lying in the tub, I could open the window and stare out at a most breathtaking scene of snowcapped mountains. It was better than *National Geographic*. Still, no matter how lovely, this was not a vacation. It was work.

The band had more than twenty members onstage, all recorded with one overhead microphone. Sun Ra was in rare form, even for him; consequently, the band was turned on and playing beyond itself. John Gilmore, Pat Patrick, and Marshall Allen (the big three) turned in amazing work. The two Dannys, Thompson and Davis, as well as Jack Jacson and Eloe Omoe completed the sax section. Sun Ra had also brought along a fellow named Reginald Hudgins, a soprano sax player from Philly. There were three dancers, Wisteria, Cheryl Banks, and Raymond Sawyer (someone new to me who was every bit as great as Bob Johnson). June Tyson was present with her voice from another planet. My former trumpet teacher Chris Capers, Al Evans, and I were one part of the brass section that was completed by trombonist Craig Harris (just out of college) and Vincent Chancey, both relatively new to the band. Akh Tal Ebah had been left in Philly, so even though both Al and Chris had played in the band before, they hadn't played with Ebah, who basically knew the arrangements. So, in a sense, things had rapidly fallen on my shoulders. I was kind of amazed at how quickly everything was moving. A little over a year ago I had joined the band, and now I was leading a section in one of the most prized Jazz festivals of Europe.

Richard Wilkinson, June's mate, was our road manager. After the concert was over, everyone was flying high from the music. Richard had given me a padded shoulder bag to hold. I hardly noticed when he did it and did not know its contents. I stopped somewhere on the festival grounds to hear another performing group and placed the bag under my chair. There were several stages at Montreux, and in each arena there was another group performing. At some point, the people in the band were notified that the Arkestra's bus was taking off. I quickly left to join the group, boarded, and proceeded out of the dream town in high spirits befitting a band of conquering heroes.

A half mile out of town I heard Sun Ra ask, "Richard, where's my bag?" Richard was sitting in the middle of the bus. I was near the back of the bus. Richard called out, "Ahmed, where's the bag I gave you?"

In the post-gig excitement I had forgotten it. The bag had all the money from the gig in it, one of the best-paying festivals in Europe, and I had left it under my seat inside the Montreux festival grounds. The driver was asked to make a U-turn. I could feel my heart pounding like a piston as we ran to where I had been earlier. There, under the chair, exactly where it had been left, was a bag with several thousand American dollars in it. I have never felt so relieved to see money.

The concert itself must have put out such powerful vibes that no one would dare touch that money. We were thus well protected. The music on Sun Ra and His Cosmo Swing Orchestra, *Live at Montreux*, released in 1976 on Saturn Records and then in 1978 on Inner City, is a most fitting musical description of what I had actually experienced in that city and on that stage. The Montreux performance stands as one of the high moments in my recorded history with the Arkestra. The recording captures John Gilmore's incredible solo on "Take the A Train," accompanied by Clifford Jarvis on drums. The intro that Sun Ra plays on piano shows he now owned the song written by Billy Strayhorn, one of the Ellington orchestra's standard signature pieces. In the wake of Ellington's passing in 1974, he also owns the position that Duke once had as the preeminent big-band leader. This was Sun Ra's first recording in a few years, and even though his Earth years were advancing (he was now sixty-two), his sense of showmanship seemed heightened as, dressed in platform shoes, a colorful robe, and a pseudo–space helmet, he played the organ with his hands behind his back.

The sound of Sun Ra's piano introduction to "El Is a Sound of Joy" still sends chills up my spine. Before I left to go on that trip, the record I had been listening to was the great album *Jazz at Massey Hall* recorded live in 1953 and released in 1956. I loved the way Dizzy (I finally got around to studying him) and Bird were playing with the incredible rhythm team of Bud Powell, Charlie Mingus, and Max Roach. I believe Dizzy's approach influenced my concept and approach to "El Is a Sound of Joy." Clifford Jarvis, drummer on the *Montreux* recording, kidded me about our being a Clifford Brown–Max Roach hookup. In my estimation, it was one of Sun Ra's best recorded live concerts.

Unless one gets hold of a video somewhere, the amazing dancing of Cheryl Banks, Wisteria, and Raymond Sawyer can now only be imagined. Wisteria was her usual swift-of-foot funky-space-ballerina self. Cheryl had a kind of perpetual-motion style that worked so well with Sunny's music. June Tyson was also particularly stunning as she sang "We Travel the Spaceways," in a haunting call and response with Sunny.

One of the most moving dance pieces did make the record. It was unprecedented as well, because Wisteria and Cheryl up to that point had primarily danced on pieces like "Watusi" and "Love in Outer Space." Raymond Sawyer came out of nowhere and danced his tail off for "Lights on a Satellite." When you listen to that song on record, understand there is an added source of inspiration in his graceful dancing.

In addition to the Montreux Jazz Festival, we also performed at the first North Sea Jazz Festival, held in The Hague, Netherlands. Two other festivals stand out, both of which were in southern France; one in Nîmes and the other in Arles. The Nîmes festival was held at a large Roman amphitheater. It was another one of the festivals that had Cecil Taylor and Sun Ra as a double bill. Cecil's really hot group included Jimmy Lyons on alto sax, Raphe Malik on trumpet, David S. Ware on tenor sax, and Marc Edwards on drums. Since they went on first, we got a chance to hear them. Their music was soaring all over the amphitheater as I walked around outside, taking in the night air and looking at this ancient structure in the modern glow of stage lights. While waiting, I came upon the great bassist Donald Rafael Garrett and his wife, Suzanne Kali Fasteau, a brilliant flutist. This was my first time meeting them. Donald Garrett, now deceased, had played bass and bass clarinet on John Coltrane's *Live in Seattle* and *Kulu Sé Mama*.

Nîmes is not far from Arles, and when we arrived in Arles we learned that our concert had been canceled. The hotel reserved by the festival ended up being filled with musicians from the Ra Arkestra and the Art Ensemble of Chicago. We all hung out at the hotel. Among the people there was Lester Bowie, a trumpeter with the Ensemble whom I had played with a couple of times before. He is one of the innovators. He has always been vocal about what he was doing and what he was going to do. I recall him saying on this occasion that he was going farther inside the horn. He surely did that and came out with an original concept. His collection of quarter tones, smears, growls, and other techniques allow him to talk through the horn in the tradition of trumpeters Bubber Miley, Rex Stewart, and Kenny Dorham.

Kunle Mwanga was the road manager with the Art Ensemble. In later years, he would work with David Murray and the Ed Blackwell Project. We all had a great time drinking, joking, and generally socializing for a few days.

One of the many things I appreciated about being on the road with Sunny was that it was usually fun. He would sometimes get involved in word games, which, on the road or off, would keep us smiling.

For instance, in asking me if I knew a song, he might say either, "You got it down pat?" or "You got it down Ahmed?" He often would do another thing on the road. If he saw a restaurant or other place of business while passing through a town, say, for instance, "Richard's Steak and Take," he'd say something like, "Oh, Richard, I didn't know you had a restaurant in this town. Maybe we should stop and have a meal on Richard?"

One of his trick questions was "How many senses do you have?" The answer would generally be "five" and he would say, "No, you forgot your sense of humor."

Sunny's sense of humor sometimes led to the spectacular. This happened while we were in Milan on that same tour. Because of his cosmic consciousness, Sun Ra attracted some of the most imaginative minds in the world. There was a man named Alfredo who used to follow the band from gig to gig.

He came up with the idea of the band performing on a streetcar in Milan while he filmed us. Of course, he wanted us to perform in full space outfits and sold Sunny on the idea. When the time came, we played our instruments while Sun Ra directed us through a series of Space Chords in the middle of Milan traffic. Alfredo had commandeered a trolley for the occasion. People stopped. Cars stopped. Heads turned in disbelief. An invasion from outer space? What an event! Sure enough, in the papers the next day the caption read, "Spettacolo," and there we were.

One night while still in Milan the entire Arkestra was invited to hear the great Sarah Vaughan, who was performing at La Scala, the well-known opera house. She had her trio of Walter Booker, Jimmy Cobb, and Carl Schroeder. This red-carpet affair had her scatting the night away.

Sunny understood a very important fact: To create means to have fun. If one really created with a childlike sense of wonder, one could easily do the impossible. There was always a sense of adventure with Sun Ra. In fact, walking down the street and looking in shopwindows could be made into a magical moment. He was especially compulsive about going into music stores in whatever city and trying out the latest keyboard equipment.

The other large festival we performed at in 1976 was in Antibes at Juan-les-Pins. I had wanted to play this festival since I had heard the recording *Miles Davis in Europe* (1964). The pictures on the cover of Inner City's *Live at Montreux* actually show the stage at Antibes, which looks as if it had been designed with Sun Ra in mind. We played with our backs facing the Mediterranean Sea.

As a result of the Arles festival's cancellation, we had two gigs added on. One of them was a recording date and the other was an extra date added to the Châteauvallon Festival, which was to be our last on the tour. At the time of the recording and the subsequent Châteauvallon gig, the band had been reduced by half. Some had been sent home, others willingly went back. What was left was the full sax section minus Pat Patrick and Reginald Hudgins, and the brass section minus Chris Capers and Al Evans. Three members of the rhythm section had been sent back as well as two of the dancers. This recording, my first in a studio with Sun Ra, was done in August 1976 in Paris.

The band was set up in a circle around Sun Ra. Sunny had this really different-sounding instrument called the Rocksichord, which emitted just the kind of spacey-sounding chords to title this album *Cosmos*. This recording reveals Sun Ra's inner understandings. It is subtle, but just as *Live at Montreux* identifies him as the preeminent big-band leader, *Cosmos* places Sun Ra in a class by himself regarding metaphysics.

Through my study of metaphysics and Sun Ra, I have come to understand how this album represents an achievement in that area and an exposition of Sun Ra's philosophies. There are twelve musicians on this album. Twelve is the number of God, as can be seen in the number of months of the year, the number of hours in the day and night, the number of astrological signs, the number of years in Chinese astrology, and the number of years an initiate must perform the austere practice of *tapas* before becoming a yogi. There are twelve tones in music. *L* is the twelfth letter of the alphabet, thus the title of one of Sunny's tunes, "El Is a Sound of Joy." El is also one of the names of God. Twelve is essentially the number of measures in the blues, the transformative music that comes from the experiences of African American people. We know that the foundation of Jazz is the blues. One needs only to observe the effect the blues has on an audience to see what a spiritually moving force it is.

Twelve can be broken down into $1 + 2 = 3$. Three is the number of God at work in the world of expression, and therefore the number of creativity. Three is known to be a number of spirituality—as in the triangle, the pyramid, the Trinity (the Father, the Son, and the Holy Ghost), or the primal trinity (Isis, Osiris, and Horus). Of course, if you multiply three by three, you get Sun Ra's number, which is nine. This recording gives coded information from Ra, Master of Metaphysics.

There is a composition on *Cosmos* called "The Mystery of Two" The paradox of the mystery is that two is one $(2 = 1)$. The mystery is that all life is an emanation of the one life and it is our illusion that creates the dichotomy. Of all the Sun Ra songs I could have recorded, I chose this composition as part of my 1987 album *Liquid Magic* on the Silkheart label. It was the first time an Arkestra member had recorded any of Sunny's tunes. The year before, I had gone to a seer and had been given information as to my incarnation objective, which included an ability to recognize Sun Ra for the advanced being he was. Although Sunny never knew of my visit, he did show his appreciation of my respect for him in recording his composition. During his last years, often-times in rehearsals or at sound checks, he would ask me to play "The Mystery of Two," even though he rarely played it anymore at gigs. He was like a father acknowledging that one of his sons had come of age.

Sun Ra also recorded a song called "Jazz from an Unknown Planet" on *Cosmos*. There are many people who play this music who have a problem with the term *Jazz*, but Sun Ra wasn't one of them; I believe he was able to see and understand Jazz for the transformative music it truly could be in the hands of a master. Besides, the letters in the word *Jazz* add up to nine. J = 10, A = 1, Z = 26, Z = 26, the sum of which is 63. And 6 + 3 = 9.

The album *Cosmos* was one of Sun Ra's favorites. Of all the albums he recorded, this one was kept on the wall at Morton Street. To this day, it's probably still hanging in the living room. Its cover has a painting of Saturn and its moons. When interviewed, Sun Ra would often speak of being from Saturn. He would also talk about having visited other planets. I always kept an open mind about what Sun Ra tended to say. We have to look past the surface of a thing to see its essence. I recognized that he was exceptional in many ways, and so my rule of *plausibility, pending further information* applied to some of what he said, while there were other things with which I was in total agreement.

Saturn, by the way, is the planet that governs discipline. It takes roughly twenty-nine years to make a complete circle of the Zodiac. Sun Ra's understanding of the need for us to develop discipline was probably why he always said he came from Saturn. And he was quite serious about instilling and enforcing discipline in the Arkestra. Not that he would be stern, but there was a point where he would break with you if you broke with discipline.

The rhythm section on *Cosmos* included a couple of young guys, Anthony Bunn on bass and Larry Bright on drums, both from Baltimore. We had nicknamed them "Bright-Bunns" because they hung together most of the time. The severe discipline that Sun Ra had put them through allowed them to stay, which worked out in the long run, as Sunny had to send drummer Clifford Jarvis packing. Clifford's taste was a little too expensive for Sunny. Whenever Clifford got an advance on whatever amount of money, he'd go to a restaurant and order lobster. He had a serious taste for lobster that bordered on an addiction. Sunny would say that no matter what he gave him one day, he'd have to give him more money the next. Finally, Clifford had to go. No discipline.

Trumpeter Al Evans, who had been playing with Sunny since the days at Slugs', also seemed to give Sunny one problem after another. Things finally came to a head one afternoon in Milan, while we were staying at a four-star hotel. The summer Olympics were being aired on a large television in the lobby. Evans, who stood six-foot three and was extremely dark-complexioned, had walked out on his balcony buck naked, totally drunk, barely able to stand straight. He had his member in his hand and was aiming off the balcony as one would a fire hose. The urine raining on the street below meant it was also raining on the front door of our four-star hotel. People had stopped looking at the Olympics, as there was a drama of major proportion occurring right outside the lobby. This incident so outraged the hotel manager that he wanted to send us all to another hotel immediately. Sunny was informed of what had happened both by Arkestra members and the manager. Al Evans had to go! Sun Ra had thus purged his band before recording *Cosmos*.

We returned to the United States in late August, just in time for me to do a gig with Clarence Curvan's band, one of the local Trinidadian groups I had been working with. We did the Caribbean Labor Day Parade on Eastern Parkway. Annually, this Brooklyn tradition serves to mark the end of summer. In those days, at least a million people would line Eastern Parkway and become part of a parade that, in its African tradition, made no distinction between spectator and performer.

I was playing on one of the floats, immersed in sound and movement, and for a brief second I looked down at the crowd of people swaying and moving to the music. The round man I spotted walking alongside the float was costumed as resplendently as the performers in the parade, and he had his own entourage. Upon closer inspection I noticed it was Sun Ra walking along Eastern Parkway! I later found out that Sunny had come to town a few days before a gig the Arkestra was to do at the Bottom Line. Apparently he wanted to experience a little of the Caribbean event. Brilliant costumes were very much a part of the atmosphere of the Parkway on Labor Day, giving Sunny a venue for exploring new ideas in fashion.

You may remember that the costumes we wore in the Sun Ra Arkestra were called plates. Oftentimes, Sunny would find material he thought particularly spacey and hem it himself. These costumes, like the music and hotel assignments, would sometimes be made especially for an individual. No one was to be on stage without a plate and they were not supposed to be worn outside of the venue. There was a ritualistic element involved in dressing up to be onstage. Big bands have done that for years. It was a swing-period thing, the suits, ties, slicked-down hair, spats. Sun Ra's costuming (though grounded in the big-band tradition), with space as a theme, set him apart in style and manner.

Stanley Crouch had this to say in *Players* magazine about that September 1976 performance at the Bottom Line:

An evening with Sun Ra and his Cosmic Swing Arkestra is an evening of mystery, joy, pageantry, and a trip through space, time, dreams, and layers of music that add up to an experience unlike any other, part sanctified church, part booty-bump-beautiful-business, part mystic giggles and satire, part swing *to the max!* The packed $5.50-a-head audience at New York's Bottom Line knew this, and if you weren't there early or hadn't gotten tickets in advance, luck had left you at the train station.

Sun Ra's music, drawing from something like forty years in the business and having been musical director to stage shows at Chicago's Club DeLisa, is a full-circle projection. It features classical Black compositions like Duke Ellington's "Lightnin'" and Fletcher Henderson's arrangement of Jelly Roll Morton's "King Porter Stomp," both from the '30s; the swinging tenor saxophone solos of John Gilmore, the bronco-busting metallic fire of Marshall Allen's alto, clarion-bold brass epics from Ahmed Abdullah and Chris Capers; the ebon beauty of June Tyson's singing; the most contemporary uses of electronic keyboards; and the dancing of three women who leap, boogie, and flip about the stage absolutely free of modern dance conventions. There are no clichés except those Sun Ra himself has invented, which are integral parts of his style with the shimmering costumes, the theatrical nature of the whole performance, and the extraordinary range of the music from the turn of the century coming this way from 1900 and the turn of the century going the other way beyond the year 2000, which is unequaled by any large ensemble playing today, with the possible exceptions of Muhal Richard Abrams's AACM Big Band in Chicago and the Duke Ellington Orchestra under the direction of Mercer Ellington.

After the Bottom Line, we did another of our reliable Midwest tours, going back to Chicago, Dayton, Cleveland, Columbus, and wherever else we could pick up shows on the way. One of the things about going to Chicago and playing at the Showcase was that if it was cold, we only had to run across the street because our hotel was right across from the club.

Producer Alton Abraham would always show up at the Chicago gigs while I was with the Arkestra in the 1970s. Alton was patronizing. The fact that we would see him only twice a year, when the band went to Chicago, meant that the vast majority of time we could manage without him. However, when he came on the scene, it was as if nothing was possible unless he tended to it. He also seemed to think Sun Ra was some kind of queer—whom he alone could help. Members of the Arkestra, I felt, were treated in a patronizing manner, as if we didn't have brains in our heads. Something like disrespect by association.

Personally, I had never met anyone like Sun Ra in my life. I had nothing but respect for the person and the angel, as he preferred to call himself. His sexuality is something no one has been able to determine. He had told us many times that he had no desire sexually for women or men. He also said that we all needed to examine this idea of calling ourselves men and women, because the historical baggage that came with either of those categories was tremendous. He preferred the terms *being* or *angel* or *angelic being*.

Certainly, his views on women were stringent, whether they were Black or white. Sometimes he'd say that women interfered with the creative process, so much so that he didn't encourage females to attend rehearsals. But then he'd make exceptions. June, for example, was one woman who was regularly allowed to sit in on rehearsals. She seemed to transcend every one of Sunny's dictums and helped to create his persona—the enigma wrapped up in a paradox. He didn't think too much of women as musicians, and yet there were two women pianists I frequently heard Sun Ra praise, Dorothy Donegan and Mary Lou Williams. In retrospect, I think Sun Ra was a creative artist who was more in tune with his feminine side. This factor not only allowed him to be the creative genius he was but also influenced him to accurately predict his music as essential for the twenty-first century, when that feminine quality of leadership would be acknowledged in the Third Reconstruction. Attention needs to be paid to Nikole Hannah-Jones's 1619 Project, the Black Lives Matter movement, Stacey Abrams, and many more women and queer people who have recently taken up the mantle.

At the beginning of 1977, Sun Ra and the Arkestra were invited to play in Nigeria at the Second World Black and African Festival of Arts and Culture, otherwise known as FESTAC. This country, sixteen years after independence and a couple of years after the bloody internecine Biafran War, wanted to improve its image in the world community. The Biafran War, with its images of starving Black people, was not a thing that would have encouraged investments in this oil-rich country. FESTAC, however, would involve sixty-two nations of the African diaspora in a monthlong series of events. It was probably the most ambitious cultural festival since the one held in Dakar in 1966 and part of a continuum that could be traced as far back as the Pan-African Congresses variously convened in Paris, London, Brussels, and New York in 1900, 1919, 1921, 1923, and 1927. In 1945, Manchester, England, was host to yet another major Pan-African Congress organized by the Trinidadian George Padmore along with Ghanaian Kwame Nkrumah. This conference was chaired by Amy Ashwood Garvey from Jamaica and W. E. B. Du Bois from the US.

The fact that diasporic connections were recognized as early as 1900 and that there were those possessing the wherewithal to time and again bring Africans together against imaginary and real cultural divides only made FESTAC that much more important.

Though FESTAC's emphasis, as the name implied, was on art and culture, its political significance cannot be overlooked. There is no question that as a people come to understand and value their cultural/artistic contributions to the world, there will be a greater appreciation of their worth as human beings, which naturally relates to political choices.

The responsibility assumed by the Nigerian government in organizing events for a monthlong festival and in feeding, housing, and transporting thousands of cultural workers during its run can be appreciated politically when one understands that nothing on that scale had been done before, nor has anything equal to it been attempted since. The US was represented at FESTAC during its second half in February by Randy Weston, Stevie Wonder, the

Troy Robinson Big Band, several dance companies, poets, play-wrights, and the Sun Ra Arkestra.

Before we left, Sunny had explained the circumstances under which we would be part of FESTAC. He told us we would have room, board, and transportation provided for two weeks but we would receive no compensation for our work. The fact that all along we had been receiving minimal payment for gigs anyway — plus the added fact of a trip to Africa — resulted in no objections. Besides, the Ra band was not a democracy and Sunny wanted to go. If money was the only thing we were after, we'd have been in different bands.

I couldn't go, however, until I had a conversation with Iyabode. Given that her name comes from the Nigerian Yoruba people and means "earth mother," I was hoping she wouldn't mind too much, especially about the money. I had come home from a rehearsal in Philly with the news. By then, Rashid and Shahid were walking and able to say a few words. They greeted me as I came in the door.

"Daddy! Daddy!" they shouted, jumping up on me. I had one on either arm.

"Well! Here's the proud papa." I recognized the voice of Rufus Taylor, Iyabode's father, coming from the living room. Our small kitchen was off to the left of the hallway as you entered the apart-ment. After taking a few steps past the kitchen you walked right into the living room. Iyabode was in the kitchen preparing the meal. She stopped to give me a kiss.

"Hi, baby. How was rehearsal?"

"Hey, Yabo," I said, kissing her back, and proceeded, chil-dren in arms, into the living room to greet her father. "Hello, Mr. Taylor. How are you?"

He was sitting at our circular oak dining table, which was hidden from view as you entered the apartment. "I'm fine, thanks. Long time no see. How you been?"

Mr. Taylor's dark oval face, even with his receding hairline, made him look as if he had spit Iyabode out. We were connected in another way, as his June 6 birthday was the same as the twins'.

"I've been good. Yabo, guess what?" I said, turning toward the kitchen again, anxious to share my news and thus answer her question.

On our living room floor was a shaggy orange rug, onto which I set the children. A piano stood against the wall on the right, and on the other side of that wall was our bedroom. The wide windows in the apartment gave us a view of the Pratt Institute dormitory. Our building, at 195 Willoughby Avenue in Brooklyn, was one of three high-rises in close proximity to one another.

"Sun Ra's got a gig in Nigeria at FESTAC."

"What? Really? Oh, you know what? That's crazy. I just heard about FESTAC," she said excitedly. "I just saw Black Rose and she was talking about going there. I heard it's really going to be something great. Wow! Sun Ra's going?"

"I don't know, baby. You may not be so excited after I tell you this part," I said, trying to break the news to her gently. "We're not getting paid for it."

Her enthusiasm was momentarily dampened. I could see her immediately adjusting to this new information. "Wait a minute. How you going to get there? That's a long way from Brooklyn. Where are you going to stay and how will you eat?" she asked with typically genuine concern.

"We're supposed to have our food, housing, and transportation taken care of," I explained.

"Oh, Ahmed, that sounds wonderful! I wish me and the boys could go," she said with a twinkle in her eyes.

Iyabode had finished cooking and we moved back into the living room.

I walked over to put on a record. We were so absorbed in our conversation, we had all but left Mr. Taylor and the children to themselves.

"You sure it will be all right? You know I'd be gone for two weeks?"

"Hey, what's that music you just put on there?" Mr. Taylor asked, interrupting a pregnant pause in the conversation. "Man, that sure sounds good."

"You like that, huh?" I asked.

"Yes, sir! That's my kind of music!"

"That's Monk. It's a really great side: *At the Blackhawk.*"

"Ahmed, this is about going to Africa. You may never get another chance to do anything like this. We been talking about Africa since we met and how much it means to us, and here you are getting an opportunity like this. Don't worry about me and the boys. We'll manage! If you go, it'll be like we went."

"Tell me something, Ahmed," Mr. Taylor interjected. "Where can I pick up this record? I tell you, I really like the way that fellow is playing that piano." Of course, coming from Mr. Taylor in Southern African American speech, it was *"pee-anna."*

"The record is actually out of print. You know, it was recorded about seventeen years ago."

"I can tell these guys know what they're doing. I sure would like to listen to it a bit more," he said.

"Why don't you take it with you?" I offered.

"Yeah, it sounds like the kind of record I could get hooked on. If I take it, I might not bring it back, you know. And you say it's out of print, huh?"

I went to the turntable, put the record back in its jacket, and handed it to Mr. Taylor. He looked at the jacket for a long time. Monk appeared as ancient and African as his music sounded. Iyabode and I were still discussing my pending trip to Nigeria. Her father got up, reached into his pocket, and put something on the table.

"When are you leaving?" Iyabode asked.

"I'm getting ready to go right now," her father answered, even though the question wasn't directed at him.

"No, Daddy. I wasn't asking you. I know you're going to have something to eat before you go, after I did all this cooking," Iyabode challenged.

"No, I better be getting on back home. You know Lucille don't like it when I eat out, if she's cooking. Besides, you folks got a lot to talk over and I want to go on home and listen to more of this here record. I'm going to say my goodbyes now. And Ahmed, I want to hear about that trip when you get back. Hear?"

He reached down and gave each of the boys a kiss, and we walked him to the elevator. We stood, the five of us, facing the closed doors, waiting in an unusually poignant silence. The elevator opened its doors, interrupting the communion. Just before he got on, he turned around and said, laughing, as the doors closed, "Oh, by the way, I left you a little something for the record, seeing as how I'm gonna keep it."

When we got back inside our apartment we saw that he had left a hundred-dollar bill on the table. It was an interesting way of saying I should go and that he had our back.

"You see? This is a sign that everything will be all right," Iyabode said, holding the bill.

It's funny how women have always been the means of my growth and development, how I've been blessed with good choices even when I didn't fully appreciate them. I could not have gone on this tour without Iyabode's consent. While I was not nearly as respectful of the women in my life as they were of me, I was in the Ra Jail and I would learn my lesson eventually.

The flight to Lagos was filled with anticipation. Here we were, a planeload of Africans being returned to our spiritual homeland by the Nigerian government. We had just come through the era of Black Power, but this was a most remarkable demonstration of that reality. It was overwhelming to think this would actually be happening after all these generations, four hundred years of Black folks being in America. Enslavement. Lynching. Rape. Jim Crow. Civil rights. I was going back to Africa to play my trumpet. I couldn't believe it until the plane landed. How would we be welcomed? What were the people like? What if the plane crashed?

There must have been many others who felt as I did, because when the plane began its descent, the collective passenger sigh gave away all of our secret thoughts. And as the plane landed, only applause could be heard.

After going through immigration, we were taken by bus from the airport, carrying our coats, luggage, and instruments to what would be our home, FESTAC Village, for the next two weeks. The tropical climate was a shock to my body, which still had New York's winter chill upon it. Gradually, I was adjusting. We were driven along a road filled with people. Long slender palm trees danced in the heat. Women balanced baskets on their heads, wearing bright material with unimaginable color schemes and patterns. Children ran barefoot alongside, in front of, or behind the bus. Men waved to us as we waved back to them, happy to be here in Africa.

The road we were on led into Lagos, a bustling city where cars were driven faster than I had ever seen in an urban enviroment, and with no traffic lights. The city sounds were exciting.

But wait. Wasn't that someone laid out in the street? And another person and yet another? Was this the Bowery of Lagos? I didn't dare ask these questions out loud, but people sleeping on sidewalks became an increasingly common sight as we got farther into the city. In 1977, pre-Reagan times, homelessness was still fairly uncommon in New York, except on skid row. Here it was rampant.

As we rode through Lagos and into the outskirts, getting closer to FESTAC Village, I began to notice a more constant military presence. Men with high-powered weaponry were standing along the road at attention and at ease. Machine guns. Bazookas. Barbed-wire fences everywhere. In fact, the gates surrounding the village itself were covered with barbed wire. This was both shocking and exhilarating. The question arose: Who is the enemy here? I had never been in a country where everybody looked like me. As great a source of pride as it was to see Black people uniformed and apparently in control, there was also a feeling of contradiction immediately evident in what appeared to be a well-financed military and homelessness coexisting so easily. It is one thing to see city cops armed with handguns but quite another to see soldiers walking around heavily armed. Certainly, Black people at the helm of government is commonplace in the Caribbean and obviously in many areas of Africa, but for those of us born in America or Europe it was a real culture shock.

My sociopolitical background had given me some understanding of what neocolonialism was. Consequently, even though I saw Black hands and faces running things, I had a pretty good idea that the major factor here was about keeping control in the hands of the colonial powers that had allowed independence to a native elite. Nevertheless, there would no longer be simple answers to difficult questions.

Back at the airport I had met up with Milford Graves. He was heading back to America after having done two weeks in FESTAC Village. Milford pulled me aside and gave me a thirty-minute course on survival in the village. While others in the Arkestra had been engaged in immigration procedures, I'd been learning about the need to be attentive to mealtimes and the importance of finding a room with proper plumbing facilities. I'd half understood what he was talking about. Now I was wondering. Milford, by the way, was well on his way to becoming a spiritual healer and knew of the relationship between fundamentals often taken for granted and the ability of an artist to create. He was one of the true priests of the Music of the Spirit. When we got to the village I better understood the necessity of heeding his advice.

The village we were to live in was a small town built primarily to house artists during the festival. After this event, it would become housing for local residents. Built by the Nigerian government, FESTAC Village was only partially completed when we arrived two weeks into the festival. Some rooms had no plumbing, no running water. The village was about a mile long, with two-story houses on either side of a wide dirt road. There were no phones or any of the other modern conveniences that people from North America were used to. In-person communication was obviously the form here.

The government fed us three meals a day, served in a large tent that had been set up in the middle of the village. Here we could eat, meet, and talk to other artists from all over the diaspora who were a part of this amazing event.

Sun Ra was in the mood to rehearse the moment we arrived, which was not unusual for him. But here, he didn't know what to do, because there wasn't the usual matching of room vibe and musician, or any form of room assignments. With no phones, the Arkestra was spread out throughout the village.

Meanwhile, I had found lots of other musicians to freely improvise with and was having a great time. Some of the musicians were African and some African American. I met a bass player named Clarence Seay, along with a drummer whose name I can't recall, and we formed a trio and played right through the day. Our playing in the room attracted enough attention that we were asked to play a gig at Lagos City Hall. Our trio played opposite a Senegalese kora trio during an African and African American fashion show.

In their beautiful long white robes, the kora players plucked the celestial stringed instruments they had made themselves. Generations of instrument makers and players had been their teachers. The women regally displayed their cultural dress, gliding to the sound of the great-grandparent of most stringed instruments. I was able to work with our trio of bass and drums in a free and exploratory way that was different for me. No directives from Sun Ra. No big-band restrictions. Here we were, presenting our collective experiences in music to a receptive African audience. Our models were showing off designs that expressed the results of their investigations into the traditional while still being informed by the present. That gig was really different!

Late at night we'd sit out in front of our respective houses, go watch other groups rehearse, or just sit around and talk. One rehearsal I saw that has been powerfully embedded in my memory was performed by a group of drummers from Burundi. Playing drums positioned on stands, the ensemble filled the African night with their full sound. On another night I met a fellow trumpeter, Rasul Siddik, who was at FESTAC working with the Troy Robinson Big Band from Los Angeles. Rasul, a brother with locks, and I talked and found we had a lot in common as far as our influences. He was from Chicago and had been a member of the Association for the Advancement of Creative Musicians before moving to Los Angeles. Being nearly the same age and, as his name implied, sharing many of the same cultural, social, and political interests helped to connect us quickly. When he came to New York years later, he would work in the ensembles of several cutting-edge musicians like Henry Threadgill and David Murray.

Sun Ra had been told about the politics occurring behind FESTAC, and had heard that Fela Ransome-Kuti, the popular Nigerian musician, was in opposition to the government in power. He had also heard that Fela's venue, the Shrine, was a kind of a smoke den. He had therefore warned the guys in the band to stay clear. Sun Ra was always tongue-in-cheek critical about how rebellious people were, so I guess he understood that if he said to stay away, some of the guys would go anyway, even while he expected strict obedience. However, one did not have to venture to Fela's to find marijuana. The local people who came out to the village had it in large supply and were pretty much giving it away. The smoke was so powerful compared to what you might get back in the States that less than half a joint would do you. This was another problem that vexed Sunny. While we were in Nigeria, I frequently heard him comment, "I don't know what happened to the fellows since we got to Africa. They just seem to want to sleep all the time." Little did he know what the reason was.

When the band finally played, we were in one of the larger venues. It was the National Theatre, which easily held five thousand people. The Sun Ra Arkestra had played in Africa before, having performed in Egypt in 1971. For me, however, this was an exciting premiere. We played our usual set, which meant that anything could, would, and did happen. We could tell we were getting to the people, which momentarily made us feel good. After about forty-five minutes, Sun Ra signaled that we were to get up and march around. This we did. Before we sat down again, however, the audience had all but left the theater. The reason for their leaving will probably never be explained. We took it as an embarrassing moment. One attempt at explanation later given was that the audience, being new to Sunny's music and style, saw us get up and thought the performance was over. Some, however, thought the music just wasn't appreciated. Others thought that the buses taking people back and forth to concerts were leaving, which meant those having to get home didn't want to be left behind. Whatever the reason, many of us were really disappointed. I mean, you don't come to Africa and have your audience leave, you know. All in all, most of us just chalked it up as one more mystery of Mr. Ra.

The next day I was able to get back into the same National Theatre to hear a performance from the acknowledged Queen of Africa, Miriam Makeba. During this period, she had been banned in America for her marriage to activist Stokely Carmichael (now Kwame Ture), which, in Africa, probably made her all the more popular. There were swarms of people outside trying to get in to hear her, and inside there were swarms of people attentively listening. She put on one magical performance. You could tell she was in her glory. African people love Miriam Makeba. It was impossible to get anywhere near Stevie Wonder's performance, though I heard it, too, was pretty amazing.

I met the South African alto saxophonist Dudu Pukwana in Lagos, as well as many other people from that area. Some questions I had been thinking about for years were answered while socializing and observing my brothers and sisters from Azania. I began to realize how deeply these Africans, much like Africans in America, had internalized self-hatred to the level of toxicity. I could also understand how the music from South Africa was a Music of the Spirit, a transformative music, designed to rise above oppression, similar to that of the African in America. Over the years, I have always included a South African song (usually by Miriam Makeba) in my sets to further recognize that connection.

The most curious thing I saw during my two-week stay was the sight of men dancing with each other unselfconsciously and with total confidence. This was pretty deep. There would be times when I saw nothing but men on the floor dancing together. I also saw men who didn't appear to be gay walking down the street holding hands. Years later, when I traveled to Turkey and Georgia, in the Soviet Union, I'd notice that same expression of emotion shared between men. It was obviously part of the cultural mores in those societies, not the taboo it is in America.

Our initial engagement had made several of us feel uncomfortable. And it probably served as the jolt we needed, letting us know that we were not on some anthropological expedition. We were actually there to play music and in some way to represent the American African. Sun Ra had to pull out the whip to get us out of our ennui. The next time we played, Sunny was able to bring out the drum in all of us. We knew the language spoken here. We were children of Africa returning after centuries of captivity to express that longing for home every child instinctively has. Our cry grabbed those who were most receptive. The others soon came around, and before you knew it, they were all waiting for the next sound to embrace what the Arkestra had to offer. Yes, we knew the language spoken here. When Sun Ra wanted to get to an audience, you better watch out, because he could put that band in gear and rev it up at a moment's notice. That night, we got much house!

The closing ceremony was yet another magical moment in artistic presentation. Every performer and group at the event marched in full costume around the huge National Stadium. Here we could see the range of colors worn by our Caribbean and African brothers and sisters. Those Africans from the States who understood the ritual of dress, as we in the Arkestra under Sun Ra's direction did, fit right into the amazing flower garden of humanity.

This is why I am disappointed at John Szwed's reportage of FESTAC in his otherwise excellent book on Sun Ra, *Space Is the Place*. The story he told suggested that our Arkestra resisted going to Nigeria because we weren't going to be paid. His account of our arrival and our levels of performance don't reflect what I experienced. The most remarkably inaccurate tale was that of the closing ceremony. Szwed's story was that we did not participate because of Sun Ra's refusal to give the clenched-fist salute of Black Power. No such demand was made. And Sun Ra did not refuse. The slogan was actually popular in America in the late 1960s to early 1970s. Here in Nigeria in 1977, there was no need for slogans, because the event *was* Black Power. Thousands of performers had created a moment together in a show of unity, the likes of which one could only dream about. I am told that there is a video somewhere of this incredible event. In either case, I was there, and we did march.

The political side to this cultural event was brought home when the newly appointed African American ambassador to the United Nations from the Carter White House, Andrew Young, paid a visit to FESTAC. His arrival, three weeks into the festival, made clear that the event was having an impact on the Western world. No doubt to elicit some form of American support was also one of the motivations behind this whole cultural event. The major thing is that if the government of Nigeria did get any support as a result of the festival, it did so on its own terms. Overall, FESTAC had been mounted with tremendous integrity, despite the fact that historians have attempted to ignore the 1970s and rewrite history when it comes to the African impact on this period. FESTAC was in fact a major historical event befitting the decade of self-determination.

When I left Lagos at the end of February 1977, I was a changed man. The essential spirit of that experience is something I have carried with me ever since.

# IV
# THE LOFT
# MOVEMENT

We must not say no to ourselves
When there is a greater deed to do,
We must not say can't
If it is not imperative that we should.
But we never should really believe that we can't
Whenever it is for our necessity good.
We must not synchronize with anything less than
　　art-wise dignity,
It is either that we are natural-constructive-achievers
Or something less than the natural self.
The rendezvous time is here
I see a prophesy:
Across the thunder bridge of time
We rush with lightnin' feet
To join hands with those,
THE FRIENDS OF SKILL,
Who truly say and truly do.
　　　　　—Sun Ra

My return to North America placed me back in the middle of a movement that had been gaining momentum for years, but which had now come to full realization. It was fitting that I should leave Nigeria's government-sponsored Pan-African arts festival to do a gig at one of the lofts that attracted musicians attempting to shape their *own* destinies. I was to work with Arthur Blythe at the Brook, a loft on West Seventeenth Street between Sixth and Seventh avenues, managed by saxophonist Charles Tyler. The gig was subsequently recorded in a double-record set for a small independent label, India Navigation. One was called *The Grip* and the other *Metamorphosis*. It was Arthur's first date as a leader. He was already thirty-nine years old and a grossly neglected major artist. When you compare Arthur's situation to that of John Coltrane's, you see the problem. Trane had ample opportunity to work and develop his craft on major recording labels; Arthur didn't.

For too many artists, this neglect was so much a condition of the 1970s that it was high time a movement in which we could take more responsibility for our vocations was ignited. There was a whole new generation of musicians, like myself, who had heard Sun Ra during his tenure on the Lower East Side. Many of the people of my generation had been influenced by his music, as well as the music of people like Ornette Coleman, Don Cherry, John Coltrane, Albert Ayler, Don Ayler, Cecil Taylor, and Bill Dixon, all of whom came to prominence in the 1960s. Their music, called free music or avant-garde Jazz, paralleled the social climate and was in turn influenced by the social movements of the period, as people sought direction and an affirmation of their humanity while venting their frustrations with the status quo. The musicians of the 1970s, mentored by that preceding generation, sought every means we could think of to bring our art to the people, too. The venues we found available were loft spaces, often with artists in residence. The music played in these lofts over the course of some seven years constituted a major movement of self-determination in the history of Jazz.

Richard Milhous Nixon, a conservative Republican, had been elected president of the United States in 1968. Earlier that year, Martin Luther King Jr. and Robert Kennedy had been assassinated two months apart. The effort to blot out any semblance of gain in the area of human rights was officially beginning.

In the sociopolitical arena we had seen the FBI step up implementation of COINTELPRO: The government program was established in 1956 to disrupt Communist Party activities and by the time of its cessation in 1971 had been expanded to seek out, infiltrate, discredit, and destroy organizations such as the Student Nonviolent Coordinating Committee, the Black Panther Party, the Young Lords, and the Students for a Democratic Society. On college campuses, we frequently saw signs of protest and unrest around the US involvement in the Vietnam War and the demand for ethnic studies, both of which were met with violent resistance.

For years, stories had circulated indicting the music industry for reacting to the overtly political music of the 1960s by suppressing the next generation of musicians modeling themselves after those who had come before. The politics of the music industry generally reflected those of the governing elite, which has in reality never veered too far from the conservative politics espoused by Nixon and others.

The African experience in the Americas, one must remember, could have happened only if there had been little or no appreciation of Africans as human beings. The labor, humanity, and the very existence of Africans in America had been appropriated by others to be used for whatever purposes. Ironically, among the things that came out of this condition is one of the most powerful forms of artistic assertions of our humanity. So much had been taken from us that after slavery our collective mission was to redefine our self-esteem. Our culture. The conditions that African Americans endured within American society, however, were also duplicated within the nation's music industry.

The stories are therefore given credence when one hears composer and percussionist Max Roach speak of how, in the late 1960s, Atlantic Records—fueled by the Charles Lloyd Quartet's gain in both audience and sales—had asked him to follow up on Lloyd's success by making a more commercial recording. Lloyd's musical concept and style had derived from and were similar to those of the John Coltrane Quartet, but were aimed at an even wider audience and were not as politically or spiritually directed. Roach, understanding our history, recorded and released *Lift Every Voice and Sing* (1971). You might think, What could have been more commercially viable than a recording of spirituals? And the answer would depend on the audience being targeted.

The African American national anthem, "Lift Every Voice and Sing," written by brothers James Weldon and John Rosamund Johnson, was influenced, according to James's autobiography, by a meeting he had with poet Paul Laurence Dunbar prior to writing the stirring lyrics. He had originally been commissioned to compose a song to celebrate Abraham Lincoln's birthday. After meeting and talking with Dunbar, whom he felt was rooted in the culture of his people, Johnson realized he, too, should write something that celebrated and inspired Black folks. "Lift Every Voice and Sing" was originally performed by 500 Colored school children on February 12, 1900.

Max Roach, politically savvy as always, thus presented a coded statement to Atlantic, which was apparently not well received. He was subsequently cut loose, his relationship with that label and every other American record label ended for ten years. During the hiatus, Roach worked in academe while continuing to record for smaller European labels and maintaining a cutting-edge presence with his own quartet despite the US ban. He also became involved in projects with Archie Shepp, Cecil Taylor, and Anthony Braxton, three of the more powerful renegades active in the 1960s and 1970s.

It appears that Thelonious Monk, another warrior, was also around this time asked to similarly compromise his artistic integrity. Like Roach, he responded with an album he could live with. But Columbia Records had a different view of the matter. *Monk's Blues* (1969), a recording of Oliver Nelson's arrangements of Monk compositions, was obviously not commercial enough for Columbia, and therefore became his last for that label. Eventually, Monk lost his band. His last regular performing group was put together by George Wein. It was an all-star group, the Giants of Jazz, including Dizzy Gillespie, Sonny Stitt, Art Blakey, Kai Winding, and Al McKibbon. After a year with this group, and with the exception of a couple of concerts, Monk chose to remain silent, both vocally and musically, for six years until his death in 1982.

Miles Davis's music throughout the 1960s had become more adventurous as he made every attempt to keep pace with the newer innovations of Ornette Coleman and John Coltrane, which were freeing up everyone. He also had with him a young drummer, Tony Williams, who had an ear and a presence in music that flirted with the avant-garde. Miles, alone among the warriors past, seemed to have had no problem making the demanded marketplace adjustments to accomotade what was described as declining sales but was in reality political and cultural suppression. He could reap great personal rewards while helping to create a music that would take a generation down a different path. Miles was on salary with Columbia, which meant they could pull his strings. He changed his music to a *Bitches Brew* (1970) and spent half of the 1970s on the label, putting out several more recordings in that same genre. Eventually, great artist that he was, it seemed he could no longer live with it, so he took a six-year hiatus from music, but not before he had influenced a generation by giving birth to a music called fusion.

The success of the Loft Movement of the 1970s and the talent of Arthur Blythe made it possible for him to go from a small independent label in 1977 to Columbia in 1978, during Miles's leave of absence. But Arthur was a much older, more mature individual by this time, and not so easy to manipulate. He was also a product of an era that seemed threatening to the industry—the era of the Afro, of self-assertion, of Black studies. People even called him "Black Arthur Blythe," because of his self-awareness.

The stage was set in 1981 for a good young trumpeter, Wynton Marsalis, who seemed to have little knowledge of recent history and therefore only partial understanding of the continuum of activism for which he would so passionately advocate, to be given a forum to misrepresent an entire era. Clad in a Brooks Brothers suit and disavowing those who had clearly influenced him, young Marsalis would rehash, out of context, the same music Miles had abandoned as he responded to the more adventurous free music of the 1960s. When Miles did return to active playing in 1981, he picked up where he had left off, playing a music that was commercially viable and that did, in rare moments, reveal the grace and beauty of his genius. His statement about his comeback, "my love for the music is greater than my hatred of the industry"—by which he meant those corporate controllers, directors, and exploiters of the music who had little regard for artistic integrity, taste, or genuine desire—spoke volumes.

At Columbia, after 1981, Miles was to find a different reality as Marsalis enjoyed a career that both supported European classical music and stagnated African American classical music. Miles Davis was no longer "the man," and his tenure at Columbia would soon end. Black Arthur Blythe's days at Columbia were also numbered, as were those of Woody Shaw, Freddie Hubbard, and the Heath Brothers, all of whom had only recently signed to the label. These gentlemen were among those who truly did represent the continuum of this music.

○

The 1970s was a decade when musicians in larger numbers than ever formed collectives; created venues, record labels, and recording studios; and generally defined themselves and developed their music on their own terms. This, of course, did not happen overnight, and perhaps a little time can be taken to look at the events that led to what is now referred to as the Loft Movement.

The efforts and combined impact of work done by several key players of the 1960s greatly influenced the 1970s. Included among these movers and shakers were Bill Dixon, Cecil Taylor, Archie Shepp, and Sun Ra, along with the Jazz Composers Guild—an integrated musicians' cooperative—Amiri Baraka with the Black Arts Movement, and John Coltrane.

Bill Dixon—organizer, trumpeter, composer, writer—had a vision based on his solid analysis of the Jazz industry. From this vision, he formed the Jazz Composers Guild. He encouraged Sun Ra, Shepp, Taylor, and white musicians (Paul Bley, Carla Bley, Mike Mantler, and Roswell Rudd for example) to join forces in order "to protect the musicians and composers from the existing forces of exploitation."

The guild was researched and founded by Dixon based "on the principles of the medieval guilds, so that one person couldn't have something that this other one didn't get a part of." In *Dixonia*, Ben Young's biography of Bill Dixon, the composer is quoted as saying, "We were politically aware, meaning that we knew that what we did—whether we were paid equitably or not—affected the entire industry." The musicians involved in the guild would agree to work in a club only if the owners of that club would hire other musicians from the guild. The intent was to turn a single event into a series of concerts designed to benefit all.

The guild had bylaws and two primary objectives: to arrange a better agreement with club owners and record producers, consolidating drawing power, and allowing for collective exposure and better contracts; and to establish independent venues to produce concerts.

New York has long been a mecca for musicians intent on realizing fame and fortune. The grim reality of it is that one person's success might often mean another's failure. One's fate is typically determined arbitrarily, rather than by talent. The musicians who were at the core of the guild did not have major reputations or recording contracts. Those affiliated with major labels such as John Coltrane and Ornette Coleman were told of the guild, but neither joined.

Since the turn of the previous century, musicians had been prey to hotel, café, and cabaret owners who had little respect for them as human beings and would use them and exploit them in every way possible. From Jazz's inception there had been a need for some organization of musicians to address artists' conditions. James Reese Europe was the first documented visionary to understand the importance of unionizing, organizing the Clef Club in 1910. Inspired by his association with W. E .B. Du Bois and the formation of the Niagara Movement and its prodigy, the NAACP, Europe's organization did for ragtime what Bill Dixon had envisioned for the free music of the 1960s.

Europe's all-Black Clef Club existed for a few years as a symphony orchestra. It significantly celebrated the uniqueness of African people. On its debut on May 27, 1910, at Harlem's Manhattan Casino on 155th Street and Eighth Avenue, the orchestra comprised a hundred musicians, including ten pianists. The ensemble's size was born of Mr. Europe's desire to hear the rich harmonies characteristic of ragtime. Besides the traditional symphonic instruments of strings and brass, he also incorporated multiple drums, banjos, and large harp guitars, adding dancers and minstrels to the mix.

The Clef Club firmly established itself as a union through which people who wanted to hire African American musicians could do so. Thus the organization set a precedent for musicians of African descent. Before the 1995 publication of Reid Badger's *A Life in Ragtime*, James Reese Europe's name and the story of the Clef Club—despite the great need the union addressed—were little-known facts of history.

By 1964, Bill Dixon had apparently come to understand that for the union to be truly effective it would need to include white musicians. They too played Jazz, and even if they were not as exploited, it was important to forge an alliance. While the Clef Club had lasted at least four years, the integrated Jazz Composers Guild, noble experiment that it was, wound up lasting less than a year. Nevertheless, its impact was felt. The guild produced over thirty concerts in lofts and concert halls during its brief tenure. Its most publicized affair was a 1964 series of concerts produced at Judson Hall (now home to the IESE Business School, on Fifty-Seventh Street across from Carnegie Hall), titled Four Days in December.

According to *Dixonia*, the attention that was being given to individual guild members as a result of their collective organizing effort meant that some musicians were offered individual contracts that were not brought to the collective body. This is ultimately what ended the guild and what prompted Bill Dixon to leave.

Without Bill Dixon and its founding Black members, the guild would quickly evolve into the Jazz Composer's Orchestra Association, producing concerts and recordings with a variety of artists. The JCOA established the New Music Distribution Service, thus becoming an outlet for many of the independent labels of the 1970s.

LeRoi Jones's BART/S, established the year after the founding of the Jazz Composers Guild, was also significant as an organization in which artists produced works by other artists. The venue was especially important in that it brought cutting-edge artists back into the Black community itself, embodying the connection between culture and politics.

It was probably the combined impact of the guild and BART/S that led the organizers of John Coltrane's last New York concert, which took place in April 1967, to choose Olatunji's school, a loft on 125th Street in Harlem, as the event's venue. Because of Trane's influence on the musicians of the 1970s, that concert was viewed by many as one of the major events inspiring the Loft Movement.

It was back in 1966 that I had taken Pat Mallory to the Village Vanguard to hear a great double bill of Trane and Coleman Hawkins. This post–*Love Supreme* Coltrane group was definitely moving in a different direction. Pharoah Sanders was playing with Trane then, as were Alice Coltrane, Jimmy Garrison, and Rashied Ali. And they played really challenging music, expanding the sonic possibilities of their instruments. There were moments when Trane and Pharoah sounded like a whole herd of elephants. It might have been a bit much for Pat. I, on the other hand, was ecstatic.

Hawkins, the father of the tenor, seemed happy to hear this modern-day tenor madness. I watched him as he sat on a sofa by the door, kicking up his heels in utter delight as he listened to the music of Trane and Co. The group Hawkins had with him featured Barry Harris on piano, Major Holley on bass, and Eddie Locke on drums. Major Holley had a way of making his voice another instrument while he bowed the bass, and Eddie Locke would often play the trap drums with his hands. No one had ever played tenor sax like the Hawk, hence his other nickname, B&O, short for "Best and Only." Harris, who had been influenced by Bud Powell, also had a style of playing that was uniquely his own. The assembled groups' style of playing as well as their concepts made the entire affair an immaculate conception. A great double bill.

When Trane extended his set a little past the allotted forty-five minutes, the club's management rudely blinked the lights, even though he was in the middle of some incredible music. One could also hear the breaking of glass during bass solos and the noise of the cash register—distractions from the business of making music by the business of making money. It was no wonder to me that the next couple of times I heard Coltrane, it was entirely outside of any club. He was an artist with a vision who apparently could not be dictated to or insulted by market limitations, even while enjoying great success in the marketplace. *A Love Supreme* quickly sold enough to achieve gold status, yet one year after its release he had gone in a completely different direction, leaving some fans and critics behind as he explored this Music of the Spirit.

Later that year, in December 1966, Trane and Ornette Coleman were again playing a double bill at the Village Theatre (later known as the Fillmore East) on Second Avenue and East Sixth Street, on the Lower East Side. Coltrane had the same band I had seen several months before, augmented now by a few more people. Rashied Ali, Coltrane's drummer at the time, spoke recently of Trane's magnetism as a beacon for younger musicians whom the saxophonist would allow to sit in. As a result, there would always be musicians around, horn in case, ready to play—cats like Archie Shepp, Marion Brown, Frank Wright, Carlos Ward, John Tchicai, and Dewey Johnson.

At the theater, Trane opened his set with "The Father and the Son and the Holy Ghost." The experience of listening to it live immediately reminded me of when I had first heard it at Jack Harris's house in Queens. Harris wanted us to hear it on earphones to get the full effect. This live set at the Village Theatre proved even fuller. Jimmy Garrison, who would be with Trane until the end, began the set with one of his long, flamenco-style bass solos, and the journey was on. LeRoi Jones's statement on the back album cover of *Ascension* spoke for me as well: "Trane is now a scope of feeling, a fixed traveler whose wildest onslaughts are gorgeous artifacts even deaf people should hear."

The other group, Ornette Coleman's trio with David Izenzon and Charles Moffett, was also incredible. Ornette, in fact, was a hero of mine in a different way from Trane. His unique style provided me with a path. He was someone I would be indebted to when I was developing my own concepts.

I recall that Sun Ra and some of the members of the Arkestra were present in the audience for this concert, a significant event for the avant-garde of the Lower East Side. Sun Ra would record his *Atlantis* album at the same venue Coltrane had performed in, the Olatunji Center of African Culture.

As mentioned above, Tunji's center was the site, in April 1967, of John Coltrane's last appearance in New York. In distinct contrast to the Village Vanguard (where there was a small audience) and similar to the Village Theatre concert, the place was packed with people wanting to hear the music. Olatunji did not have an exclusionary policy at his center, but Harlem, post-1964 rebellions, was not a place that too many people besides Africans wanted to frequent. There were standing-room-only lines of folks waiting to get in to hear Trane play a concert billed as John Coltrane & Quintet in Roots of Africa.

Before he passed in July 1967, Trane was taking steps to do two noticeable things in relationship to his art: First, he had taken his music out of the clubs and was now working in areas where there was tremendous support for what his spirit demanded he do (the story is that he, Yusef Lateef, and Olatunji were working on a partnership that would ensure the creation of more venues such as Olatunji's); second, he had made a move toward starting his own record label. These moves brought him closer to Sun Ra in philosophy and action and were probably influenced by the Jazz Composers Guild as well.

In one of Trane's last interviews with Frank Kofsky, published in *Black Nationalism and the Revolution in Music*, Kofsky posits, "Yes. Sun Ra is quite bitter, and claims that you've stolen all of your ideas from him, and in fact that everybody has stolen all of their ideas from him. [Laughter.]" Coltrane responded with, "There may be something to that. I've heard him and I know that he's doing some of the things that I've wanted to do."

Speaking personally, from the time I had first heard Trane at Birdland until he passed, I was under his sway; much of my foundational interest in the music and movement of the 1970s came from John Coltrane, which, in turn, eventually led me to Sun Ra.

I had another friend on the Lower East Side, Al Blackman, who changed his name to Dahoud and skipped out of the military before he could be sent to Vietnam. We had met at one of the many political rallies I attended in those days. It was around this time (about 1967) that I, too, was set to be drafted into the army, probably to fight in Vietnam. A couple of people I grew up with had already died there, and it seemed that this was to be the fate of anyone sent to that unpopular war. Up until this time, the fact that I was continuing my education had been a source of protection. School, however, was no longer happening for me, so I was going to have to deal with the draft.

By then, I knew enough to realize that the military was not an option for me. One of the sources of my knowledge was the hero of the day, Cassius Clay, who had recently become Muhammad Ali, a member of the Nation of Islam, publicly voicing his opposition to the war in Vietnam. He was subsequently stripped of his heavyweight championship title, arrested, and sentenced to five years, pending an appeal he would eventually win. Ali's refusal to engage in an unjust war against a people who were not his enemies—and the clarity of his opposition, which at the same time gave voice to the feelings of many—was extremely encouraging.

The day before I was to go down to the induction center at Whitehall Street for a physical, I went to my sister's apartment. Now a nurse, she prescribed Ritalin as a pill to help me to achieve the desired effect. I took several of these pills and then went to Whitehall Street. The plan was to make myself unappealing enough to get a psychological deferment. When I arrived at the induction center, I probably looked like someone who had been rejected from the Bowery for slovenliness. They took one look at me and sent me to the psychiatrist, just as I had wanted.

When I got to his office, I started running around and yelling out, "Birdshit!" I thought myself clever and that I was especially good in this role. The psychiatrist, however, did not buy it. He asked me a few questions, took a long look at me, and declared me mentally fit.

One of two things was going on here: He had either seen a lot of cases like mine or he assumed this to be normal behavior for a Black person. Whichever it was, I was assigned a military escort, who took me to the front of an incredibly long line of potential soldiers. I thought they were going to have me sign up and then arrest me. It was either the Ritalin or an enormous sense of fear that had my heart beating so fast and irregularly that when I was examined, I was found to have a heart murmur. I was given a 4F, a physical deferment.

Dahoud and I had a friendship based on other mutual interests than our anti–Vietnam War attitude. Being a drummer, Dahoud modeled himself after Milford Graves and had developed a makeshift set of drums closely resembling Milford's.

We also both loved John Coltrane. In fact, I think I listened to more Coltrane at 377 East Tenth Street, where I was living at the time, than I have in any other period of my life. When Dahoud eventually got an apartment in that same building, we listened thousands of times to tapes of the Coltrane Quartet playing at the Half Note. Dahoud had a series of air checks on an old reel-to-reel tape player taken from the Jazz DJ Alan Grant's show.

It was through Dahoud that my interest in metaphysical and occult literature developed. He made me aware of Weiser's Bookstore, then situated in a basement on Broadway, between Thirteenth and Fourteenth Streets. Being a Scorpio, Dahoud seemed naturally drawn to that which was hidden or different in some way. One book in particular that he turned me on to, *The Sufi Message: The Mysticism of Sound* by Hazrat Inayat Khan, was said to have been read by both John Coltrane and Sun Ra. Dahoud would introduce me to more literature of a mystical nature or to people who were themselves mystics. He was so intense that whenever he had something to share with me that was of special interest (which was often), his eyes would be wide with excitement as he'd say, "Brother, this is it!"

He was usually right. Plus, he had an uncanny ability to find the most interesting music. He turned me on to both of Dizzy Gillespie's extended works, *Gillespiana* and *Perceptions*. Dahoud was also searching for the philosophical underpinnings of Trane, Sun Ra, and life in general. As a result of our friendship, I too became thus engaged.

It was with Dahoud that I heard the recording *Other Planes of There*, the music that ultimately made me aware of Sunny's exceptional approach. This recording, unlike the first Sun Ra recording I had heard the year before, was done by the Arkestra in 1964, in New York. It included a version of Sun Ra's composition "Sketch," a piece with unusual intervals blending into a steady swinging groove. It was through this recording and that composition that I was able to hear why Sunny was so special. John Gilmore's playing on that particular track has wings; his amazing saxophone work takes off and allows you to go with him as he patiently and logically explores every crack and crevice of the song, taking you to other planes you never thought possible. He gets sounds out of his sax that are just unbelievable.

Frank Kofsky's interview with Trane in *Black Nationalism* quotes Coltrane as saying, "I listened to John Gilmore kind of closely before I made *Chasin' the Trane*, too. So some of the things on there are a direct influence of listening to this cat, you see. But then I don't know who he'd been listening to."

The sound that Pat Patrick gets out of his baritone on "Pleasure," another track on *Other Planes*, is so juicy you just want to revel in it. No wonder Sun Ra spoke of musicians as being tone scientists. I was turned on to this album right around the time of Coltrane's funeral, which both Dahoud and I had attended as if Trane were a member of our immediate family.

*Other Planes of There* was a signpost, telling me what direction I needed to take now that Trane had gone. Because of his strong interest in the metaphysical, Dahoud had spent a considerable amount of time around Sun Ra too, and it was he who had informed me of Sun Ra's call for a hundred musicians to join him in a presentation at Central Park.

If there was any question about Sun Ra's ability to bring people together, the park demonstration rendered it moot. A few hundred people were on hand to witness this sound and sight phenomenon. With Ra, it was never just about music.

Dahoud and I went out there for that concert, though neither of us joined in. I was just getting into it, so there was no way for me to think I was ready for someone like Sun Ra. Nor did I have any idea how one could get the sounds I was hearing out of those instruments. Many other people weren't ready for this concert either, just as so many folks were hardly ready for Coltrane's *Ascension*, which had been recorded on June 28, 1965, and was an obvious nod in the direction of Ra. The music of *Ascension* was collective in nature, with strong individual voices emerging from the body whole. Little musical notation was involved, though I understood the musicians had definitely been given some direction. Trane, in a sense, was presenting his own musical-social-political strategy, a communal one, rooted in an interdependent paradigm that, if practiced, would enable musicians to find a new sense of freedom. A. B. Spellman's excellent liner notes to *Ascension* point to Sun Ra as a source of influence for Trane. It seemed that what Sunny was going to prove once and for all, with his hundred-piece assemblage, was who the true source really was. He had at least eight times the number of musicians as the *Ascension* date. Sunny's was an endless sound exploration.

◖◗

My first live-in relationship was now on the outs. Besides the difference in age and political awareness, Pat and I had some difficulty understanding one another. I didn't know quite what I wanted to do and frankly didn't understand myself. Pat was about to go off to Tanzania to finish school, and I was about to drop out of school. I had long owned my own trumpet and had a deep interest in music, but I wasn't quite ready for the commitment it would take to really play my horn. This lack of purpose and direction had an effect on our relationship as well.

One day we had a fight about nothing in particular, but, due in large part to my ignorance about women, it proved devastating. After the fight, Pat went off to Cleveland to stay with friends for two weeks. I was so angry with her I didn't call her once. I had thought from the heat of the argument that we had had it, that it was over between us. Little did I know, all the time she was in Cleveland, she had been waiting for me to call. I later learned that it was because I hadn't called—not because of the fight—that we broke up. I learned a big lesson.

It wasn't long before my relationship with Pat ended that another woman, Ellen Coaxum, entered my life. Ellen, who, like my father, was from North Carolina, had been working for the telephone company. We hit it off pretty good, but before I knew it, she had moved in with me, along with her four-year-old son, Oba. We formed a family quicker than I thought possible. Ellen had been involved in the Nation of Islam. As such, she was insistent that people call me Ahmed Abdullah, and her efforts truly made this name mine. It was with Ellen that I also made tremendous progress as a musician. During the time spent with her, I practiced incessantly, oftentimes in the bathroom, so as not to disturb folks, with the door closed late into the night, and all day in the open. Fueled by the memory of Ra's Central Park concert as well as by all the music I had been listening to, I was playing catch-up.

We were still living on East Tenth Street when tenor saxophonist Frank Wright came to New York. He had found an apartment on Avenue B, right around the corner from us. Frank had come from Cleveland in a big white Cadillac, ready to conquer New York City. He was eventually given the nickname Rev, apropos to the preaching he did with his tenor saxophone. Shortly after he had arrived, he put together a really great sextet and recorded for ESP-Disk. The front line of this album, *Your Prayer*, included Algerian-born trumpeter Jacques Coursil and alto saxophonist Arthur Jones. Rashied Ali's brother, Muhammad, played drums.

Through Frank I met Arthur Jones, who was a player in the Eric Dolphy tradition. And man, could he sing through that horn! We shared a love for the music of Billie Holiday, and his lady at the time, Dorethea, and Ellen were really good friends. The four of us would spend evenings together listening to music and talking. Arthur was one of the first really accomplished musicians to befriend me, encouraging me to get my act together. I went to his gigs wishing that I was good enough to be up onstage with him. He, along with Frank Wright and a number of other players, left to go to Europe in 1969 seeking better work opportunities. They all returned intermittently. When I went to Paris with Sun Ra in 1976, Arthur, Frank, and another special saxophonist Noah Howard were among the musicians I would check out. I found Frank and Noah, but was told that Arthur had been committed to a mental institution outside Paris. I saw him for the last time in 1984, when we played together, and then I lost contact with him.

Marion Brown was another saxophonist I admired and would frequently see on Tenth Street, heading east toward the apartment of Bennie Maupin, who lived on East Tenth between C and D. Marion was one of those guys who walked like he played. To my mind, he was already a star, having recorded on *Ascension* with John Coltrane, and on *Fire Music* with Archie Shepp. Though I appreciated him from a distance, I would not meet him for several years.

Shortly thereafter, Ellen and I moved to the Bronx, where we lived until sometime in 1970. Two months after we moved into our Manida Street apartment, we thought the world was coming to an end. When Martin Luther King Jr. was assassinated, I was a young man, almost twenty-one. I had been made more politically aware by association and study, and fully understood the implications of the strife and turmoil in America. The Vietnam War was still going on, and the King of Love had been shot dead.

The group of people that I hung out with in college, however, did not hold MLK in high esteem and it would take years before I would truly appreciate his genius. At the time, I agreed with my college buddies. We felt that nonviolence did not work and that King's death was the actual proof of our belief.

While I stayed in touch with them, I had left college in 1967 to seriously devote myself to music on a full-time basis. I was beginning to feel encouraged enough to take my horn out to sit in. The first place I did this, interestingly enough, was in Harlem at the 135th Street YMCA. Baritone man Charles Tyler had recently worked with Albert Ayler and was now leading his own band. Included in his group was Arthur Williams, one of my friends from Queens College. Knowing Arthur made it easier for me to summon the courage when Charles allowed folks to sit in. There was another trumpeter in the house who also sat in and spoke to me afterward. Complimenting me on my attempt, Chris Capers offered to give me some much-needed trumpet lessons. He, by the way, had just finished a couple of years working with the Sun Ra Arkestra.

Chris was my first real trumpet instructor, and he showed me the rudiments by making me aware of several trumpet method books. We worked out of Arban, Saint-Jacome, Schlossberg, and Charles Colin's Advanced Lip Flexibilities series. Through Chris I was able to read music and play with more confidence. Once I made up my mind as to what I was going to do, things began to happen.

I eventually found opportunity with a collective group about to be formed, and it was Arthur Williams who once again was my connection. The band featured Joe Rigby on saxes, sometimes Mustafa Abdul Rahim on bass clarinet, Les Walker on piano, either Luis Angel Falcon or Ben Hanson on bass, and Steve Reid on drums. The two-trumpet/two-sax front line was different and powerful enough to give us the right to call ourselves the Master Brotherhood. We felt, and in Joe Rigby's case most especially, that we were continuing the music of Coltrane. As a result, we worked many of the cultural institutions that had developed in the late 1960s to provide a forum for the new consciousness. By then, LeRoi Jones had moved back to his home in Newark and had changed his name to Imamu Amiri Baraka. He had also opened Spirit House, a cultural institution we played at. We also did gigs at Black Power conventions and conferences, at the East in Brooklyn, and at the Far East in Queens.

Arthur Williams, Joe Rigby, and I would often go to drummer Eric Brown's house for sessions. Eric lived in Hollis, Queens, and he was yet another drummer to be deeply influenced by Milford Graves. Eric, unlike Dahoud and Milford, used a standard set of drums, but he played them in a completely unorthodox way.

Many of the musicians back then would make the trip out to Queens from Manhattan, Brooklyn, or the Bronx to play at Eric's. I once met Albert Ayler's brother Don out there. I had actually met the Ayler brothers earlier, during my days on the Lower East Side. I remember an extraordinary set that the Ayler brothers did at Slugs' with Milford Graves on drums. Outside, after their offering, I also remember listening in on one of the oddest conversations I've heard in my life.

"I felt it again! Did you see it, man? Did you see my third eye comin' out this time?" Albert asked of Don.

"Yeah. I could feel mine's comin' out too. It came out a little more this time," Don replied.

What was most startling to me, the young, impressionable observer, was the seriousness and total sincerity of this conversation. Notwithstanding my inability to understand the exchange, Don Ayler had one of the biggest tones I had ever heard. I learned something about sound projection from him the one time we jammed at Eric's. As we played, I could hardly hear myself. It was as if the sound of his trumpet swallowed my own sound whole. I practiced hard for several weeks after that. Fortunately, before I had moved from the Lower East Side, Walter Bowe (who had been arrested in the Statue of Liberty conspiracy) had finally come out of prison. Walter is a trumpet player whose advice was to prove invaluable to me . He suggested a trumpet teacher named Carmine Caruso.

After I studied with Chris, I looked up Caruso. Though a saxophonist himself, he had developed a trumpet method that was a sure thing. It was kind of like weightlifting for the chops. Caruso suggested that students play long tones in every interval, starting with half steps and going up as far as they could in both intervals and range. This method, which I practiced diligently, helped me develop a good round tone. Of course, the best thing for me was to play, and for a period Eric provided the forum for that. He, however, would live out one of the many tragic scenarios I have witnessed in this music.

For all his sophisticated drumming technique, Eric was a really simple guy. He didn't play publicly too often, but at that time, none of us did. I suppose that, as a drummer, he saw himself as the center of a cell, and thus expected people would come to him. But when we had all moved on to the next phases of our lives, Eric was still out there in Hollis waiting for people to come and jam at his house. I don't know exactly when he snapped, but the last time I saw Eric he was riding the F train with a look in his eyes that didn't indicate any sense of cognition. I had heard that he had lost his wife, child, and house, and had flipped out.

In 1970, an organization was initiated to attempt to address some of the problems musicians faced. The group, the Collective Black Artists, was spearheaded by bassist Reggie Workman and trumpeter Jimmy Owens. It had as its major goal the purpose of making musicians more self-sufficient; as well, it served as a much-needed forum in which like-minded artists could meet. The opposition to creativity in this society can be so overwhelming that one must set up the necessary supportive environment to continue the work. As a result of the CBA, musicians would produce gigs for musicians in different venues and generally take more responsibility in relation to their vocations. You might say this was an extension of the concept initiated by the Jazz Composers Guild. There is, I believe, a great benefit that awaits any artists who take steps in the direction of self-determination. In spite of the fact that there might be limited support for creative work, artists have the ability to respond in an organized fashion by meeting regularly, sharing information, and strategizing effective solutions.

The Jazz Composers Guild, though short-lived, became the catalyst for ESP, due in no small part to Bernard Stollman, the label's founder, who was able to see the real need for artists to have their work documented.

Sun Ra felt that one of the failures of the Jazz Composers Guild was the inability of its members to respect one another enough to choose a leader from among themselves. The implication was that the white members were reluctant after Bill Dixon had left to choose any of the Black members as leader of the organization. The CBA, however, made an attempt by definition to circumvent those cross-cultural disagreements.

We met at percussionist Warren Smith's loft at 151 West Twenty-First Street, organizing to produce concerts at Long Island University in Brooklyn and at many other facilities. Because it was created with a particular intent, the CBA was for a time able to provide work for many musicians. While in existence, it was an effective organization. It was through the collective that I met saxophonists Charles Brackeen, Hamiet Bluiett, and many other musicians.

Bluiett is a musician for whom I have a great deal of respect. I have known him since our days at the collective and in 1970 I was invited to be a part of the group to mark his first New York appearance as a leader at the East. The East and the Collective Black Artists had similar interests in organizing and in self-determination, which meant that many of the musicians from the CBA played at the East.

Bluiett and I had an interesting connection in that my oldest sister, Marilyn, was a close friend of his former wife, Ebu. In effect, Ebu knew me before I knew myself. The incredible thing is that while we did not recognize each other, I always felt close to her. My mother told me one day that her friend Grace Starks's daughter Helen (Ebu Bluiett) had married a saxophonist. My mother couldn't quite recall the man's name; she said it was one she had not heard before. As my mother butchered it and finally came up with "Blue something or other," I eventually figured it out. Bluiett, by the way, is one person I have always been able to rely on for pearls of wisdom. While we were rehearsing for that first gig, he dropped one on me that I will always remember.

It was 1970 and Sun Ra had left New York to live in Philadelphia. Someone asked, "Where is Sun Ra these days?" Bluiett's reply was, "I don't know, but, wherever Sun Ra is, that's where the music is!"

The day I met tenorman Charles Brackeen, he was looking to form a band, and he came to one of the CBA meetings with this as his agenda. Charles was a different order of being, and he dressed the part: He had on a black cape that hung off him like Zorro's, and a tall conical black hat. Trick or treat? When the meeting was over, he went about purposefully choosing musicians to play his music, which he had with him in a black leather briefcase. Charles is a unique voice within the music. His sound is a mixture of Sonny Rollins, Ornette Coleman, and Albert Ayler, with a lot of Charles Brackeen thrown in. His writing is also distinct. One of the first of his songs I played that day was "Rhythm X," the title tune of his Strata-East date produced by Clifford Jordan. The group he used on that 1968 date, Don Cherry, Charlie Haden, and Ed Blackwell, would gain popularity ten years later as Old and New Dreams, except that Dewey Redman would be on tenor instead of Charles.

On this particular day after the meeting, Charles picked me and two Detroit musicians, bass player Hakim Jami and drummer Shams Mutadir, and we went to rehearse. I liked his music from the beginning, so much so that after the rehearsal we exchanged phone numbers. We were at that time living right near each other in the Bronx. Charles had a drummer named Roger Blank with whom he had been rehearsing. A few months later, when we started practicing on a regular basis, I had already moved again, this time to the Crown Heights section of Brooklyn, at 520 Crown Street, and Charles had, interestingly enough, moved from the Bronx to the very block I had first moved from, East Tenth Street between Avenues B and C. We rehearsed in Williamsburg at a loft space shared by Roger and Rashied Ali, Coltrane's former drummer. Roger had managed to maintain a relationship with his ex–Sun Ra rhythm section mate bassist Ronnie Boykins.

Ronnie had come to New York in 1961 with the Arkestra and worked with Sunny for quite some time. He had a falling-out with Sun Ra over a couple of compositions he claimed were his and for which he got no royalties and no acknowledgment as composer. He later won a legal battle and a settlement.

During the early 1970s, it appears that Sun Ra had an arrangement with ABC Records to do a series of albums. Ronnie's lawsuit might have been one of the things that allowed ABC to back out of the deal with Ra. I understand from various conversations with him that far more records were to have been released than were actually issued. Many of the Sun Ra recordings made in the 1950s, as touted as they are, basically capture rehearsals, and many of the people on those dates never did receive payment. Ronnie Boykins was the only person who came forward with a gripe. One can only imagine the position of a record company anticipating the can of worms that would be opened if news of Ronnie's victory got out.

What Sun Ra had in his favor was that many of the musicians who stayed with him over the years had actually exchanged services for room, board, and a real sense of family. We understood that there was an unwritten and unstated understanding that once you were part of the band, you could always count on it. Ronnie Boykins proved to be an exception to the rule.

For me, Boykins was a great teacher in the group we formed, the Melodic Art-Tet. He was a real taskmaster who expected me to be up to snuff in making the chord changes in the tunes we played. When and if there was a passage that I did not make on a gig, I would be sure to hear about it afterward, and I could hear it coming because he would start out with, "Now, young man," with a lecture to follow.

Generally, we played Charles Brackeen's music, which was freer and had great presence and presentation with a sense of ritual to it. When Charles didn't show for a gig, we would either play Ronnie's songs, my own, or some standards we had previously included in our repertoire. We might even use another saxophone player's compositions. I recall saxophonists Lyman Reynolds, Bugs Dyer, Marvin Blackman, and Bill Saxton all making gigs at

different times. All of them were good, and the music we played
with them was your basic club music. Good, straight-ahead Jazz.
Charles and I, however, had a special chemistry. I have been able
to document our playing together only on recordings issued
under my name, which is great for archival purposes but doesn't
necessarily tell the whole story.

The Melodic Art-Tet was a special group with original music
by Charles, Ronnie, Roger, and me. Roger handled all the business, booking the band, securing rehearsal space, and so on. He
was also a good drummer, having studied with both Charli Persip
and Ed Blackwell.

Roger and Charles had an odd kind of relationship. Both were
sensitive and therefore prone to arguments that would reach the
point of headache. Once we were going to do a record date and
we had invited the quick-witted trumpeter Don Cherry to record
with us. So Roger and Charles were in their arguing mode, going
back and forth and back again as if no one was in the room but
them. Don looked at me, looked at them, looked back at me as if
to ask, *What in the world is going on?* Finally he shook his head
and said, "Man, y'all either need to get married or y'all need to get
a divorce, and I don't know which one, but I'm gone!"

The presence of Don Cherry was natural because we were
using Ornette Coleman's concept as a point of departure as
opposed to Trane's. But Cherry split and we never did the date.
Yet what we had planned was a thing to behold. We were going to
use Charles's music, which spoke to another level, given the truly
gifted composer that he was. Often he would use a suite-like form
for his compositions, and the solos would leap out at you from
long ensemble passages. While we did do quite a few gigs together,
we never did do an actual recording. But in 2013, a Melodic
Art-Tet performance from 1974 on WKCR radio was released on
NoBusiness Records, with William Parker replacing Ronnie.

The Melodic Art-Tet, however, prepared me to work with Sun
Ra, what with Ronnie Boykins keeping on my case about learning how to play on changes. The music that Ronnie composed
and that we played when Charles was not around was seriously

advanced bebop. And when I went outside of the form of a particular composition without really knowing what I was doing, Ronnie would be right there, as critical as he could be.

I had come into the music listening to some of the most adventurous and exploratory sounds possible. To my way of thinking, freedom was the path, yet here was Ronnie Boykins, who had spent years with Sun Ra and had played some of the most way-out music in that ensemble, telling me that in order to really be free, I needed discipline. This was a wisdom I had come to acknowledge primarily because of my respect for Ronnie. I didn't know it at the time, but this was also a major concept that Sun Ra pushed. In my search to learn more about music, Ronnie had become the catalyst.

Cal Massey, an influential composer, arranger, and big-band leader, also directed me to a better understanding of music. My meeting with Cal would come as an indirect result of an ad. During the fall of 1968, I had bumped into a *Village Voice* ad for a job working with children at 1310 Atlantic Avenue, a daycare center in Brooklyn. The mission of the center, which was run by Rupert Vaughn, was to prepare young minds by instilling in them a sense of pride in their own culture before they reached school age. Rupert was seeking people who loved children and were primarily interested in making a difference. What he got was a staff of committed artists of varied academic backgrounds who were pretty much aware of their culture and loved children. This was my first effort at teaching, and as it turned out, I would be there for four years.

Previously a two-story garage, 1310 Atlantic Avenue was huge. Inside it, two great Brooklyn artists named Jokula and Tejemola, had painted a Wall of Respect with images of heroes from African American culture that you could see as soon as you walked into the New Directions Day Care Center.

Rupert, the director, had been educated at Brooklyn College and was a native of Barbados with a flair for the dramatic. He seemed to have been caught somewhere between the Afro-centered and Euro-centered approaches to life, probably exactly what was then needed in the directorship. Many of the parents who dropped off their kids were middle class or had middle-class aspirations; in that context, this meant that they were not necessarily interested in having their children taught about being from Africa or in being called African Americans. For the most part, they wanted babysitters for the ten to twelve hours a day that they were busy with their own careers. The center was partially funded by a private white donor. When he later withdrew his funds, mobilizing the parents to deal with the increased fees necessary to continue the program took a truly major effort.

Though many of the parents were hardly interested in an Africa-centered educational focus, they did need the daycare center. In terms of self-sufficiency, I believe it would have taken a person a little more grounded and streetwise than Rupert to have successfully taken this innovative concept to the next phase. It was, however, Rupert's vision that had initiated this concept, and we were bound to deal with him. And what a vision it was!

The school had actually set new standards in day care. Rupert's mother, Mrs. Vaughn, was a midwife who had developed an impeccable method for the care of infants as young as three months. This method would actually be adopted by the city as word of it spread. The teaching staff had, among other things, developed an alphabet creatively designed to aid children in reading and identifying with their own culture (i.e., *A*, African American; *B*, Black and beautiful; *C*, Colored people; *D*, dignity; *E*, education; *F*, freedom; *G*, generous, etc.). We made up songs for the children to sing and firmly implanted these words and alphabet into their consciousness. On any given day I would arrive at the center at 7 a.m. and stay until eight or nine at night. It was a real community center, and we saw ourselves as building an institution that spoke to the needs of our community. Besides my paid job of working with the children, I was able to practice my horn, rehearse with the Master Brotherhood, read, or just socialize with a wide cross section of people.

Around the corner from the center on Nostrand Avenue was a sign elevated from the street level proclaiming a music school. One day in 1969, desirous of a firmer understanding of chord changes, I walked up the flight of stairs to the music school and met a fellow named John Stephenson. He asked me to play his song "Assunta," to see where I was at musically. After I had played it, he told me he would recommend me to Cal Massey, the composer of the composition. He felt that I was too advanced for him and that Cal would be a better teacher for me. I didn't know at the time what a tremendous opportunity I was being offered. I had not taken the time to notice that Cal Massey was the composer of "Bakai," a song on the first Coltrane record, *Coltrane*, on Prestige, that I had fallen in love with during my days at the Donnell Library. Cal had also written music recorded by Charlie Parker, Freddie Hubbard, Lee Morgan, Jackie McLean, Philly Joe Jones, McCoy Tyner, and, later, Archie Shepp.

John Stephenson had assured me that he had given Cal my information as he had done likewise with me regarding Cal. The Massey family house was at 235 Brooklyn Avenue, close to St. Johns Place.

On a hot spring day that year, I rang the bell and was greeted by a tall, graceful, pretty brown lady with long black hair and big beautiful eyes.

"Hello. My name is Ahmed. I'm here to see Cal Massey?"

"Hi. Come on in. I'm Charlotte," she replied, turning completely around. With her back to me, she said, "Cal, there's someone here to see you."

I looked past her and could barely make out the figure of a rather large man in the next room, sitting on a piano stool in a hunched position. As I walked into the space, I noticed manuscript paper sprawled on top of the upright piano. The man was seated in his undershirt. He had long curly hair combed back from his forehead. His eyes looked through me as he checked me out from head to toe. I was nervous without even knowing why.

"Hi," I stammered. "John Stephenson said I should come by to talk with you."

"Who?"

"John Stephenson said he talked to you about me," I said, rephrasing my intro.

"Uh-huh," was all he said. A long silence followed as he began to peer through me even more intensely.

"So, whatcha want?"

"John told me I could probably learn something about playing on changes and writing music from you."

"I don't know nuttin' 'bout no music," he replied. He was now looking straight at me with his penetrating eyes. Like his wife, Charlotte, he could easily have been mistaken for a native of India.

I was to learn later that their oldest daughter was in fact named India and that their four other children, Taru, Zane, Singh, and Waheeda, had similarly different names. But now Cal was checking me to see, no doubt, what I was made of. He was probably wondering if he'd be wasting his time, while testing me to see if I could handle the pressure. The music that people called bebop was a tough music, and the guys who played it learned it the hard way, through just this kind of process and through a more stringent one on the bandstand. The wisdom of this music was not passed on easily. You had to pay your dues.

"I see you got your ax with you. Let me hear you play something," he finally said.

I slowly and nervously pulled out my horn and began to play. I was too anxious to do anything but play from my heart. He listened, almost as intensely as he had been scrutinizing me before.

"Who you been listenin' to?" he asked.

By now my list of influences was considerable. "Miles Davis, Donald Byrd, Clifford Brown, Freddie Hubbard, Kenny Dorham, Don Cherry, Dizzy Gillespie . . ." When I came to fellow Philadelphian Lee Morgan, I finally got a response.

"Yeah. Lee's warm, man."

"Booker Little . . ."

"Booker Big," he said.

"Booker Big?" I asked.

"Yeah. Booker Big. With a sound like his, that's what he shoulda been called. Wasn't nothing little about Booker," he added.

This finally broke the ice. Booker Little, you see, was a kind of secret trumpet player, hardly known, and the fact that I had spent time checking him out indicated to Cal that I was possibly worth the effort. Other than his son, Zane (who is now a powerful tenorman), Cal never had another official student. Eventually, I understood why, with the kind of lessons that went on all day.

What Cal did primarily was write out patterns that I then had to transpose through the keys and play in as many permutations and combinations I could conceive of. I would return with the patterns worked out, and he would play the chords on the piano as I'd go through them.

The other lessons I got from Cal were on life. True to the bebop culture he'd been raised in, it was always a thing for him to try to get extra money from me. Initially, I didn't mind, because the lessons were endless, and it wasn't about money anyway. It was a mind game that he'd play, and when I realized that my role in the game was to resist in order to strengthen his game, I felt the classroom I was in. I never considered myself a bebop player, and becoming one really wasn't my intention in studying with Cal. What I learned from him was a technique that enabled me to make more coherent, logical, and lyrical musical statements.

The other part of my relationship with Cal Massey entailed my learning something about concert production. Cal had developed a reputation as the person to see about putting on a benefit concert. He had a magnetic personality and an amazing ability to get people to participate in or to come out for the events he produced.

At some point late in 1969, while I was still studying with him, someone had proposed the idea to Cal of a benefit for the Black Panther Party. I happened to be working at the perfect location for that affair. I introduced Rupert Vaughn to Cal Massey. As a result, one hell of a great benefit for the Black Panther Party was put on at 1310 Atlantic on February 21, 1970. Quite a bit of money was raised, and Cal Massey became a person whom once again people started to notice.

Because of his frankness and temper, and most of all because of his decision to control his own publishing, Cal Massey was avoided by many of those who controlled the music establishment. When I met him, Cal was no longer that active as a performer, although from time to time he would pick up the flugelhorn. His major source of income was the royalties he'd receive when people recorded and released his compositions. His aggressive way of hounding the record companies about when records were to be released appears to have been seen as a threat. The threat was that other musicians would eventually understand the kind of money they could make if they owned the publishing companies themselves. For this is the one toehold that guarantees the income that accrues through record sales and other forms of royalties. Consequently the delicate balance of control would be challenged.

Massey saw that many recordings made by other musicians adapting his compositions were often shelved for years, thus cutting him off from projected royalties. Cal was unique to his generation. There weren't many musicians who understood the importance of owning their music as he did. There are stories of musicians strung out on drugs, selling their compositions to record producers just to get high. Cal's position was revolutionary by comparison. He felt a real affinity for the Panthers and their brand of militancy. He would, however, prove a bit much even for these young firebrands.

Cal got excited whenever he produced mammoth events like the benefit for the Panthers. On this occasion, he was dressed in a long dashiki and was perspiring heavily, as it was an unusually warm February day and he had just gotten offstage. The center had a ramp leading to a back room that acted as a dressing room. The back door opened onto Atlantic Avenue just before you got to the dressing room. The door, guarded by a young Panther, had been opened to provide ventilation for the few thousand folks who had packed into the space.

Cal walked up the ramp, sweating profusely; the dampness of his skin caused the dashiki to stick to him. The Panthers, with their uniforms of black leather jackets and berets cocked to the side, had a reputation for being tough.

"My brother, could you close the door? It's too much of a draft coming in," Cal said to the guard.

"My orders are to keep the door open and to guard it, sir," he replied.

"What? Hey, man, close the door, will you? I'm all wet and shit," Cal said testily.

"I gotta check with the Secretary of Communication, because I got my orders."

This fellow obviously did not know who he was talking to, nor did he see the rage rising in Cal and about to visit upon him. Cal let out a roar and yelled, "I said, 'Close the goddamn door!'" I had never seen someone move as fast as that young Panther did.

One of the things that would be interesting to find out through the Freedom of Information Act is if the benefit done for the Black Panther Party at 1310 had anything to do with the fact that the private donor's monthly stipend of $10,000 ended soon after. This money was in effect the lifeblood of the center. At the time, no one thought twice about it; there was too much work to be done to make up for this huge sum of money we were told had come to its inevitable end.

As a result of the projected deficit at the center, Cal Massey was once again called in to produce a benefit, this time for the New Directions Day Care Center itself. This fundraiser, Jazz on Grass, was produced in association with Staten Island Community College on July 19, 1970. It was advertised with a design that smacked of Peter Max, quite psychedelic.

Being around Cal during this time taught me another important thing: Anyone is reachable. He would get on the phone and charm you into doing whatever he wanted. His opening salvo was always, "This is Cal, baby!" and then he'd proceed with an appeal you couldn't refuse.

He put together a show that probably would have been impossible to do today because of the fees involved. And it was pretty incredible in 1970 to have Carmen McRae, Pharoah Sanders, Leon

Thomas, Babatunde Olatunji, McCoy Tyner, Freddie Hubbard, Lee Morgan, Eddie Gale and His Ghetto Music, along with the Last Poets and Cal's seventeen-piece Ro-Mas Orchestra (named after Cal and arranger/composer Romulus Franceschini) on one program. For my efforts, I was awarded a slot for the Master Brotherhood. And what an event it was. Eight hours of compelling music. Everyone showed up and performed wonderfully. One of the secrets to Cal's successful affairs was that they were actually Jazz parties that people would attend simply because they knew other people would be there. This particular party, however, did not attract nearly the number of fans it should have, given the budget and lineup involved. Perhaps this was due to the location, the Staten Island Community College campus, which was supposed to have been a cost-effective site. The success, however, was in the music, not in the profits. Consequently, the result was one more nail in the coffin that would be the final resting place of the center. But what a way to go!

Cal's decision to find support with a younger, more radical audience was well timed. He would soon write an extended work called "Liberation Suite," and dedicate it to Malcolm X, Huey P. Newton, and Eldridge Cleaver. He would also work on a really great album by Archie Shepp, *Attica Blues*, which would document the uprising at New York's Attica Prison in 1971. If you listen to Shepp's music before *Attica Blues*, you might be given to believe that the addition of Cal Massey brings something to the fore that was not heard before in Shepp's music. One thing I know for sure is that *Attica Blues* is a bona fide classic.

Cal Massey, principled and fearless composer and arranger, was in many ways like Sun Ra, capable of pulling large numbers of conflicting and complementary personalities into one cohesive and collective unit working together for the common good of the music. While they both knew how to take advantage of an opportunity, they were never opportunists, but maintained and nurtured the principle of integrity with everything they did. Not that they were saints, but they did hold on to a basic ethos regarding the spirit found inside their music.

Roughly a year and a half after that glorious benefit, in the early morning of February 20, 1972, I was awakened by a phone call. It was Cal.

"My brother, Lee Morgan has just been shot, and he's dead!" A shared silence followed.

"What?"

"Yes!" Another longer pause ensued before he hung up the phone.

Lee Morgan was someone I studied and admired, and who had recorded a number of Cal's compositions. He was one of those rare individuals we both felt a great deal for. It happens that on the evening before that phone call, he had been shot by his wife at Slugs', where he was playing a gig.

Later that same year, Cal continued working with Archie Shepp. They had already traveled to Europe and Algeria, where they briefly met with Eldridge Cleaver, who at the time was still in exile. Somewhere in that mix of gigging and traveling, Cal and Archie began collaborating on a play Aishah Rahman had written and for which Archie and Cal would compose the music. It was called *Lady Day: A Musical Tragedy*, and it premiered at the Brooklyn Academy of Music on October 25, 1972. On that night, however, Cal Massey was stricken with a fatal heart attack, which in itself was a tragedy, as he was just beginning to get the kind of exposure and recognition he had earned long ago.

While at 1310, I also met this fellow by the name of Chuck Jones. He had a magnetism about him that attracted women. We used to often meet at parties because we traveled in the same circles. He had a day job at the Spofford Youth House in the Bronx, not too far from where Ellen and I lived. Chuck, however, lived in Brooklyn on Eastern Parkway, and would often come around

1310. There would always be a bunch of pretty women at the center, and they all loved this guy. Ellen also worked at 1310 with me, which kept my own wanderlust down to a minimum. One day, this fellow Chuck told me he could play trumpet. Plausibility pending further proof was usually my unspoken response. It didn't take long before I heard him and knew he was serious! His name is now Olu Dara, and he is one of the truly great artists of our generation—he's also the father of well-known rapper Nas.

Dancer/choreographer Dianne McIntyre also used to come to the center to rehearse with the Master Brotherhood. She seemed to enjoy dancing to our energetic music. Because of my affiliation with the center, we often rehearsed late into the night without interruption, which was a great service. Dianne would eventually use Joe Rigby as the saxophonist for her innovative dance company Sounds in Motion.

Author and now television host Iyanla Vanzant worked at 1310. I remember her as Rhonda, a young mother involved in African dancing, trying to get her life in order. Obviously she succeeded.

Sometime after the Jazz on Grass concert, the Master Brotherhood split up as an ensemble. I moved on to form my own group and had the opportunity to premiere it at 1310. The affair was put together by an organization called the African Mobilization Committee, whose activist chairman, Samori Marksman, later became the program director at New York City's Pacifica radio station, WBAI. The event was billed as the African Liberation Movement Symposium, held on May 13, 1972. The music was provided by Baba Ishangi and Dancers, Kwame Nkrumah (the musician), and my new group, which I named Abdullah. There were speakers as well, including two powerful intellectuals, Walter Rodney and Courtland Cox, along with Elombe Brathwaite, founder of the 1960s African Jazz-Arts Society and Studios and later the Patrice Lumumba Coalition, and historian Yosef Ben-Jochannan, affectionately known as Dr. Ben. For me, the event was baptism by fire.

The timely formation of my own group coincided with a movement of musicians in New York that was beginning to converge. The inspiration for this was coming from Studio We, an organization in existence since 1968, run by James DuBoise, Juma Sultan, and Ali Abuwi. Duboise came from Pittsburgh, where he had been nurtured by various musician collectives. When he arrived in New York in 1967, it was natural for him to form an organization that would act as a supportive arm for the struggle that always accompanies the creative process.

By 1972, the struggle to be waged was against George Wein, who was relocating the Newport Jazz Festival to New York and excluding many musicians active in the metropolitan area. The New York Musicians Festival was organized to counter this slight. The University of the Streets at 130 East Seventh Street, at the corner of Avenue A, had just recently opened its doors and became the meeting place at which to strategize. With little money and a lot of heart and support, the effort of more than 500 participating "other" artists, Black and white with many stylistic differences, the New York Musicians Organization put on its own festival, seriously impacting George Wein's event. Sites all over the greater metropolitan area were included. The publicity garnered for this musicians' festival could not have been paid for; it was the local media's contribution to our worthy cause.

The New York Musicians Festival was thus a huge success, and the power of our collective effort was clearly in evidence the following year, when George Wein negotiated directly with the NYMF. Without fully understanding the significance of our victory, one individual as opposed to a committee was sent to talk to Wein. This individual was offered a sum of money that he accepted on our behalf before checking with the collective body. As a result, the New York Musicians Festival came under the umbrella of Wein's Newport Festival in 1973. It was essentially co-opted, never again to emerge.

But one good thing to come out of our 1972 counterfest was the decision by Sam and Bea Rivers to open up a loft at 24 Bond Street, Studio Rivbea, and present musical programs in their basement, which turned into one of the premium sites for our festival. On its opening night, Roger Blank, Ronnie Boykins, Charles Brackeen, and I worked there as the Melodic Art-Tet, opposite the Clifford Jordan Quintet.

The following year, 1973, the Newport Jazz Festival placed the New York Musicians Festival at Lincoln Center's Alice Tully Hall. On the surface, this might appear as an honor, royal treatment even. But further investigation reveals that at the same time we were scheduled to be at Alice Tully Hall, with little name recognition and even less publicity, we were up against major names like Ray Charles, Ella Fitzgerald, Stan Getz, and the like at Carnegie and Avery Fisher Halls. Wein's effort was not just about co-option.

During his post-festival press conference, George Wein told an uninformed public how much money he, the great benevolent impresario, had lost trying to support the avant-garde musicians who had been relegated to Alice Tully Hall. If his interest in broadening the audience for more adventurous artists had really been sincere, the way to go would have been inclusion and integration, not a neo-apartheid separation between stars and prodigies. What about having a lesser-known artist open for a well-established one, thereby building an audience for the range of newcomers? Even with vision exploitation can occur. But no. His intention was to obliterate the new heat.

During this second festival, I managed to appear at Alice Tully Hall with two groups. My own band Abdullah, though only a year old, was nevertheless included in addition to the Melodic Art-Tet. Abdullah featured Frank Lowe on tenor saxophone, Richard Dunbar on French horn, Aerol Henderson on bass, and Rashid Sinan on drums; and the Melodic Art-Tet again had Charles Brackeen, Ronnie Boykins, and Roger Blank on board.

In spite of, or maybe because of, the attempt to obliterate our movement, many of the musicians became stronger but in a completely different way. We didn't have the level of organization demonstrated in 1972, or that which was evident with the Collective Black Artists or the Jazz Composers Guild. What did occur, however, was the proliferation of individual efforts unfolding in the recently abandoned industrial buildings that would later be identified as the Loft Movement.

Around 1974, Studio We became the site for a rehearsal big band. These workshops brought together musicians who wanted to share music, new arrivals to New York, and those already here. They allowed anyone who so desired to bring music to a rehearsal and have it worked on by the group regularly attending. This inspired guys to write for larger ensembles and got us working together as a big band. The musicians had a lot to do with this growing movement, which had long since started but was now taking on a new momentum. Regulars included baritone saxophonist Charles Tyler, tenor saxophonist Frank Lowe, alto saxophonist Oliver Lake, multi-reed man Joe Rigby, trumpeter Ted Daniel, and myself, along with drummer Steve Reid, guitarist Mel Smith, and bassist Richard Pierce. There were many others who joined the workshops on various occasions, like Arthur Blythe, Hamiet Bluiett, David Murray, Kazutoki "Kappo" Umezu, and Olu Dara. Consequently, quite a few gigs came out of these workshops, but they mainly offered a chance for musicians to come together to develop musical and networking skills. Back then, when musicians would first come to town, they'd often be referred to this workshop, as David Murray and Arthur Blythe had been.

A couple of gigs this group did were coordinated by trumpeter Ted Daniel. When we worked under Ted's direction, the group was called Energy. On at least two occasions, Olu Dara and Lester Bowie (whom I had heard about through the Jazz press and from other musicians) were part of the trumpet section when we did the gigs at Sunrise Studio and at New York University. There were more than enough musicians around to make the big-band idea most appealing.

On several occasions, Bluiett also put together a big band from this pool of musicians. I remember one concert we did at Stanley Crouch and David Murray's loft space, on the corner of Second Street and the Bowery, right over the Tin Palace, a club that would later be a hot spot for the music. There were some extra musicians added to this band. Drums for instance, were played for a time by Phillip Wilson and Stanley Crouch, with bassists Fred Hopkins and Brian Smith, and the people who would later be known as the World Saxophone Quartet: Julius Hemphill, Oliver Lake, David Murray, and Bluiett. Olu Dara, Malachi Thompson, and myself played trumpet. The music was so powerful that someone called the police. That, of course, put a damper on the spirit, even though this concert did get a favorable review in *DownBeat* magazine. Throughout the era, Hamiet Bluiett and Ted Daniel continued organizing other spectacular events at the Brook, Ali's Alley, and Environ, a club on Broadway.

The music that was happening in the lofts was in fact affecting the mainstream of Jazz. Working in an environment that supported the growth and possibilities of their discipline, musicians were going into bands with a renewed sense of confidence and exploration. In the mid-1970s, both Bluiett and Olu Dara had found employment in bands run by legends in the music. Bluiett was working with Charlie Mingus, and Olu was working with Art Blakey and the Jazz Messengers. Both of these bands were more challenging and adventurous than either Mingus or Blakey had led before. Much credit is due to them for being open and to Olu and Bluiett for being true to the muse.

My work with Sun Ra, who had established himself on the fringe of the mainstream, was also a direct result of the activities in the lofts. By 1974, two years after they opened their doors, Sam and Bea had made Studio Rivbea, at 24 Bond Street between Lafayette and the Bowery, the most well-known of all the lofts. If it weren't for the activity around Rivbea, this cobblestone street would have been totally lifeless at night; it was a really dark street, especially as you got closer to Lafayette. The industrial firms on Bond Street were closed at night and their employees long gone by the time music started.

During the month of December 1973, Studio Rivbea presented concerts with musicians and groups whose contributions to the music were being recognized by larger audiences. The venue also presented musicians and groups that were relatively unknown, some performing in their first New York appearances. The studio ended the year with an all-day holiday music festival from December 21 to 31, presenting two exciting groups each night beginning at nine and ending with a jam session in the early morning hours. Each weekend in December, Studio Rivbea would also present an art and photography exhibition with works for sale by Ron Warwell and Clarence Eastmond.

A sample of the groups offered were those of saxophonist Keshavan Maslak with trombonist Ray Anderson and drummer Steve Reid; pianist Errol Parker's quartet with percussionists Samuel "Sticks" Evans and Ray Mantilla; Flight to Sanity with drummer Harold Smith and saxophonist Art Bennett; Muntu with Arthur Williams, saxophonist Jemeel Moondoc, pianist Mark Hennen, William Parker—the last bass player for the Melodic Art-Tet—and drummer Rashid Bakr; and the group known as Apogee, featuring saxophonist David S. Ware, pianist Gene Ashton (now known as Cooper-Moore), and drummer Marc Edwards. That New Year's Eve, drummer Norman Connors's Dance of Magic was featured with saxophonists Carlos Garnett and Byard Lancaster, vocalist Dee Dee Bridgewater, bassist Alex Blake, trumpeter Charles Sullivan, pianist Onaje Allan Gumbs, and percussionist Nat Bettis.

For January 1974, a sample program included my group Abdullah, the Karl Berger Group, Ken McIntyre, and the Melodic Art-Tet, all doing two nights each. Also running through the month of January was a play, *Offering Black Mass*, by the Caribbean playwright Edgar White, featuring, among many actors, Mary Alice and Laurie Carlos. Later, Ntozake Shange traveled cross-country from California to present *For Colored Girls...* at Rivbea. Joseph Papp came to see it there and took it to Broadway for its historic run.

For my performance there in January 1974, I used recently arrived alto saxophonist Arthur Blythe as well as French horn player Richard Dunbar, guitarist Masujaa, bassist Aerol Henderson, and drummer Rashid Sinan.

For a time, Studio We on Eldridge Street was at the forefront. It had a rehearsal studio, a recording studio, and its owners had the wherewithal to produce concerts. In addition to other recordings made at this facility, my first two releases as an improvisational musician were recorded at Studio We.

The first one, done in August 1975 (four months after I had joined Ra's band), was called *Seikatsu Kojyo Iinkai*, which means "life improvement committee." The organizer and leader of the date was a Japanese visiting artist named Kappo Umezu, who played the saxophone. It featured Rashid Sinan and William Parker as well as Kappo's friend from Japan, pianist Yoriyuki Harada. The music played on this date was for the most part freely improvised with minimalist structure provided by our melodies. It had a definite Cecil Taylor influence. We had done one performance together before we went into the studio to record at another loft space called the Sunrise Studio, on Second Avenue between Seventh and Eighth.

Although Kappo had produced the date, handling music, fees, and all on his own, the album cover photo was a group shot that included the engineer Ali Abuwi. This inclusive gesture on Kappo's part reflected the ideal of the era that was in contradistinction to the reality I experienced during my second recording done at We.

In March 1976 (four months before Sun Ra's *Live at Montreux*), I was recording with the disbanded Master Brotherhood. We had agreed to make an album together to document our existence as a group. We were donating time and expertise to the project without compensation because it was something we all wanted to do. After we had labored collectively to make the recording, I was genuinely shocked, angered, and disappointed to find that without consulting or seeking agreement from the other players, Steve had taken the liberty of putting his picture on the front cover and had called the album *Steve Reid/Nova Featuring the Legendary Master Brotherhood*. The liner notes read like it was his date with no mention of anyone else's input.

While we had known the album would come out on Steve's Mustevic label and under his name, we had recorded with the understanding that it was to be a collective venture. It was a collective ensemble from the beginning, and a collective date. Two of the album's five compositions were mine, with saxophonist Joe Rigby contributing one, and pianist Les Walker and Steve (with Luis Angel Falcon) also each contributing a piece, yet the cover and liner notes pushed individualism at the expense of collective motion. Steve's actions exemplified a fundamental problem that surfaced throughout this period.

The problem of individualism versus collectivity is one that arose frequently in the 1970s. If you could pinpoint any cause that continually affected the Loft Movement from within and minimized its outward impact, I'd say it was the failure to comprehend the need for collective sensibility in order to work interdependently. As artists, we develop our individuality and oftentimes go through life that way, while the forces in opposition to our being are multiple. But these can only be countered through a collective response.

Sam and Bea kept up their mixture of programming through 1975, but just before I went to Europe with Sun Ra in 1976, there was a great deal of excitement generated by another series happening on Third Street near where Slugs' had been before it closed in '72. Produced by a fellow named Amos Rice, it was called the Music for Cartographers series and was scheduled to take place during the same time Sam Rivers was producing a festival at Rivbea. And so the clamor. Some people were scheduled to participate in both festivals. The festival at Sam's, backed by a record company, was offering guaranteed money. The Music for Cartographers series offered only a share of the door. The clamor eventually turned into a smoldering resentment among a few musicians toward Rivbea, particularly toward Sam. Many of the people in the Music for Cartographers series, as well as many of the performers at Rivbea, were new to New York. Since early 1975, the city had seen an influx of musicians unlike ever before. Most of the new arrivals had no awareness of the history of the movement that they were suddenly and dramatically a part of. There was little understanding among them when the Music for Cartographers series was cut short due to lack of audience and media attention. Several of its concerts were subsequently canceled, leaving some bad feelings, a bit of controversy, and many rumors that cast aspersions on the work done by Rivbea.

Despite the conflict, the *Wildflowers* sessions that were recorded there remain among the most well documented statements on the movement of the 1970s coming out of the loft spaces. Not only had Sam and Bea Rivers started Rivbea in 1972, but Sam was also connected to the full continuum of collective efforts up to that point, namely the New York Musicians Festival, the Collective Black Artists, and the Jazz Composers Guild Orchestra of 1965. Their perspective had to be different from those of the recent arrivals to New York, and so misunderstanding came to replace clarity.

The live recordings at Rivbea, the *Wildflowers* sessions, occurred between May 14 and May 23, 1976, and were produced with Sam by Alan Douglas, a collector and producer of eclectic tastes for his Douglas label, distributed by Casablanca records. Douglas was a collector, in particular of Jimi Hendrix's and Eric Dolphy's music. Sam's relationship with him stemmed from Douglas's interest in Hendrix, as Sam had done a project with that great guitarist that had never been released.

Alan Douglas had broad enough taste to also have produced a record date with Duke Ellington, Charles Mingus, and Max Roach (1962's *Money Jungle*), as well as a couple of Eric Dolphy and Art Blakey recordings for United Artists. Taking note of the potential market in the music developing from the lofts, he, along with Sam Rivers as his liaison, documented the music, choosing Rivbea as the site for the historic sessions.

These recordings represented a move forward, in that Douglas had much better access to distribution than any of the musician-owned or independent labels that had arisen since 1970. Therefore the music that had been heard only in major metropolitan areas such as New York, Philly, Chicago, and Oakland would be heard throughout the world. There were more than twenty groups and close to seventy artists recorded on five volumes. The liner notes for this recorded event read:

> Many of the most important changes of the 1970s are now taking place in the loft performing spaces that have emerged in New York as an alternative to the commercially oriented clubs and concert halls. Run cooperatively by the musicians themselves, these lofts have become centers of creative activity by providing an environment outside the inhibiting pressures of the music business for the ongoing experimentation that is the lifeblood of the music. In the ten years or so since the first lofts opened their doors, the players have used their independence to hone their musicianship, develop their individual voices and distill their music down to a readily communicable essence. In the process, they have attracted a large audience of listeners responsive to the relaxed informality of the loft ambiance and give and take between performer and listener, a shared enthusiasm that contributes to the music's characteristic high-energy good feeling and lyricism.

The musicians who participated in the sessions as leaders were paid double union scale. Each group was asked to perform a forty-five-minute to one-hour set. The bonus of this really innovative project was that the leader of the session was allowed to keep the master of the unused performance material for whatever purpose. Charles Tyler's entire performance was for some reason not used, and he sold the whole tape the following year to an independent label.

The *Wildflowers* sessions created a great sensation in the music community that lasted a couple of years. For many of us, it was our first recording as leaders or so-called sidemen. We were well into the 1970s, but this was the first major documentation of the era.

As I had been traveling the Spaceways by then, my relationship to Sun Ra played a role in this recording. My composition "Blue Phase" (on the third volume of *Wildflowers*)—with trumpet and saxophone riding the waves of an ostinato bass line laid down by electric and acoustic basses, with drums freely creating—was published through Sun Ra's company, Enterplanetary Koncepts. The musicians used were Charles Brackeen on tenor and soprano, Masujaa on guitar, Richard "RaDu" Williams and Leroy Seals on bass, and Rashid Sinan on drums. The review we received in the June 1977 issue of *Cadence* magazine, written by Carl Brauer, read:

> The next performance shows just why these recordings are so important. It's a piece entitled "Blue Phase" (12:37) played by a group called Abdullah. Except for Brackeen all the musicians are new to me and they deserve to be heard. The piece is out of the neohard-bop camp but with a great deal of rhythmic activity produced by the guitar, two basses and drums. Abdullah's trumpet solo comes out of Clifford Brown with similarities in tone and improvisational approach to another young trumpeter, Hannibal Marvin Peterson. Brackeen and Masujaa also have good solos. At times the sound gets too cluttered (the two bassists sometimes intrude on one another) but I find this to be an exciting group.

My use of two bass players on this date had to do with John Coltrane using that combination effectively on a few recordings. It was also related to the fact that bassist Fred Hopkins was playing with a group called Air, and that night they were playing opposite us. Some of the musicians on the *Wildflowers* session were new to me, as far as their musical capabilities were concerned. I had heard about most of them but hadn't actually heard them. The group known as Air, with saxophonist Henry Threadgill, Fred Hopkins, and drummer Steve McCall, was an interesting ensemble I would later come in contact with up and down the eastern seaboard while working with Sun Ra from 1976 through 1978. I had actually met Henry on one of my trips to Chicago while he was still working at Transition East, with Muhal Richard Abrams's wonderfully inventive big band. Henry and Fred had not yet moved to New York. In fact, only Steve McCall was here. But when Fred finally arrived in New York, he was the bass player of choice for a number of groups. The *Wildflowers* sessions reflected this, as he is heard on many of the tracks.

During the first days of the recordings, I had gone to check out some of the music at Rivbea. The performance space of the studio had now moved upstairs, and there was a duplex loft area right above the music area. I remember sitting and talking and being distracted in my conversation by the insistency of the bass. I knew one guy could not have been playing all that bass, so I went down to check to see what was happening. Sure enough, it was one guy, Fred Hopkins.

He had my ears humming with his sound and my mind working overtime. I was not to be outdone in my own town. I had been part of the loft scene from the beginning and knew that with the way Fred played I had to do something. So I added an electric bass player, Leroy Seals, who had been playing with Masujaa. I felt ready.

And there was much exciting music to be heard. There were groups led by artists including Kalaparusha Maurice McIntyre; Ken McIntyre; Sunny Murray with Byard Lancaster; David Murray; Khan Jamal; Anthony Braxton with George Lewis and Barry Altschul; Marion Brown; Leo Smith and the New Dalta Ahkri with Oliver Lake, Anthony Davis, Paul Maddox (now Pheeroan akLaff), and Stanley Crouch; Randy Weston with Alex Blake; Andrew Cyrille and Maono with Ted Daniel, David S. Ware, and Lyle Atkinson; Hamiet Bluiett with Olu Dara, Billy Patterson, Juni Booth, Charles "Bobo" Shaw, and Don Moye; Julius Hemphill with Abdul Wadud; Jimmy Lyons with Karen Borca; Roscoe Mitchell with Jerome Cooper; and many more. "The New York Loft Jazz movement continues to grow," read the review in *DownBeat*. "Eliminating the middlemen of the music biz (agents, managers, club owners, concert entrepreneurs, etc.), musicians have seized control of their destinies by producing their own music in environments unfettered by commercial considerations."

This, by the way, is exactly why many people did not know about Sun Ra until fifteen years after he had been creating with the

Arkestra. It is one of the byproducts of being independent. The collective effort over the years was finally making a difference, but because there was no real sustained organized strategy to consolidate it all, only a few individuals would benefit.

Arthur Blythe was one of the musicians who wasn't included in the *Wildflowers* recordings. I recall having a conversation with him down the street from Rivbea during those live recording sessions. He was a little upset that he had been left out of the proceedings. I felt it might turn out just as well that he wasn't included with the pack, so to speak. After all, he was working in a situation with an established musician, Chico Hamilton, which separated him from the rest of us anyway and gave him a larger profile. It is interesting that the year after we did his live date at the Brook, he was chosen as the first among us to be signed to Columbia.

# V
# LEAVING

Somebody else's idea of somebody else's world is
not my idea of things as they are. Somebody else's
idea of things to come need not be the only way to
vision the future. What seems to be need not be what
need had to be; for what was is only because of an
adopted source of things. Some chosen source as
was need not be the only pattern to build a world on.
—Sun Ra, "Somebody Else's World"

The summer of July 1977 saw lots of activity for Sun Ra and
the Arkestra. In New York, Sunny was invited to perform
at the Axis-in-SoHo. Part art gallery, part club, the Axis was one
of the places that had come into being through the downtown
activity around the Loft Movement. Sun Ra's presentation of a
solo piano concert was part of the Newport Jazz Festival and was
produced by Paul Bley, a connection from the Jazz Composers
Guild. Sunny, however, had asked several Arkestra members
to come sit in. John Gilmore, Danny Davis, June Tyson, Eddie
Thompson, and I were all to be featured in a video produced by
Bley's company Improvising Artists that documented the event.

By 1977, Baltimore and Washington, DC, had also discovered Sun Ra. Consequently, we began to work in the South more
frequently. We were first brought to Ed Murphy's Supper Club in
DC, on Georgia Avenue close to Howard University. There were
a number of devoted fans in the nation's capital, and the relationship between Sun Ra and Duke Ellington's city of birth intensified
during these years.

Some of us, including Ra, in an effort to save money, were
staying at the home of a fellow named Andre, a friend of the band
and a lover of the music. One day during our stay, in an effort not

to disturb my housemates, and desiring privacy, I walked to the nearby campus of Howard to find a practice room. While there, I heard a pianist in the next room who sounded so good I knocked on the door to say hello. The brown-skinned young lady abruptly stopped practicing, opened the door, and invited me in. She was studying at Howard and was familiar with Sun Ra; and, yes, she would be delighted if I could leave her name at the door. She did come to the club that evening. Today, people know her as Geri Allen, one of a new generation of musicians who were listening to and influenced by Sun Ra.

The article that Stanley Crouch had written for *Players* magazine the year before had helped give Black communities outside New York insight into what Sun Ra was doing. There was an organization in Baltimore, the Left Bank Jazz Society, that had been in existence for at least thirteen years by 1977, when Sun Ra was invited there for the first time. John Coltrane had performed his very last concert there in May 1967. The society produced Sunday afternoon concerts complete with Sunday dinner. The site they used, the Famous Ballroom, was a huge space. They did an excellent job of getting people to support their endeavor. Every time we played there, the ballroom was packed with hundreds of people. After the first Arkestra gig, we were invited back at regular six-month intervals. In both DC and Baltimore we were playing primarily to Black audiences.

In July 1977 we made a trip out to the Midwest, to play in Bloomington, home of the University of Indiana. There we worked a club called the Bluebird. Sun Ra had been working on his solo piano efforts and recorded a breathtaking version of "Somewhere Over the Rainbow" at this club, which was released on Saturn Records. Eleven years after that gig, I was in Chicago when pianist Michael Weiss, a student at the U of I in 1977, who went on to work with Johnny Griffin and Charles Davis, and who has transcribed a great deal of Sun Ra's music, told me that he had been in the audience for that performance.

After the *Wildflowers* recordings came out in 1977, things started
picking up in New York. Charles Tyler was managing a club called
the Brook on West Seventeenth Street. Pianist John Fischer had
opened Environ on Broadway, close to Canal Street. Farther west
on Canal was the New York City Artists' Collective, headed by
drummer Tom Bruno and singer Ellen Christi. A few hours outside
of the city, in Woodstock, vibraphonist Karl Berger had opened
the Creative Music Studio. Studio We was still happening; singer
Joe Lee Wilson had opened the Ladies' Fort down the street from
Rivbea. Bass clarinetist Mike Morgenstern was running Jazzmania
uptown on Twenty-Third Street, and drummer Rashied Ali had
opened Ali's Alley. Earlier loft spaces like Ornette Coleman's
Artist House on Prince Street and George Braith's Musart on
Spring Street had long since come and gone. All these places,
current and past, provided opportunities for musicians to work
together and to develop concepts.

June 1977 saw the second New York Loft Jazz Celebration, the
first having occurred the year before, in June, after the *Wildflowers*
sessions were finished. The first festival garnered an overwhelming response. The lofts involved in this effort to coordinate events
were Environ, the Brook, Jazzmania, and the Ladies' Fort.

Consider this excerpt from a preview written by Robert Palmer
in the June 3, 1977, issue of the *New York Times*: "Several hundred
people had to be turned away from some of the loft events. Even
better, listeners who first encountered the lofts during the festival
kept coming back. The public support has allowed the jazz lofts to
keep up performance schedules of unprecedented scope. Environ,
for example, has presented about three hundred concerts during
the past year, a record unmatched by any other loft."

One of the reasons for the success of the lofts was the broad
range of Jazz styles. At that year's festival one could hear celebrated vocalist Eddie Jefferson and Dakota Staton at the Ladies'
Fort. Among the groups offered at Environ were Fischer's group
Interface, Malachi Thompson's Brass Proud (eight trumpets plus
a rhythm section), pianist/vocalist Amina Claudine Myers, gifted
tenor-saxophone veteran Roland Alexander, and groups led by

drummers Phillip Wilson (featuring Olu Dara) and Sunny Murray. At Charles Tyler's Brook, folks could hear Indian percussionist Badal Roy, Arthur Blythe, and my band. Jazzmania had Keshavan Maslak, Bennie Wallace, and the two "most impressive baritone saxophonists in town, Pat Patrick and Hamiet Bluiett."

The summer of 1977 at Rivbea saw an even better-produced festival than in previous years. I worked there with Abdullah, opposite Jimmy Lyons's band. Our double bill was on August 31, 1977. At the time, I was using tenorman Arthur Doyle, violinist Ramsey Ameen, Masujaa on guitar, RaDu on bass, and Rashid Sinan on drums. With altoman Jimmy Lyons playing opposite us, we were graced with the presence of Cecil Taylor in the audience. Jimmy Lyons had a relationship with Cecil similar to the one John Gilmore had with Sun Ra—that is, Cecil had built his band around Jimmy.

Cecil heard Ramsey and found good use for him in one of his more extraordinary groups, which also featured Jimmy Lyons on alto sax, Raphe Malik on trumpet, Sirone on bass, and Ronald Shannon Jackson on drums. This group made three much-touted recordings, *The Cecil Taylor Unit*, *3 Phasis*, and *One Too Many Salty Swift and Not Goodbye*, all recorded the following year, 1978.

Ramsey had been a friend of mine since 1967. We'd met during a time when we were both working at the Seagram Building on Fifty-Third and Park. It was one of my early jobs: I was working as a clerk, and Ramsey was working as a data analyst. I was in the habit back then (in my effort to catch up) of carrying my horn everywhere I went. I missed no opportunity to practice, so at my day gig, during lunch, I found an isolated place in the basement of the building where I could play. On one such day, Ramsey was sitting in the lobby when I got off the elevator carrying my horn under arm. He had a violin case nearby and was busy writing music.

"Hey, man, what you got in that case?" I asked.

"It's a violin," he said, looking up from the manuscript paper. "You work here?"

"Yes, down the hall in the Xerox room. Mine's Ramsey. What's your name?" "'Round here they call me Leroy, but my friends call me Ahmed. What you writing?"

"I was trying to write out this composition by a pianist named Thelonious Monk. It's a pretty incredible piece of music. I think he's really a genius. I can hear a parallel between his compositions and improvisations and some of the through-composed European music I've studied. Have you ever heard his music?"

"I think I might have heard a thing or two by Monk," I said, with a thinly veiled attempt at sarcasm. "Who else have you listened to?"

"Well, I just saw a record by Charlie Parker I was going to purchase. . . ."

"Man, you hip to Eric Dolphy?"

I went on to list a number of other musicians, most of whom Ramsey was unfamiliar with. It was obvious, however, that he had a background in European music, which I was totally ignorant of. He had done extensive study of the music of Bartók and Bach at the City College of New York. From the meeting at Seagram's, and for at least the next decade, we would share across the rich cultural divide that separated our respective backgrounds.

Ramsey had been raised in Flushing, Queens, by a Jewish mother and an Egyptian father. He had attended the competitive Bronx High School of Science. With a highly developed background in the sciences, he was also skilled as a pianist and a violinist.

When I talked with Ramsey in later years, he reminded me that our relationship had grown to include jam sessions at his various apartments after I had taken him out to drummer Eric Brown's house in Queens. I brought him in touch with the musicians with whom I had already developed relationships, people like those in the Master Brotherhood, Joe Rigby, Arthur Williams, Mustafa Abdul Rahim, and Steve Reid. He recalled that one of our greatest sessions had occurred when Arthur Jones, an extraordinarily advanced saxophonist, had come by.

Once when we played at his apartment on East Ninety-Fourth Street, between Second Avenue and First Avenue, we had indulged in some marijuana. We had damn near a big band in the apartment that day and had created enough excitement to bring the police to the door. Ramsey, indignant at the intrusion, almost got us all arrested. Mustafa had smoothly and suavely intervened and let New York's Finest off the hook with his gentlemanly manner. We all in our own way tried to hip Ramsey to the streets, but we never meant for him to challenge the authority of the police. Of course, that wasn't true of everybody. Drummer Rashid Sinan, who lived with Ramsey for a brief time, used to brag about his escapades in various courtrooms. Once, when asked by a judge what his name was, Rashid was said to have replied, "You sittin' up there like you know so much, why don't you tell me what my name is?"

When Cal Massey needed extra hands to write out parts for his "Liberation Suite" the night before he premiered it at 1310 Atlantic Avenue, Ramsey and I helped him out. We stayed up all night and wrote and hung out, indulging in Cal's diet pills that made you feel so cool. Cal called them "mellow fellows." Man, did we get the job done.

Once, Ramsey turned me on to a place on Twenty-Third Street, Brodwin Piano Co., where I could rent a piano with the option to buy. After five months of payment, I had fallen behind and was asked to come in to see the manager. In our conversation in his office, the manager determined that I was passionate and serious about my music. He told me he was a communist and didn't believe in extracting payments from people in the way that was done at this establishment. He then told me I should keep the piano and needn't make any more payments, and that he would handle the paperwork. I never received another bill for my blond Carl Fischer piano, which I still have.

Arthur Doyle was also in the 1977 band at Rivbea. We had met during the same period that I'd first met Ramsey, back in 1967. Arthur was from Birmingham, Alabama. We met at a big-band rehearsal that Jothan Callins had at Olatunji's Cultural Center in Harlem. Both Jothan and Arthur, satin-hued 'Bama natives, were working with Sun Ra by then. Arthur has an incredible sound and is a well-studied musician; he had developed the concept of playing off the harmonic series of the saxophone in a manner akin to that of Pharoah Sanders. By 1977 he was still playing written music, but eventually, through association with Milford Graves, he would move beyond any semblance of Western influence in his sound. Whenever possible, I would set up jam sessions at Ramsey's and include Brother Doyle. Once Arthur had brought a fellow native of Birmingham, trumpeter Frank Walton, to one of the sessions. Frank was living in Chicago at the time and had a style and tone so close to Booker Little that I was stunned.

By fall 1977, the Loft Movement had made enough of an impact in Europe for Sam Rivers to take a seventeen-piece big band to the Nancy Jazz Pulsations festival in France. Sam had thought up an innovative concept for this event. He decided upon a double rhythm section, two drummers and two bass players. The big band would break down into small groups with designated players choosing a group of any size from the pool of musicians available. There would be three small ensembles featured each night, with the evening's climax arriving in the form of Sam directing the large ensemble. This approach allowed for those among us who had leadership ability or potential to exercise it.

The personnel of the group changed a couple of times before we made the trip. Sam's original plan included four saxophonists who had figured prominently on the *Wildflowers* dates and had recently become known as the New York Saxophone Quartet: Julius Hemphill, Hamiet Bluiett, Oliver Lake, and David Murray.

One of the problems that surfaced, though it was not completely spoken, was an old one: Who would be the declared leader of the Loft Movement? Sun Ra had said this was one of the problems with the earlier Jazz Composers Guild. This problem could only be resolved through a total understanding of the dire circumstances that had initially given rise to the Loft Movement, or that would cause any generation of artists to define, present, and control their art.

The fact that most artists live in an ego-centered universe while subliminally controlled by collectively conscious exploitive practices on the part of conglomerates makes it difficult to address problems where and when the need is most pronounced. A shift in consciousness was and is still definitely needed.

By 1977, Sam Rivers had been presenting concerts at Rivbea for five years. Rivbea and Studio We seemed the only lofts organized enough to apply for grants and subsidies. Yet the New York Saxophone Quartet seemed not to want to lend their collective support to Sam, which would more than likely have placed him in a much stronger position as the leader of the Loft Movement. Sam, however, was not involved in the coordination of this year's or the previous year's Loft Jazz Celebration. Viewed in hindsight, these are the things that might have given the loft era a longer run.

One can say, however, that the generation of musicians who had come to prominence during this period was self-made in a different sense from musicians in other eras. While Bluiett worked with Mingus, Olu Dara worked with Art Blakey, Arthur Blythe worked with Chico Hamilton, and I with Sun Ra, we were the exceptions. Most of the other musicians from our generation were not connected to the musicians who had come before us.

Sam, on the other hand, though no less a genius at music, was quite a different person from Sun Ra in that the younger musicians who were around him were not compelled to learn life lessons from him. Sam treated us as if we were his equals. To be in Sun Ra's band, however, one had to have communion with him. As a result, something of the history that he represented had to be respected, at least while we were associated with him. No such requirement or demand was placed upon those in Sam's band.

The fact that the saxophonists of the quartet, for whatever reason, had decided not to make this gig in Europe signaled a serious break in the continuum. Each generation in Jazz had been built upon the generation before it. This was just as true well into the decade of the 1970s. This incident, however, a harbinger of the 1980s and 1990s, would be exactly the thing that would affect the cultural and political gaps manifesting during those decades.

Sam Rivers was not to be stopped; he found another group of saxophonists, some of whom were not on the *Wildflowers* date (Chico Freeman and Rene McLean), some of whom were (Byard Lancaster and Kalaparusha). The other members of the band included George Lewis and Charles Stephens on trombone, Abdul Wadud on cello, Dave Holland and Brian Smith on bass, Don Pullen on piano, Barry Altschul and Charli Persip on drums, with Frank Gordon, Youseff Yancy, and myself on trumpets. The attention that the Loft Movement had been receiving brought people to Nancy from all over Europe on those five days—from October 11 to 16—to observe this exciting ensemble. Sam, a brilliant notator of music, chose on this occasion to use no musical notation. He gave indications of texture, dynamics, and tempo changes by writing out his desire in words. It was a real innovative stroke, and people went wild over this effective approach to presenting energizing music that was so free and yet so well organized.

Out of the larger ensemble, I was able to direct a sextet featuring Freeman, Stephens, Wadud, Smith, and Persip. The response I got was enthusiastic. It felt good to lead a band in front of thousands of cheering people. In fact, the very next day, photos of Chico and me had made it into the local paper. We were the stars of Nancy for a day, and I was now feeling that ego-itch, not to mention the fact that I was making more on this gig with Sam than I would probably ever make with Sun Ra.

◖◗

Storyville was a club in Manhattan on East Fifty-Eighth Street between Madison and Park. In late July 1977, the Sun Ra Arkestra worked that room, and we were asked back for late October. During the time that Sun Ra was rehearsing for the gig, I was in Europe working with Sam Rivers. We got back from Europe a few days before the October 24 gig at Storyville.

My life in music up to that point had included working in a variety of different settings, and most folks I worked with didn't mind. Sam's gig was different. As an innovative leader of a big band, he was rivaling the position recently established by Sun Ra, and Sunny seemed to perceive Sam as a challenger of sorts. Several times Sunny would turn to me and say curtly, "I'm not fattening frogs for snakes, you know." When I got to Storyville, there was a young trumpeter I noticed who was watching my every move. And he had some of his own, too. Michael Ray, from Trenton, New Jersey, with a rhythm and blues background, had been recruited for the purpose of being made over into the image of Ra.

The trumpet chair in the Sun Ra Arkestra had been the least stable of all the valued lead instruments. From Art Hoyle, Phil Cohran, and Hobart Dotson in the 1950s to Martin Banks, Eddie Gale, Walter Miller, Al Evans, Chris Capers, Kwame Hadi, Akh Tal Ebah, Longineu Parsons, Randall Murray, Roy Burrowes, Tommy Turrentine, Robert Rutledge, Cecil Brooks, and many more, the trumpet chair was an ever-revolving position. This probably had as much to do with the nature of the instrument and its particular practitioner as anything else. The trumpet is a martial instrument; it is direct and requires a great deal of confidence on the part of those who would dare master it. The phrase "bold as brass" is specifically applicable to trumpet players. The history of Jazz is loaded with stories of the lives of trumpeters that speak to the grand and uncontainable individualism that comes with the territory of trumpet.

The kind of submission, putting your own goal under someone else's, that Sun Ra demanded did not attract trumpeters to the Arkestra for extended stays. The saxophone, on the other hand, had developed a culture of its own, and much credit was due to John Gilmore for remaining long enough to help realize that. No trumpeter would ever be in that position.

But now, Sun Ra seemed intent on disciplining me and making life uncomfortable, deliberately spending more time developing the new kid on the block. Ebah was still in the band when we played at Storyville from October 24 to October 29, 1977 (*Unity* on Horo records), but he was now slowly fading. Michael's presence and the attention Sun Ra bestowed upon him might have indicated to Ebah that things would never quite be what they used to be. They did to me, but I had other options to explore.

During Thanksgiving week, 1977, the Arkestra was in Chicago, at Joe Segal's Showcase on North Rush. Dimly lit, with velvet carpeting throughout, the Showcase had tables and chairs arranged in stair-step fashion so that the audience could look down in descending rows on the small bandstand. The bottom row was at eye level with the band, which was miraculously squeezed onto what was called a stage. There was one aisle on the left and one on the right of the stage that led up to the bar in the back. A full mirror on the wall behind the bar gave the room the illusion of being larger.

The band was pretty much the same as the one Sunny had at Storyville, minus a couple of players. Ebah had been fasting for thirty days. He was thin and hardly looked like he was there. He got up to take a solo and walked right up to the mike and off the bandstand up the aisle to the right, up the stairs, and right out the door, still playing. It's true that Ebah was a little different, but even for him this move was odd. It was Thanksgiving Eve. When we finished the set and Ebah had not returned to pick up his music, we knew something was wrong. In the Sun Ra band, no one leaves music on the stand when the set is over. We were instructed not to.

On Thanksgiving Day, we got news that Ebah had tried to put himself in an oven. He had managed somehow to do this and suffered severe burns over his body as a result. Sun Ra always talked about the forces getting to people and taking them out of the band if they didn't belong or when their time was up. Well, this case was so weird I could have believed anything. That was it for Ebah; he would never play in the band again, although he lived at least a couple more years.

◯

Back in New York, I was again playing with Rivers, who now had brought his Nancy big-band concept to Rivbea to close out 1977.

It had been a great year, and we celebrated by playing on New Year's Eve.

Once again, I was given an opportunity to lead an ensemble at Rivbea. Earlier that year, in February, I had recorded with Arthur Blythe, who used a cellist on that occasion. I was consequently so struck by the sound of the cello that I'd looked forward to working with Abdul Wadud again in Sam's band. For my gig at Rivbea, on December 23, 1977, I came to use another cellist, Muneer Abdul Fatah (then Bernard Fennell). Muneer had an unusual way of playing the cello. He had a long peg, which allowed him to play standing up with fantastic technique. That helped bring an African sensibility to an instrument that has generally been regarded as European. He had studied with the one of the quietly known legends of the music, cellist Calo Scott. I had heard Muneer at Rivbea working with tenor saxophonist Dewey Redman, and I looked forward to working with him.

I also used tenor saxophonist Kalaparusha. He was a member of the Association for the Advancement of Creative Musicians, as were many of the musicians coming to New York in the mid-1970s. The AACM, originating in Chicago, is an important independent organization. Kalaparusha and I met through Sam's big band in Europe. I had played in a quartet that he led at Nancy, and now I was asking him to play in Abdullah. While the gig we did wasn't exactly exceptional, it helped me to develop as a leader in my own right.

○

I knew I could not continue much longer with Sun Ra. He was doing things to make that even more apparent to me. Late December 1977, I had heard that Sunny was planning to go to Europe that following January with a small group. He was going to take John Gilmore, Luqman Ali, and the new trumpeter Michael Ray. I couldn't believe that after almost three years of working with him, sometimes for little or no pay, an opportunity had arisen for me to actually make money in a smaller group, and he'd chosen someone who had hardly been in the band three months. I was infuriated and hurt. But I remembered that I had seen a similar thing happen with Ebah when I had joined the band. And now Ebah, probably as a result of putting all his hope in Sun Ra, was lying near death. In my hurt, I was determined that my fate would be different.

I was preparing more and more to lead my own ensemble, anyway. One of the places that had become available as a result of the Loft Movement and Rashied Ali's initiative was Ali's Alley. I had known Rashied since the days when I rehearsed with the Melodic Art-Tet. I struck up a deal with him.

"Rashied, I'd like to bring a group into the club, man."

"Okay, Ahk. I'm down. When do you want to do it?"

"What's the deal?"

"It's like this. You can get all the door on Sundays; we got the bar. Now I see that look in your eyes, Ahk, but the door don't have to be a drag. Cats are makin' pretty good dough off the door, man."

"Yeah, man. I'm just thinking 'cause I been using six pieces," I said.

"So, man, all you have to do is cut down. Make it a quartet if you want," Rashied replied.

"You know, I been thinking about doing something with Arthur Blythe, 'cause I did a recording with him this year."

"What you mean, Ahk? Y'all gonna play together or do it as two separate groups?"

"I thought a double bill would be hip for a Sunday afternoon. Suppose, Rashied, we used that to kind of test the waters. So we do a concert in January, a double bill with Arthur's group and my band, and then we set up something for February pending the January gig."

"Okay. Solid. Let me go check the calendar."

Rashied Ali was easy to talk to and easy to do business with. No contract, just a handshake and trust. He had dreamed of having a place to play, like so many of the musicians of the day. The difference, of course was he had taken steps to make his dream a reality.

Rashied Ali had been the drummer in John Coltrane's last band. He had played the concert at Olatunji's, which signaled that the music had to move in a different direction. He was there to see firsthand and learn that in order for the music to evolve unhampered by commercial considerations one had to take control of one's own product. Ali's Alley was probably the largest club in the city, a spacious ground-floor venue owned by a musician. It was at 77 Greene Street, between Spring and Prince, in what is now SoHo. Because of the high ceiling, as soon as you entered the space, you sensed a feeling of roominess.

Working with quartets, quintets, and sextets when he first opened in 1974, Rashied Ali used the space as a vehicle for his own bands while also providing a good quantity of work for musicians. He had basically built the club himself with help from bassist Benny Wilson, who worked in many of the ensembles Rashied would put together. He would often have Don Pullen or Charles Eubanks as pianist and a front line made up of Jimmy Vass, Bob Ralston, Carlos Ward, Marvin Blackman, Lee Mixashawn Rozie, and Byard Lancaster. I would sometimes be added as a trumpeter. His impact on the era can be seen by the fact that two other drummers (Sinan and Bakr), younger than he, both changed their names to Rashid, out of respect for him. By 1977, he had started to book other musicians into the club. Our conversation and deal yielded a concert that came off quite successfully in January 1978. Stanley Crouch reviewed us in the *SoHo Weekly News* on January 19:

Ali's Alley: On a Sunday afternoon, I heard Arthur Blythe's trio and Ahmed Abdullah's sextet. Abdullah's band sounded very good, particularly his trumpet playing, the French horn work of Vincent Chancey and the drumming of Rashied Sinan. Arthur Doyle's tenor saxophone always went to the same places, the guitarist and the Fender bassist were journeymen of the contemporary language and the compositions showed tasteful variety and a penchant for stomping and insinuating swing. In fact, it, like the band of Blythe, is one of the fresher ones I've heard.

As planned, we followed up with a weeklong gig from Tuesday, February 21, through Saturday, February 25, 1978. I was determined to make use of the attention brewing around this music. I used a slightly different group than the one I brought into Ali's Alley the month before. Remembering the impact that Chico Freeman and I had made together when teamed in Nancy, I decided to use him as opposed to saxophonist Arthur Doyle or Kalaparusha, who had done the last couple of gigs with me. I was also going to use Vincent Chancey, the French hornist I had introduced to the Sun Ra Arkestra. As well, Muneer Abdul Fatah had begun to add an important element to the band with his cello.

Rashid Sinan, the left-handed drummer/boxer, the backbone of the band, had been with the group from its inception six years earlier. The new additions to the group were bassist Jerome Hunter and vibraphonist Jay Hoggard. Jerome was working with singer Betty Carter at the time, and Jay had been working in Chico's band. This septet filled the house at Ali's Alley every night we played, doing quite well with the door. Friday night, Jay Hoggard had another gig and couldn't be with us, but it was also the night that we recorded. The recording was released three years later on Cadence Jazz Records as its premiere album. It would actually be my second documentation as a leader.

The week's performance fulfilled its goal with lots of attention. The first paragraph of Robert Palmer's *New York Times* review on February 27, 1978, was already placing my relationship with Sun Ra in the past tense:

Ahmed Abdullah used to sound like a conservative when he played solos with Sun Ra's Jazz orchestra. Instead of the cracked tone, skittering runs and huffing intensity favored by so many trumpet players in avant-garde contexts, Mr. Abdullah always displayed a bright brassy sound and a more measured flow of inspiration.

Mr. Abdullah continues to provide crisp, well executed trumpet improvisations to a variety of group situations. But during the past few years he has been developing as a bandleader, and the group he led at Ali's Alley over the weekend—like all his bands, it was called Abdullah—was simply magnificent. The combination of trumpet, tenor saxophone, French horn, cello, vibraphone, bass and drums was an unusual one, and it gave Mr. Abdullah the chance to try out an intriguing variety of scorings—playing off trumpet-vibraphone leads against horn, cello and saxophone, for example. But the best thing about this edition of Abdullah was the way it allowed each musician to improvise on his own terms while channeling everyone's energies toward the creation of a distinctive group sound.

The *Village Voice*, the *SoHo Weekly News*, the *New York Times*, and smaller publications like *Cadence* and *Coda* magazines were the major media sources covering what transpired in the lofts. *DownBeat* would write an occasional article, but its major concern seemed to be around what happened in Chicago or with artists from that town.

The review we received in the Canadian publication *Coda* (April 1978) by Roger Riggins, one of the few Black Jazz critics, was also encouraging:

Abdullah, led by trumpeter Ahmed Abdullah, is a welcome new unit on the modern music scene. On this particular occasion one was doubly lucky, for the band was augmented by the fine young reedist Chico Freeman. The band leans toward tightly knit "arrangements of sound" and there is a sonoric quality in the ensemble segments that is at times quite beautiful.

For several years since 1973, I had been working with dancer/choreographer Dianne McIntyre. I had inherited this gig from Joe Rigby, my former front-line partner in the Master Brotherhood. Before she formed her original concept of live improvised music and dance, Dianne used to come to 1310, where she rehearsed with our band; eventually she would create an original concept that was influenced by those rehearsals. She called her company Sounds in Motion.

I followed Joe Rigby as the music director of that ensemble and was given the responsibility of directing the musical trio that she usually hired to accompany her dancers. When I started working with Sun Ra in 1975, oftentimes gigs with Dianne and Sun Ra would crisscross, but somehow they never conflicted. When required, I did performances and workshops with Dianne. It was great working with dancers, but being in the company of women so confident in using their bodies was sometimes quite a turn-on. I had eyes for one dancer in particular, Mickey Davidson.

Mickey was from Long Island—Wyandanch, New York, to be exact. She had completed her studies at the University of Illinois in Urbana-Champaign, and had returned to live on East Fifth Street on the Lower East Side. Physically, Mickey and Iyabode were different, but spiritually, they were very close. They were both outgoing, intelligent, indefatigable, resourceful warrior women rooted in their culture.

A light-brown-complexioned woman with an abundance of energy, Mickey was a little bit more than five feet tall, with a fiery disposition. She stayed in dance classes and taught and wrote about dance. She lived through her craft. That was important for me to observe at a time when I could feel a transition occurring.

When we were on the road I would constantly make a play for Mickey. She always roomed with dancer Bernadine Jennings, the two of whom I dubbed "the last Girl Scouts." They would carry pots, pans, and hot plates on the road to cook their own food during our stays at various hotels. As much as I thought them odd to go through the challenges they did of preparing home-cooked meals wherever we went, I would be right there knocking on their hotel room door trying to get me some.

"Who's that?"

"It's me, Ahmed."

"Chile, it's hot lips. Thing smells the food before we even get it ready." Bernadine, a fabulous dancer, and one of God's most sensuous creatures, had a habit of calling people "thing." Dancers, I discovered, like musicians, had a language and a world all their own.

"Oh, no, he didn't. He didn't knock on our door again for something to eat. Baby, I think you got the wrong restaurant. Big Mac's across the street, darling. And besides, wasn't it you I heard smirkin' and signifyin' about pots and pans clankin' and shit?" Mickey was rough.

Leon Brown, Philip Bond, Lonnetta Gaines, actress Gwendolyn Nelson-Fleming, percussionist Babafumi Akunyun, along with Mickey and Bernadine were the major participants in Dianne McIntyre's Sounds in Motion dance company.

"I didn't come empty-handed, now. I did bring a bottle of wine."

"Oh, and since you did bring a bottle of wine, what we suppose to give up?" Mickey mockingly challenged.

"Well, what would you like to give up?" I shot back. One of the things I appreciated most about being in the company of these two was their openness. They worked at their craft in a way that allowed them to be free. In a sense, they embodied what Sun Ra spoke of when he said that one needed discipline in order to understand freedom.

Though she was being facetious at the time, Mickey would tell me later that it was the fact that I didn't come empty-handed that night that finally broke down her resistance. She also explained that she had just ended a relationship with one trumpeter and was not at all interested in getting involved with another. One night in Columbus, Ohio, before I was to fly back to a gig with Sun Ra, we consummated our relationship. And from that day on, for almost a year, we would sleep together whenever the opportunity arose.

We were also on the road together, both with Dianne's company and with the Arkestra as a result of my introducing her to Sun Ra. In the Arkestra at the time, John Gilmore and Marshall Allen were the only others with the band who had the extra benefit of sharing rooms and developing relationships with the dancers traveling with us. John and Cheryl Banks usually roomed together, while Marshall and Wisteria shared a room. Bringing Mickey into the Arkestra and having her on the road with me made me feel as if I'd attained equal status with Gilmore and Marshall, who were among those I admired most.

We often worked in Ohio, Dianne's home state, where she had been educated and still retained strong ties, familial and otherwise. April 1978 had us in Athens, Ohio. I wasn't slick enough or deceptive enough to figure out a way to keep Iyabode from calling me when we were on the road. But then again, maybe unconsciously I was getting tired of the subterfuge.

Iyabode had called one night, and for some reason the hotel operator hooked her up with Dianne's room. Dianne innocently had the call transferred to our room. Mickey answered the phone. The only thing that Iyabode wanted to know was, "Who was that woman who answered your phone?" I was caught! And big-time!

When I got back home to Brooklyn, Iyabode had my bags packed. She didn't care where I went, but I was not staying with her. I loved Iyabode. I loved my kids. I loved Mickey. I guess I wanted it all and didn't expect to have to choose. I had never envisioned the scenario I was in, and as a result, I refused to take responsibility for it. I thought it was my right as a man to deal with more than one woman at a time and really couldn't understand what Iyabode's problem was. I mean, after all, we were African people; she understood that. We both knew that there were many cultures in Africa where polygamy was the norm. So why all the drama?

When I had met Iyabode, I'd been living with Ellen Coaxum. Iyabode and I met December 9, 1972. I will always remember the day we bumped into each other on Sixth Avenue and Eighth Street in Greenwich Village. I was so taken by her beauty that I dropped my horn and broke one of the handles. That meeting led to a night out that led to an all-consuming passion we shared; we found every means of being together (usually in hotels), in spite of the fact that I was living with Ellen. Our passion led to her pregnancy and to my leaving Ellen.

This had become my modus operandi, hound that I was. When things got too close in one relationship, I'd find a new woman and tried to juggle the two. It kept me from committing myself while allowing me to flirt with a false notion of polygamy.

The problem, however, was that I was deathly afraid of committing to a relationship. I now believe that fear stemmed from the loss of my oldest sister during my adolescent years and was then easy to rationalize given an available belief system that suggested it was permissible for a man to have a relationship with more than one woman.

Polygamy, if you could call it that, as practiced by the African in America, did not give the woman the right to choose. My understanding of the practice, which probably doesn't exist in today's Africa either, is that a polygamous relationship would occur when one woman would bring another woman into the partnership. The understanding behind this was rooted in the fact that men generally went off to war and killed one another, leaving women with children alone and unprotected. Polygamy existed in some societies as a means of addressing an imbalanced condition. It was created in most cases by men and originally sold as an act of compassion, from one sister to another. And it was the woman who was empowered to make the choice that would affect her family and her society.

All of this was lost on me at the time, because my ideas were rooted in a disempowering and prevalent concept practiced by some American Africans, especially, but not exclusively, coming from my distorted understanding of women's role in Islam. Here I saw women as being submissive; in fact, many men with whom I've conversed had encouraged me in this most distorted view. In the culture of the Arkestra, for instance, women were more often viewed as appendages to men.

Ultimately, this concept means we sacrifice half of our potential in a relationship that benefits only a single individual. In thinking this way, it is hard for us to see how we perpetuate a system of disempowerment as a reaction to perceptions of powerlessness. Essentially what is practiced is a win-lose paradigm when what is needed is a win-win understanding.

I didn't see it then, and the women I was attracted to were never submissive. These warrior women wouldn't go for it either. I was caught between buying into the distortion and being attracted to strong women.

While I was out of town, Iyabode had moved with the boys from our place at 195 Willoughby Avenue to 345 Clinton Avenue. Since I did not have the keys to this new apartment it was easy for her to get rid of me.

It happens that Mickey invited me to share her apartment at 209 East Fifth Street, on a beautiful tree-lined street between Second and Third Avenues. Her building was connected to and behind another in the rear, meaning we had to walk down a long dark corridor under one building and come out into an opening that led to my new home. We would walk up a few steps and enter a hundred-year-old three-story building. The first room was the kitchen, which also contained the bathtub. Adjoining the living room was a bedroom. All in all, we shared four rooms. Mickey's son, Malcolm, nine at the time, was six years older than Rashid and Shahid, who were not quite three.

The rents on the Lower East Side were still reasonable in 1978 — that is, for those who were living in rent-stabilized situations. Even at that, I noticed that prices had generally tripled since I had left in 1968. The rents, though rising, still kept many artists in the neighborhood. My next-door neighbors were David Murray and flutist James Newton. David had already been married to and divorced from poet/playwright Ntozake Shange. To make this work, I was going to have to contribute to my new family and send money out to Brooklyn. I was in the process of procuring work with Dianne McIntyre, with my group Abdullah, and doing some work with Sun Ra. With my weeklong performance at Ali's Alley and the *Wildflowers* recordings on the market, I was slowly establishing myself as a leader. And there was only one thing to do now; just as when I'd left my mother and father's house at eighteen, there was no looking back.

Cobi Narita, a woman of Japanese descent, had been one of the few female members of the Collective Black Artists, the group that Reggie Workman and Jimmy Owens formed in 1970. Cobi had created a one-woman operation, the Universal Jazz Coalition, aiding artists in the production of their own concerts. In her efforts to help artists become more self-determined, she provided mailing lists, helped design flyers, and was able to get reduced-rate ads in the *Voice* while producing her own newsletter. Cobi patiently walked anyone who wanted to learn how to become more independent through the process.

I had the help of my sister Lorraine and her daughter Angela in the production of my flyers. Lorraine's pen-and-ink artwork was striking and immediately caught people's eyes.

My next gig was on Monday, April 17, 1978, at Art D'Lugoff's Village Gate, part of a series Cobi had produced there. I brought a sextet with the same personnel I used at Ali's Alley, minus vibraphonist Jay Hoggard. As well, Hamiet Bluiett would come to sit in with us on a couple of selections.

The review I received in the *Amsterdam News*, April 29, 1978, by Yusef Salaam, was captioned "Ahmed Abdullah moves the Gate." He did make some mention of my relationship to Sun Ra, but mostly, he positively described the music we presented.

○

By May 1978 I had stayed away from Sun Ra for most of the year. He was, however, going to do a concert at one of New York City's newest venues, Joseph Papp's Public Theater. Technically, I hadn't quit the band. Nor had I been fired. I was just angry with him. Plus, I wanted to blame my separation from Iyabode on someone; so Sun Ra was a good choice. After all, hadn't he gone to Europe with a small group, leaving me without work while taking new trumpeter Michael Ray? Well, it happened that Sun Ra called me and asked me to come to the gig and to bring Mickey as well. I went with less than love in my heart, but I did the gig anyway.

Sun Ra could always find a place for a talented dancer, and he wanted Mickey to be in on this one, which is why he asked me to play. "The band can reach a certain level, and they can't go any further 'cause they been educated on an Earth plane," Sunny would say. "So, therefore, when I start moving out on a cosmic plane, they can play up until a certain degree, but they gonna have to leave it to movements or to silence, because silence speaks too. And dancers are people who can express something with their hands and their eyes like they do in the East. Therefore, if I wanted to say some things, I had to have dancers too, and they could take up where the musician couldn't go any further."

One of the problems with Sunny's form of negotiation was that he would present the Arkestra, musicians and dancers, as a package deal, which often resulted in our getting less money than was possible. With Mickey, he saw an opportunity to get a dancer and a musician for the same price.

For this gig, Sunny had a plan in mind that didn't quite sit right with me. He demanded complete submission on the part of the band members. I, however, had played with other bands and had led my own even while I had been playing with the Arkestra, and Sunny didn't like that. It upset his sense of control, especially as I had done the gig with Sam Rivers, whom he viewed as encroaching on the realm of Ra; but he wanted Mickey and therefore had to include me. So on this gig, Sun Ra was going to pay me not to play while he featured my new lady dancer. I was relegated to playing an occasional space chord in between songs.

He had rearranged most of the music I had previously been featured on and for the most part had given the solos over to Michael Ray. Sunny had a way of making you feel like you were a jilted lover, as a new person took over his attention. Song after endless song went by that I used to play on—"Images," "Velvet," the Fletcher Henderson stomp "El Is a Sound of Joy"—and when those came, Michael would jump up and down like an irrepressible mannequin encouraged by Sun Ra. Halfway into the concert, I'd had it. I wasn't taking any more of this. There was a moment in Sun Ra's composition "Shadow World" that I knew was mine. I stood up, with no prompting, to express myself.

A couple of phrases into my stolen moment, eyes closed, I heard Sun Ra's voice yelling across the room, "No trumpet! No trumpet!"

I could feel someone discreetly pulling at my pants legs, motioning me to sit down. Some who weren't as discreet said loudly, "Sunny said sit down, man!"

I tried to act like I didn't hear, but it was obvious that everybody in the theater had, so I sat down and packed up my horn. Not wanting to bring any more attention to myself, I stayed until the end of the set. When I left the theater with Mickey, after being paid, I vowed never again to play with the Sun Ra Arkestra.

# VI
# KEEPING IN
# TOUCH

Sometimes you should appreciate
The work of Nature's God
The work of Nature's God
The work of Nature's God
Lightning, sunshine, wind,
the leaves on the trees
Lightning, sunshine, wind,
the leaves on the trees
A place for nature's breeze,
the leaves on the trees
A place for Nature's breeze
    —Sun Ra, "To Nature's God"

The concert series at Joseph Papp's Public Theater began in the spring of 1978, providing another venue for many of the musicians coming out of the Loft Movement and, ironically, helping to end it. The Public Theater was an upscale cabaret setting, complete with professional lighting, guaranteed money, larger audiences, better publicity, and contracts for performers. Booked by a young Andy Plesser, formerly of the Axis-in-SoHo, a club Sun Ra had performed at the previous July, the Public soon became the choice place to work.

Outside of the 1976 and 1977 loft festivals, the lack of information exchange and coordination of efforts between the New York independents meant that the musicians who arrived to New York in droves in the mid- to late 1970s basically found themselves part of a movement with no direction. As in the past, many musicians came to New York during this period to find work and to develop a reputation, not to help build an organizational structure that could become the means to that end.

In July 1978, yet another proposed summer festival was to take place at Studio Rivbea. This was Rivbea's seventh year in existence, and Sam and Bea Rivers had managed to continue their tradition of sponsoring up to four seasonal festivals each year. I was again scheduled to participate in this festival on another double bill with Arthur Blythe. At the beginning of the year, the double bill had worked quite successfully at Ali's Alley; I saw no reason why it wouldn't work again at Rivbea.

The difference between this year and previous ones, however, was that the loft down the street from Rivbea, the Ladies' Fort, which Sam had helped vocalist Joe Lee Wilson to open, was now being booked by drummer/writer Stanley Crouch, who had arrived in New York from California three years earlier. Sam had learned that some of the same musicians he was using at Rivbea were being asked to play at the Ladies' Fort. In his instruction to us younger players, Sam would often say we needed to leave months between our gigs at various establishments due to that fact there was a limited audience for the music. We were basically drawing from the same pool of people. What Stanley was proposing—in terms of having the same musicians at the Ladies' Fort, days after or before they performed a block away at Rivbea—was an economic disaster.

A call of alarm went out to some musicians who doubled as gangsters and who loved and respected Sam Rivers. They saw Crouch's encroachment as an affront and, like well-bred New Yorkers, were ready to make a move.

The situation was in effect a recurrence of the problem that had surfaced in 1976 between the Music for Cartographers series and the *Wildflowers* sessions. Sam and Bea were producing this festival with little or no financial backing. They didn't see the practicality of having two festivals with some of the same people at the same time without a system, an organized plan, or any coordination to equitably tap into the same audience. Disagreements between the two producers intensified and became public knowledge. The papers were calling it the "Loft Wars," but Sam decided it wasn't worth the fight. He said his wife and family had not wanted to stay on the Lower East Side anyway, and that he had convinced them to stay for the sake of the music. This war with Crouch, however, was the last straw. The festival never happened. Sam and his family subsequently moved to New Jersey and eventually to Florida, and a whole era was on its way to obscurity, courtesy of encroaching opportunism.

The Loft Movement was also doomed because of economic reasons and changes in the laws governing lofts. The SoHo area, where most of the lofts were, soon became much-desired Manhattan real estate. SoHo is just south of Greenwich Village. When most of the lofts opened as performing venues, the district had been in the middle of a shift away from the industrial businesses that had been there since the turn of the twentieth century to residential spaces and galleries that began to manifest during the mid-1960s. There were no laws dealing with what was taking place. Local real estate interests, fearful of losing potential profits from this new artists' village of co-ops, galleries, performance and work spaces, and living quarters, moved to have the rent laws changed, with the result that many artists were eventually forced out, the lofts gradually shifting to house more lucrative commercial enterprises.

Rashied Ali actually owned the building that housed Ali's Alley, and therefore was able to keep the doors of his club open a little longer than the rest. With the confrontation between Studio Rivbea and the Ladies' Fort, Sam Rivers and Stanley Crouch had effectively eliminated themselves from the business of providing much-needed venues. The Ladies' Fort never had the kind of reputation Rivbea had, and Stanley's only purpose seemed to have been to make life miserable for Sam. In that, he was effective. Stanley ended up booking the Tin Palace, the venue downstairs from where he lived on the Bowery, near Bond Street.

I rushed to Rashied Ali to attempt to secure another week at his club. My first week there, during the previous February, had been well enough attended for Ali to offer me the week of July 11 to 15, 1978. For this gig, I used a different band. I got Frank Lowe, the tenor saxophonist from Memphis (by way of California) who had worked with Alice Coltrane back in 1970. Along with Frank, I chose violinist Billy Bang, a New Yorker. Though a relatively new name to me, Billy was then emerging as a powerful talent. This was the first of many projects we would be involved with together over the years.

On bass was Leonard Jones from Chicago, a member of the AACM. The rhythm section was completed by two musicians I had used before, vibraphonist Jay Hoggard and drummer Rashid Sinan.

In April 1978, an article on me written by publicist/teacher/writer Arnold Jay Smith came out in *DownBeat*. This bit of exposure in what was still considered the premier Jazz publication was significant in that little coverage was given to the music or musicians coming from the Loft Movement. Arnold later explained that in order to have that particular article published, he'd had to write several articles they wanted in exchange. This one made a direct impact on my vocation in that a couple of record producers, Alan Ringel and Larry Shengold, read it and thought I'd be a good bet for their new label, About Time Records. They came to the Ali's Alley performance in July and we set up plans to talk.

Meanwhile, with places to play becoming more and more scarce, I decided to continue to work my band by producing my own concerts. Mickey Davidson served as coproducer, assisting with flyers, press releases, and newspaper ads, while I organized musical arrangements and rehearsals. We also had to find a good venue where we could attract a decent audience. She helped by collecting money at the door and working the sound and lighting.

The concert we produced took place on August 18, at the St. Marks Playhouse, home of the Negro Ensemble Company. The ensemble, founded by Douglas Turner Ward, had been housed at this theater since January 1968. Mr. Ward had a vision for the ensemble, combining professional performances by a resident company with an extensive training program for promising actors, playwrights, directors, and managerial and technical personnel. This was similar to what had been articulated by Loft Movement groundbreakers as part of the struggle for Black cultural expression in all its various modes. Our connection to the space was through a woman named Susan Watson, Dianne McIntyre's road manager. We were able to rent the venue and a sound system on a Saturday and put the concert on in a wonderful theater. For this gig I included the brilliant alto saxophonist Oliver Lake and the amazing bassist Vishnu Wood. Vishnu previously had a long run with spirit-catcher Randy Weston. The other people in the group had become my regular choices, cellist Muneer Abdul Fatah, along with Jay Hoggard and Rashid Sinan.

In December 1978, an article written by Stanley Crouch in *Musician* magazine on the music called "Freedom Swings: The New Avant-Garde" dealt with many of the leaders of the new music including people like Don Pullen, Chico Freeman, Rashied Ali, Beaver Harris, Oliver Lake, David Murray, James Newton, Olu Dara, and myself. The following year, I was ready to go into the studio to record for About Time Records. I was able to book a series of gigs in March and April to develop material I would later record in May. I went back into Ali's Alley for five days, March 13 to 17, 1979. That gig, coupled with one at the Sounds in Motion dance studio in Harlem and a gig at New York University's Loeb Student Center, prepared the group for the record date. I had developed a concept that combined what I had learned from the three-year stint with Sun Ra, the studying I had done with Cal Massey, and my own on-the-job experience as a leader in the Loft Movement, all of which blended well with my extensive studies of spiritual culture.

Just around the end of our time together, Iyabode had found out about a person named Brother Ra, also known as R. A. Straughn, who was teaching classes in a Harlem brownstone on 138th Street, at the Rosicrucian Anthroposophical League. The street directly north of the league was Strivers' Row, a historic landmark block peopled by Harlem's professionals. The classes, offered out of generosity, bore no connection to Rosicrucian teachings. Initially I had gone to the classes as a means of getting back with Iyabode. After much begging and pleading with her to let me come back home, I agreed to go to these classes with the intent of regaining her trust. At least that's what I thought I was doing. I had already been opened up to spiritual teachings as a result of my relationship with Sun Ra; now I was on the path without knowing it.

Every Friday at 8 p.m., Brother Ra would give lectures on what he called "spiritual culture." He would often speak for an hour and a half or more without notes. Subjects included meditation, diet, the Kabbalah, hatha yoga, astrology, and the Egyptian Mystery System. The lectures were open to all people; even some white folks would brave their way up to Harlem to attend. No money was ever asked for. Brother Ra believed that if money changed hands as a result of his teachings, then the higher spiritual forces would not present themselves. He always received materially, however, because spiritually, he was always giving. People would buy his books and voluntarily make donations to his organization, while life itself would somehow provide whatever he required to continue. At that time, he was working on a third book, *The Realization of Neter Nu*, synthesizing the ancient wisdom and making it applicable to today.

Despite my stated purpose for attending his classes, I found that my intellect was being profoundly affected by the material. And even while I was attempting to reconstruct my relationship with Iyabode, I was still living with Mickey. For me, there was no contradiction. In many ways I was naive while trying to deal with both women. What I didn't realize was that Iyabode was not about sharing me with anyone. As long as I was living with Mickey, she was not going to have anything to do with me. Yet on quite a few occasions she would let me stay with her and my sons after these Friday night lectures. This, I would later understand, was only to encourage me to get a place of my own, i.e., cut Mickey loose.

In any event, when I went into the studio that May, the work I had been doing in spiritual culture was beginning to inform my approach to the music. Sun Ra understood that music could be a healing force if the composer was aware of that possibility. I found myself choosing the most soothing instruments I could think of—French horn, cello, vibraphone, bass violin, and, of course, my sometimes muted trumpet. The musicians I used, Vincent Chancey on French horn and Jerome Hunter on bass along with Muneer

Abdul Fatah, Jay Hoggard, and Rashid Sinan, had begun to sound like a group. I called the album *Life's Force*, the title referring to what is called *kundalini* or *chi*—that is, the energy present in all of us that allows us to accomplish Thy will. It was the first album for About Time Records, which had given it the number 1,000, and my first one as well.

Around this time, a couple of years past my thirtieth birthday, I ended up learning how to drive a car. I had never attempted to drive before, having never been in a situation where a car was available. Mickey, being from the suburbs of Long Island, had an advantage over an inner-city person. She could drive and she always owned a car. I had never thought driving was all that necessary or that learning how to drive would be much of a problem, given all the millions of people I had observed doing it. Sure enough, it wasn't at all difficult, not even for me at my age. I was going to need to drive in order to go back to school. There was an interesting new program at Kingsborough Community College, whose campus was situated right off the Atlantic Ocean near Coney Island, a good twenty-six miles from where I was living in Manhattan. I had heard good reports about this program, which was being run through the Musicians Local 802 and masterminded by Dr. Bernard Shockett. It was especially designed for people like me, who had been working professionally.

The program offered conservatory-level training in music, which included ear training and dictation, classes in theory, private trumpet lessons, orchestration, big-band workshops, orchestra training (where I played my first opera), plus a range of academic courses, all in a two-day intensive setting.

My days with Sun Ra, master that he was, showed me how much there was to learn about music. What I didn't realize at the time was that Sun Ra and I learned best from within, rather than in institutions. I reenrolled in school just a few months before my first recording was due out.

*Life's Force* turned out to be the first of two recordings I did in 1979. In late November of that year, I was asked to be part of a quartet formed by Ed Blackwell, a drummer I had been listening to on the Eric Dolphy–Booker Little collaborations done at the Five Spot in 1961. I was honored to be asked.

This was my second time working with Mr. Blackwell. When we previously worked at Wesleyan University in 1974, Blackwell's group included Charles Brackeen, David Izenzon, and Azzedin Weston (Randy's son). After that memorable gig, I met alto saxophonist Marion Brown, who was at Wesleyan working on his master's. I had been an admirer of Marion since my early days on the Lower East Side.

On this occasion, Blackwell's group was working at the Tin Palace on the Bowery at Second Street, a half block from Sam Rivers's now-defunct Studio Rivbea and the Ladies' Fort. The Tin Palace had been the hangout bar for most of the musicians involved in the Loft Movement. As the loft sites began to dwindle, the Tin Palace intensified its bookings.

It turns out that Charles Brackeen had been contacted by Ed Blackwell to put music together for that gig at the Palace. Charles called me and we started rehearsing. Blackwell already had a bass player in mind. Mark Helias had been working with him in pianist Anthony Davis's quartet and they had developed a solid connection. The gig at the Palace served as a prelude to the record date, Blackwell's first as a leader. We played a weekend at the club and then went into the studio to record. The whole project took less than a week, from the end of November into the first days of December.

The recording was done for Sweet Earth Records, run by Rick Jeffery and Nancy Weiss. They had done some other recordings, one with Amina Claudine Myers interpreting the piano music of Marion Brown. All the music on Blackwell's date was Charles Brackeen's, and it was the first time in the nine years we'd been playing together that I had an opportunity to record his music. But this recording never went beyond the studio and has yet to be released.

With many of the lofts now closed, Joseph Papp's Public Theater became the preferred performance venue. I had been booked into the Public twice by Andy Plesser. I used the opportunity to expand upon the concept I had used in Abdullah, including the use of poetry by Fatisha and the dancing of Mickey Davidson, working with a six-piece ensemble. Fatisha had an original way of expressing her poetry. I always thought that if Billie Holiday had been a poet, she'd sound like Fatisha. If there was any poet to inherit Billie's mantle, it was Fatisha.

When Nancy Weiss took over the Public's bookings, I couldn't reach first base in getting a gig there. Things were changing. Musicians were no longer in charge, and this new group of people, out of touch with the music, had their own people to push. Attending all this was a fear over job security, i.e., making the error of booking people that those self-appointed critics might not like. The only thing for many of us was to continue self-producing.

Gradually, as doors shut in our faces, the myth would take root that nothing noteworthy had been produced in the 1970s — no real music, no Loft Movement, no continuum between fusion and rap. Then it was back to bop, via an ill-informed rising star, Wynton Marsalis.

◖◗

The first smell of spring was in the air by March 9, 1980, as I followed Mickey in her red-and-white 1955 Ford Falcon. She had been driving a rented car ahead of me, and we were returning it to its home at LaGuardia Airport. We had rented the additional car for some long-distance work we had to do, as we didn't believe that the Falcon would hold up.

We had just come off the Williamsburg Bridge and were heading toward the Brooklyn-Queens Expressway. As the Falcon mounted the ramp, I suddenly felt as if I had nothing in my hands to steer anymore. I tried the brakes but I had lost control of the car. The best I could do was watch, frightened, as it rammed into a light pole and spun back onto the road at an angle perpendicular to oncoming traffic. I turned my head to the right and fearfully noticed the cars behind me heading straight for a broadside hit. They stopped within seconds of the Falcon. There was deathly silence for a couple of awful moments.

Mickey came running to the car from where she had halted in front of me. She had seen the whole incident in her rearview mirror. I was dazed and bleeding profusely from a cut inches from my right eye. The car was totaled. We left it to go to Lenox Hill Hospital's emergency ward, where I got thirteen stitches for the cut. My guardian angel was looking out for me.

When *Life's Force* finally came out in 1980, I decided to have a record release party at the Jazz Gallery. The gallery, the artist studio of John Spaulding (brother of James) and Cobi Narita's latest site for concert productions, was on West Nineteenth Street in Manhattan, between Fifth and Sixth Avenues. The people I chose for the group, except for Vincent Chancey, were completely different from those who played on the recording. I asked saxophonist Henry Threadgill, pianist Bob Neloms, bassist Brian Smith, and drummer C. Scoby Stroman to do the gig with me.

It happened that the record release gig missed a major New York transit strike by a couple of days. The strike, which started on April 1, paralyzed the city. Our gig was mercifully spared from what could have been a disaster, especially for an independently produced concert.

*Life's Force* was getting good press. Somehow, I naively thought, things would become easier as a result. I was soon to learn, however, that having just one recording to your name was only the beginning, and that by itself a single record would not make any significant difference. Perhaps if my first recording had been on a major label, things would have been different. About Time Records, however, was also on its own virgin voyage as a record label. Alan Ringel and Larry Shengold seemed to expect me to sell the records through public performances, just as I expected them to sell me through skillful marketing ideas. Both of us had a lot to learn about our individual approaches.

Over the past few years, I had been using all my resources to produce these concerts, and I was determined to do one more self-produced concert. Once again, I'd be at the Jazz Gallery, this time with a different set of musicians. I chose poet Earlene Smith as well as Fatisha. Earlene sang her poetry while Fatisha read in her inimitable style. Mickey Davidson was also on board for this ride. The band was similar to the one I had used earlier that year. I felt I had really learned from Sun Ra how to effectively weave music with poetry and dance.

The gig was one of my most successful productions, with intent yielding solid results. I wrote music for Earlene's poetry that further emphasized the contrasting styles between her and Fatisha. Mickey danced magnificently through it all. The musicians, Vincent Chancey on French horn, Masujaa on guitar, Brian Smith on bass, and Rashid Sinan on drums, did an excellent job complementing one another when there was a need to and being forceful when it was called for.

◖◗

The thing that really changed America in 1980 was the election of Ronald Reagan, who began his campaign earlier that year in Philadelphia, Mississippi, the place where civil rights workers James Chaney, Andrew Goodman, and Michael Schwerner were murdered in 1964 for attempting to register locals to vote. Reagan was sending out a thinly veiled message regarding the new agenda.

In May 1981, I went to Italy with Sounds in Motion. Dianne also used drummer Charli Persip and pianist Sharon Freeman. I ended up celebrating my thirty-fourth birthday in Rome with this group of musicians and dancers. We had gigs there and in Milan, Pisa, and Sardinia. While in Milan, I made a visit to the office of Giovanni Bonandrini, who ran Black Saint and Soul Note, and picked up a copy of the Sun Ra record on the Horo label, *Unity*, which was unavailable in the US. The album documented the performance we did in October 1977 at Storyville in New York, and proved to be a compelling testament to my relationship with

Sun Ra. The recording also documented the performance where I found out that Michael Ray was being groomed to take my place in the Arkestra. I had gone out of my way to procure the album, somehow understanding its importance.

Isio Saba, who had booked the Italian tour for Dianne, was a native of Sardinia. His bookings there always included the five cities that made up the island. We went to Sardinia overnight by boat from a place near Rome called Civitavecchia. Isio had also previously booked the Sun Ra Arkestra, which actually worked to our advantage because he knew I was a member of that group. The reputation of the Arkestra as tough guys was to Dianne's and my own advantage in that Isio was careful with me. He frequently upset Dianne in business matters, and I was often asked to come to her rescue. Personally, I didn't like being placed in a situation where I had to renegotiate what had already been agreed to— rebuilding bridges, as it were. The only other choices were to stick my head in the sand or stand and watch the wood drift away. Despite a few tense moments, things worked out well.

The tour ended up being an emotional roller coaster with some bright artistic moments. Most memorable to me was the fact that "Liquid Magic," a song I had composed and premiered in New York earlier that year, was performed on this tour. In composing this song, I had experimented with a method of turning a spontaneously improvised line into a fixed composition. During rehearsal, I taped everything. After the rehearsal, I wrote out the melody for "Liquid Magic," which would one day become the title song on one of my records. The musicians on the Italian tour with whom I first created the song included Sharon Freeman on piano and French horn and the great Charli Persip on drums.

The Loft Movement and the era of self-determination were being looked at differently now. I had spent a year and a half at college and was really fed up with what I was supposedly learning. While I appreciated the conservatory-style training at the school, which kept me immersed in music for seven to twelve hours, two days a week, I was not as enthused about the Eurocentric perspective presented there.

By this time, I had started to drive a cab. Initially I drove part-time on weekends, with the idea of getting enough money to pay for school and subsidize musical projects. I made another effort at putting out music by selling a tape to Bob Rusch's Cadence Jazz Records in Redwood, New York. The tape was from a performance at Ali's Alley, which had taken place in February 1978. By now, I knew it was important for me to document the music of the loft years, as they were quickly fading.

Cadence Jazz, like About Time Records, was just getting started as a record company. Once again, I was the first on a label. Cadence Jazz Records, at least, had a publication and a distribution arm, so all was not completely lost. I did an interview for the affiliated *Cadence* magazine that was released as the cover story of its September 1981 issue.

There was one new loft space that had come into being outside of both the Lower East Side and the musician-run format that had characterized the lofts of the 1970s. This place, Soundscape, managed by Verna Gillis, was on West Fifty-Second Street between Tenth and Eleventh Avenues. Basically, Soundscape was working out of a different system. It wasn't operated by musicians, and there was no booze to peddle. In 1981, I did two concerts in this room, which would have easily been forgotten except that I had used saxophone player Booker T. Williams, who was quite exciting to my ears, along with Bob Neloms on piano. The bassist was Saheb Sarbib, someone I had worked with on occasion in his Multinational Band. Masujaa was back on guitar and Rashid Sinan on drums.

Musically, around this time, I began to move in the direction of forming or working within a collective ensemble. The group I helped form included my neighbor, bassist Sirone. Born Norris Jones in Atlanta, Sirone is an incredible bassist who had by then most recently played in the Revolutionary Ensemble with violinist Leroy Jenkins and drummer Jerome Cooper. Among his impressive credentials were stints with Ornette Coleman, Archie Shepp, Pharoah Sanders, and Marion Brown. He lived right around the corner from Mickey's Fifth Street apartment on Cooper Square.

We saw each other frequently and conversed about what we were doing.

In our exchanges I came to understand that Sirone and I shared an optimistic attitude regarding our ability to conceive a project and execute it. We agreed that if musicians came together with the intent of organizing music and took a hands-on approach to the business, the world would be ours. We had both seen it happen too many times to believe otherwise. So the next step to forming a band was an easy one. Kalaparusha, the saxophonist I had met in Sam Rivers's band, and Rashid Sinan, the drummer from Abdullah, were also chosen to be part of what we called New Dimensions in Music. The group was one in which Sirone, Kalaparusha, and I would contribute original compositions and arrangements.

The first gig we did, in November 1981, was actually meant for Abdullah, but I chose to feature this collective instead. The gig was at the State University at Binghamton, New York, booked by a college group called the Harper Jazz Project. One of the students who belonged to that organization was Mitch Goldman, who would play an important role in my life in later years.

The music we played synergized the approaches of the three of us who contributed compositions. There was much dynamic energy expressed by Kalaparusha, Sirone, and Rashid as individuals. The band needed only to work and rehearse more to focus that energy into a group sound.

I drove us all upstate in a used station wagon Mickey and I had just recently bought. After a successful gig and on our way back home, I stopped to purchase some gas, asking the attendant to fill it up. One of the problems with our car was that the indicator for the gas tank was frozen. I gave little notice to the amount of change I got back from a twenty-dollar bill and actually thought nothing of it until, in the middle of nowhere on a dark and deserted New York State Thruway, I heard the telltale sound of a car without gas. The attendant had obviously not filled it up. We managed to walk back to another gas station, where we got gas. That was the first of a series of incidents that should have warned me away from the project.

Around this time, I had moved from part-time to full-time cabdriver. I was growing more and more frustrated over seeing my sons some weekends and then having to take them back to their mother. After three years and several failed attempts to get back with Iyabode, I had resigned myself to creating a family where I was. Rashid and Shahid were six years old by now; Malcolm, Mickey's son, was twelve. Malcolm was taking Suzuki piano lessons at the Third Street Music School Settlement, which, oddly enough, is located on Eleventh Street. To create some stability and regularity for myself in relation to my sons, I decided they would begin taking piano lessons as well. For a while the lessons had the desired effect, helping them develop a sense of discipline. But the most difficult thing was always taking them back to Brooklyn. The return trip left me feeling depressed. Sometimes I would take them out in the cab with me when I went out to drive. They seemed excited by this for a while, especially when passengers would give them tips.

On a night in February 1982, I stopped driving early and went to hang out at the Village Vanguard, New York's oldest Jazz club. There was a tall dark woman sitting at the bar who reminded me of Iyabode. We made conversation quickly and effortlessly. I offered her a lift up to her Harlem apartment and soon began what turned out to be another triangular relationship. This one was complicated by my own unacknowledged depression, which easily lent itself to a severe case of drug abuse. Cocaine and I soon became solid partners.

One of the most remarkable things about this entire period bounded by a two-term conservative Reagan administration was the easy availability of drugs. I had been using some form of intoxicant, mainly marijuana, since I was a teenager. In the 1980s, cocaine became the drug of choice. In 1982, when I first met Charlene, it was still expensive. But the cab business was thriving. She had a pretty serious love affair with cocaine as well as the good connections necessary to procure the white powder. Charlene, like Iyabode, was a social person. As we spent quite a bit of time together, cocaine correspondingly burned a hole in my money pocket.

○

Even though I had been rehearsing with New Dimensions in Music on a regular basis, I hadn't given up my band Abdullah completely. In fact, Charlene, with whom I had now been dealing for about a year, came through with a gig at Sweet Basil. Horst Liepolt, a German producer and part owner of the club, had developed some interest in the new music and had put together a series called Music Is an Open Sky.

Charlene convinced him that I should be a part of this series, which would be taking place at Sweet Basil on the Sundays and Mondays of February and March 1983. It would be the first intensive flurry of activity around this music in years. Since many of the musicians chosen to participate had also been involved in the Loft Movement, doing a gig at a club like Sweet Basil seemed to signal a kind of new hope for the music.

Among the bandleaders given a two-day play were Olu Dara, Muhal Richard Abrams, Amina Claudine Myers, Saheb Sarbib, Craig Harris, Henry Threadgill, Joseph Jarman, and Don Moye. I was given March 13 and 14 to work my sextet.

For this occasion, I chose a different ensemble, as I was working on some different music. I had written a piece to premiere, "Suite Songbird." The instrumentation of violinist Billy Bang, cellist Muneer Abdul Fatah, and bassist Brian Smith, along with Bob Neloms on piano and John Betsch on drums, was a new one for me. This combination gave me an opportunity to work with some of the textures I had been exposed to at Kingsborough College.

We got the attention of Gary Giddins, who gave us a *Village Voice* Choice, and Jon Pareles of the *New York Times.* Pareles had this to say in a March 15 review of our concert: "Half of the sextet of the trumpeter Ahmed Abdullah was strings—bass, cello and violin—when the group played Sunday at Sweet Basil. That lineup gave the proceedings a woodsy, almost rustic sound, and the gruff tone of the strings neatly complemented Mr. Abdullah's clear trumpet phrases."

Later on, Sirone came up with the brilliant idea of producing a film with the band in a performance situation at the Village Gate. The film, titled *New Dimensions in Music*, was set to be shot on March 28, 1983. There were four cameramen lined up, including Doug Harris, McClinton Karma Stanley, Ronald Grey, and the director Teppe, who had worked with Miles Davis and was quite good in his role.

Rehearsals and filming at the Village Gate went well. The problem occurred in the editing of the film. Sirone, who was not a filmmaker, and Teppe, who was, were at odds every step of the way. Their disputes were such a drag that they drove everyone else away, including me. Thanks to my confused state, I contributed $1,000 to the project, and with the conflict between Sirone and Teppe, the money was just thrown away. Only recently have I seen what the completed film looked like. It is an amazing documentary of a group and period of time in this music.

Meanwhile, Charlene, working at Sweet Basil, had developed such a relationship with the people there that I was able to get more work out of that club. These gigs were like tokens—just enough to frustrate me even more. I never got a week's worth of work at any one time, and the effort it takes to build yourself up to perform one-night stands is really the same effort it takes to do a week. Isolated one-night gigs were not very appealing. They became temporary breaks from driving a cab and then I would go right back to the grind again.

Some of the guys from the Loft Movement, like Arthur Blythe, David Murray, and Oliver Lake, were able to move into the regular weeklong rotations at Sweet Basil. I thought I should be getting more regular work, too. Of course, my increasing cocaine dependency was not helping; neither was my depression or my feeling of stagnation. I had in a sense forgotten all about the principle of doing for self and was prepared in my drug-induced state to go the way of the plantation. In October 1983, the Reagan administration ordered a military invasion of Grenada. Under the pretext of aiding American medical students while actually aiding in the assassination of Maurice Bishop, the invasion of this English-speaking country marked a return to the gunboat diplomacy that has ever characterized the United States' relationship to Caribbean countries.

I was aware of the political reality of the Grenada invasion even while the cocaine I was using was narrowing my vision to just one preoccupation — my continued sexual relationship with Charlene. That was a factor in my decision to leave Mickey and move in with Charlene, which I did two weeks before the invasion. We got a place together on 120 Gates Avenue, in the Clinton Hill section of Brooklyn. Of course, moving back to the borough put me closer to my sons. Iyabode didn't have the problem with Charlene that she did with Mickey, so eventually I was able to see Rashid and Shahid more regularly.

The fact that I had given up on self-production and had now attempted to become part of the system, with Charlene as my entree, also factored into my leaving Mickey. Previously, whenever I moved in with somebody it was a fifty-fifty split, bills and all. But between Charlene's body and the shape of her pocketbook, the coke in my head and the possibility that I was on the edge of regular employment as a musician, I was not only ready to leave Mickey but also to take on the entire cost of moving, putting up the required month's rent and security deposit on my own.

There was one major problem I didn't have to face right then: Mickey. She had gone to Europe with Cecil Taylor's ensemble, and while she was away, the coward in me decided it was a good time to move. My conscience ate at me because I really did care for Mickey. She was more than a lover to me; she was my friend. I could not have her come back from Europe to an empty apartment.

Her tour with Cecil lasted five weeks. When she came back to town just before Thanksgiving, I went to Fifth Street and spent the next two nights with her. She saw that my things were gone, and we talked about it. For the most part, those two days continued that way. We talked. She cried. We talked, she cried. It was emotionally wrenching for both of us and the beginning of a painful personal descent into hell for me, during which all my demons would come to feast. The next day, when I went back to Brooklyn, I found myself locked out, all of my clothes, along with most everything I owned, including my horn, piled up in the hallway. A letter on yellow paper sat upon my things.

11/22/83
Ahmed,
Please move this stuff as soon as possible. None of it is damaged and it's everything you had here. Call when you want to pick up the piano and bring $250 cash for long-distance calls you made to Europe. Also, I want $100 for money I lost due to your indiscretion. Don't fuck with me about this. Just go. Here are your cab keys.
Sayonara,
Charlene

I banged on the door. No answer. I banged again. Still no answer. Slowly, I began to lose it, angered by the insanity and ridiculousness of the situation. So I broke the lock. And in that instant I became a raving lunatic rushing into the house looking for her. I can't remember exactly when I saw her or what I did. I can only say that I physically hurt her. When I came back to my senses, I was hurting myself.

That Wednesday, Thanksgiving Eve, marked a full month that Charlene and I had been living together. The next day, I was back with Mickey in Manhattan. I spent Thanksgiving with my parents. When I went back to Brooklyn on Friday to move my stuff out, Charlene showed up and called the police. Her face was so bruised that she could have convinced anyone I needed to be put away, which she did and which I was. The police handcuffed me and took me to the Eighty-Eighth Precinct on Classon Avenue. Charlene went to the station, sneering contemptuously at me and savoring the moment, watching me in handcuffs. It was hard to believe that just a week ago we had been lovers.

I was kept at the station house for a while and eventually taken, handcuffed, to central booking in a van with other prisoners. There, I was fingerprinted and jailed. As it was the Friday after Thanksgiving, it was quite possible that I would remain in jail until the following Monday without seeing a judge.

I was permitted the obligatory single phone call, and so I contacted Mickey to let her know that our car was parked outside of my Brooklyn apartment and that I was in jail. She understood that despite the horrible crime I had committed, jail was not where I belonged. She promised to raise bail.

I stayed locked up overnight, totally depressed, thinking, wondering. There was a *Time* magazine that someone had left in my cell. In it was an article on Wynton Marsalis. Reading this article made me even more depressed. It was more than symbolic that the rise of this trumpeter was occurring in the Reagan era, one of the most conservative periods of this country's recent history. And here I was observing the phenomenon, locked up. I couldn't have been in a lower state of existence. But when you know you're at the bottom, there is only one direction left open to you.

I began trying to understand what had led me to believe that it was okay to lay my hands on a woman. Drug abuse was not enough. I had to pry deeper into my soul's recesses to come up with answers so that I would never again find myself in this state of complete disempowerment.

On Saturday, Mickey came and bailed me out. I was given a date on which to return to court. Eventually, however, Charlene dropped all charges. Despite that, I had to live with myself, and I knew I needed help. I went to one of the Lower East Side centers and found a therapist at a reasonable fee.

Therapy was helpful in some ways, but for the most part I wouldn't or couldn't allow anyone to get to know me well enough to help me help myself. The mission I was on led me to Carl Jung's *Memories, Dreams, Reflections*. That book helped set me back on the path to recovery. Jung explained the dual nature we have as human beings. He presented a theory that we're all both male and female, and suggested that many of our problems result from our refusal to acknowledge this fact. Given a social structure compounded by both white supremacy and patriarchy, defined by racism and capitalism, it would stand to reason that most folks in general, women in particular, and Black men and women especially, would be hard put to emerge from such a system unscathed. In actuality, one-sided perceptions of reality are not healthy for anyone.

A structure that has white men dominating white women and dominating every other ethnicity and color is one in which little opportunity for growth can occur unless one seeks information outside the existing paradigm. Everything in the culture is going to reflect a white male patriarchal position. What would constitute revolutionary thought would be to suggest that someone other than a white male might hold the job of president of this country.

At the time, I was sharing a cab with a driver who was studying to be a librarian, and who happened to be white. I told him about the incident with Charlene in an effort to talk to someone other than a doctor. I didn't know what kind of response I expected, but I didn't think I would be ridiculed. However, my partner spoke to me like I was some kind of idiot, saying, "Man, don't you know how to use your goddamn brain? The only thing you know how to do is strike out."

His totally unempathetic response was probably why men don't express their true feelings to other men. We're afraid to be confronted by our own adamancy. Yet my partner's response made me think more. Was I missing something?

Gradually, I settled for a self-imposed therapeutic method that included reading books written by women. I deduced that if I came to respect men as a result of time spent absorbing their thought processes via books, music, etc., I could do the same with women via female writers, musicians, composers, artists. I set out on a deliberate reading campaign that brought me in touch with the works of Toni Morrison and Alice Walker. I read Morrison's

*The Bluest Eye, Sula,* and *Song of Solomon.* I read Walker's *The Color Purple* and *Meridian.* This effort allowed me to open a part of myself that I had always suppressed, or at least was totally ignorant of. The perspective I began to adopt and the questions raised by these women propelled me to acknowledge the work I had yet to do.

Fortunately for me, Charlene (who was well-read) and I resumed our relationship, which eased my anger at her for having the judicial system punish me. I knew it was time to take a look at the man in the mirror.

In 1984, bassist William Parker, a former member of the Melodic Art-Tet, and his wife, choreographer Patricia Nicholson, organized the Sound Unity Festival at a community center called Cuando, then on Second Avenue above Houston Street. I was asked to bring a group to this festival, which gave me a reason to finish up a suite I was working on, a kind of swan song to music. It was difficult for me to live with myself then. The coke was still right there beside me. It was still a constant that didn't help. Somehow, this upcoming gig gave me a reason, and so I finished my suite, "Reflections on a Mystic," which was inspired by Carl Jung's book and which I saw as the way I would exit the world of music.

Arthur Jones, the alto saxophonist I had not seen since he left for Europe in 1969, had been deported from France and suddenly appeared back in New York. Things had changed in Europe just as they had in the States. Conservatism was back on the rise, and there was little tolerance for musicians who embraced the avant-garde and who were not seen by the authorities as positive contributors to the art, much less to society. Arthur, a brilliant saxophonist, returned to the States with his saxophone in a bag, homeless and broken. When I saw him, I immediately thought about how fortunate I was to have stayed here. If I thought my condition was deplorable. I had only to look at Arthur to realize how blessed I was.

I took advantage of the one opportunity I would have to work with Arthur and recruited him into my ensemble. Mickey also danced with us. While I began with the idea that this would be my last concert, the more involved I became once again organizing music and musicians, the more revived I felt. Music has always been a healing force and had now taken over. The reaction to our presentation at that festival was encouraging. From a review by Bob Rusch published in *Cadence* in August 1984:

> Saturday welcomed the largest crowds of the entire event and the music did not disappoint. Jimmy Lyons set a precedent for alto sax; Karen Borca, bassoon; Raphe Malik, trumpet; William Parker, bass; Paul Murphy, drums. Lyons' compositions offered their customary short, frenetic, tightly arranged heads before loosening up and allowing plenty of solo space for each musician. The front-line voices were particularly impressive, never permitting the emotional power of the music to waver for a second. Abdullah's trumpet was in fine form as he ran the gamut from free form to the melodically sublime. The real treat, however, was the reappearance of Arthur Jones following his apparent ten-year absence from the music scene.

Next, I reached out to Sun Ra. I had long since gotten over my anger at what I believed was his mistreatment of me and had never actually severed our ties. From 1978, when I left, I continued to keep the lines open. In fact, in 1979, I went back out with Sun Ra when he did the second Atlanta Free Jazz Festival in Georgia and the Ann Arbor Blues and Jazz Festival in Michigan. From then on, whenever he worked in New York and I was available, I would show up trumpet in hand, whether at Soundscape, the Squat Theatre, or Jazzmania, and he, in turn, would give me a uniform and tell me to get up on the stage. And I'd get paid for it, to boot.

There was a phenomenon I couldn't help but notice. If I knew Sun Ra was performing somewhere with the Arkestra, and I decided not to show because I preferred to drive my cab to make better money, something would invariably happen to the cab. The whammy! You know what I mean? Flat tires, stolen meters, broken windows, and an assortment of other unexplained occurrences. They happened with too much regularity and frequency to simply ignore and they were always connected with Sun Ra's appearances.

After the Sound Unity Festival, I decided to come back into his fold in order to refocus. With Charlene still in contact with Sweet Basil, I had inside information that the owners would be receptive to a Sun Ra performance there. After I informed Sun Ra that this was the New York hot spot, he sent Danny Thompson to inquire about the Arkestra working there. Danny's mission resulted in a series of Monday concerts projected for July 1984.

Prior to that, in June, I had gone back on the road with the Arkestra. There were some changes in the band's personnel. Philadelphia-born trombonist Tyrone Hill was new to me, as was drummer Don Mumford from Lawrence, Kansas, where Langston Hughes grew up. Danny Davis was no longer part of the Arkestra, and his diabetic condition would soon take him off the planet. Ronald Brown from Kansas City, a newcomer on trumpet, added a good sound to the ensemble.

Mickey Davidson danced with the band on this tour as we traveled to England, Belgium, and Germany for two weeks. Though Mickey and I had gone back to living together, my relationship with Charlene was still going strong sexually. Mickey and I always had an artistic passion we shared, which allowed us to survive most situations. Things had changed somewhat between Charlene and me since our botched live-in situation, however. She had moved to her mother's home in Queens, which meant that in order for us to be together, I usually had to rent a hotel room. We would then have wild coke-fueled sexual marathons. The type of relationship we had would run its course in time, but while we were in it, that was all that was happening.

On the road in England, the Sun Ra Arkestra performed at the Brixton Academy in a concert produced by John Cumming's

Serious Productions. In Germany, we worked the cities of Hamburg, Bonn, and Landshut. We played Antwerp and Brussels in Belgium. In Brussels, we were the last group to play at the club Bloomdido.

A concert was organized at a farmhouse in Antwerp by a Jazz lover named Klaus. At the reception he had for us at his house, we were treated to this man's record collection, which matched his enormous size. He was obviously a tremendous fan and a great lover of the music. I mean, he had everything and everybody you could think of. In Belgium, of all places. Amazing!

When we arrived back in New York for the Kool Jazz Festival, we played Carnegie Hall opposite Dizzy Gillespie. The Sun Ra Arkestra, to me, had never sounded tighter than at those European gigs. We were psyched to go into Carnegie Hall and we hit hard. And so I will never totally understand why Sun Ra permitted a drunken Al Evans to make this gig and singularly destroy the work and arrangements that had been so carefully created and so wonderfully developed during our two-week tour. The condition that Al Evans was in at the gig—falling-down drunk, interrupting arrangements by playing right through them with solos that were uncalled for—was not an unusual one for him. One would have thought that the tour had been meant to hone the music that would be presented at its best here at Carnegie Hall.

Al had little self-respect and never spoke of Sun Ra with any degree of respect either. What was remarkable was that knowing this about Al, Sun Ra still allowed him to get onstage with the band. At the end of the concert, John Gilmore, whom I had never heard oppose Sun Ra publicly or privately, issued a threat that if a similar thing ever happened again, he was gone. But Sun Ra had his way; he always allowed Al to play with the band, whatever his condition, and paid him for it, too. He appreciated something about Al's playing, and Al did have a unique trumpet style. My problem was that his chops were rarely in shape, and he was frequently too drunk to make sense. Sun Ra somehow saw past all of that and heard music even in what most people would think of as a series of failed attempts.

I can only speculate that Sun Ra's concept was really so much his own and so far beyond ours that even a gig at Carnegie Hall, which others might have deemed highly prestigious, was to him just another gig. He had the amazing capacity to allow Al Evans, or whomever, to be who they wanted to be in his world, because, after all, it was his world. With his conceptual brilliance, he would create other equally important opportunities.

After coming back to the US, Sun Ra had the idea of putting together a hundred-piece ensemble once again. This one was to be performed indoors, and he had a coconspirator in a Hungarian by the name of Péter Halász of the Squat Theatre. Péter was as out there in his theatrical concepts as Sun Ra was with his music.

When the Squat Theatre was closed to make way for urban renewal, with a Cineplex Odeon movie house on Twenty-Third Street, I actually watched Péter build another theater on East Twelfth Street with his own hands. Like Sun Ra, he was unstoppable. The site where Péter had proposed to produce the hundred-piece Omniversal Symphonic for July 19 and 20, 1984, was a catering house of another day called the Lennox Chatelet. Located on East Second Street between Avenues B and C, this venue was right around the corner from Slugs', where, eighteen years before, Sun Ra had made his first legendary impact on New York.

Word spread that Sun Ra was doing something innovative, and sure enough, all sorts of dancers, poets, artists, and musicians began showing up. Billy Bang, Frank Lowe, Charles Tyler, Rashied Ali, Gary Bartz, Kalaparusha, Wilber Morris, Earl Cross, and Earle Davis were among the musicians who moved in fast. Sun Ra was like a beacon radiating energy throughout all of this. When they hit, the concerts proved a tremendous event and were the talk of the town. Many of the musicians who had come aboard at these concerts would join in at the Sweet Basil Monday night concerts or would travel with the band, proving once again that Sun Ra could create his own legend. As exciting as it all was, I was not quite ready to limit myself by working only with Sun Ra.

He had gotten me out of a severely depressed state, for which I was grateful, but now I would try to find my own way again.

Late in the summer of 1984, Charlene's connections helped me to get a gig at the third Greenwich Village Jazz Festival. Horst Liepolt of Sweet Basil was booking groups into the Bitter End, the club farther east on Bleecker Street known primarily for its folk music. The Greenwich Village Festival, produced by Mel and Phyllis Litoff, Horst Liepolt, and WBGO radio personality James Browne, sought to bring together all the clubs doing Jazz in the Village for an end-of-the-summer festival. The venues advertised collectively and set up discount prices for patrons who attended more than one event at each of the several participating clubs.

A place like the Bitter End obviously saw the advantage in such a deal, given the greater publicity available, and therefore suspended its regular folk-music policy for the length of the Jazz festival. For my gig at the club, I planned to put together an exciting Abdullah unit. I called tenorman David Murray. We'd known each other since he came to New York at least ten years before but we had never worked together in a small group. He agreed to do the gig. I also got Bob Neloms to play piano, Muneer Abdul Fatah on cello, Brian Smith on bass, and John Betsch playing drums.

The problems I'd been experiencing in my personal life had not been fully worked out, so it should have been no surprise that I was going to be tested in some way by the choices I had made for this gig. I had not yet understood how deeply my music reflected who I was. The first sign of distress came in the form of a call from Bob Neloms. He was in a bad state. He couldn't leave the bathroom of his apartment because whatever he had eaten couldn't decide whether to exit from his mouth or from his backside. I received this call just as I was on my way out the door to do the gig. It was nine o'clock on Saturday night. Who could I call that late to make a gig with no rehearsal possible?

After a few failed attempts, I thought of Amina Claudine Myers. I appreciated her soulful, bluesy approach to the music and knew that spiritually she would be right. Fortunately, she could make it, but she wasn't going to get there until the second set. So we played the first set without the piano, relying instead on Muneer's cello work to provide additional color. The music worked well and, without the piano, allowed another kind of urgency to be present. So we had one really good set, even if it wasn't what had been planned.

The other problem was Brian Smith, who had two gigs in one night. Brian had been leading a bass ensemble with this huge bass that he had to get up on a ladder to play. He was scheduled to play that with Roscoe Mitchell's ensemble up the street at Sweet Basil. Rather than cancel one of the gigs, Brian decided to make both gigs by leaving a bass in each club and running back and forth between breaks. I don't know how Roscoe Mitchell fared, but for my gig it didn't work. I believe Brian had mentioned something about this potential disaster to me, but I was led to believe he had worked out all the snags. If I had known from the beginning that he hadn't, I would have gotten another bass player. After he played the first set with us, he left the club to play a set with Roscoe.

Amina showed up at the end of the first set, and I went over the music with her. Because she had not played my music before, I wanted to give her every advantage that the presence of a bass player would afford. By the time Brian showed up, I was thoroughly pissed off, the audience had grown impatient, and the group had lost some of its momentum. Nevertheless, Amina worked out brilliantly and through it all she learned the music and helped to make an incredible set. It had all the excitement and drama of a mystery novel.

During the fall of 1985, I read an article in *New York* magazine. The Racketeer Influenced and Corrupt Organizations Act had been passed by Congress in 1970, ostensibly directed at organized crime. Under the RICO statutes, people allegedly involved in some form of racketeering could be arrested and held without bail while awaiting trial. The statutes themselves created their own controversy in light of similar detention laws in place in the Union of South Africa during the apartheid era and the fact that this was practically unheard of in the United States of America. But what made it all the more compelling to me was that, according to the article, the first people to be arrested under the RICO statutes were a group of Black and Puerto Rican community activists collectively known as the New York Eight. The federal prosecutor, a theretofore-unknown Reagan appointee, US Attorney Rudolph Giuliani, had with much pomp and circumstance brought a 101-count indictment against the activists.

As I continued reading the article, I became amazed by the Orwellian scenario, in which a group of young people were charged with doing nothing more than thinking about revolution. To make the indictment happen, the government had spent millions of taxpayer dollars to shadow members of the New York Eight, which initially included Viola Plummer, Coltrane Chimurenga, Roger Wareham, Colette Pean, Omowale Clay, Robert Taylor, Ruth Lateefa Carter, and Yvette Kelley. Jose Rios was eventually added as a ninth defendant.

What caught my attention was *New York*'s description of each group member's background. These were highly intelligent people, well educated at such prestigious institutions as Barnard, Harvard law, Columbia, and Rutgers and mostly engaged as working professionals.

The following year, when they were tried, I took my sons to have them witness this debacle on the part of the government and the courageous stance that the New York Eight were taking in direct opposition. Inside the courtroom, we heard sworn testimony from a government agent as to how a hundred agents had been deployed in a single day at a cost of thousands of dollars to follow Coltrane Chimurenga from Connecticut to New York, with nothing to report. Meanwhile, the problem of homelessness in America was even then completely out of control.

The New York Eight were eventually cleared of all charges and permitted to walk. However, its members paid a dear price, losing jobs, homes, and so-called friends in a process that took practically two years, part of which they spent imprisoned for their commitment to struggle against the oppression they saw.

The political landscape seemed to have influenced artistic choices as well. Very little opposition had been mounted against the widespread celebration of bebop as the music of the 1980s. The various styles of Jazz are as much related to sociopolitical influences as they are to artistic evolution. Until the 1980s, in fact, each generation had created a music that reflected the period of its creation by infusing that of the preceding generation with the contemporary. Thus, we evolved from ragtime to swing to bebop/ hard bop to free Jazz and loft-era music/fusion. There is no question that bebop and hard bop represent a high artistic achievement for the era they were created in. The lack of alternative spaces meant that those musicians who played certain clubs had to play what was demanded of them. Artistic statements representing the current evolution of the music were a secondary consideration. By the 1980s, an art form that from its inception spoke of revolution through evolution was now effectively Madison Avenue's child, with bebop or hard bop as the music most chosen by club owners.

It was in this atmosphere that in 1985 a musicians' organization was once again summoned into being. The people who made it happen were veterans at organizing musicians, including Lester Bowie, Oliver Lake, and Cecil Taylor. The organization was called the Musicians of Brooklyn Initiative (MOBI).

The leadership was an interesting combination. Taylor, a New Yorker by birth, was a member of Bill Dixon's Jazz Composers Guild. Bowie was one of the early presidents of the Association for the Advancement of Creative Musicians. Lake was a founder of the Black Artists' Group (BAG) from St. Louis. All of them had recently become Brooklyn homeowners, which helped to create a stabilizing influence. In actuality, MOBI represented the first large-scale organizing effort to occur among musicians since the 1970s. The social conditions had become so stifling that an organization was a must.

I was informed by Lester Bowie that the next meeting of MOBI was to be held in Brooklyn Heights, at St. Ann's Church. I went, and it was packed. Seated at the table in the front of the room were Cecil, Lester, and Oliver along with a smallish blond woman dressed in purple. Her name was Philippa Jordan. Musicians I had never seen before were present, too. There was an excitement in the air as if something was going to really happen!

The internal structure of the organization that would allow for funding had already been worked out by another group of folks, including the musicians mentioned, along with Philippa, Phillip Bither, and Burl Hash. Burl by then had been programming the music at Brooklyn's Prospect Park Bandshell for several years.

Folks who came to the meeting were advised that plans had been made to produce a festival and a regular concert series. Committees had been formed, and those present at the meeting were encouraged to get involved by joining one of them. I opted for the communications committee.

Lots of activity began to occur as a result of MOBI. Concerts of adventurous, cutting-edge music were organized on an ongoing basis at the Prospect Park Picnic House, as well as at the bandshell. Meetings were regularly scheduled and there was a good cross-cultural thing happening. I was inspired by this model to do some organizing on my own. In the early part of 1986, through conversations with my neighbor Sirone, I organized a band known as the Group. The band featured Marion Brown, Billy Bang, Andrew Cyrille, Sirone, and me.

To a large extent, the network of connections we made use of evolved around Marion, who, having worked with John Coltrane and Sun Ra, was held in high esteem by many. Besides working as a musician, Marion had also written and published a book, *Reflections*, on his life as an artist. He had recently become a painter, and his account of his transition from music to visual art was simply that he decided he wanted to do it and did it. When Sirone and I began to select musicians for this ensemble, I mentioned that I'd recently had a conversation with Marion and that he would be open to joining up with us. Marion and Sirone had both come from Atlanta; they had a recorded history that went back to Marion's early dates as a leader. Andrew Cyrille had also worked with Marion on *Afternoon of a Georgia Faun*. Billy Bang and I had some history. He worked in my band Abdullah several times, and in September 1984 he had asked me to play on his *The Fire from Within*.

I called everyone together for a meeting at our place on Fifth Street and had photographer Raymond Ross come by to take some pictures. At the meeting, we came to an understanding as to how we would produce our first concert. All the guys were given a choice as to whether to get a fixed salary or to share profits after expenses. Fortunately, everyone chose the latter, which was the plan that Sirone and I had conceived, understanding that the first thing one must do is to get musicians who want to play together regardless of money.

The Group's premiere was to be May 3 at the Greenwich House on Barrow Street. Kwame Shaw, a concert producer, was doing a regular series there. He had selected the venue because it was right across the street from Sweet Basil. Kwame was helpful in suggesting things to me that aided immensely in the promotion of our first concert. Marion Brown had good friends, such as Kwame and E. L. James, who were willing to lend support to our effort.

James, a producer for WBAI, the local listener-sponsored outlet for Pacifica Radio and one of the few places where one could get genuinely alternative views, assisted us in many ways in promoting the event. Having the advantage of being on the radio, E. L. arranged for actress-vocalist Novella Nelson to interview us on the air, as well as to plug the event as a regular public-service announcement, and he assisted with our mailing. The only payment he required of us was to list his company Conscious Comedy as a coproducer of the show, which we willingly did. Every step of the way, this premiere was well planned and well executed.

We rehearsed diligently and worked on our presentation of the music, bringing in arrangements of our own materials as well as works by others. The music was tight and reflected a wide range of possibilities. We were on to something unique.

The concert was huge success. Gary Giddins, in his *Voice* Choice of May 6, 1986, wrote: "The Group: Here's an uncommonly promising new quintet bringing together five formidable musicians whose careers span most of the history of post-bop Jazz."

The article that Robert Palmer had written for the *New York Times* on Friday, May 2, ensured the full house that we had. Palmer had interviewed me and paraphrased me as having said that the Group was an important indication of the state of the music, as "the time demands it." He implied that the Group had tapped into something that many other artists were feeling at the time as a plethora of collective groups had come into being. Among them were those put together by Ornette Coleman and Pat Metheny for their *Song X*; the Leaders, with Lester Bowie, Chico Freeman, Arthur Blythe, Kirk Lightsey, Cecil McBee, and Don Moye; and Sphere, with Charlie Rouse, Kenny Barron, and Buster Williams. Old and New Dreams, which had preceded us, was still going strong with Dewey Redman, Don Cherry, Charlie Haden, and Ed Blackwell; the World Saxophone Quartet, too, continued to thrive.

The attention Mr. Palmer gave us, and the comparative associations he made, gave our promotional efforts a major boost. With the success of this concert, I had come back from the depths of my own despair, using the cab as my major source of income but not allowing myself to be frustrated by the choices I had in fact made for myself. The work was hard, but in the end it paid off. Here I was, in the throes of a mini-movement, without even realizing it.

# VII
# RETURNING

People have to be open to hearing new kinds of music, just like learning a new language. I'm talking to them about their potential through the music. They'll be surprised by their new potential at first, but the way will be opened to them to move in a creative and positive way. When their minds become universalized, they'll hear it. Everything in the universe loves music. When we play in my house in Philadelphia, even the spiders come down the walls to listen, because they love music, too.
—Sun Ra

Nineteen eighty-six was in many ways a banner year for me. The premiere concert of the Group in May brought me into contact with Philippa Jordan, who had heard me before at a concert with Lester Bowie's Brass Fantasy at the South Street Seaport. She later admitted that she had made inquiries to Oliver Lake about me. At the time we started talking, Philippa—who represented Amina Claudine Myers, Ronald Shannon Jackson, Frank Lowe, Lester Bowie, and Oliver—was working with a group of flashy Antiguans who called themselves the Burning Flames. They were popular on their island and in the Caribbean. Philippa was convinced they would do as well in the US, given the kind of assistance she could provide.

She had a winning way about her, a good sense of style, giving off the impression of being from the British upper class. She had been born in Edinburgh, close to the end of World War II, when the bombing of London was a constant reality. Her parents were in enough of a stable financial position to settle eventually in a rural part of England, a village called Much Hadham. She had been raised by a mother, athletically inclined, who taught horseback riding, and by a father who was a lawyer.

Philippa once explained that the area in which she grew up had no Black people in it, and that she hadn't met Black folks until she was an adult in London. We seemed to find an immediate chemistry, both personal and professional. At our first meeting, she proposed helping me with the Group, offering to become our business manager, booking, promoting, and generally representing us, alleviating many of the responsibilities that I had taken on. Certainly, after the effort it took to launch the Group's premiere, I was ready for anyone to relieve me of the non-musical side of the production work. What I hadn't expected was that this petite blonde and I would also become lovers. Of course, this was complicated by the fact that I was still living with Mickey.

Two months after our affair began, Philippa asked me to accompany her to Antigua for Carnival, which was scheduled for that August. I had never been to the Caribbean before and wanted to go. But I knew that going there with Philippa, a white woman, while living with Mickey, might be the last act of my natural-born life. It wasn't easy for me to feel comfortable out in public with Philippa, either. Until Philippa, I'd hardly had to deal with this contradiction to my public persona as an African-centered self-aware individual. But Philippa was quickly moving me into another area, demanding more than merely sleeping together. And me, I wasn't sure what I wanted to do. I knew that ultimately the choice was mine and that taking the proposed trip would mean coming out of a closet.

I decided to consult a seeress, a Black woman I had heard on the radio while driving my car, who seemed honest and sincere. Because I felt pretty desperate, I gave her a call and made an appointment.

Without being told anything, this woman knew exactly why I had come and told me more than I'd expected. She reminded me of something Brother Ra had said many years before, that the Creator provides us with a means to know that which we are ignorant of.

The first thing she said was that she did not believe in cross-cultural relationships of the kind she saw me getting into. Be that as it may, she saw a meaningful and undeniably karmic relationship between Philippa and myself. She was not encouraging it, she said, only speaking on what she was seeing. She also revealed to me that the name Solomon had a powerful vibrational force in my life and suggested that I might consider using it. She further stated that I had a priestly responsibility to the music, and that I was avoiding it through my dissipation with drugs and sex, the combination of which did not allow me to reach my full potential. She also gave me another name that I would come to use later, one that she told me I should not reveal to anyone until then. And finally, she told me to pick up a copy of a book known simply as *The Kybalion.*

Buoyed by the seeress's reading, I went to Antigua with Philippa. The island was such an African country, it reminded me of being in Lagos. For here, too, one could see dark-hued women dressed in an array of bright colors, carrying bowls and baskets on their heads, walking with poise and dignity. Philippa had been here before and even had a lover who lived on the island, to whom she introduced me.

We stayed at the touristy Jolly Beach Hotel. It was a uniquely odd experience for me to feel like a tourist in an African Caribbean country. One memorable vision of that trip was that of following the Burning Flames around the island and watching folks dance in the most expressively wild manner to such infectious music. I had never seen such dancing!

After five days I was set to go back to the States, leaving Philippa with her Antiguan lover while I went back to New York to be chopped into pieces by a none-too-happy African American lover. Fortunately for me, Mickey had taken her rage out on my straw hat, which she'd cut up into little pieces and left scattered for me to see. With Mickey, I could be assured of one thing: Her fiery scorpion temper would compel her to react in a harsh and stinging way. An undeniable level of passion had always existed in our relationship, onstage and otherwise. During the time we were together I had been seeing two other women, but Mickey, not at all passive, had herself shared space with two other men. Nevertheless, neither of us was able to handle the other's indiscretions. And for my indiscretion, I had to pay with my hat. I liked that lid, too.

Meanwhile, I was making a tremendous comeback with the development of a band that had created interest and commanded respect. The next concert the Group performed in New York was even more successful and even better attended than the first. I enlisted the services of Cobi Narita, who now had a place of her own, the Jazz Center of New York, on Lafayette Street between Third and Fourth Streets. We played there on Friday and Saturday, September 12 and 13.

Suddenly, I was being called on to do gigs with other people as well. On a couple of occasions during the year, Lester Bowie had asked me to play in his Brass Fantasy. In November, Frank Lowe, whom I had not played with since he worked with my band Abdullah in 1977, called me to make a gig with him at the Painted Bride Art Center in Philadelphia.

The band that Frank organized for this one-night stand included Lester's younger brother, trombonist Joe Bowie, along with pianist Walter Bishop Jr., bassist Fred Hopkins, and drummer Charles Moffett.

Frank put this group together with just one rehearsal between him and me. It happened that Joe Bowie lived in Maryland at the time and the rest of the guys were unavailable. So Frank had to do it that way and communicated the details of the rehearsal to the others.

I was already familiar with some of the personnel. I had met Fred Hopkins ten years earlier when he first came to New York City as the bassist with Air. We had done some work together in big bands, but it was only recently that we'd worked in the same small ensemble together.

Earlier that year, right after the Group's premiere, Marion Brown had organized a couple of gigs for the band at Wesleyan University, in Connecticut, and at the Iron Horse in Northampton,

Top:      Ahmed's father, Lubia Bland, ca. 1980s.
Middle:  Ahmed's oldest sister, Marilyn Bland, ca. 1960.
Bottom: Iyabode, ca. 1980s.

Ahmed Abdullah with his twin sons, Rashid and Shahid Taylor-Abdullah, on Bowery and East 4th Street, New York, 1978.
Photo:   Gary Halperin.

The Sun Ra Arkestra at the Village Gate, 1976.
Left to right:    Sun Ra, Ahmed Abdullah, Marshall Allen, Danny Davis, Eloe Omoe,
                  Jack Jacson.
Photo:    Val Wilmer.

The Sun Ra Arkestra at Storyville, New York, 1977. Sun Ra (*Rocksichord*), Akh Tal Ebah (*trumpet*), Eddie Thomas (*drums*).

The Sun Ra Arkestra at the Five Spot, New York, June or August 1975.
Left to right:    Cheryl Banks, Wisteria el Moondew (Judith Holton), June Tyson, Sun Ra, Ted Thomas,
                 Akh Tal Ebah.
Photo:    Raymond Ross.

Left to right:   Sun Ra, Danny "Pico" Thompson, Ronnie Boykins, Marshall Allen, Pat Patrick, Danny Davis,
                John Gilmore, Eloe Omoe.
Photo:   Raymond Ross.

The Sun Ra Arkestra at the Montreux Jazz Festival, Switzerland, July 9, 1976.
Left to right:   ' Pat Patrick, John Gilmore, Ahmed Abdullah, Marshall Allen.
Photo:    Leon Collins.

The Sun Ra Arkestra at the Jazz Showcase, Chicago, November 1976.
Left to right: RaDu ben Judah, Sun Ra, John Gilmore, Ahmed Abdullah.
Photo: Hal Rammel.

Bring in the Sun Year with -

# SUN·RA

&

His SPACE archestra

## March 19·20·21

Fri·Sat· 10pm    Sun·8pm

good food! good folks!

good vibes!

at the
# EAST

a cultural and educational center for people of african descent

10 Claver Pl., B'klyn, N.Y.
tel. 636-9400

Flyer for Sun Ra and His Space Archestra [sic] at the East, Brooklyn, March 19–21, 1971.
Courtesy the Alton Abraham Sun Ra Collection at the University of Chicago.

The Sun Ra Arkestra at the Bottom Line, New York, ca. 1976–77.
Left to right:   Wisteria el Moondew, Cheryl Banks, Sun Ra.
Photo:   Adger Cowans.

The Sun Ra Arkestra at the East, Brooklyn, ca. 1973.
Photos: Basir Mchawi.

Milford Graves (*top*) and Mtume (*bottom*) at the East, ca. 1973.
Photos: Basir Mchawi.

Pharoah Sanders at the East, ca. 1973.
Photo:    Basir Mchawi.

An audience at the East, ca. 1973.
Photo:   Basir Mchawi.

Flyer for African Street Carnival at the East, June 8–July 4, 1974.
Courtesy the Juma Sultan papers at Columbia University Library.

256

African Street Carnival, Brooklyn, 1976.
Photo:   Marilyn Nance.

African Street Carnival, Brooklyn, 1976.
Photo:   Marilyn Nance.

258

Milford Graves (*center*) and Nadi Qamar (*far right*) with Nigerian artists at FESTAC Village, Lagos, 1977.
Photo: Marilyn Nance.

The Sun Ra Arkestra rehearsal at FESTAC Village, 1977.
Left to right:    Vincent Chancey, Danny Davis, unknown drummer, Marshall Allen, RaDu ben Judah,
                Danny "Pico" Thompson, Sun Ra.
Photo:    Marilyn Nance.

The Sun Ra Arkestra rehearsal at FESTAC Village, 1977.
Left to right:    June Tyson, Wisteria el Moondew, Cheryl Banks, and unidentified dancers.
Photo:    Marilyn Nance.

The Sun Ra Arkestra rehearsal in Lagos, 1977.
Wisteria el Moondew and Cheryl Banks dancing in front of observers and musicians Marshall Allen,
Vincent Chancey, Danny "Pico" Thompson, John Gilmore, Ahmed Abdullah, and Sun Ra.
Photos: Marilyn Nance.

Ahmed Abdullah, Danny "Pico" Thompson, and Jack Jacson at FESTAC '77.
Photo:   Marilyn Nance.

June Tyson at FESTAC '77.
Photo:    Marilyn Nance.

The Sun Ra Arkestra at FESTAC '77.
Photos:  Marilyn Nance.

Ahmed Abdullah at FESTAC '77.
Photo:   Marilyn Nance.

The Sun Ra Arkestra at FESTAC '77's closing ceremony.
Photos: Marilyn Nance.

The Sun Ra Arkestra at FESTAC '77's closing ceremony.
Left to right:    Marshall Allen, Wisteria el Moondew, unknown, Sun Ra, John Gilmore, unknown,
                Cheryl Banks.
Photo:    Marilyn Nance.

The Sun Ra Arkestra at the Public Theater, New York, May 1978.
Sun Ra (*keys*), Luqman Ali (*drums*), Michael Ray (*trumpet*), Marshall Allen (*saxophone*), Ahmed Abdullah (*trumpet*), Danny Davis (*flute*), Vincent Chancey (*French horn*), John Gilmore (*timbales*), Craig Harris (*left trombone*), Artakatune (*rear percussion*), Danny "Pico" Thompson (*saxophone*), Eloe Omoe (*flute*), and other musicians.
Photographer unknown.

The Sun Ra Arkestra at the Bottom Line, ca. 1980s.
Danny "Pico" Thompson (*alto saxophone*), Ahmed Abdullah (*trumpet*), Noël Scott (*tenor saxophone*).
Photographer unknown.

The Sun Ra Arkestra at Left Bank Jazz Society, Baltimore, year unknown.

# A BLACK FESTIVAL

A BENEFIT FOR THE
NEW YORK PANTHER 21
produced and managed by
CAL MASSEY in cooperation
the COMMITTEE TO DEFEND
THE PANTHER 21.

Lee Morgan Quintet

McCoy Tyner Quintet

Freddie Hubbard Quintet
Louis Hayes—Cedar Walton
Junior Cook—Wayne Dockey

Cedar Walton Trio

Pharoah Sanders Quintet
featuring Leon Thomas

Alice Coltrane

Sonny Reid

Jackie McLean

Archie Shepp Quintet
with Cal Massey

Eddie Gale & his
Ghetto Music

Bill Lee &
the Bass Choir

Cal Massey - His Mas
Orchestra including
Curtis Fuller
Wilbur Ware
Bob Cunningham
James Spaulding
Clarence C. Sharp
Charles Davis
Bill Hartman
William Bennet

Julius Walton
Cedar Walton
Alice Coltrane
Rasheed Ali
Eric Chambers
Noel Pointer

Elvin Jones Trio

Roland Alexander
"Kianazawadi Quintet"

Joe E. Wilson

(straight from Paris)
Creative Construction Company
    A.A.C.M. Group, including:
Anthony Baxton
Leroy Jenkins
Steve McCall
Leo Smith

Chris Capers Septet

Romulus

Buddy Enlow

Lawrence Tucker

China Lynn

Grachun Moncur III

"New Day Unlimited"
Presents a One Act Play
by Bernard Pearson

Fashions by "Ile"

Poetry Reading
Archie Shepp
Bernard Pearson

Master of Ceremonies
Ed Williams &
Al Roberts
of WLIB

Young People's Concert

Eric Chambers—Bass
(Paul Chambers' son)

"Number One" Group

Zane Massey—Alto Sax
(son of Cal Massey)

"Clovell & the Bells"
    plus
Sebastian at the piano

Olive Pointer with
Noel Pointer &
William Pointer

"The Auction"—dance
by Olive Pointer

Master of Ceremonies
Master Carl Walton
(Cedar Walton's son)

SUNDAY, FEBRUARY 22    5 p.m.—5 a.m.    $5 donation at the door

COMMUNITY DEVELOPMENT CENTER

1310 Atlantic Avenue

Brooklyn

NO ALCOHOL PERMITTED

Committee to Defend the Panther 21

37 Union Square West

New York, N.Y. 10003

243-2260

Flyer for A Black Festival, benefit for the Panther 21, Community Development Center, Brooklyn, February 22, 1970.

Dewey Johnson and Rashied Ali with an unidentified man at Ali's Alley, New York, ca. 1975–78.
Photo:    Raymond Ross.

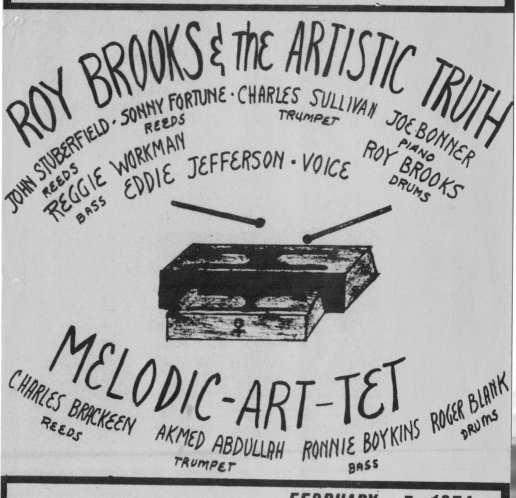

Flyer for Melodic Art-Tet at Wollman Auditorium, Columbia University, New York, February 3, 1974.

# melodic·art·tet

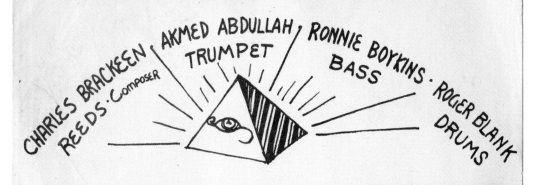

CHARLES BRACKEEN REEDS·Composer / AKMED ABDULLAH TRUMPET / RONNIE BOYKINS·BASS / ROGER BLANK DRUMS

**MEDGAR EVERS COLLEGE** ◆ 1130 Carroll St. BROOKLYN (Crown St. Enter) ◆ **MAY 3** *FREE* FRIDAY 7-9 P.M.

**GERALD'S JAZZ CLUB** ◆ 227st / LINDEN BLVD CAMBRIA HEIGHTS, N.Y. ◆ 10:00 p.m. **MAY 3 & MAY 4**

**N Y U** BLACK STUDENTS ◆ LOEB CENTER La Guardia Pl. ◆ **MAY 29** *FREE*

**MELODIC-ART-TET** CULTURAL STORY • 1-7 pm

* **Percussionette** . . . . DOUG HAMMOND...COMPOSER
ROGER BLANK
JEROME COOPER
MICHAEL CARTY

* ART SHOW... RAY GIBSON
GYLBERT
CAROL BLANK
OMILAYO

* **POETRY** . . . JOHN FERRIS

Flyer for Melodic Art-Tet concerts in New York, May 1974.

Abdullah at Studio We, New York, ca. 1973.
Left to right:    Aerol Henderson, Masujaa, Ahmed Abdullah, Arthur Blythe, Richard Dunbar, Rashid Sinan.
Photo:    Karma Stanley.

erformance at Black Student Union Kwanzaa celebration, Pratt Institute, Brooklyn, 1975.
hmed Abdullah (*trumpet*), Clifford Adams (*trombone*), Lawrence Northington (*alto saxophone*),
haroah Sanders (*tenor saxophone*).
hoto:    Marilyn Nance.

Abdullah at the Summer Festival of New Music, Studio Rivbea, New York, 1977.
Left to right:    Richard Williams, Ramsey Ameen, Rashid Sinan, Ahmed Abdullah, Arthur Doyle, Masujaa
Photo:    Raymond Ross.

Poster advertising performances by Arthur Blythe and Abdullah at the Summer Festival of New Music, Studio Rivbea, July 3, 1977, designed by Dorrie Ameen.

The Rashied Ali Quartet at Ali's Alley, 1977.
Nick DiGeronimo (*bass*), Byard Lancaster (*left saxophone*), Rashied Ali (*drums*), Ahmed Abdullah (*trumpet*), Lee Mixashawn Rozie (*right saxophone*).
Photo:    Raymond Ross.

Poster for Abdullah at Ali's Alley, July 11–15, 1978, designed by Ahmed's sister Lorraine Logan.

Ahmed Abdullah at Ali's Alley, February 1978.

Flyer for Abdullah concerts at St. Marks Playhouse, New York, August 18–19, 1978, designed by Lorraine Logan.

Abdullah at St. Marks Playhouse, August 1978.
Left to right:  Muneer Abdul Fatah, Oliver Lake, Rashid Sinan, Ahmed Abdullah, Vincent Chancey,
               Vishnu Wood, Jay Hoggard.
Photographer unknown.

Second Annivesary Concert

# THE
# GROUP

| SIRONE | MARION BROWN | BILLY BANG | ANDREW CYRILLE | AHMED ABDULLAH |
|--------|--------------|------------|----------------|----------------|
| Bass | Alto Saxophone | Violin | Drums | Trumpet |

AT

## GREENWICH HOUSE
### 27 BARROW STREET
(AT 7TH AVENUE & BLEEKER ST.)
### SATURDAY MAY 7
### SHOWS: 9:00 P.M. AND 10:30 P.M.
FOR TICKET INFORMATION CALL: (212) 874-7738

*All Seats $12*

Poster for the Group's concert at Greenwich House, New York, May 7, 1988.

The Group, ca. 1986.
Left to right:    Ahmed Abdullah, Fred Hopkins, Andrew Cyrille, Billy Bang, Marion Brown.
Photos:    Desdemone Bardin.

Arthur Jones and Ahmed Abullah at the Sound Unity Festival, Cuando Community Center,
New York, 1984.
Photo:   Raymond Ross.

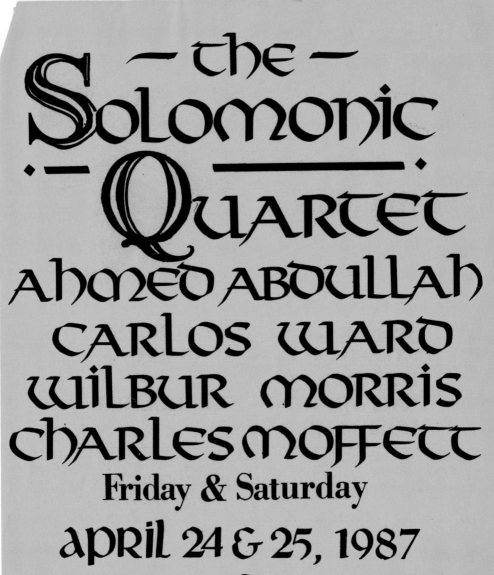

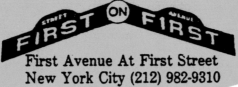

Poster for the Solomonic Quartet at First on First, New York, April 24–25, 1987.

# An Evening of Poetry and Afro-American Folk Rhythms

ABDULLAH AND LIFE FORCES
WOMEN OF THE CALABASH
LUIS RIVERA
SAFIYAH HENDERSON HOLMES
ROSE MARI MEALY

Where: Kenkeleba 214 E. 2nd St (btwn. Aves. B and C)

Take "F" train to Second Avenue and Houston. Walk east.

When: Sept. 27, 1980  8-12 midnight

A BENEFIT IN SUPPORT OF LOCAL 882, INTERNATIONAL CHEMICAL WORKERS UNION
LAUREL, MISSISSIPPI

Admission—$4.00

Albums, poetry and instruments on sale. For more information, call 840-6184.

Poster for An Evening of Poetry and Afro-American Folk Rhythms at Kenkeleba, New York, September 27, 1980.

Sun Ra and June Tyson on the set of David Sanborn and Jools Holland's *Night Music*, New York, 1989.
Photo:   Adger Cowans.

Solomonic Sextet, Carnegie Hall shelter concert series, State Office building in Harlem, New York, ca. 1990.
Left to right:   Atiba Wilson (Kwabena), Billy Bang, Charles Moffett, Ahmed Abdullah, RaDu ben Judah, Masujaa.
Photo:   Desdemone Bardin.

Solomonic Sextet backstage with the mayor of Thessaloniki, Greece, 1991.
Left to right:    Masujaa, Ahmed Abdullah, Charles Moffett, Konstantinos Kosmopoulos, Billy Bang, John
                 Ore, Carlos Ward.

Charles Moffett, Ahmed Abdullah, David S. Ware, and Fred Hopkins backstage at the Knitting Factory, New York, 1987.

The Sun Ra Arkestra on a flatbed truck in Istanbul, April 1990.
Ahmed Abdullah (*trumpet*), Elson Nascimento (*drums*), and Noël Scott (*saxophone*).
Photo:   Cem Akkan.

The Sun Ra Arkestra performing on a flatbed truck in Istanbul, April 1990.
Photo:    Cem Akkan.

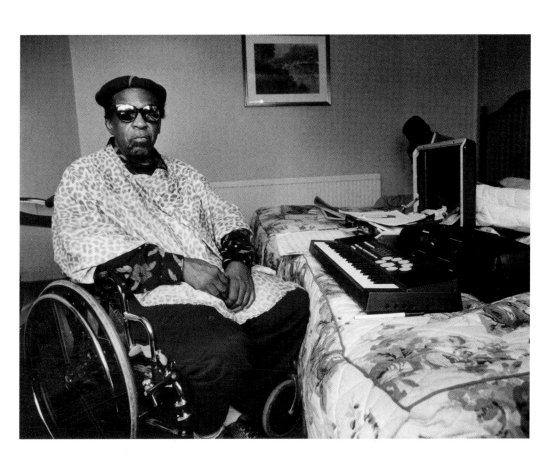

Sun Ra, Grafton Hotel, London, September 1991.
Photo:   Christian Him.

The Sun Ra Arkestra under Marshall Allen's leadership, the Paradiso, Amsterdam, ca. 1997.
Bruce Edwards (*guitar*), Marshall Allen (*saxophone, standing*), Michael Ray (*trumpet*), Yahya (*saxophone, seated*), Art Jenkins (*drums*).

The Sun Ra Arkestra in Oakland, California, August 1995.
Left to right:  Unknown, John Ore, Bruce Edwards (*guitar*), Marshall Allen, Tyrone Hill, Michael Ray
(*left trumpet*), Noël Scott (*baritone sax*), Wisteria el Moondew (*silver hat*), Craig Haynes
(*drumsticks*), Ahmed Abdullah (*middle trumpet*), Jack Jacson (*bassoon*), Eddie Gale (*right
trumpet*).

Top:     Michael Ray and Ahmed Abdullah delivering a lecture demonstration in Oakland, August 1995.
Bottom:  The Sun Ra Arkestra concert in Oakland, August 1995. Bruce Edwards (*guitar*), Eddie Gale (*top with purple circle*), Marshall Allen (*saxophone*), Wisteria el Moondew (*silver hat*), Ahmed Abdullah, Craig Haynes (*percussion*), Jack Jacson (*vocals*).

Ahmed and Monique's wedding, Taplow Court, Maidenhead, UK, September 27, 1992.
Left to right:    Kazuo Fuji, Robert Rutledge, Ahmed Abdullah, Monique Ngozi Nri, Diana Penny.

Top: Ahmed Abdullah with cousins in Vanceboro, North Carolina, ca. 2007
Bottom: Ahmed with sons Shahid (*left*) and Rashid (*right*) at an Ebonic Tones concert, Bob Myers's Up Over Jazz Cafe, Brooklyn, ca. 2002.

Danny "Pico" Thompson and Ahmed Abdullah at the International African Arts Festival, Boys and Girls High School, Brooklyn, ca. 1997.

Ahmed Abdullah and Marshall Allen backstage at Central Park Sumerstage, New York, ca. 2003.

Massachusetts. Sirone had a prior commitment and was unavailable for either gig. Since Andrew Cyrille and Fred had a close working relationship, we all agreed that Fred should replace Sirone on these gigs. Back in September, at our Jazz Center gig, we'd used both Fred and Sirone, which was an exciting move. So it was great to work with Fred. Trombonist Joe Bowie had his own group, Defunkt. He and I also had worked together in large ensembles before, and this too would be our first time together in a small group. Joe had just proudly and amazingly finished running in the New York Marathon, a twenty-six-mile race through the streets of New York City.

Some of the other members of Frank Lowe's ensemble were new to me. Walter Bishop Jr. had been only a name to me before this gig, but on our way down to Philly in a van we got into an interesting conversation about the music. Walter had played with Charlie Parker and many other musicians from Parker's era, so I took the opportunity to learn from a firsthand source what that had been like. I found out that Walter was a poet of sorts. During the trip down, he shared a poem he had written for the great percussionist Max Roach, which he called "A Roach Named Max." It was a comical and insightful piece Walter proved to be open and rooted in the music of his generation, which made for an interesting gig, personally and professionally.

◖◗

The most important connection that came out of this once-in-a-lifetime performance was my getting to work with Charles Moffett, someone I admired greatly. Born September 11, 1929, in Fort Worth, Texas, Charles had grown up right alongside one of the major innovators of the music, Ornette Coleman. In 1962, he was a member of one of Coleman's great bands, a trio that was rounded off with Dave Izenzon on bass, and that produced several wonderful recordings. One of them, the live *Town Hall, 1962*, on ESP, featured the sweet and mournful "Sadness," an Ornette composition I had listened to countless times. Charles was also the drummer on the much-acclaimed live *At the "Golden Circle" Stockholm*, on Blue Note Records. I had seen him play with Ornette at the Village Theatre in 1966, opposite John Coltrane. This was, in fact, the same Ornette Coleman Trio that had been asked to play at John Coltrane's funeral in 1967. So for me, it was an honor to be a part of this group that Frank Lowe had put together.

The night of the gig, there was a moment when we had some time before we went on.

Charles was setting up his drums, and I was checking my sound out with the microphone.

"What kind of horn you got there?" he asked.

"It's a Conn," I answered.

"Man, that Conn is a hard horn to blow, isn't it?" his Texas accent singing in the comment.

"Yeah, Jack! I gotta be sure to do long tones every day, 'less it kick my ass."

"Ha-ha-ha!" Charles' laughter was real robust, and everything around him seemed to light up with it. "I used to play trumpet, you know. Still do, sometimes. With the students I got at school, so I know about them long tones, man."

"You play trumpet?" I asked incredulously.

"Uh-hum. I got a son that plays too."

"Oh yeah? Y'know, I remember hearing the Charles Moffett Family Band at the Tin Palace, oh, about ten years or so ago. And I remember seeing Charnett, he was a little guy then, playing a bass that looked twice his size. And there was another one of your sons playing tenor; another playing drums, and if I remember right, your daughter was singing. But I don't remember no trumpet player."

"Mondre. He's the trumpet player. Lives out in Oakland. But that was Charles Junior on tenor, Codaryl on drums, and Charisse, my baby girl, singin'."

"Man, that was some concert y'all gave. That must be great, having a band with your children, huh?"

"Yeah, it sure is," he said proudly, and continued meticulously tuning his drums.

The concert we hit with received tremendous appreciation from a Philadelphia audience that even demanded an encore. Owing to our limited repertoire, we ended up playing one of the pieces we'd just gotten through doing, Ornette Coleman's "Jayne," written for his former wife, poet Jayne Cortez.

We gave them what they wanted, got a good and solid response, packed up, and began our trip back to New York—all of us, that is, except Joe Bowie, who lived in Maryland. Charles, who had driven down with his drums in his Cadillac, offered me a ride with him, which gave us a chance to talk, and me an opportunity to learn more about him. Besides working with Ornette, it turned out that Charles had also worked with Eric Dolphy, Sonny Rollins, Sonny Simmons, and Archie Shepp. He had been in semiretirement from performing, spending most of his time teaching. But after that reception in Philly . . .

Having taken the Verrazano Bridge into Brooklyn, he drove past where he lived before dropping me off in Manhattan. "I want you to see something," he said, pointing to a gate.

"What's that?"

"This where I live. I want you to know that, 'cause we gonna make some music together," he answered.

Prophetic. Just like that, he said what he had to say, and eased the car back out of the driveway of his building complex, and took me into Manhattan.

That symbolic gesture made a big impression on me. Charles Moffett was a giant, but one you could talk to. And because he put on no airs, you could easily make the mistake of disregarding the stature of the man.

◖◗

In December 1986, I received a call from Keith Knox, executive producer of Silkheart Records. Based in Stockholm, this new label was interested in recording the most adventurous music available.

The owner of the label, Lars-Olof Gustavsson, an investment banker, had been a longtime fan of the music. He had heard Charles Brackeen and me perform during the loft years when we were members of the Melodic Art-Tet. He remembered us well enough to tell executive producer Keith Knox to record us for the new label. The music had apparently inspired him enough to invest in the two of us fifteen years later.

I was facing a tough choice. I was asked to do one recording as a leader and to participate in another as a sideman. At the time, the money being offered, I thought, was good. The hook, however, was that I had to give up royalties against the record sales while retaining the publishing rights and royalties to my compositions. Back then, I believed that you should get as much money up front as possible. The chance of seeing money afterward meant you had to rely on the honesty and integrity of the people in the industry, which was from slim to none. So here I was being told, "Don't even think about it! What you see up front is all you'll get."

Tough as it was, it was actually a deal I could live with, or so I thought, because I was being given a choice.

In reality, Jazz is a music that has to be measured by long-range sales. Music of the 1920s, '30s, '40s, and onward is still being reissued and sold with little overhead. Because of deals similar to what I was being offered, the profits go to everyone except the artist on the recordings. So it behooves the artist to have a vision beyond the immediate.

To prepare for the recording date, I formed another group to work the music out with a live audience. Charles Moffett was to be the drummer, his prophecy in effect becoming reality. I also returned the favor to Frank Lowe and called bassist Wilber Morris as well. Philippa helped me with producing the rehearsal/concert by lending me money and designing the flyers. It was with her that I had brainstormed the name Solomonic, which was the unit I would use to express my music for the next ten years. Yet another prophecy of the seeress had unfolded.

This prophecy engaged me all the more, as I had been receiving communications from an imprisoned musician who called himself Dr. Elliot Emanuel Cola. A few months before, just after doing the Group's concert at Cobi Narita's Jazz Center, Dr. Cola had sent the first of a series of letters and songs to Cobi's mailing address. The publicity we created for the Group's concert had obviously found its way upstate to Fishkill prison, where Dr. Cola was incarcerated. In his letter to me via Cobi's address, it was clear he knew about the Group and about our concert.

The song he sent, actually a command, "Walk with God," had biblical references from the Book of Revelations. In his letter, Dr. Cola described himself as a musician more advanced than Mingus, Monk, Ellington, Coltrane, and Sun Ra. He said he could play a number of different instruments well and could write for all of them. He spoke of how we could work together, like Ellington and Strayhorn, and create really special music. What was most intriguing were his references to Solomon in his letters.

At first, I didn't do much more than play around with the tune on the piano. It was a fascinatingly simple modal blues. As opposed to dealing with traditional blues changes moving from the I to the IV and V chords, it alternated between the I and II chords of the mode, placing the feeling of the blues in the melody rather than the harmony. By the time we were ready for the prerecording concert the following February, I had decided to include this tune in our repertoire. Thus, the Solomonic Quartet was given life on February 10 and 11, 1987, at First on First, a Lower East Side club. The two nights were subsidized by money I had earned cabbing, along with the money Philippa had put up. Working out the music in New York turned out to be a brilliant idea, since I wouldn't have an opportunity to do it with the guys I was to record with later in Dallas. I did, however, send them a tape of the music we were to record that had been played by the quartet.

The personnel for the recording date, however, were unfamiliar with my music and had been chosen by Silkheart Records. Though Charles Brackeen and I had played together for several years with the Melodic Art-Tet, he rarely, if ever, played my music in that ensemble. He had recorded with me on the *Wildflowers* sessions, but that was eleven years before. We'd last played together with Ed Blackwell in 1979, but that too had been all Charles's music.

By February 1987, Charles had been living in Inglewood, California, for a few years. He used to play on the streets of New York and, being a complete original, he'd bring his peculiar flair to his street work, as he did onstage. He would improvise with windup toy monkeys while they moved. Something as harmless as that managed to incur the wrath of a member of the police department to whom Charles had no human rights the cop was bound to recognize. The cop insisted that Charles move from his spot. Charles's refusal to comply with local fascism quickly led to a beating, an arrest, and a lengthy stay in the mental ward at Bellevue Hospital. Fortunately, Roger Blank was able to get him out. Charles left New York and didn't want to hear nothing about coming back. That, coupled with the use of Texas-born multi-instrumentalist Dennis Gonzalez as the coordinator of the date, was why Dallas was chosen.

I had never before played with bassist Malachi Favors or drummer Alvin Fielder, the other two men on the date. I had met Malachi in France in 1976 while touring with Sunny. He was with the Art Ensemble of Chicago, which made me familiar with his playing. Alvin, a friend of Blackwell's, was at least aware of my work and had gotten a tape of the Sweet Earth recording that Charles and I had done with Ed. To round it all off, I brought Philippa along as my companion and as a contractual negotiator with Keith Knox.

Our February 16 recording session went smoothly. The title tune, "Liquid Magic," was the same one I had previously written for Sounds in Motion. I got to play piano on "Reflections on a Mystic." As I mentioned earlier, Jung's *Memories, Dreams, Reflections* had gotten me through a time when I was on the verge of abandoning music entirely. This song helped to acknowledge that.

*Liquid Magic* also gave me a chance to record Sun Ra's "Mystery of Two." He had granted me permission to do this, yet appeared both surprised and honored when I gave him a copy of the recording after its release. After returning from Charles Moffett's place of birth, I went directly to his apartment to let him hear the tapes of the session he'd had helped me hone. It was now my turn to be prophetic, and I told him, "You gonna be the drummer on the next record I do." He smiled and said, "Oh, yeah, A'med?" as only he could.

I had also sent a recorded copy of "Walk with God" to Dr. Cola. He got so excited that he began sending me letters damn near every other day. Some of them included music that he also wanted me to play. In his letters, he indicated that he would be getting out of prison soon and gave me a number in the Bronx where he would be staying, so I could contact him when he was out. We set up an appointment for him to come by our apartment on Fifth Street at noon the day after he was sprung.

The building Mickey and I were living in had only four floors; all of the people in it were artists. None of us got up early, unless we really had to. But Dr. Cola showed up promptly at 10 a.m. and repeatedly rang every bell in the house. I didn't know whether or not it was for me until I heard him yell, "Abdullah!" I got up and quickly ran downstairs to greet him.

"I'm the only musician who can show you what you need to know," he began, with no other introduction. "You got some good ideas. I can see that! But you gotta be careful, 'cause people duck the real thing. And don't you be among them!"

"Hey, man, I thought our meeting was for noon. It's only ten," I said.

Without losing a syllable, he continued, "You might wonder why I was in jail? Read Revelation 2:10. Before W. C. Handy was, I am," he said.

Dr. Cola was a tall man with horn-rimmed glasses dressed in a brightly colored zoot suit looking like both he and it had come off the rack back in the 1940s.

Oh man, I said to myself, I better not take this cat upstairs. He's either a nut or on his own mission. And he did make sense, even inside his monologue style.

"My song is free. No money feeds my soul. The blues is food enough for me. For blues is God's reply to souls that music cry, and there's hope for all when man can hear a song."

I thought I had better take this guy back to the train station or to wherever it was he came from. But I knew I had to be delicate with him, as he was obviously a sensitive human being, even in his insensitivity. Throughout our session together, he never stopped talking long enough for me to say anything, so I gradually guided him out of the courtyard of 209 East Fifth Street, and over to the Fourteenth Street train station.

"Like Monk said, 'Straight, No Chaser,'" he continued. "Like Miles said, *Someday My Prince Will Come*. Like Coltrane said, 'The Father and the Son and the Holy Ghost.' Like Mingus said, *Better Git It in Your Soul*. Like Dolphy said, *The Blues and the Abstract Truth*. Like you said, 'Reflections on a Mystic.'"

When we finally arrived at the subway stop, he momentarily stopped to enter this world and asked for carfare. After I gave him more than enough for a token, he returned to his mission.

"Blessed is the man who walks not in the counsel of the ungodly, nor sitteth in the seat of the scorner. But his delight is in the Law of the Lord. And in His Law doth he meditate day and night. And he shall be like a tree planted by the rivers of waters. His leaf shall not wither and whatsoever he doeth shall prosper. I'm gonna leave you with that, my brother. It's taken from Psalm 1:1."

"Hey, man, we can keep in touch," I said, not really meaning it.

"There are seven colas of Asia: The Cola Nut Tree. Royal Crown. White Rock cola. The Pepsi Generation. Coke, the Real Thing. Like cola. Seven Up cola," he answered, and descended the stairs.

Throughout 1987, the Group, still consisting of Andrew Cyrille, Marion Brown, Sirone, me, and Billy Bang, stayed together. In fact, we began the year at 1369, a club in Cambridge, Massachusetts.

Marion still had the connection to the Iron Horse, so we did both venues up there before driving back to New York through a blizzard to do yet another gig at Sweet Basil. We had decided to drive back that night instead of relaxing in Cambridge and returning with daylight beside us. I drove the van.

There was hardly anyone on that road at 4 a.m. No one else was obviously foolhardy enough to hit a highway that had not yet been cleared. As a cabdriver, I would go out under the most hazardous conditions and believed the best way to deal with that kind of difficulty was to face it head-on. It gave me a sense of adventure, of going against the forces of nature, or, as Sun Ra would say, doing the impossible.

It was all quiet, with most of the fellows in the van nodding out into their own sleep. After a few hours heading into Connecticut, I must have dozed off myself for a microsecond or so. Luckily, I was able to shake it off and wake up, but in that instant, realizing I had been asleep, I immediately slammed the brakes and in doing so swerved off the road. The van went right into a snowbank on the side of the road, almost overturning. No one was hurt, but everyone was obviously shaken and annoyed. For me, it was another case of my guardian angel's protection.

The following evening, we opened at Sweet Basil and did two nights. Gunter Hampel, a friend to both Marion Brown and the Group, videotaped our performance.

After my return from Dallas, we regrouped and made it through 1987 working at Temple University in late February. Scheduled in the middle of the week, the show—produced by Paxton K. Baker, a student in his last year there—was packed. Paxton would later become a concert impresario with a vision, creating Jazz festivals in the Caribbean, where there were none before. He went on to become a senior vice president of BET on Jazz.

At the Temple University gig, the Group had demonstrated tremendous drawing power for a Philly event; it was attended as well by quite a few of the fellows from the Sun Ra Arkestra.

Later that May we returned to the Greenwich House to do what we hoped was an annual concert. We had not yet recorded by this time, and we could see that our audience had dwindled compared to the turnout we had the previous year.

I got us a gig at the Helsinki Festival in Finland for that coming September. This turned out to be our best-paying gig to date, but that was because I finally acted on a long-held belief: In order to get good money, one had to ask for it. I asked for $10,000 for the concert, and the person I talked to agreed. Of course, after agreeing, the promoter realized what he had done and asked us to play another concert in the nearby college town of Tampere.

On the way to Helsinki, we stopped in Stockholm and were treated royally by Lars Gustavasson, who had no connection with our tour. Yet he paid for our hotel, treated us to dinner, and made our overnight stay in the beautiful city quite comfortable. The next day, we took the Silja Line, an overnight ferry, from Stockholm to Helsinki. Oftentimes when traveling I get an urge to wander around and investigate things. On this boat, I came upon a table and sat down. Food was offered and served. I ate and quite honestly thought the meal was included in the ferry ticket. I left the table and strolled away. I ran into Billy Bang and Andrew Cyrille, who were similarly investigative. I pulled their coats to what I thought was a free meal. They went to the same table and did the same thing. For some reason, however, things weren't the same for them. When they left the table, an alarm was triggered and they became food fugitives.

People were notified that two Black men had not paid for their meals. A description of Andrew and Billy was given out, and they were hunted down. We were resting in our cabins when men came and charged Andrew and Billy with eating without paying. Nothing at all was said to me. After some arguments between musicians and officials, Andrew and Billy paid their tabs.

Though the concerts in Finland were well received, we were still not making progress toward recording. By November, I once again had taken the initiative to produce three days of concerts on Grand Street at the Henry Street Settlement's theater. The fee was reasonable for the site, which was slightly inaccessible and not used frequently enough to generate the kind of audiences we needed. We put out flyers, did a mailing, radio blurbs, and even placed ads in the *Village Voice*. Yet, what with the weather dipping into winter mode, the turnout was light enough to result in us barely breaking even.

The one good thing about this concert, besides the high level of music, was that Lars Gustavsson showed up again. This time he got a chance to hear the band. We hoped that he would want to record the Group, but apparently he didn't think we were adventurous—i.e., avant-garde—enough. Our tendency to stick with well-disciplined arrangements even with our free music background did not seem to impress Lars.

He was, however, interested in setting up another recording date that he would once again let me produce. I had suggested a quartet to him that would include alto saxophonist/flutist Carlos Ward, bassist Fred Hopkins, and Charles Moffett. Lars had in turn informed Philippa, who was still working with the Group, that he would send her the money and that the session was on.

The first problem I encountered was that Carlos had a prior commitment in the Caribbean with Don Cherry. Since we had been given money for a particular set of personnel and since changing the date was not an option I could consider, we had to find out who the Silkheart label would agree to as a replacement for him.

They gave me a list of names, out of which I focused on David S. Ware. Though we had never played together, we knew each other. We had shared the same cab over a period of time, and David had lived near me on Seventh Street. Like Mickey Davidson, David was also a Scorpio, having been born on November 7, and even though my relationship with Mickey (born November 6) was waning, we always shared a strong artistic passion of the kind I would hear in David's playing. I thought he was a good choice, as he, too, was a veteran of the loft era. He had played in Cecil Taylor's Unit and had in fact worked with Andrew Cyrille on the third volume of the *Wildflower* sessions.

I decided to follow my own lead and once again use a live concert to prepare for the actual recording. This time, however,

I'd be using the same personnel for both. I booked a couple of days at a new place in town, the Knitting Factory. My quartet, which was now known as the Solomonic Quartet, consisted of Moffett, Hopkins, and Ware.

As I started rehearsing with David, I realized our respective tones were startlingly different. David was used to playing in a trio format, where he was the sole horn, and consequently, his was a different sound for the ensemble. Now I had to make another decision, this time, without asking Keith Knox.

I added Masujaa's guitar to absorb and balance the front-line sound. This was a totally musical consideration, one that the Silkheart people might not like, oddly enough, primarily because of the commercial implications. Like many others who consider themselves Jazz purists, they were not particularly fond of electric guitar. David S. Ware's sound had created just the right challenge to require a balance between quartet and quintet numbers on the recording. In short, Masujaa's guitar was vital.

Philippa and I worked together on the choice of studio and engineer and the person to write the liner notes. We got engineer David Baker to commit before we went into the A&R studios on West Forty-Eighth Street (now home of Local 802, the musicians' union); Robert Palmer—who had championed my efforts throughout the days of the Loft Movement—was to write the liner notes. As recently as that July, he had done a *New York Times* review of the Solomonic Quartet's gig at Carlos One, a Village club. Under normal circumstances, his job at the paper would have prevented him from doing liner notes because of an implied conflict of interest, but he was leaving his job there anyway to do research on Mississippi Delta blues.

The piece I felt strongest about recording here had come to me by way of a tape, a gift from a friend. The album, *O Canto Dos Escravos (Song of Slaves)*, concerning enslaved Africans in Brazil, included "Canto II," a folksong presented by Clementina De Jesus. The song touched me when I heard it. There was depth in the music, speaking to the human condition and the possibility of spiritual transcendence of a condition as horrific as slavery. The first time I heard it, I felt the connection to people of the African diaspora. The lyrics, written in a kind of Portuguese patois peculiar to the Brazilian African, were translated for me by a woman I knew only as Françoise. They convey the story of a little child freed by her parents from a slave village. The emotions of the child's parents serve as the basis for the song, which mixes sadness over never seeing the child again and happiness over the fact that the child, unlike themselves, will be free of slavery's chains.

I could feel the special power invoked in this song. All the musicians were also much in tune with the thematic material. The process of arranging "Canto II" for that recording grew into a spiritual endeavor. And in keeping with the name Solomonic, there were three Davids in the studio, including poet David Dunn. The resulting recording became *Ahmed Abdullah and the Solomonic Quintet, featuring Charles Moffett*, produced on December 3 and 4, 1987, with Philippa's assistance from beginning to end, and with an original painting by Marion Brown on the cover.

Musicians rarely get credit for producing or directing their own art. We are judged only by how well we "star" in our scripts in relation to others. Too often we read that the leader of a date had been "outplayed by his sidemen." Very rarely is our intent, the most important aspect of an artistic creation, even considered.

The Solomonic Quintet was a continuation of the process that had begun for me with the Master Brotherhood. Fundamentally, I was still asking how I could get maximum performance from the group without subordinating the players to my will. I had, in a sense, stumbled on a methodology that allowed me to do what I had seen Sun Ra do repeatedly over the years. I had found a way of allowing musicians in my ensemble to have their voices completely and particularly heard within the context of a group sound. That this method worked with the *Solomonic* recording is evidenced by the acclaim it came to receive, but most specifically by the praise given to Moffett and Ware, both of whom had been heard in many instances prior to this date but without as much critical notice—that is, with the exception of Charles's work in the 1960s with Ornette. It obviously wasn't their playing that was being "discovered," but the context in which it was heard. David was subsequently able to come out of semi-obscurity and record numerous albums for Silkheart Records, eventually moving to DIW before going over to Sony.

The people at Silkheart did not seem pleased with the album (it was my last one for them), but for me it was a wonderful experience. To capture all of the drum sound David Baker made sure there were enough mikes on Charles Moffett. Drum master that Charles was, I never had to do much more than play him a song or hand him the music, allowing him to interpret it. He and Fred worked especially well together, and with Masujaa woven in, they formed a formidable rhythm section.

A couple of weeks after the recording, my life took yet another turn. Mickey and I started arguing again. Of course, she had not been happy about my relationship with Philippa over the past year and a half, and I had been similarly at odds with her over a relationship she was having with a trombonist in Count Basie's band. There didn't seem to be any point in our staying together, so by Christmas our arguments ended with her telling me to "just get out!"

While Philippa had invited me to stay with her, for me, that option recalled too closely the scenario I was just exiting, so I declined. I swore that I would never again put myself in a position where I would be asked to leave a woman's house. From then on, I would keep a place of my own.

I was still driving a cab; in fact, I had a deal where I could keep the cab twenty-four hours, seven days a week. I was virtually living in that car until one day, toward the end of the year, I was at Philippa's when she discovered a *New York Times* ad for an apartment in Brooklyn at 17 North Elliott Place. I drove to this address on New Year's Eve and met the owner, William Hock, who seemed like a good person. On January 1, 1988, I gave him the deposit he requested, and on January 10 I moved into the first apartment I'd had on my own in twenty years.

The year before, I'd been contacted by Mitch Goldman, a student at Columbia University and a staff member at WKCR, the school's radio station. I had met Mitch at Binghamton, when I did a gig there with New Dimensions in Music a few years back. WKCR has aired some of the most informative Jazz programs in the world. The station produced marathon events on different artists throughout the year. On the occasion of the births or deaths of people like Roy Eldridge, Billie Holiday, Bix Beiderbecke, Charlie Mingus, Duke Ellington, Miles Davis, John Coltrane, and Coleman Hawkins, one can hear their music played for twenty-four hours without commercial interruption. During the conservative 1980s, WKCR was right there providing alternative programming that spoke to the complete history of Jazz.

Mitch Goldman had teamed up with Charles Blass and Andy Rotman (the three Sun Ra fans were all student DJs) to do 114 hours of Sunny's music. Even for WKCR, given to doing marathons, this was exceptional. Since I had recently reached another level of appreciation for Sun Ra's genius, as well as his contribution to my life, I totally encouraged them in their efforts. They were, however, not getting much encouragement from Sunny himself.

One night, while I was hanging out at my favorite spot at the time, Sweet Basil, the three of them came in looking totally dejected. They had talked to Sunny, who seemed to have nixed the whole marathon idea, something about keeping a low profile. I told them they shouldn't be swayed by that, because after they'd pulled it off he would be the first to sing their praises. Since they had done most of the work already, they were relieved to hear that it was still possible to do.

When it finally did hit in April 1987, the show was probably the most exposure Sun Ra had gotten since ABC/Impulse had released the Saturn label records back in the early 1970s. Though Charlie had been responsible for most of the organizing efforts, along with Mitch and Andy, the trio deferred to Phil Schaap when it came to interviewing Sun Ra.

Schaap was the resident historian at WKCR who, like another DJ there, Sharif Abdus-Salaam, had long since grown past his student days, staying on because he was committed to the music. Every morning, Phil Schaap would do his show on Charlie Parker. With his knowledge of the music, Phil was able to pose questions to Sun Ra that had never before been asked—and Sunny had been interviewed by some of the best, all over the world.

The interview lasted several hours, during which Sunny revealed many things about his past that had not quite come into focus before. I listened to the entirety of the interview while cabbing it around New York City. Sunny talked about his early life in Birmingham, his time with Fletcher Henderson, and his beginnings in New York; he also discussed key principles of his musical philosophy that, over the years, I rarely heard him speak on, except during rehearsals. It was an amazing event in the history of that station and a significant one in the history of Jazz.

The new year, 1988, found me back in Brooklyn, in a neighborhood close to where my sons, Rashid and Shahid, were living. Shortly after I had moved in, I brought them around to show them my spot. They were now twelve years old. Upon entering my brick-front ground-floor garden apartment, their first comment was, "Daddy's got a bachelor's pad!"

"Yeah. Sure does!"

Once I settled in, things began to happen quickly for me. Mitch Goldman, who thought I could make some money on the side as a model, referred me to a friend of his who worked for the William Morris Agency doing print ads. On my first time out at an audition, I was selected to do a Benson & Hedges commercial, which was shot that spring.

Though I declined the offer of the chauffeured limousine, it nevertheless indicated the level that this commercial was on. The upscale shoot for which I was chosen as one of the principals, along with actor Dean Irby, took place at a club in SoHo known as Greene Street.

The shoot took most of the day, as everyone and his mother was trying to tell me how they thought I should hold my horn. When the director finally decided he'd had enough, he whispered in my ear that I should do something that no one had suggested I do up until that point—play my horn. This worked absolutely. The sound of the trumpet took everyone else by surprise and caught them off guard, creating the most natural poses imaginable. I made more money in one day than I had made in most musical situations in months.

It was around that spring I had a dream about Sun Ra, who appeared as my teacher, giving me serious instruction. At first when I awoke, the dream didn't make a lot of sense to me. I didn't normally remember any of my dreams, and that bothered me. But, dig, I had the *Liquid Magic* recording coming out shortly, and before long the recording I'd done at the end of the previous year, with the Solomonic Quintet, would also be out. Of course, working with the Sun Ra Arkestra was not the place for me at this time. Then again, what I had unconsciously discovered in the process of my last recording revealed to me that I had more work to do. I needed to fine-tune some things and Sunny was a source. The dream helped me to see that I needed to be back in his band; after all, he didn't have that much time left, and I had more lessons to learn. That May, I was called to do a gig with the Arkestra in one of my favorite cities, Washington.

We were going to play at Blues Alley in Georgetown. It felt good to be back in this band that was becoming more of a family to me. No matter what, there was something connecting us, something imperceptible that kept bringing me back. The gig in DC was a good one. Brother Ah, whom I hadn't seen since my first years in the band, had moved to the District and had come out to hear us. A welcome surprise. We talked briefly.

On our way back to New York by bus, I sat in front of John Gilmore, which gave me an opportunity to chat with him. In the course of our conversation, he mentioned that he thought this time I should stay with the band. This, coupled with the dream I'd had, made me seriously consider his proposition.

It wasn't long before I was once again traveling the Spaceways from city to city, country to country, planet to planet. That July, Sun Ra was for the first time asked to come to Japan to play at the Live Under the Sky festival. Even though Richard Wilkinson was on the outs as band manager for whatever reason, he was the person who negotiated the business for Japan.

I was in a bit of a conflict, as I had been asked by the William Morris Agency to hold open a block of time that corresponded to the time we were to leave for Japan. The Benson & Hedges people wanted to use me for some billboard ads they were shooting. The modeling industry expected models to commit a block of time with no guarantee of money and with no reasonable assurance that they would be used during the period reserved. They did this knowing that other models would gladly take your place. But I was also a musician first. I decided to go to Japan, and Dean Irby, the actor on the original shoot, took my place as the poster man for Benson & Hedges, with his image plastered all over town. A joke that he and I later shared concerned the fact that the poster shot had him holding the trumpet incorrectly. Since he wasn't a trumpet player, they couldn't rely on a "natural shoot."

Before the trip, I had purchased another copy of *The Kybalion*, which the seeress had told me to read a couple of years before. It's a book on Hermetic philosophy, covering the principles of life said to have been conceived by Hermes Trismegistus. I'd bought this copy for Sun Ra and gave it to him as a present. He read it during our flight, and in our discussion of it he said, "You know, sometimes it seems like I wrote that book myself."

He then began to talk about the person he was named for, a magician who was called Black Herman. Thanks to the lively discussion we had after he read the book, I was beginning to see why I was supposed to be back in the band.

Live Under the Sky 1988 had scheduled groups led by Dave Sanborn, Pat Metheny, Charlie Haden, Miles Davis, and Sun Ra. At our first concert, in Tokyo, a very young Marlon Jordan was also featured. Marlon is the trumpet-playing son of saxophonist Kidd Jordan of New Orleans. His brother, Kent, a wonderful flutist, was a sideman with Marlon. Kidd Jordan is said to have been instrumental in providing the first gig that ultimately established the World Saxophone Quartet.

I had no idea what an incredibly modern city Tokyo had become, or in fact how well developed the rest of Japan was. The four cities we visited were teeming with life, and their hotels were the first ones I'd seen in which computer cards were used as hotel room keys.

In Tokyo, we performed at Yomiuriland, an amusement park, for a crowd of about 40,000 people who paid the equivalent of $40 a head. Prior to our performance, we came into the open-air concert ground to do a sound check. The Miles Davis band was on but without the maestro, who obviously didn't do sound checks. Sun Ra, on the other hand, seemed to relish sound checks, as they permitted him to rehearse the Arkestra prior to the actual performance.

The dressing rooms we were taken to afterward were equipped with televisions so we could view a live telecast of the onstage concert.

This being his first trip to Japan, Sun Ra was out to dazzle his new audience. We had two drummers, Samarai Celestial and Buster Smith. Rollo Radford, who plays some crowd-pleasing yet uncompromising bass, was on hand as well, with guitarist Bruce Edwards rounding out the rhythm section. Tyrone Hill, Michael Ray, Martin Banks, and I were the brass section. Martin, a first-rate trumpeter from Austin, had played with the Arkestra at Slugs' back when I was watching the band as a teenager. The saxophone section included John Gilmore, Marshall Allen, Eloe Omoe, and Danny Thompson.

I call the Sun Ra method of communication at festivals the "blitz." He would have us walk on stage in a burst of energy, completely mesmerizing audiences with music, dance, vocals, solos, duos (any combination of free flow, discord, harmony, and/or unity). He would then make his entrance after we had tuned up folks, as he would say, having built the audience to a fever pitch. Then he would choreograph us to the next level, which would be a fast-paced selection of songs that would cover the complete history of Jazz, from ragtime to no time. Thus, the Arkestra, under his direction, would pull out all the stops, and just as quickly as eyes could blink and mouths fall agape, be gone before anyone fully realized what had happened. This was standard festival procedure and one of the central characteristics that led to the Sun Ra Arkestra being voted the leading big band in the *DownBeat* Critics Poll for the following two consecutive years. Critics, by the way, haunted festivals in form, and their reviews of festival bands often made the difference in future attention.

Later that night, after the gig, a group of us were hanging out in the lobby of the upscale Tokyo Prince Hotel, where we were staying. Several of the guys were from Miles's band, among them alto saxophonist Kenny Garrett. In the course of our exchanges about the various performances, compliments and conversations just kept whizzing by. Finally it was suggested we all go and get something to eat. Since I was hungry and free bus transportation was being provided, I went along. We continued with big fun and merriment on the bus, but when we got to the restaurant, things quieted down, and I felt a sudden sense of apprehension in the air. "We're here!" someone yelled.

We got off the bus one at a time and walked into a chic, lavishly decorated restaurant. The simple black-and-white check-ered scheme of the room belied the quiet elegance of the setting. The mood had shifted from our prior gaiety on the bus to a frightened awestruck inertia. Someone whispered, "Miles!" as we were escorted into a back room with one long dining table and a low round table in a far corner. Every other chair was laden with a package. At the head of the table was a person perched in throne-like splendor, dressed in the same color scheme as the room, only in a style even more lavish and elegant. Here, with silk and cotton topped off by a shoulder-length weave accenting his odd and characteristic forehead that contrasted with the stony and perfectly etched Black beauty of the remainder of his face, was the "Prince of Darkness." It was then that I realized what all the anxiety had been about.

As people entered the room they were seated. The guys who were part of the Miles band all went to him and acknowledged his presence by bowing or kissing his hand or his cheek.

I'd had no idea we were going to a dinner party hosted by Miles Davis. I quickly understood my faux pas and tried as quietly as possible to find an unoccupied and undesignated seat.

Though he probably wouldn't have remembered, I had met Miles Davis eighteen years before when he played the Club Baron on 132nd Street in Harlem as part of a double bill that included Dizzy Gillespie's band. Like most of my musician buddies, I was fascinated by Miles. He was still playing phenomenally at that time, with a band that included Wayne Shorter, Chick Corea, Jack DeJohnette, and Dave Holland. Back then, his was one of those must-see gigs.

Later that night at the Baron, my friends and I were standing outside between bands and saw Miles and approached him as he stood on the corner. We didn't know what to say to this master, but one of the guys said something like, "Mr. Davis, could you tell us what to do as musicians?"

"I'm gonna tell you one thing," Miles replied in his characteristically gravelly voice. "If you ever get a gig, don't ever turn it down. Just ask for more money!"

Having dropped that pearl, he glided away. We were astounded that he'd spoken at all. Having met him that one time, I realized he was at least human. So here in Tokyo, in late July 1988, I took a seat that I thought was okay and relaxed.

A few minutes later one of Miles's reps came over to me and said real quietly, "Miles would like you to sit at that table."

The table he pointed to was across the room, all the way in the back and on the other side of the long table where the majority of people had been seated. At the smaller round table were three attractive women. This didn't seem like a bad place at all. So I sat down, relaxed, and talked to the ladies, sitting there with my back completely to the host, who was at the head of the long table.

Suddenly, I felt a steely viselike grip on my shoulder, and in my ear hear a rough voice. "Who in the fuck are you? And who invited you?"

Though whispered, it was suddenly for me the loudest sound in the room. After picking up my heart from my toes, I managed to blurt out something like my name and "Your band invited me."

"Who?" Miles asked, with gravel-voiced persistence. "Which one of these muthafuckers? Bobby! Did you do this to me? Did you fuck me up again?"

He was speaking to Robert Irving III, a relative and keyboardist with his band.

By this time, I'd had enough. I was extremely uncomfortable being the butt of this perverse joke. I stood. "Look, okay. I'm uninvited and I'll leave, man," I said, making a move for the door.

Quicker than mercury and smoother than butter, Miles changed up and said, "Naw, man! Sit down! Have some champagne. Enjoy yourself!" He then left the room, only to return in a few minutes and menacingly stand over me with his huge gravity belt inches from my face.

"Man, you all right," he said, and then walked back to his royal seat at the head of the table. Within minutes of sitting, he was up again, walking past me, this time saying nothing, and then he left.

The party, such as it was, went on without the host. I stayed a little longer, answering questions like, "Why'd he do that to you?" Questions I didn't have answers for. Finally I got up and left.

On the way back to the Tokyo Prince Hotel, I shared a cab with Kenny Garrett and asked him about Miles's behavior, having already formed the opinion that the great trumpeter was totally uncool.

"Man, how could you work with that cat?" I asked.

"Miles is cool, man. He probably dug you, too. Don't think anything of that. That's his usual thing, man." I did think a lot about it. And I no longer regarded him with the same reverence I once had.

The next day, I got up and went to Sunny's room to recount my adventure. Sunny was appalled and told several members of the band about the way "that no-good" Miles Davis had treated me.

One of the cats Sunny related the story to was one of the other trumpeters in the group. This trumpet man was an excellent section man, soloist, and reader. He had spent time as part of Harlem's Apollo band in the 1960s. While he worked at the Apollo Theater, he also worked with Sun Ra at Slugs', which is where I first saw, heard, and began to admire him from a distance. He used to ride around on a motorcycle, a gig bag containing his trumpet on his shoulder.

He hadn't played with Sun Ra for a while until the months prior to the Japanese gigs. Apparently he had a history of alcohol abuse, and on this trip he was supposedly going to abstain. For some reason, however, he seemed to think that sake, the Japanese drink, would not affect him, and from the time we got off the plane, he started indulging. It was in the city of Fukuoka that his past caught up with him. He had been drinking sake the night before and into the next day as the temperature rose above a hundred degrees. We were playing outdoors in the heat. From the time of sound check, both Michael and I were trying to keep him cool despite the fact that he, a dignified man when sober, became a totally despicable and belligerent character under the influence of alcohol. We could see that the sake had gotten to him when he became so erratic onstage during the performance that he had to be escorted off.

Sun Ra, seeing the trumpeter's behavior, just shook his head in disgust. When we finished our set, we found that he had passed out. He had to be taken to the hospital, where he almost died from the combination of sake and hundred-degree-plus temps. Sunny was furious and wanted nothing to do with him. In fact, he tried to make arrangements to send the man back on the first available flight after the Fukuoka gig. When that could not be accomplished, he wanted to put him in a separate hotel from us. Of course, that was also impossible. This really brilliant trumpeter never played with the band ever again, and Sunny managed not to speak to him for the rest of the tour.

What was interesting about Sun Ra's reaction was how different it was from his response to Al Evans's usual drunkenness and especially the incident that had occurred at Carnegie Hall back in 1984. It seemed as if things were changing for Sun Ra during his seventy-fourth year on the planet. He was on the verge of getting fuller recognition for what he had been doing for the past thirty years. Yet, even as he was moving on, some of the same forces that helped him get where he was would continually come forward to embarrass him.

# VIII
# NEW HORIZONS

> And I was trying to tell them about the Creative Universe, but now I'm talking about the Creative Omniverse, you see. I'm moving along the spiritual planes of evolution. At first I was talking about music being the universal language; now I'm saying that music has stepped up to be the omniversal language, you see. That's the eternal—well, the eternal everything, you might say.
> —Sun Ra

Our last gig of the Japanese tour ended at the Pit Inn, Tokyo's well-known Jazz club. We had come full circle, having performed in Osaka, Yokohama, and Fukuoka. The Pit Inn gig was recorded live on 8/8/88 and we returned to the US the next day.

On the flight back I ran into Robert Rutledge, an old friend and fellow trumpeter, who also had been working in Japan, with Lionel Hampton's band. We took up common space in the back of the plane, flirting with flight attendants and drinking cognac and beer. While filling Robert in on the years since we had not seen each other, I was also able to reflect on the circumstances around being back with Sun Ra.

A few weeks later, many of us were summoned to Birmingham for a special occasion in August. Sun Ra had not played in his hometown since he left in 1946. One of the gigs set up for the band was not exactly the kind of red-carpet treatment a returning prodigal son would have expected. Nevertheless, Sun Ra called in all his people. Carl LeBlanc and Michael Ray came from New Orleans; Samarai Celestial from Knoxville, Tennessee; June Tyson, John Ore, Buster Smith, Billy Bang, and I from New York; and TC III from Philly, to join regulars Gilmore, Allen, Omoe, Scott, and

Hill. We were to create maximum impact at the Nick, a Southern bar complete with pool table and bluegrass music.

The Birmingham gig was so hot that Jothan Callins, a Birmingham native who was in the audience and hadn't played with Sunny since the 1960s, heard the band and was immediately ready to drop everything to go on the road with us. Jothan, a talented trumpeter, pianist, bass player, composer, arranger, and educator, was working at the time as a pianist at a club we visited upon our arrival in town. Another talented local, ex-Temptations falsetto crooner Eddie Kendricks, was also in the audience digging on Sun Ra's "Birmingham Blitz."

Traveling with the Arkestra now was quite different from my tenure in the mid-1970s. I had returned to the band with two recordings that were to be released in 1988, making it now four recordings under my name since I had left in 1978. Although it was but a small accomplishment, in comparison to the fellows who were considered the "stars" of the band, it was tremendous.

John Gilmore had but one recording, *Blowing in from Chicago*, and Pat Patrick had *Sound Advice* with the Baritone Saxophone Retinue. Marshall Allen had never recorded as the leader of an ensemble. Michael Ray and Tyrone Hill, both of whom had developed reputations as major soloists in the Arkestra, were also at that time without any albums under their own names.

This gave me a sense of self-importance, which for me was absolutely necessary when working with someone who said he represented the Creator of the Universe. Talk like that left me wondering about my own identity, despite what I had achieved on my own. Jazz writers around the world tended to portray members of the Arkestra as a marginalized fringe with no individuality and generally unworthy of even being mentioned, much less critiqued. This resulted in an unspoken but definite feeling of disempowerment. An interesting contradiction. You see, this Music of the Spirit is one of the most empowering artistic disciplines ever created, and one of the few areas traditionally open to African Americans for expressing our humanity.

As well, this music provides the artist working as part of a collective the space for individual style and identity. Yet in the Arkestra, only the leader received attention, and then only after decades of high artistic innovations. It's a compelling triad of contradictions. On the one side, the music is effective and powerful. No question. But that has to do with the artistry and level of achievement brought by the gathering of individual musicians into one collective force.

Then there is the genius of the leader himself. When Sun Ra was achieving only the barest recognition, the individual members of his group received none; then, just when critics and producers finally granted Sunny his due, the members of the Arkestra were still not awarded due recognition for their musicianship. Thus the sense of disempowerment and lack of self-esteem. For me, this feeling manifested most obviously in the rampant drug addiction into which I descended during my second time around with the Arkestra. Some band members, myself included, had moved from smoking marijuana to using cocaine. Many of these guys had also begun smoking cocaine, something I had not attempted nor felt a desire to try. I had learned vicariously that smoking cocaine was like shooting heroin, and I wasn't even hardly curious. It was bad enough snorting it, I thought, even as I moved to get some more.

It's been said that drug use expands one's state of consciousness. That is something I can agree with; however, the user typically is not paying attention to the often more costly side effects: the time spent attempting to achieve and regain that state. It is a search, moreover, so personally centered that it is characterized by a selfish myopia. Like, I got to get some now, not for *us*, but for *me*. On the road with the band, this search would play out whenever we reached a new city. Aside from working the gig, for most of us, our primary interest was to get high.

The astounding thing was that Sun Ra was working at the highest level that he had ever worked at before, in terms of visibility, artistic vision, and pay. And everywhere we went in the US, if there was a housing project to be found, cocaine was easily available.

Crack cocaine, a concentrated pure rock, had by then been made freely available in Black and Latin neighborhoods around the country, creating a new and more dangerous addiction that rapidly reached epidemic proportions. Years later, in August 1996, we'd learn from a series of articles in the San Jose *Mercury News* by Gary Webb that the CIA—in its illegal support of the Nicaraguan counter-revolutionary group known as the Contras—had aided in the marketing and sale of crack cocaine in the 1980s throughout African American and Latin communities.

Once the fear of a people is established through constant rein-forcement and manipulation via the media, it's easy to understand how drugs could be allowed into the country and predominantly distributed in their neighborhoods.

There are a number of reasons why these neighborhoods are targeted for drug distribution. The first is that another community of interest profits financially from these drug sales. Many of the decent people who live in the areas where drugs are placed can't cope. They subsequently abandon their own communities, where they could have developed voting strength, and move into "better" neighborhoods, where they then in effect form part of a minority.

The local sale and use of dope are both one-way streets lead-ing to the penitentiary or the morgue. In the prison–industrial complex, a modern form of slavery is thus reinforced. Slavery existed as long as it was profitable; it provided a free and exploit-able source of labor. Addiction and imprisonment is like the chattel system; it is essentially the same state of affairs. An added dimension to this modern form of slavery includes the fact that felons (and in some states ex-prisoners) lose their right to vote and are thus systematically exploited as a cheap labor force through corporate privatization of prison systems. The political implica-tions of drug abuse become clearer as one is freed from its clutches.

Ronald Reagan, while president for eight years, had a not-so-hidden agenda to turn back the hands of time. Because of his support of the Contras (though financial support had been outlawed by Congress) and his opposition to the Sandinistas (the revolutionaries who had overthrown the Somoza regime in

Nicaragua), he looked the other way as financial support for the Contras came from drug sales. His vice president, George H. W. Bush, continued this policy as president—drugs and guns, buy and sell, smuggle and exploit, all easily accomplished through money laundering, which kept the banks afloat.

◖

I thought I had a problem with drugs until I returned to the Arkestra and witnessed firsthand how severe the problem had gotten, both throughout the country and in the band. During the Chicago Jazz Festival of September 1988, this reality hit me hard.

Chicago was still a second home to the band, and we were staying at the Blackstone Hotel on Michigan Avenue, a few blocks from the festival site in Grant Park. The Blackstone was the official festival headquarters, with most of the participating musicians staying there. In the lobby of the hotel was the new home for the Chicago festival's central club, the Jazz Showcase. No longer on North Rush, the club provided an arena for late-night hangouts and jam sessions for musicians during the festival. Of course, this was also where you found the local drug dealers quietly taking care of business.

Those in the Arkestra had a tendency to travel as a family and hang together and generally stay away from others, especially when private business was at hand. There was a room at the hotel where many of the cats in the band who were into smoking cocaine would go. The room was kept dark night and day, and you could smell the unmistakable scent of cocaine burning as soon as you got off the elevator. There were guys who probably did not leave their rooms (except to play the gigs) for the five days we stayed at the Blackstone. Most of their money went to their dealers, who probably made more off this festival than the entire Arkestra combined.

Despite all of what this implies, there was still a high level of artistic innovation coming from Sun Ra's vision. Prior to Chicago, we had done the Montreux-Detroit Jazz Festival, where Sunny had premiered the new Arkestra. By then he had augmented the band with other dancers, a singer, and percussionists. In addition to June Tyson, Sun Ra brought in Don Juarez, a percussionist and singer. As well, he found two male capoeira dancers, Loremil Machado and Gato, both of whom danced and played (Machado the berimbau and Gato various other percussion instruments). The capoeira exhibitions they performed were breathtaking. Don Juarez engaged the audience in a call-and-response exhibition that was fabulous.

Sunny's regular festival trap drummers Samarai Celestial and Buster Smith were accompanied by percussionist Elson Nascimento, who in turn hired several other Brazilian and African American percussionists. As well, Sunny began using master drummer Kwasi Asare, a Ghanaian who lived in Manchester, UK, but who had been doing workshops in the Philadelphia area.

Both the Chicago and Detroit festivals were wonderful arenas for local support of this African American art form: The two outdoor events were well financed and free to the public, with thousands of people present.

That year, the Chicago organizers gave special acknowledgment to that peculiar saxophone sound that had evolved out of a Chicago tenor tradition through the likes of Johnny Griffin, Von Freeman, Gene Ammons, Clifford Jordan, and John Gilmore and company. In fact, a performance of leading Chicago tenormen playing together was one of the festival's featured presentations. Among the more thrilling moments of the Chi fest was hearing saxophone master Sonny Rollins play at his peak.

Before Rollins got up there, John Gilmore had remarked in a conversation with me that Rollins, a native New Yorker who had spent some time in Chicago, was totally aware of the rich tenor saxophone history there and would come prepared to get house. Mr. Rollins's set was nothing short of incredible and was the talk of the festival among those who congregated later at the Showcase.

Sun Ra's music also went way beyond anything I had heard the band do. Unlike Rollins's set, ours was recorded for radio, and thus the extraordinary event documented. Our Sunny was moving into a significant new area. The audience sensed this, as the crowds at both Detroit and Chicago went wild over the ensemble.

One of the things that kept my nose clean and my head clear in Chicago was a romantic adventure with Belinda Kay Holmes. Born in Albuquerque of Navajo and African American parentage, Belinda, then residing in Denver, was a law student on vacation with a couple of female friends. With my new bachelor status firmly in hand, I had been eyeing this trio of fine ladies for a couple of days. One morning, while strolling along Michigan Avenue, I happened to meet Belinda. Because of the ease with which we engaged in conversation, I figured she had paid some attention to me as well; so when I suggested that we spend some time together that afternoon, she didn't hesistate in replying in the affirmative.

I had heard about the Velvet Lounge, saxophonist Fred Anderson's club, as a place I should check out. I'd been told that this musician-run club was a hangout for local musicians and meeting place for those, like myself, who were visiting the area.

On a Sunday afternoon in September, Belinda and her friend from Toronto drove me to the club where bassist Malachi Favors and trumpeter Billy Brimfield were playing with drummer Ajaramu and some other musicians I didn't know. The music was on the scale of adventurous bop, and after a while I was encouraged to sit in and did so. We all had a good time, and I could tell there was something happening with the chemistry between Belinda and myself. As I was sharing my hotel room with another musician, I had to find another space that night for Belinda and me, which I did.

Belinda went home to Denver after the festival, and we kept in touch by telephone; it didn't take long for us to begin a torrid cross-country relationship. Through our exchanges, she knew we were going to stay in Chicago for another week to fulfill an engagement at George's, an upscale supper club in a different part of the city.

Our stay at the Blackstone was only as good as our work at the festival, so we were moved to a motel on the South Side where, sure enough, we were in the hood. Belinda flew back to Chicago and hung out with me for a couple of days while we played George's; the romance simmered with its own steady heat.

A true indication of the fact that I had really returned to the Arkestra was my inclusion on a Sun Ra West Coast tour later that October 1988. I had up until this time, managed to avoid these trips out West, which were usually done in a couple of vans in questionable condition. On this tour, however, the Arkestra was traveling by Amtrak, making a wonderful three-and-a-half-day journey across the 3,000 or more miles that would bring us to Seattle.

On our way out, on October 22, we celebrated trombonist Tyrone Hill's birthday. I was able to make only part of the tour with the Arkestra, doing gigs in Seattle, Portland, and several stops in California. After a gig at Palms II, a quaint club near the University of California, Davis, I left them to fly back to do a gig in New York. While I was in New York, they continued with work in Texas, Omaha, and Kansas City. After a few days, I flew back to Denver, where the Arkestra was to do a performance on Election Day. With Belinda living in Denver, I thought my trip out there would be well worth the expense. I played the gig and hung out a few days with Belinda while the band went back by train.

Years later, Sun Ra critics would report that Sunny had voted for George H. W. Bush in that year's presidential election. Whatever the basis for such a rumor, I can only say that unless he had carried an absentee ballot, it could not have happened.

○

I was moving into places I had never been before, both in social and business matters. I found myself dealing with too many women while not wanting to commit to any of them. The relationship with Belinda, more like a fling, all but ended as quickly as it had begun shortly after my trip to Denver. Obviously, I was being too noncommittal in matters of the heart.

Back in New York, I was hanging out on University Place, at Bradley's, a piano bar that for years had been a choice spot for musicians. Bradley Cunningham, who started the club, had passed and his wife, Wendy, was currently operating it. Some of the most excellent pianists, bassist, drummers, and horn players were hired to play this room. On any given night, one might find pianists Hank Jones, Kenny Barron, John Hicks, Ronnie Mathews, Kirk Lightsey, Michael Weiss, or Joanne Brackeen; bassists Cecil McBee, Ray Drummond, Don Pate, or Rufus Reid; and horn players George Coleman, Bobby Watson, Gary Bartz, or Roy Hargrove playing a gig or just hanging out.

Bradley's had the great advantage of being open until the wee hours. The excitement that a good set can stimulate makes it hard for some musicians to go home and go to bed like ordinary people after a day's work. Oftentimes, musicians would come to Bradley's after their regular sets to get loose and jam. There was an air of expectancy always present because you never knew who would show up or what might happen. Many a night would roll into morning as musicians and friends of the music strolled in and out of Bradley's as late as 5 a.m.

One night, I met Amber Taylor there. A redhead from Los Angeles who worked behind the scenes in film and television, she had worked on the innovative television miniseries *Lonesome Dove.* Having seen and enjoyed it myself, I was able to get with her in some seriously deep conversation. Amber turned out to have a great interest in and love of music and had a remarkably impeccable memory of the lyrics to almost any song.

The powerful attraction we had, I was to find out later, was based on the fact that Amber was a practicing Buddhist. Mickey Davidson had also begun to practice Buddhism during the course of our relationship. They both practiced the Buddhism of Nam-myoho-renge-kyo. A practitioner of this belief system chanted to a scroll known as the Gohonzon in order to bring forth the inherent Buddha nature. Philippa, too, had been brought into Buddhism while working with drummer Ronald Shannon Jackson before I knew her. Even though she was not practicing at the time I knew her, she still kept her enclosed Gohonzon in full view at her apartment.

The practice of Buddhism is based on mystic law, which moves and acts in ways that are not always immediately revealed. Back then, it was not obvious to me why I felt a need to deal with so many women. A surface rationale came up years later in therapy, when it was revealed to me that I was reacting to the fact that Iyabode had gotten married and had a child. I had deluded myself into believing that all those years I was away, she had been waiting for me to return.

When I did return from Japan in 1988, and before leaving for Chicago, I got a call from Iyabode about Shahid being in a hospital in Staten Island. It happened that he had cut his finger on a swimming-pool grate while on a day-camp outing and had to be rushed to a local hospital with his finger dangling by a virtual thread. In the waiting room, while we were sitting together for the first time in years, I discovered that Iyabode had recently given birth to a third child, a daughter by the name of Merakhu. My suppressed internal reaction to this news was a sudden desire to distance myself from both her and my sons.

Shahid came out of it all right, having received a series of stitches to keep his finger in place. I didn't come out of it as well. My totally uncalled-for resentment toward Iyabode became heavy, leading me to justify what grew into a more distant relationship with the three of them. It didn't matter that I had given myself permission to deal with as many women as I could, including white ones. Yet, on another level, these women became the key to unlocking the mystery of my life, as I gradually moved closer to understanding my mission.

Before the year ended, 1988 provided a couple of other new arenas for Sun Ra. During the last part of November, the Arkestra did a week at the Village Vanguard. On November 30, we were playing the club when the news broke that both Charlie Rouse and the Baroness Pannonica de Koenigswarter—two people closely associated with Thelonious Monk—had died that day. The Village Vanguard was also closely linked with Monk's career, and that week Sun Ra had used drummer Art Taylor and bassist John Ore, two other people closely aligned with Monk and his music.

Sunny acknowledged the deaths by having John Gilmore play a spiritual version of Monk's classic "'Round Midnight" in quartet format. The spirits of Rouse, Nica, and Monk were definitely in the room that night.

To emphasize the connection, on December 5, 1988, we were in the studio recording *Blue Delight* for A&M Records, a major label. Being in on this one was a big step in terms of distribution possibilities for Sun Ra's music. The thing I found most curious, however, was the presence of Billy Higgins in the studio. It turns out that Art Taylor, who had done the entire week at the Village Vanguard, had a problem with the money he was offered to play drums on the recording. So he decided not to do the date. The spirit moves in mysterious ways.

John Ore and drummer Billy Higgins hadn't played together on record since April 29, 1960, when they did one of my favorite records, Monk's live *At the Blackhawk*. And now, here they were together again on *Blue Delight*; and I, too, would be in on that one.

While *Blue Delight* is not necessarily one of Sun Ra's greatest recordings, it was notable both for the Monk connection and for the presence of trumpeter Tommy Turrentine, who had just dropped by the studio with Al Evans and managed to get in on the date. Trombonist Julian Priester was there (it was my first time playing with him); altoist Noël Scott, who joined the group in the early '80s, had come back; and guitarist Carl LeBlanc of New Orleans was there beside Bruce Edwards. Regulars John Gilmore, Marshall Allen, Danny Thompson, Buster Smith, Eloe Omoe, Tyrone Hill, trumpeter Fred Adams, and now Elson Nascimento were all on hand, with Sunny on a variety of keyboard instruments.

While sales for *Blue Delight* were good given A&M's distribution, it was neither vintage nor current Sun Ra. The session went well but it was mostly standards or vehicles for a series of solos with very few of Sunny's arrangements or even the exciting rhythmic mixtures that had characterized our most recent festival performances.

One night, in 1989, the Solomonic Quintet was working at Carlos 1. Our eponymous recording had been out for a while now, and the quintet was beginning to get some work. For the club gig, I used Carlos Ward, Masujaa, bassist Vishnu Wood, and, of course, Charles Moffett. Philippa had booked the gig, so it was natural that she be present. But in the course of the night, Mickey, Amber, and Belinda (who surprised me by flying in from Denver) were all in the same room at the same time. The pressure was there, in the air and in me. With three of the women I was seeing having the Gohonzon, the ultimate object of worship in their homes, it was only a matter of time before I had to make profound changes in my life.

Carlos 1, run by a Black man from the Caribbean, deserves much credit for the venue it offered. The club was centrally situated on Sixth Avenue near West Tenth Street, with a lovely wood-paneled interior that came complete with a view from the street. This site allowed passers-by (as in the case of Sweet Basil) to just drop in. Carlos 1 functioned as a Jazz club for about three years, from 1986 to 1989. I was able to work there on quite a few occasions with either the Group or the Solomonic Quartet/Quintet.

The owner's taste was eclectic. He would book Benny Carter, Clark Terry, Harry "Sweets" Edison, Oliver Lake, Lester Bowie, Jay McShann, or Geri Allen at any given time. Billy Bang was once hired to play the room with his own band after the Group had performed there; his gig was recorded and later released as *Live at Carlos 1* on the Black Saint/Soul Note label. Hamiet Bluiett also documented the club's existence with a session that was taped in that room.

The weeklong gig I did there, from April 25 to 30, 1989, was previewed by Gary Giddins with a *Village Voice* Choice, and reviewed by Francis Davis in a full-page article in *7 Days*, a new publication. Davis showed up on opening night and in the next month's edition his article appeared with the following lead:

I don't know if a concept like *mainstream* is still applicable to a music as internally torn and alienated from mass taste as Jazz, but if it is, Ahmed Abdullah's high-minded but inviting music is mainstream Jazz in its ideal state at the end of the 1980s. Abdullah is a 42-year-old trumpeter with a radiant sound and a penchant for growling notes a semitone flat; his solos are remarkable for their unlikely combination of sardonic dissonance and melodic glow. Though Louis Armstrong, Miles Davis, Lee Morgan, Freddie Hubbard and Fats Navarro were the names he volunteered when I asked him about influences during a recent conversation, the trumpeter Abdullah most reminds me of is the late Kenny Dorham—he has Dorham's sense of lyrical continuity, a quality that makes it seem as though he's thinking out loud.

I got a copy of the news magazine while driving my cab a week after we did the gig. Immediately, I pulled over to the curb and read it and became so excited that I told the next passenger who got into my car about it. The article gave me the right push just when the Solomonic Quintet had been booked to play two festivals in Europe—at the Ulrichsberger Kaleidophon in Austria and a festival in Eindhoven, Netherlands. This was my first tour as a leader since going over with Sam Rivers in 1977. We left New York on a real high because the review in *7 Days* came out just before we took off to perform.

For this tour I wanted the same cats who were on the recording, and fortunately, they were available. We were, however, running into some resistance from Alois Fischer, the festival producer in Austria, regarding my choice of Fred Hopkins. The year before, Fred had caused some concern over there when he had not been able to play and had almost died. His problem with alcohol and its resultant effects were similar to what had occurred in Japan with one of Sunny's trumpeters. Fred was my choice bass player, and as an advocate for second chances, I was determined to have him make these gigs. Alois Fischer, however, was so insistent on not having Fred play that he advertised Reggie Workman, who had worked with the band but was not going to be in on this gig.

I won out. And as it turned out, it was truly the best thing. Just before we left, we had gotten news that Steve McCall, Fred's longtime partner in the innovative group Air, had passed. When he arrived at the airport, we could see that Fred was visibly shaken. The advantage we had on this tour was Charles Moffett, who was much like Steve McCall in spirit. They were both powerful and melodic drummers, a rare and interesting combination. Fred and Charles had already worked together in the studio as well as on that initial gig with Frank Lowe three years before. The result was that they played beautifully together, and with Fred knowing he was under scrutiny, he played with even greater brilliance.

Cheryl Banks, a former dancer with the Arkestra and John Gilmore's partner for many years, was also performing at this festival with vocalist Jeanne Lee. Theirs was an exciting set, and, as it turned out, Cheryl's presence proved to be good for Fred, as he was constantly hitting on her. While at the Austrian festival, it fell on me to convey the news of Steve McCall's death to another one of his closer friends, tenor saxophonist Reverend Frank Wright, whose group was also featured there.

Frank and I used to hang for a while. I had known him since the 1960s, just about the same time he and his Cleveland homeboy, alto saxophonist Arthur Jones, had made their way to New York. When I first met Rev, he had driven his white Cadillac to the city, seeking fame and fortune. He had managed to play alongside Coltrane on one of John's legendary performances at the Village Gate. He had recorded twice on ESP, once with a trio and later with a sextet. Not long after, around 1969, he moved to Europe, where he fared better in developing a strong audience for himself with a consistent group including pianist Bobby Few, bassist Alan Silva, drummer Muhammad Ali, and sometimes alto saxophonist Noah Howard. Now and then he would keep an apartment in New York, trying to do the same thing here. The audiences here, however, were not as open to him as those in Europe.

As it turned out, years later, his New York base happened to be in the same Manhattan building where Philippa lived, at 2350 Broadway. Whenever he was in the city and I was visiting with Philippa, I'd hear his horn through the shaftway, call him up, and go down to his apartment to hang with him and exchange good vibes. So here we both were at this rather obscure festival in the Austrian countryside leading our own groups, and it was on me to tell him about Steve McCall. Usually, news of the death of a musician of Steve's caliber traveled fast, but the expression of profound shock on Rev's face when I told him indicated that he hadn't a clue.

For me, the festival was a major step; for Rev, it was like the news I had to drop on him, signaling the approaching end of a hard-traveled road. Later on in March 1990, when I visited with him at his New York apartment, he was excited about the fact that after all the years he had been playing, he was finally being offered a gig in the US that paid reasonably well. They were to do a tribute to Albert Ayler, also from Cleveland, at the New Orleans Jazz and Heritage Festival in April. Rev got to play that gig. A month later I heard that he had died in Germany.

The Solomonic Quintet's European premiere in Austria was fairly well received, though we were not at our best as we were plagued by problems with the sound system. Basically, performing groups are often not permitted enough time to do a proper sound check at these festivals. Instead, you'll get a quick line check just after you take the stage. If this is not performed correctly, the result can be an unbalanced sound. With European audiences in particular, if you don't get the clamor for "More! More," characterized by some foot-stomping, hand-clapping enthusiasm, you know you haven't done your job. And so it went in Austria.

Fortunately, we had another engagement somewhere else on our mini-tour through which we could redeem ourselves. Unfortunately, because of our tight schedule, I didn't get a chance to hear Reverend Frank Wright's group.

Our second gig was in the Netherlands, and we had to leave Austria immediately. On her way home, Cheryl Banks, who at the time lived in Wuppertal, Germany, accompanied us part of the way, much to the delight of Fred, who was still chasing and hitting on her. At the time, I imagined his flirtation as a way to lighten things up for himself, given that the death of Steve McCall marked the end of a long and close collaboration, spanning well over fifteen years.

We were slightly apprehensive about the Netherlands gig because we'd never received a verified contract. The guy supposedly representing us was a Belgian who had come to us from Silkheart Records. As our relationship with Silkheart was a good one, Philippa and I had no reason to distrust this agent. But the contract he sent us, outlining the conditions of payment for the gig in the Netherlands, was written out in German, not in English, and the fellow who had hooked it up was Belgian, not Dutch.

We couldn't understand why someone would do that or what the contracts meant. What we could see was that the price for the gig, given by the festival, was different from the price quoted by the agent. This was a common exploitive practice, which gave the agent a percentage of your fee plus the difference between the actual fee for the gig and the amount the agent quoted on his contract.

Although this was my first European gig on my own, I wasn't a fool, and Philippa was in my corner. We suspected skullduggery. The money we had gotten from the Austrian gig was used for transportation, so that our net salaries would have to come out of the gig in the Netherlands. I had a group of musicians traveling with me for whom I was responsible. They didn't know what was going on, but they expected to get paid at the end of the day, and I didn't appreciate the discomfort.

We arrived in Eindhoven by train the next day and were met at the station by a crew from the Eindhoven Festival, who took us to a nearby hotel. After we checked in to our respective rooms, Philippa came to mine and we got a call from our Belgian agent. I had never met this man in person, but by phone he sounded insulting and condescending. "Mr. — —, I don't believe we have a contract for this gig," I said.

A long silence on his end was followed by, "What do you mean you don't have a contract? I sent you one!"

There was something about his hesitation and the nastiness in his voice that told me all I needed to know. "Yes, but it's in German," I replied, as if he didn't know.

"Well, don't worry about anything. I have your money. Everything is fine! All you have to do is play good music," he said patronizingly.

"But I am worried! And if you have the money, I would suggest that you bring it to my room now!" I said testily.

"Who do you think you're talking to? I've been in this business for years; I've worked with some of the greats and you're a nobody! Who do you think you are addressing in this way?"

"Listen, muthafucker!" My Harlem/Lower East Side/ Brooklyn roots were coming out now. "If you got my goddamn money, bring it to my fuckin' room now! You understand that shit?" I demanded and hung up the phone.

Sometimes I lose my temper and say things I might want to retract later. But the truth was, I didn't know who this man knew, nor did I know what his true position was in relation to the festival, but I wasn't going to let myself be nobody's "boy," either.

Philippa hurriedly put in a call to the festival producer. We told him that we needed to be paid before we played and that if our agent had the money, as he said he did, it was the festival's responsibility to get it to us. Once you play, you have no bargaining power. That's something I learned years ago.

We found out that our agent was bluffing. The festival had given him no money and was perfectly willing to pay us before we played. At sound check that afternoon, we were paid in full—$500 more than what the agent had told us the gig was paying. Because of the insulting way this agent had dealt with me, the person he was working for, my intention was to not give him a dime.

The concert took place late that evening. After the day's excitement, which had me in war mode, it took a couple of songs before I was able to get into playing. We were the closing act of the festival, following a bass and cello duet that featured Muneer Abdul

Fatah and Peter Kowald. Peter was living in Wuppertal, where Cheryl Banks was staying. I had not seen Muneer, the world's only standup cellist, in years. He had been living in Freiburg teaching martial arts and music.

The first song we played, "Mayibuye," was a giveaway for me. I was barely into it. We came back a little stronger with Charles Moffett Jr.'s "Gypsy Lady"; I then let David S. Ware blow some, as I could feel he was ready to fly and I had been holding him back. The perfect vehicle for him was "The Dance We Do," which he played on stritch, the E-flat instrument that looks like a bass clarinet and sometimes sounds like one, too. After David went way out there, which is his wont, we came all the way inside with the blues, "Walk with God." I was feeling like I had gotten over the war, and after a rendition of Paul Laurence Dunbar's epic poem "When Malindy Sings," I was ready to play.

Saxophonist Bill Saxton, an old friend, was also in Eindhoven. He had worked with pianist Errol Parker the day before, but I could tell when I met him earlier in the day that he hadn't gotten his thing off. When I called "Walk with God," I saw him walking toward the stage ready to play. When I finished the poem, I called him up and from then on the concert soared to another level.

I was playing songs from the last two Silkheart albums, so next I called "Liquid Magic," the lyrical title tune that had become a vehicle for some incredible bass work by Fred Hopkins. That piece flowed into "The Ruler," a dedication to John Coltrane, which unleashed the energy of the combined forces of Ware and Saxton, with Moffett, Hopkins, and Masujaa exploding as well. The audience and festival producer loved it. I wanted to make sure that if that agent was in the audience he would never make the mistake of playing me cheap again.

The cat, however, didn't let the matter drop. Even though I had no idea whether or not he was at our concert (he hadn't identified himself), he wrote a footnoted dissertation of several pages about how he was robbed and how no one in their right mind in Europe should ever book me again. In an attempt to "white-list" me, he sent it to as many festivals and promoters as he could, as well as to Silkheart Records. The letter I received from Keith Knox, at Silkheart, confirmed the agent's anger at me and gave every indication that he (the agent) would have his revenge if I didn't apologize. I didn't understand why I should have apologized for preventing someone from ripping me off. So I faced the consequence of a two-year stint without working in Europe and the possibility of not recording for Silkheart again.

Earlier that year, in February 1989, I had participated in a concert at the Bottom Line in New York in which Sun Ra premiered music devoted to Walt Disney songs. It was a brilliant idea, because those songs, like some of Sunny's own compositions, touched that childlike quality in a person. They had universal appeal. The infusion of the Disney material into a regular repertoire tended to bolster Sun Ra's already growing support and popularity.

Interestingly enough, later in April, the month before I was to appear there, Sunny had played Ulrichsberg and had done an entire show of Disney material, which eventually was posthumously released on Leo Records.

In early May, while I was in Europe with my band, Michael Ray was still working with the Arkestra, and Sun Ra did the New Orleans fest opposite Miles Davis again. It was also in New Orleans that Michael met Gloria Powers and renewed his relationship with Kool and the Gang; those two events took him out of the Arkestra for a few months.

Sun Ra was not only doing new and different music by now but he had also radically changed his way of doing business. He was being booked by Jack Reich in Rhode Island and the Brad Simon agency in New York. While Sunny had never trusted white folks enough in the past to allow them to fully represent him, he was currently distrustful of the Black folks he had known for years. The excesses of Richard had rendered him ineffective as Sunny's road manager. And Danny "Pico" Thompson, his righthand man, Sun Ra later found out, had married and kept it a secret. This had created a situation in which Sunny ended up severing ties with Pico, one of the people closest to him. With the combined forces of Reich and Simon, the Sun Ra Arkestra was moving into places we had never been before.

From late June through the first of July 1989, we toured Canada, playing festivals in Toronto, Edmonton, Calgary, Vancouver, and Victoria. Brad Simon booked the tour. Of course, it didn't hurt that the Sun Ra Arkestra had won the *DownBeat* Critics Poll as the number one big band for that year, or that, with A&M Records promoting *Blue Delight*, Sun Ra had become a somewhat acceptable freak.

Throughout all of these gigs, we were playing at a high level. Touring Canada for the first time, I became aware of other things. Like the fact that in Edmonton it never quite got dark at night. During that time of the year, there's only a perpetual after-evening twilight through dawn.

While in Calgary, I went to a club, sat in the audience, and witnessed the effect that the folk song "Iko Iko" had on people. From that day on I added it to my own repertoire. On another occasion, percussionist Don Juarez and I made the front cover of the *Calgary Daily*; we were pictured warming up before the concert. The most memorable place we visited was Victoria, British Columbia. It looked like a paradise on Earth and was vastly different from any place I have ever seen. There was a museum in Victoria that abounded with Amerindian artifacts. Walking through it, you could feel a most profound presence that spoke to the fact that despite their bloody demise, theirs was a spiritual existence.

Our most memorable performances took place in Vancouver, where we played a large hall. It was a most relaxed yet impassioned performance. The producers allowed us the time to stretch out, and these West Coast Canadians were apparently a lot more familiar with the band.

Our last gig in Canada was at the Toronto Jazz Festival. One of the volunteers at the festival, Carmen Arguelles, an artist, would later become a good friend to both Jothan Callins and me. After I told Carmen about my encounter with Miles the year before, she gave me a photograph of him and her, one visual artist meeting another.

During this time, I was experiencing the best financial situation with Sun Ra ever. While I understood it was important for me to be around him for spiritual reasons, I also knew that you couldn't let Sunny take you for granted financially or you were finished. He had a way of changing the price on you, even now, when we were working more. It was his way of controlling things.

Our gig in Toronto was the day before a bank holiday in Canada, the first of July. After a lot of waiting around, Sun Ra got payment by check. Those of us who didn't live in Philly would not see him until the next gig, which was scheduled to take place July 19 at the Lone Star in New York, or so I was told. As the number of gigs we were doing began to blur one into the other, I realized that I might never see the money for any one of those separate gigs. It was for this reason that I couldn't play the Lone Star gig without first getting paid for the Toronto gig. So I went to the New York club prepared not to play. I had been through these battles with Sunny many times before; this time, with Michael Ray not around, I knew I had the upper hand. Sunny the tiger became Sunny the pussycat as he handed me my money no sooner than I said, "Sunny, I need to get paid for Toronto!"

Jack Reich had booked the gig at the Lone Star, a rock club then located on Fifty-Second Street in Manhattan. It was indicative of the kind of domestic venues he had added to our itinerary. With Jack's contacts (he currently booked NRBQ, a white rock group), we found ourselves working in the South quite a bit. These tours were done on a sleeper bus with rows of bunks for up to twenty people to sleep in, sandwiched in between lounge areas with tables in front and back. While we had been traveling this way in Europe since the 1970s, it was a new American reality for the band. Previous gigs in the US had rarely paid enough to allow the Arkestra to consistently afford the luxury of a bus complete with driver. We had been used to making stateside gigs in several vans, sometimes rented and other times loaned by a hanger-on or a member of the band.

Since becoming Sunny's agent, Jack would regularly book us in college towns like Durham, North Carolina; Athens, Georgia; and Columbia, Missouri. While traveling on the sleeper buses, Sun Ra oftentimes sat alone, unless June Tyson or I shared a table with him at the front of the bus. He never slept in the compartments but always found a table to put his music and books on. It was on these journeys that I began staying up nights talking with him. Most of the other guys would retreat, as they had always done on these long trips, and get high, out of sight. In keeping with my "bad boy" status in the Arkestra, there is no question that I would join them from time to time. But I was also serious about spending time with Sunny. I took these talks as leadership training sessions and realized, remembering my dream, that my purpose in the band was to learn all I could from him so that I could become a more effective leader.

A new addition to the 1989 Arkestra was the brilliant Pittsburgh trumpeter, sixty-two-year-old Tommy Turrentine, older brother to the popular saxophonist Stanley. In one of our conversations, he told me he had roomed with Miles Davis during their tenure together in Billy Eckstine's great band. That band boasted a mean trumpet section, at times including Dizzy Gillespie, Fats Navarro, and Kenny Dorham. Eckstine's sax section just as gloriously included the likes of Charlie Parker, Dexter Gordon, Gene Ammons, Frank Wess, Sonny Stitt, and Leo Parker. Add Art Blakey and Sarah Vaughan to this and you get the type of band that is the stuff of legends. Tommy had also worked in the Benny Carter, Dizzy Gillespie, and Count Basie big bands. Max Roach, Jackie McLean, and Charlie Mingus (with whom he shared the same birthday, April 22) were other great musicians Tommy had recorded and/or worked with. Having Tommy in the band as a section mate was a delight for me. He played so beautifully I would sometimes forget to come in with my horn, so engaging was his gorgeous sound. And check this out—he'd been playing a trumpet modeled for students! Man!

Tommy had been attracted to Sun Ra's band for a number of different reasons. One was that he had correctly gauged Sunny's incredible musical ability. Another was that Sunny had provided him with a place to stay in Philly. And finally, always an advocate for musicians, Sun Ra would find a space in the band for a player as good as Tommy, even if for just a short while.

Tommy, like his friends Al Evans and Martin Banks, had years of alcohol abuse behind him. He couldn't drink without getting drunk, and when he was drunk he was a different person. Most of the time he was lots of fun, but he would also do some of the craziest things. I remember one gig we had in Miami. Tommy had managed to climb atop one of the big speakers in the theater and perch on it in the middle of the show, just sitting there with his horn in his hands. Sun Ra, who tended to treat him like a child, demanded that he come down that instant. He climbed down in complete obedience, giving the audience the impression it was part of the act. Tommy worked with us for about six months, doing this odd tour from the middle of 1989 until its end.

Sunny had other, more serious problems that revealed the state of dysfunction within the band, one of which was with bass clarinetist Eloe Omoe. Eloe had joined the Arkestra before me. We were around the same age and had always had a pretty good rapport. I noticed, however, that since I'd been back Eloe was on another mission, the crack pipe, and that he was in the grip of a serious addiction that came to a head on one of our Southern tours.

We were doing lots of work in the Deep South, in Atlanta and Athens, Georgia; in Durham and Raleigh, North Carolina; in Miami and Key West, Florida, traveling by sleeper all the way.

Another addition to the band was Spencer Weston, a substitute teacher from Philly who had been around the Arkestra for years. He was a good friend of Pico Thompson and therefore had an inside track on Sunny. Because of Spencer's relation to Pico, Sunny saw him as a natural replacement aide-de-camp. In that position, Spencer was responsible for keeping records of all outgoing expenses, including payments made to musicians, road costs, etc., and for serving as a general liaison with booking agents.

Spencer had previously served as mentor to Paxton Baker (for whom I had done the Group's Temple University gig); by then, Paxton was living in Miami and working with Philip Michael Thomas of the popular television series *Miami Vice*. Philip had transformed a local movie theater into a glorious recording studio/ performance venue that he called the Miami Way Theater. Both Paxton and Philip were aware of the importance of Sun Ra, and one of our gigs on the tour was to be at that theater.

Throughout the tour, Eloe would rarely come out of his compartment. He wasn't playing and he was barely eating. When we got to Miami, Paxton's sister, a nurse, had a look at Eloe. He was found to be seriously ill, suffering from brain cancer and need-ing immediate hospitalization. When we got back to Philadelphia, Eloe was placed in Germantown Hospital and given a few months to live. As much of a hard time as Eloe sometimes gave Sun Ra, I'm sure Sunny recognized him as a valuable member of the team. As a dancer and musician and a person with great stage presence, Eloe was irreplaceable. Before we'd go out to gigs during the time Eloe was hospitalized, Sunny would organize visits to our ailing band member. There would sometimes be four or five of us in the room at the same time. Eloe's family soon opted to take him from Philadelphia and drive him to Chicago, but by that time it was only a matter of days before he would leave the planet. Eloe became likened to a sacrificial lamb, his death a warning that things had really gone too far in this country, and in the band whose leader represented the Creator of the Omniverse.

Robert Rutledge and Cecil Brooks were two other trumpet play-ers who had come into the band for a short period in 1989. Robert was an old friend whom I later found out was another practitioner of the Buddhism of Nam-myoho-renge-kyo. He was born on May 8, 1948, in Birmingham, Alabama. His place of birth made it easy to convince Sun Ra to use him for a couple of gigs. Sunny had a thing for Birmingham musicians because he knew them to be well trained. Robert made one of the gigs in Cambridge, Massachusetts, at a club called Nightstage, and another one at the Blues Alley in Baltimore. The Nightstage gig had Robert, Tommy, and me in the trumpet section. Three Taureans playing together turned out to be a special treat!

Many years before, Bob Rusch, in an interview for *Cadence* magazine, brought to my attention an oddity about people who worked with Sun Ra: the double-initial syndrome. Rusch pointed out that there was Pat Patrick, Danny Davis, Chris Capers, and me. Since that interview, I learned to pick up on its consistency. Look at this in alphabetical order, starting with myself: Billy Bang, Chris Capers, Danny Davis, Field (Fielder) Floyd, Jack Jacson, Jimmy Johnson, Pat Patrick, Rollo Radford, Robert Rutledge, Ted (Thaddeus) Thomas, and Tommy Turrentine. Twelve in all, an interesting phenomenon that I came to call a "twin thing."

Later that year, in October, we played Soviet Georgia's third Tbilisi Jazz Festival. We had to arrive in the capital city via Frankfurt and then through Warsaw. Planes from Warsaw went to Georgia twice a week, so we had a day layover. Gabby Kleinschmidt, who booked a number of other artists, including Art Blakey, handled Sunny's European bookings.

While in Warsaw, we were invited to the internationally acclaimed Jazz Jamboree and treated to a concert by Mr. Blakey and his expanded Jazz Messengers. Blakey's touring that year had been billed as his seventieth birthday celebration. For that tour, he had brought back Jackie McLean, Curtis Fuller, and Benny Golson, all former Blakey band luminaries, along with current regulars Frank Lacy, Brian Lynch, Dale Barlow, Javon Jackson, Geoff Keezer, and Essiet Okon Essiet.

Through the years, Blakey had consistently kept very exciting ensembles beside him. The power of a Blakey performance was always thanks to the strong individuals who made up his bands, many of whom went on to become bandleaders themselves, their talents heightened by his dynamic drumming. In contrast to Sun Ra, Art Blakey probably rivaled Count Basie in terms of the number of musicians who had left him to go on to lead their own bands. My theory in regard to that is that neither Blakey nor Basie were extensive composers of written music. One could argue that the so-called Jazz musician is a spontaneous composer, as improvisation demands. Be that as it may, my point is that those musicians who are composers but don't write out their compositions (like Blakey and Basie) afford to other composers or arrangers who do the opportunity to step up to the plate. Thus, by bestowing a position of responsibility on a person, people like Blakey and Basie help create new leaders who may well bring more potential into this music.

When we finally arrived in Tbilisi on a gray day, I was struck by the grandeur of the buildings and boulevards. A large and well-populated city, Tbilisi gave off an air of impoverishment. Perhaps that was due to the hotel we stayed at, which was a joke to the well-traveled middle-class Americans we had become. There was no TV, no radio. No toothpaste, no shampoo. We had to ask for soap, and washcloths weren't even considered. While there, I was able to see how much the American lifestyle and propaganda had also influenced my thinking in regard to a fear of communism. I had to force myself to leave the hotel and go out on adventures as I had done in other places. Since we were being chaperoned most everywhere, this took some doing.

We had come to the Soviet Union at a turbulent time in its history. In fact, some Georgians I met were insurgents who claimed not to be part of the Soviet Union at all. There was a fierce independence to these people, who seemed to identify readily with African Americans. During the week that we stayed there, I was invited into the homes of several people I had met.

In those abodes, I was filled in on the rich history of a people who had been subjugated but not broken by an oppressive Russian government long before the Bolshevik Revolution. I was taken to a museum, where I was familiarized with Georgian culture and presented with this statement of Georgian history: "Numerous invaders attacked this country and its capital, trying to destroy it, to enslave freedom-loving people. The strong souls of Georgians always prevailed and these proud people have managed to preserve its religion, traditions, language, alphabet, history, culture and music."

Being very musical, Georgians respond to every new wave of music regardless of genre. Thus, Jazz has always been popular with them. Similar to Italian names and names found in various African countries, many Georgian names end in vowels. According to their oral tradition, people of African descent have lived along the eastern shores of the Black Sea since "time immemorial."

Among their other traditions, Georgians accompany their wine drinking with a series of toasts. At each of the homes I was invited to, my hosts brought out several bottles of wine, all of which we drank as we toasted everyone at the table numerous times. The tradition appeared to be to find the most encouraging thing to say about the person being toasted, and most everyone would be so toasted before the dinner was finished. I was impressed and definitely understood how such a tradition could strengthen a people.

At the home of Gregory, one my hosts, I was given a huge and beautiful book on the work of Georgian artist Niko Pirosmani (1862–1918). Gregory told me that the common saying among Georgians is, "Why do we need Picasso when we have Pirosmani?"

He inscribed the book, "For my great friend from America. I was very happy when I saw you! I think you will always remember Tbilisi and me! Thanks a lot, Gregory."

My fond memories of Georgia included listening to Les McCann and Eddie Harris perform while I sat in the balcony next to Sun Ra at Tbilisi's equivalent of Carnegie Hall. Sunny liked their performance so much he wanted to go backstage to tell them. He asked me to serve as his emissary, as he wanted to ensure he would receive a warm reception. It turned out that both of them had such tremendous respect for Sun Ra that they welcomed the opportunity beyond what Sunny had expected. Eddie Harris, in fact, was an old friend of Sunny's from Chicago back in the 1950s;

they would rarely see each other except at airports, train stations, or festivals.

Later on, at a dinner in their honor to which we were invited, I found out that Les McCann was also a visual artist with a sense of humor that allowed him to laugh at himself. In fact, he had us all rolling with his natural wit.

Les, a rather corpulent man, and I were seated next to each other at a table. There was an attractive Georgian woman who kept staring our way. I began eyeing her and Les, noticing this, turned to me and said, "You think she's lookin' at you? Man, she ain't lookin' at you. You got to be a big man to get somebody like her! Man, she's lookin' at me!"

Among the others participating in that Georgian festival was Freddie Hubbard, who had played the night before we got there and was already gone—so we missed him. We did, however, get to hear Jimmy Smith, whom I was catching live for the first time in my life. I thought it was pretty incredible that for as long as he had been around I would end up hearing him for the first time so far away from home. Art Blakey's seventieth anniversary band, an event in itself, was also part of the Georgia gig.

A bright moment occurred late one night at the hotel as I rode in the elevator with Blakey. The festival had set up jam session possibilities every night after the concerts by having a drum, piano, and bass available with a sound system in the designated banquet room. The artists were supplied with champagne, caviar, and other morsels. We were riding in the elevator with saxophonist Dale Barlow. Art checked me out and asked, "Man, where's your ax?"

"It's in my room," I answered.

"Go on and get it, and come on back down and let's play some, man. Dale," he added turning to Barlow, "go get the other cats."

What a spirit Art Blakey had! Here he was at seventy, organizing a jam session at two in the morning with musicians thirty and forty years younger than he was. I was thrilled over the only opportunity I got to play with this master. We jammed, but it was only for one solid bebop tune, after which Blakey let the "youngsters" have it, as he turned in.

When the Sun Ra Arkestra played, we did it with a streamlined brass section consisting of Tyrone Hill and myself. Sun Ra had also run into problems with bass player Juni Booth, whose bass got caught up at customs when we arrived. Then, on the day we were to play, Juni missed Sunny's sound check/rehearsal. Sunny got so angry he used local Georgian bass player Tamaz Kurashvili, who was only supposed to be bringing his bass for Juni to use. That bass player was one happy chappy as he made sure his friends and family took as many pictures as they could with the band. It was an average Sun Ra set, well received especially by our new friends. The incredible thing is that we had been on the road for a week but got to play just that one set. One of the things I paid close attention to was the treatment of the Georgians I encountered by the Russian soldiers/police. It became obvious after a time that we were only performing for a select group of professionals (doctors, lawyers, teachers, etc.) in Tbilisi.

Those who wanted to hear the music but who were not in that particular class were brutally kept out by armed guards. I couldn't even walk people in as my guests without them being beaten down. Whatever the ism practiced by the dominant culture, it didn't result in anything more than the win/lose paradigm that also characterizes American reality.

On our return trip we reversed ourselves, stopping in Warsaw and then going on to Frankfurt. At the huge Frankfurt airport, after waiting several hours for our connecting flight, we were suddenly and suspiciously asked to board a bus that took us to a plane that had apparently been waiting at the runway for some time. There was no way our baggage was going to be put on this plane (even though we were promised it would be); it was not our scheduled flight and was just about full and ready to take off.

Consequently, when we arrived in New York, our luggage didn't. Frankfurt is one of the centers of international espionage, so we were hardly surprised when our luggage, looking as if every item had been gone through, arrived two days later. Our reaction to this inconvenience was somewhat neutralized when Pan Am, our airline host, gave each of us a flight coupon valued at $2,000, redeemable within a year.

If it was as we had suspected, this was probably one of the last acts of that Cold War–espionage charade between the US and the USSR. By the end of the year, the newspapers were filled with photos of Soviet people marching in the streets in opposition to government domination. The crumbling empire had to yield to the will of another tune.

Earlier in October, as a result of our Japanese tour the year before, Dave Sanborn, who had toured opposite us, got to hear and appreciate Sun Ra's music. Dave had a syndicated music show on NBC-TV, *Night Music*, produced by an old Sun Ra fan, Hal Willner. Willner had been involved with *Saturday Night Live* back in 1978 when the Arkestra had performed on that show. This time, Sun Ra was asked to be on *Night Music*, but without the band.

Sun Ra's understanding of his own power at the time became one of my most important lessons from him. He refused to do a solo piano performance, as that was not what he wanted. The leader of *DownBeat*'s number-one big band was going to have at least a ten-piece ensemble. The producers conceded, and while it was not the full Arkestra, it was ten times the original offer. He chose stalwarts John Gilmore, Marshall Allen, and Jack Jacson to populate a reed section complemented by Tyrone and myself as the brass section. Juni Booth, Buster Smith, Elson Nascimento, and June Tyson rounded out the tentet.

Sunny made up for the group's small size by deliberately refusing to cooperate with the cameramen. They wanted to lock shots in based on the placement of the band according to the compositions we were playing. Every time we rehearsed, Sunny would either come up with something different or just change the piece entirely. The camera crew looked frustrated and puzzled. They had obviously never seen anyone do what Sunny was doing in preparation for commercial TV. Exasperated, they decided to follow Sun Ra, allowing him to do whatever he wanted with no commercial interruption. As a result, Sun Ra got twelve uninterrupted minutes on network television.

Toward the middle of November we headed out to the Midwest for a tour. For the most part, I was accustomed to dining with my family on Thanksgiving. My sons always looked forward to those meals because it gave them a chance to get away from the strictly vegetarian meals their mother prepared. One of the few times I had missed this ritual was when we were in Columbus, Ohio, closing out a tour. A couple, who were fans of Sun Ra and the Arkestra, invited the entire group to their house for dinner. They seemed to have every Sun Ra recording available, so we spent the day bathed in the wonderful sounds of the old recordings along with the good vibes generated by our hosts. Sun Ra acted as the king on his throne, as a beautiful array of food was laid out in this lovely atmosphere with camaraderie galore.

Shortly following the tour, just before the end of November, Sunny asked me to come to Carroll Music Studio for a rehearsal. I was surprised to find Don Cherry there. He was going to make a record with the Arkestra as the featured soloist. The next day, at BMG Studios on Forty-Fourth Street, I would be further surprised to see Jothan Callins and Michael Ray arrive. The recording that became *Purple Night* also included former Arkestra members Julian Priester and James Spaulding. As well, Brooklyn baritone saxophonist Reynold Scott was there. It turns out that he did his first and only gig with Sunny that day. Rollo Radford was flown in from Chicago to play bass along with John Ore. The ensemble was strong with all the regulars included.

Don Cherry improvised on a couple of songs during the session. Even though he had worked with the Sun Ra All-Stars Band back in 1983 and 1984, this was his first performance with the full Arkestra. He didn't sit with the large brass section, but sat next to Sunny and had the freedom to improvise at will. His role was like that of anyone playing their first gig with the Arkestra. Some of the other numbers without Don were quite spontaneous and powerful as well.

What was, in fact, an incredible date in the studio later fell victim to some seriously awful mixing. The power of the performance is still somewhere on the tapes for that session, but the evidence didn't make it onto the release. Once again, the documentation on this major label revealed nothing of the true contemporary range of Sun Ra. However, because of what I had heard played in that studio I was pleased to know we hit hard. Dave Sanborn's *Night Music* show aired December 10, 1989, and got rave reviews in the *Village Voice*, opening up even more doors for the seventy-five-year-old bandleader.

The Philly "sub-teenagers," as Sun Ra called them, had by then begun to come around the house on Morton Street, having gotten hip to Sun Ra after that show. Of particular interest to them was his version of "What Do You Do?" also known as "Face the Music," which we delivered with funky conviction behind Sun Ra's space rap, apparently striking a responsive chord with the new hip-hop generation. It was a great ending to a great year, even while the recording didn't cut it.

# IX
# THE FALL AND
# THE RISE

It's taken me fifty years to write the Music for the
21st century. It's like a newspaper. Headlines for the
Destiny of Nations. They change every day, so does
the music. I'm always creating, because we don't
know how long the world will last.
—Sun Ra

For some time now, I'd been checking out how different Robert
Rutledge had become. We'd done a couple of gigs together with
the Arkestra and got to hanging pretty tough. Having known him
since the mid-1970s, I was now beginning to recognize a certain
confidence in him, a focus and directness that I hadn't noticed
before. Gradually he began to share his source, encouraging me to
read publications he had around his apartment, and eventually he
invited me to a Buddhist meeting.

The first meeting I went to was in Karen Falcon's apartment
in downtown Manhattan. Karen was a jolly redheaded woman
whose dancing bright eyes, surrounded by the blue rims of her
glasses, reflected an eager attitude. When we got to her apartment, Robert immediately went to sit next to Karen. There were
others at the front of a group of fifteen people facing a scroll with
bead-wrapped hands clasped together. I was encouraged to hang
out in the back of the room, where I walked around people seated
on the floor, listening to them read from a small book, *The Liturgy
of the Buddhism of Nichiren Daishonin.* I found out later that
Robert was a group chief, which explained why he was among the
few who sat at the front of the room.

The people I sat next to were very friendly, and I was aided
here and there in the endless recitation, which was in Japanese.
Every time I thought it would stop, it began again. I had a difficult

time getting comfortable, first trying to balance myself on my knees, then sitting on the floor on my rear, all the while being guided through some words in a language that made no sense to me. Finally, to my relief, it was over.

"Welcome to the Gracie Mansion, sadhakai!"

"Yea!" Hands clapped.

"Do we have any guests?" asked our host.

"Yes, I brought a friend and fellow trumpet player, Ahmed," Robert volunteered from the front of the room.

"Welcome. Is there anyone else?"

There were two other people, introduced respectively by those who had invited them, two men named Joe and Bob. Karen and the rest of the group acknowledged and greeted one another. She then came back to me, "How do say your name, Ach-med?"

"Yes. Ah-med."

"I'm sure Robert, Joe, and Bob have already told you all about the practice," Karen said, addressing all three of us. "But I'll just mention a few things here," she continued. "First, what we've just participated in was Gongyo, which we do morning and evening. *Gongyo* means 'assiduous practice,' and essentially we read from the second and the sixteenth chapters of Buddhism's highest teaching, the Lotus Sutra. These chapters we have just read explain how each individual holds the potential for enlightenment and that life itself is eternal. Our primary prayer or chant is Nam-myoho-renge-ryo. *Nam* means 'devotion.' *Myoho* is the 'mystic law.' *Renge* is the simultaneity of 'cause and effect.' And *Kyo* is the 'sound' that is in every living thing."

I had heard this phrase over the years. I can't count the number of times throughout the last twenty years that someone had come up to me and asked if I had heard of it. Usually I tried to get as far away from them as quickly as possible. I remembered once I did go to a meeting and chant with a saxophonist named Claude Bartee. But that had been years ago. That Robert didn't try to give me a fire-and-brimstone sales pitch on the practice got me interested enough to attend this one. I could sense that Robert's being had been profoundly affected somehow, and it was this that had whetted my curiosity.

"In this practice of Buddhism," Karen went on, "faith is based on experience. We call it 'actual proof' of the teaching's power. To develop faith we must take action. We strengthen our vital life force by actualizing our Buddhahood each day."

When she said *life force*, I immediately recalled my first album called *Life's Force*; for me it was interesting that she had used the term.

"The practice of Buddhism consists of two parts," she continued, focusing on her three guests.

"Practice for ourselves and practice for others. Practice for ourselves is primarily the chanting of Nam-myoho-renge-kyo. Practice for others consists of action based on compassion to help give the means to make fundamental improvements in their lives. This is similar to what we're undergoing in our own engagement with the teachings. In other words, that is why Robert brought Ahmed, why Bob brought Joseph, and why Joe brought Walter to the meeting.

"You see," she elaborated, "the goal of Buddhism is ultimately the achievement of world peace, and we feel this can be obtained by helping people to achieve their desires in life. When one chants for one's dreams to be realized, a higher life condition becomes the fringe benefit, so that a person's desires become a source of enlightenment while helping that person attain fundamental happiness. Buddhism has primarily been spread by positive personal interaction. There is no history of Buddhist crusades or jihads."

With this she really struck a responsive chord in me. I remembered reading about Christian crusades and Islamic jihads and always wondered how it was possible to kill someone in the name of religion. What God, what Creator would beg for the death of its own creatures? And what kind of person would worship such a god? Of course, one might find a contradiction as far as the history of Buddhism is concerned, as well. I was, however, open to what I was hearing in the moment. This was the Buddhism of Nam-myoho-renge-kyo.

It was also interesting to me that this was a white woman speaking and that I was listening. Six or seven years before, that would not have been possible; my experiences would have caused me immediately to reject what she was saying just because she was white, and in the Western world I was not expected to see her humanity beyond that one fact.

My relationship with Philippa Jordan over the past four years had allowed me to appreciate her as a human being beyond the category of white woman. As a result, by this time it was a lot easier for me to listen to what this woman was saying and to acknowledge the wisdom of it. It immediately made sense to me that there should be a spiritual path such as this one, wherein all one's desires in life could be realized. My study of Sufism back in the 1960s and the work I'd done with Brother Ra in the 1970s—in fact, everything in my life up to that point appeared to prepare me for this moment.

The meeting followed a format. After the guests were welcomed, a study topic on Buddhism was presented. Next, one of the members told of a personal experience that related to the topic presented. After that, others at the meeting joined in what became a provocative and profound discussion.

Leaving the meeting, Robert and I stood outside Karen's apartment building for a few minutes before we settled on a place to eat. Robert had one of those "I told you so" looks on his face. He was right. But my mind was racing, making connections to all I had just heard and to what I had experienced throughout my life. And I knew that at this moment that something was about to change in my life.

I thought about the seeress of four years before and her advice and guidance in relation to Philippa. She had said she saw deep karmic ties between us. Perhaps this connection to Karen through Philippa was what she was speaking about. I thought about that seriously because Philippa had asked me to accompany her on another journey, this time to Europe.

Later that month, February 1990, Philippa and I went on vacation to Paris, spending a week there right around Mardi Gras.

Philippa was of the view that I was playing too much of Sun Ra's music and not enough of my own. She had hoped that our trip to Europe would be one of both business and pleasure, and a way to pull me into my own creativity. Away from Sun Ra, if you will.

As it turned out, while walking one day along a Parisian thoroughfare, we drifted into a music store and I decided to try out a few trumpets. They happened to have some editions of the French Besson, a horn that I loved but didn't think was available anymore because I thought the company had gone out of business. The only Bessons I had seen on the market were used ones. The storeowner assured me that they were now making the Besson mostly by hand, just as they had in the past, and that I could purchase one if I so desired. Quickly, I put a down payment on a most wonderful-sounding instrument that was going to be delivered to me some time later. That incident alone made this a rewarding trip.

We got no gigs in Paris, and no contacts we made paid off, but we had plenty of fun. We went to hear music at several clubs and visited a couple of musician friends. It was during this trip that I began to chant regularly upon waking up every morning.

Buddhism appealed to me for reasons that were related to efforts I had made six years before as a result of reading Carl Jung. I needed to understand why I could be so abusive to a Black woman, as I had been to Charlene. I had gone to see a therapist, but it didn't work for me, so I gave it up. My search for a clearer grasp of myself led me to read a lot more. The writings of Toni Morrison and Alice Walker helped me a great deal, as did the writings of Jung. But there was still more to be done, and Buddhism provided me another door. Here was a belief system I could live with, one that allowed for the totality of human expression without judgment.

If a person is convinced of the importance of the practice, as I was, the next step is to be sponsored to receive a Gohonzon, the ultimate object of worship in this form of Buddhism. Nichiren Daishonin, founder of the Buddhism of Nam-myoho-renge-kyo, had inscribed his enlightenment in the form of a mandala, a scroll, some seven hundred years ago. Over the years these scrolls (or mandalas) have been duplicated by priests and given to people who desire them as a means of attaining their own level of enlightenment. There is a ceremony attached to receiving the Gohonzon. On March 4, 1990, I took part in one such ritual. The purpose of this ultimate object of worship is to realize the highest state of being possible—Buddhahood, the enlightened life condition of the universe. It is important to understand that the potential for enlightenment exists within each of us. In any true belief system, one understands the Creator or the Supreme Being to be all-wise, all-powerful, and omnipresent—everywhere. How, then, could the potential for enlightenment not exist in all beings? What a Buddhist does through the daily ritual of Gongyo is increase the possibility for realizing that potential state.

From the time I left her apartment, Mickey Davidson and I nevertheless continued to work together, and on rare occasions we even slept together. That March, we were offered an opportunity to develop a program of lecture demonstrations in dance and music that we would execute in the public and private schools of Buffalo and the surrounding area. Artpark, an arts organization, sponsored this three-week residency, providing us with a car and separate rooms at a residential hotel. Our ability to work together on our craft had only increased through the years, and the passion we always showed on stage was sometimes matched by passion in our hotel rooms.

During our stay in Buffalo, I checked in with Sun Ra and found out that the band was going to play in Boston at Northeastern University on one of the weekends Mickey and I were in residency. It wasn't possible for me to get to Boston, because I had already made a commitment to Iyabode and my now-teenage sons, who were both about to enroll at Brooklyn Technical High School. On the weekend that Sunny was playing in Boston, I was to have a class reunion at Brooklyn Tech at the same time the school was hosting a program for incoming students. I took the bus from Buffalo to New York City and got to hang out with my sons and some old schoolmates.

My relationship with my sons over the past couple of years had been less than satisfactory. I'd been running away from my responsibility to them and in conflict with myself over that fact. In a sense, I had been punishing them for something neither they nor anybody else but me had anything to do with. They had reached out to me by phone, desiring contact, but I had avoided their calls. This reunion became an opportunity for me to tune into them, and it was only because of them that I had made the effort—it wasn't because I had fond memories of Brooklyn Tech; there were none, really. However, the trip to New York and back up to Buffalo was a good way to break up the three-week residency.

On the last day of our stay in Buffalo, Mickey and I were surprised when we returned from our gig and entered the lobby to see the Sun Ra Arkestra checking in. The Arkestra had been scheduled to work at a place in Buffalo called the Tralfamadore, which was pretty incredible in itself since the gig was slated for our last day in the city. Still, I hadn't expected that they would be staying at our hotel.

I hadn't seen Sunny since the recording we'd done with Don Cherry that previous November. I was told what room he was in, and Mickey and I went up there immediately to find it in complete chaos. Sunny had apparently not been well for days, and his situation had reached another low point upon his arrival at the hotel. I was surprised to see how bad he looked. He appeared as if he had not slept for a while. Unshaven, with deep bags under his eyes, he talked as if he was out of breath. It was shocking to see him in this state. Apparently, June Tyson, Buster Smith, and Art Jenkins had been taking care of him.

Even with Sun Ra's alarming physical condition, the synchronicity of the Arkestra's appearance in this same town and in this same hotel without any prior arrangement on either of our parts was heavy stuff. Occurrences such as this one deepened my belief in the mystic law, the power of the practice of Buddhism, and my connection to Sun Ra. It is said that when you chant, you place yourself in tune with the forces of the universe. I definitely felt in tune.

By showtime, Sunny had recovered a bit. Mickey and I joined the Arkestra in their performance at the Tralf, as it was locally called. We had made some friends while in town, so we had in effect developed our own fan club. A new edition to the Arkestra for this gig was Jothan Callins, who had been trying to hook back up with the band since our Birmingham gig in August 1988. The friends we made in Buffalo had never heard Sun Ra before, so they were quite amazed to see the two of us, people they had one vision of as teaching artists, transformed within the context of the Arkestra into costumed performing artists.

After Buffalo, the next Sun Ra gig was in Erie, Pennsylvania. Mickey and I again joined the band on that one. We followed the Arkestra's vans in our rental car.

In effect, these events allowed Sunny and me to reconnect, and 1990 would turn out to be one of the most exciting years I would ever spend with the Arkestra. Sunny had summoned many of the players he had put time into, along with some new ones, to come together that year in an eloquent conspiracy to celebrate his greatness.

Besides Jothan, Michael Ray had come back, his stay with Kool and the Gang over, as had Noël Scott. Marshall and John had been holding it down all along. Tyrone Hill was there, as well as June Tyson. The addition of drummer Clifford Barbaro working with Buster Smith also proved exciting, with Elson working his percussion trio with Ron McBee and Jorge Silva. As I had been apprised of the significance of this time for me, I began keeping a diary, which I had purchased on the way to Europe.

After the Erie gig, we were headed to Stuttgart for a festival. We arrived in Frankfurt early on the morning of Friday, April 13, but had to wait six hours at the airport for transportation to Stuttgart. Eventually, we got into town and found the festival, which was being filmed for German TV, to be a really excellent one.

Cecil Taylor was there and scheduled to perform. Backstage, before we went on, I couldn't make out whether Sun Ra was kidding or not when he asked Cecil to play in the Arkestra. Cecil declined, but in another unusual gesture, as if to show he could handle having another keyboardist, halfway into the performance, Sunny beckoned Michael Ray to come over and play the Korg synthesizer, which he did quite well. In addition to Michael, the brass section also included Chris Capers, another one of yesterday's trumpeters who had come back for this mini-tour.

Cecil Taylor's presence naturally led to some late-night hanging out. A couple of people I had not known but who were obviously familiar with my work were in Cecil's dressing room. Among them were Oliver Belopeta, who ran a festival in Skopje, and Velibor Pedevski, a journalist from that part of Yugoslavia. Meeting them turned out to be a good connection for the future.

After Stuttgart, we left for Istanbul, where an organization of Jazz enthusiasts, Positif Vibrations, was just getting started as a major producer of Jazz in Turkey. Cem Yagul, a shortish blond blue-eyed Turk, and the brothers Mehmet and Ahmet Ulug (both dark), also happened to be Sun Ra fans. They had seen Sunny on a number of previous occasions and had developed an innovative approach to get Turkish people, who had never heard of Sunny or his music, to attend the concert. Their plan was to have us check into our hotel, immediately put on costumes, and go out, with instruments and all, to ride around a major thoroughfare of the city on a flatbed truck, playing.

It was dramatic and different enough to completely captivate the people. We rode through the streets playing music and singing, which appeared to pique their interest. After pulling off that bold move they treated us to a meal at the wonderful Pera Palas Oteli, where we were staying. That hotel was said to have been where Agatha Christie had written *Murder on the Orient Express.* The owners of this historic hotel would name rooms after famous guests who had frequented the premises. There was one for Agatha Christie, one for Kemal Atatürk, and one for Jacqueline Kennedy, among others.

A store across the street from the hotel, stocked with traditional and adventurous Turkish outfits, catered to tourists. I happened to

go there and stumble upon some vests. They were of black material or red or green, all with gold embroidery and a scattering of
tiny mirrors. When I brought back my brand-new vest to Sun Ra's
room, suggesting it as a new stage outfit, he immediately went for
it and authorized me to go back and purchase twenty-five more.
Against a set of black shirts and pants, the colorful vests worked
well and gave the band a new look for the 1990s.

Ahmet, one of the festival producers, and I would get into a
few conversations here and there. It turned out that during one
of his visits to the United States a few years before, he had heard
me play with both the Group and the Solomonic Quintet at New
York's Merkin Hall. This too would later prove to be another
valuable connection. A mystic who knew the producers used his
connection to make a special request to have an audience with Sun
Ra. This fellow brought a huge pile of papers for Sunny to read.
He called it *The Book of Information*, and told us it was a channeled document that spoke of space travel, future conditions of
the planet, and extraterrestrial beings. After reading a few pages,
Sunny got very excited and began dispensing unbound copies to
other members of the Arkestra.

It didn't take long for Sunny to realize that he had not given
out copies of the book but had given away whole chapters. He
spent the next week putting the book back together again so that
he could decipher the entire message it contained. A visit to his
room at any time would mean that one would interrupt his perusal
of the chapters he was slowly getting back in order. For the next
couple of weeks he became obsessed with the book. Even after we
got back to the States, he called me a few times and asked if I had
given him back the part he had given to me. His fixation with this
book was indicative of something else that was soon to manifest
itself. Back in the States, we were scheduled to play at Wolf Trap
in Vienna, Virginia, on April 21.

I had arrived in Philadelphia by 8 p.m., as we were supposed to
leave at about ten that night to arrive in Virginia at 2 a.m. The trip
from Philadelphia to Vienna was at that time about four hours,
but if you ever traveled with the Sun Ra Arkestra, you would

know that a four-hour trip could easily take twelve. Four out of the twelve would be taken up with getting Sunny's bags packed and another four would be used getting the cats together. We actually left Philly around the time we were supposed to arrive at Wolf Trap.

On this trip, one of the vans was driven by Jack Jacson (I was the designated driver for the other van). Jacson had assumed the role of "straw boss" in light of the fact that John Gilmore was ill and was not going to make this gig. Jack, who was pained over the loss of his buddy Eloe but would never admit it, had the kind of military background that didn't allow for mistakes, even when he was making them. In either case, he insisted on taking the lead and I followed. We arrived in the vicinity of Wolf Trap just about daybreak. The route to the site was tricky, but Jacson didn't know it. The problem with driving at 5 to 6 a.m. is that the average body goes out at this time and it's difficult to concentrate, especially when a person has been up all night. We ended up driving around trying to find the right exit for a couple of hours, with Sunny visibly distressed and obviously overtired before we finally got to the hotel. We checked in at about seven in the morning.

Jothan, June, Sun Ra, and myself were booked at the same hotel while the rest of the band was across the street at another one. We were supposed to stay at the hotel only until the 11 a.m. checkout time. Much of that had already been eaten up first by leaving late and then with finding the place.

After catching about two hours of much-needed sleep, I got up and went to Sunny's room to find him hardly able to get around.

"Sunny, how you doin'?" I asked.

"I'm tryin'," was his response.

Try as he might, however, there was a powerful force working against him. Healthwise, he was in no way ready to leave the hotel, and we had about an hour before checkout time, with no place for him to go or to rest.

"Sunny, don't you think you need to see a doctor?" I asked, a bit half-heartedly, knowing his answer was going to be no.

"I just need people to do what they 'posed to," he said, in a series of gasps. "I need people to learn how to follow the leader." Then he added, in between his rasps, "Ain't no doctor gonna understand that, much less cure it."

I tried to help him organize his clothes and costumes, manuscript papers, etc., astonished that in just a couple of hours he had managed to empty his bags and strew their contents about. I was relieved when June Tyson knocked on the door and came in to assist, as I was completely inept at dressing the boss.

"Maybe you should take a vacation?" I offered, looking into Sunny's face.

"I ain't got no time to take no vacation. Too much work to do. We gotta go out to the West Coast next week. Gotta get to Oregon, Washington, San Francisco, and a bunch of other places. Some we ain't never been to before. I ain't got no time for no vacation," he repeated.

Sun Ra had an answer for everything, and probably even if more people had asked him questions, as I just had, it wouldn't have made much of a difference. But the fact was that more often than not, no one would bother to ask. It was obvious to me that his condition was serious and that he needed immediate attention.

Finally, with all of his things packed, and after communicating with the rest of the band across the street, we left the hotel and went over to the concert site. We parked ourselves, instruments and all, in the band/rehearsal room that had been assigned to us.

The room was much like a college lecture hall, with ascending rows of seats surrounding a central area that served as a rehearsal space and a dressing room off to the side of the stage. We all spread ourselves throughout the hall and hung loose for the rest of the afternoon and into the early evening, with June and I keeping a close watch on Sunny, whose physical condition had become more and more disturbing to me. He had a look in his eyes that seemed to indicate he wasn't conscious of much going on around him, where he was, what he was doing, or how he was feeling. Here and there, June or I would try to solicit a response from Sunny, but his answers would be brief, their delivery showing him to be out of breath. Personally, I thought it would have been better for him to remain in his hotel room bed that afternoon, but since that hadn't been arranged for, we were stuck with the rehearsal space. I supposed this was in part an effort to save money, but to what end and at whose expense?

It could be said that Sun Ra was not so much exploited as he was a victim of his own actions. He didn't have anyone around him he was willing to listen to. Richard Wilkinson and Pico were gone, and Jack Reich and Brad Simon, who had booked this gig, didn't have that kind of relationship with Sun Ra. The other guys in the band had him on such a pedestal that most of them, even after seeing his condition, were unable to respond effectively. And June, a woman, didn't count in Sun Ra's eyes.

At gig time, Sunny, in his usual manner, began a tune at the piano. At the point that the band was to come in with the melody, his head was literally on top of the piano keys. It was frightening to see the master of focus and concentration so completely unable to maintain any level of it. Instinctively, we shifted gears and managed to cover up Sunny's lapse by calling tunes in between his nods. In this way, we played until he was able to come back in and play something else on the piano. It was virtually impossible for the audience not to have noticed the leader of the Arkestra with his head resting on the piano, but, nevertheless, we got through the concert. And, in spite of Sunny's condition, we sounded good. Music we could always do.

The heavy thing about this concert was that it was the only time I remember doing a gig with the Arkestra without John Gilmore. This was at a time when someone who was truly respected by everybody else in the band needed to come forward. John apparently had been too ill, and his was a telling absence.

On the way back to Philadelphia, we had to stop every half hour or so to allow Sun Ra to get more air. We'd keep the window lowered for him, which he needed, but the rush would be too much and as he was hyperventilating, we'd have to pull over to the side of the road to allow him to regain his composure. Since there were two vans, we decided that one should go on to Philly and the other could continue with Sunny at his own pace.

Jacson went on with most of the band and equipment. Marshall Allen, Fred Adams, Art Jenkins, Tyrone Hill, and I stayed with Sunny at a hotel that our manager Spencer Weston had taken the liberty of paying for before he continued on with Jacson. Art stayed in one room with Sunny while the rest of us shared another one. To me, the most amazing thing about the entire trip was how Sun Ra was constantly being asked by various band members if he wanted to do this, that, or the other, when it was apparent that he was in no way able to make decisions about his condition.

Art had been given the nickname "Art Smart," which he truly earned that night, as he was the only person among us ready to initiate some kind of medical care. When we were leaving in the morning, Art announced to us that Sunny was better because he had administered one of his mother's home remedies—salt.

It turned out that Sun Ra had been suffering from a severe case of untreated high blood pressure. The first thing that is usually demanded in those cases is a salt-free diet. When we got into Philly early the next morning, April 22, Earth Day, Sun Ra was still resisting going to the hospital. As good fortune would have it, a medic happened to park behind us in an ambulance as we stopped at a health-food store. From my driver's seat, through the rearview mirror, I noticed the ambulance and went over to persuade the medic to have a look at Sun Ra. Sunny was still insisting on his own home remedies, which were to be purchased at the health-food store. After the medic took Sunny's pressure, which was 200 over 120, he warned us that Sun Ra was a very sick man. Finally, we were able to take Sun Ra to Germantown Hospital.

He had both high blood pressure and weakened kidneys, but at Sunny's insistence, he left the hospital within a week, ready to meet the West Coast commitments already made. He felt comfortable on the train, so we took another three-and-a-half-day trip to California. No one challenged the logic of this, because Sun Ra, ill though he was, was still in charge. But the incident at Wolf Trap spotlighted how ineffective the Arkestra was without Sun Ra giving orders. There was absolutely no mechanism in place to deal with the inevitable recurrence of what we had experienced.

Unfortunately, the belief system that permeated the Arkestra was in line with the assumption that Sun Ra would always be there to provide for everyone. Not the least bit of consideration would be given to any other reality.

◖◗

On Duke Ellington's ninety-fifth birthday, we left from Grand Central Station for our westward journey. On this second trip west with the Arkestra, every time I looked around at the faces of these guys, I was reminded how much this felt like a family. But before I could get into a lovefest feeling, the alarm was sounded — someone had forgotten the medicine that had just been prescribed at Germantown Hospital for Sunny. When the train made a brief stop in Charleston, West Virginia, Tyrone Hill and I made a mad dash to telephone Philly and speak with Fatima, a woman who frequently helped out the band, asking her to send the medicine to Alton Abraham in Chicago.

Chris Capers made the trip west with us and proved to be a valuable comfort, acting as a personal attendant to Sun Ra. Chris, though often the butt of jokes within the band for being overly health-conscious, was a compassionate person, waiting on Sun Ra as was needed throughout the journey.

I had made this train trip a year and a half before, so the second time around was not as exciting. In Chicago, Abe showed up right on time with the medicine. We changed to a double-decker train, the California Zephyr, that would take us the rest of the way across the country. While on this second train, I found myself a baggage car to practice in. I knew I had to get my chops in shape since we were scheduled to arrive in San Francisco and get to Slim's with just enough time to hit the stage.

We arrived at Slim's on May 2. Just moments before we were due to hit, we were met by Wisteria — whom we hadn't seen since Japan in 1988 — and Mary Vivian, another dancer and longtime friend of the Arkestra. Ronald Wilson, a saxophonist who dated back to Sunny's Chicago days, was also waiting for us. With the added troops and three days traveling together, we were tight and inspired, and the audience responded in kind.

Mary Vivian, a satin-hued beauty, was always a good friend to me. The guys in the Arkestra believed that she and I had much more going on than we actually did; we always had such a good rapport, hanging together after gigs, conversing about almost everything. Wisteria was an actress, a playwright, as well as a choreographer and dancer. Ronald Simmons was the only tenor I ever heard Sun Ra give major blowing room to even with John Gilmore also present, but then again, Ronald had played with Sunny before Gilmore arrived on the scene.

Wisteria brought an acupuncturist to treat Sunny before we played the Koncepts Cultural Gallery in Oakland. That worked fine for a couple of days until, while in San Luis Obispo, Sunny sprained his ankle while getting into or out of the van. Fortunately, Sun Ra was a senior citizen, so we had no difficulty obtaining him a wheelchair to move around in.

The gig we did on May 9 was in La Jolla in the penthouse of a hotel, which held about 125 people. We had to carry Sunny in his wheelchair through the crowd in order to play. Sunny's semi-invalid condition had a way of affecting the band, so much so that our performance before this well-heeled audience was less than solid. The one consolation of that day was that our rooms were in the same hotel.

Sun Ra continued in this state for the duration of our California trip, and by the next night the band had grown used to seeing him that way. When we did the two shows in Los Angeles, at the Palomino Club on the tenth and at Club Lingerie on the eleventh, we even worked out a proper entrance for Sun Ra, making the wheelchair appear as a throne, with the bulk of the band playing from the stage as four of us regally carried him onto the stage and placed his wheelchair in position.

On the tenth, I was treated to one of the best birthday parties I ever had. The guys really did make it special for me, many of them bringing me drinks, which really touched me, and, man, did we play incredible music that night. Once again, the trip had made this Arkestra feel like a family.

After that night's gig, I hung out with a fellow by the name of Bruce Hollihan and his girlfriend and buddy. Bruce was a DJ and a fan of Sunny's music who had a thing for recording every live set he could on a DAT machine. As it turned out, he had taped the gig we just did and promised to come to our North Hollywood gig at the Lingerie the next night to tape that as well. He offered to send me copies, which, true to his word, he did. As a birthday gift, he gave me a wonderful book, *Labyrinths*, a collection of essays and short stories by Jorge Luis Borges.

Born in Argentina on August 24, 1899, Borges was a free-thinker, a visionary, a poet, and a mystic. His writings, I was told, were close to the impressions Bruce got from listening to Sun Ra's music. I was intrigued by a Borges quote delivered in 1946, when he resigned from the regime of Juan Perón: "Dictatorships foment subservience, dictatorships foment cruelty. Even more abominable is the fact that they foment stupidity. To fight against those sad monotonies is one of the many duties of writers."

On May 11, I made a note in my diary about the dinner I had with John Gilmore at a restaurant not far from our hotel in North Hollywood. John was such a recluse, a real loner, that this single act of dining with someone without the entire band, of enjoying an after-concert meal together, was an occasion unto itself. John acknowledged both my birthday and my playing the night before. He also noted the amazing way people were reacting to the music. He could feel the interchange of warm vibes among the cats, which created a reciprocal response with the audience. My dinner with John reminded me that another great tenor, Charles Brackeen, had been living in Inglewood, California. Before we left from Union Station en route to Denver, I made sure to give Charles a call. Our conversation was short, but it was good to touch base with him again.

Our gig in Denver was produced by a classy couple, Craig and Lisa Steinmate. They had booked us into a beautiful hotel. We performed at a renovated theater, after which they prepared a feast for us. The respect and hospitality they showed us had a profound effect on everyone. Sunny expressed his appreciation by doing his "Ra dance," which, in fact, was more like a funky wobble.

Being in Denver led to much reflection on my part. We had been here before, a year and a half earlier, when I was passionately involved with Belinda Kay Holmes. She had since moved to Chicago, where she was continuing her studies in law. Just two years before, Eloe was still alive and Pico was still in the band. Yes, things were really moving fast.

While we were on the West Coast, my French Besson trumpet, which I had purchased three months prior, finally arrived. Knowing that I might not be in town, I'd had it delivered to Philippa's address. My first gig with this trumpet, interestingly enough, was one I did with Sun Ra when we got back to New York. The wedding we played at the Central Park Boathouse was an unusual affair, even for the master of oddities. To add to the unusualness of it all, the bride and groom had requested that the Arkestra play Henry Purcell's "Wedding March." After we complied, space became the place as we performed a standard way-out-there Sun Ra set. To add to it all, I was not the only one with a new trumpet. Not to be outdone, both Chris Capers and Fred Adams showed up to this gig with brand-new horns.

I got another chance to work out with my new instrument, practicing the music of Louis Armstrong that Memorial Day weekend, preparing for a show with Mickey Davidson that was set for later that week. We had organized a special program to celebrate the New Orleans trumpet maestro. We were supposed to play in the backyard of the Armstrong home in Corona, Queens, but because of rain we had to perform at a local community center. Right after that event, I got word that Sun Ra was setting up another European excursion. He was going to England with fifteen other musicians and he also wanted to take me along. After much back-and-forth discussion, Jack Reich called me after Sunny had left for the UK to inform me that there was a Virgin Atlantic round-trip ticket waiting for me at the airport. Since he could not get the all-important work permit for me, my visit had to be vacation related.

Trying to leave my house in enough time to get to JFK Airport, I got my key stuck in the lock and couldn't get it out. It had broken off inside, and the front door to the building was still open. I had to call a locksmith, but that also meant I was going to miss my flight.

By the time the locksmith came and got everything together, it was nine thirty, and my flight had left at eight that evening. I called a pissed-off Jack Reich, who told me how much trouble he had gone through to get that ticket. The ticket, he said, was not refundable and consequently was just money down the drain. He didn't know that he couldn't have been any more disappointed or pissed off than I was about not making the gig. I called Sun Ra in London and talked to him. Sunny was calm, talking about the forces and how one always had to be on guard. I told him that somehow I was going to make it there, and after talking to him I truly believed I would, directly because his understanding made me want to make it.

It occurred to me after I hung up that I still had a $2,000 coupon from Pan Am that was redeemable for one year. It had been in October 1989 that we'd been in Soviet Georgia and received the coupon. Now it was June, only eight months later. The next day I went to JFK armed with the coupon and the attitude that I was somehow going to get to London. First, I went to the Virgin Atlantic desk and confirmed that I indeed had no chance of obtaining a refund for the missed flight. It was clearly stated on the ticket. Then I went to the Pan Am terminal, swapped my coupon for a ticket, and got the first flight to London. The thing they don't tell you about the coupons, however, is that regardless of whatever the flight cost, once you use your coupon, that's it. So for a $600 round-trip ticket I had to give up my $2,000 coupon. I took the loss and got to London.

The Londoners who had booked this tour were affiliated with the Blast First label. They had entered into an agreement with Sun Ra to release a 1968 recording, *Out There a Minute*, and had set up this particular tour for the Arkestra to help promote its release in the United Kingdom. So for the first two weeks in June, we had gigs scheduled in London, Liverpool, and Manchester.

Philippa, whose ears had been getting filled with road stories every time I'd come back from one of those Sun Ra adventures, decided she would go with me to find out for herself what was really happening. We worked out a plan where she would take another flight and carry my horn to London. Having a British passport, she didn't need a work permit. This trip would also give her an opportunity to see up close why I was so willing to travel with the band despite her continual insistence that I should be doing my own thing.

Even though he did change the people who were booking him, Sun Ra had not changed so radically that he was now ready to have a white woman traveling with his band; however, in this case, he understood that Philippa was doing me a favor.

The morning after I arrived, Philippa flew in from New York and came to our hotel in enough time to leave with us on the train to Liverpool. We were assembling in the lobby when Sun Ra first came downstairs and saw Philippa and me sitting together in the hotel parlor. The strange look on his face spoke volumes without him actually uttering a sound. He was quick to size up situations and I think he realized that this was the woman I'd told him about who'd brought my horn through customs. Sunny was cordial.

So Philippa traveled with us by train from London to Liverpool. I was more than a little uncomfortable, but I was cool. On the journey, we were joined by writer Graham Locke, who was doing an article on Sun Ra for *The Wire*, the British publication. He also took time to interview some members of the Arkestra.

Our gig in Liverpool was at the Bluecoat Arts Centre on June 8, two days after my sons' fifteenth birthday, which also marked the span of my involvement with the Sun Ra Arkestra. Sunny appeared to have fully recovered from his twisted ankle, and the band, as in most of the performances to date this year, was in top form. The percussion section was augmented by Clifford Barbaro, Buster Smith, and Kwasi Asare, along with Ron McBee, Jorge Silva, and Elson Nascimento. Sun Ra had developed a cosmo-drama around the percussionists, having Elson and company follow him around the stage while he did his "Ra dance."

After returning from Liverpool, we had a scheduled gig at London's Brixton Academy, but it had been canceled for some unknown reason. To compensate for that, the Blast First group put together an impromptu concert for us at the University of London. For an event with such short notice, we had a good turnout. The next gig was at the Mean Fiddler. At sound check, we were joined by a local dance group, the Jivin' Lindy Hoppers, who were going to dance with us later that August on a scheduled return engagement to the UK. This would be the only opportunity they had to rehearse with us. Our actual performance at the Mean Fiddler was recorded by Blast First Records and issued that same year as *Live in London 1990*.

We returned home for a short visit soon after the recording. The rare privilege Philippa had been afforded of traveling with the band and hearing us night after night had more than the desired effect. Not only was she no longer on my case about leaving the band and doing my own thing, but she had also become one of Sun Ra's biggest fans.

For the latter part of June, we were once again in Europe working at the Lugano Estival Jazz. Lugano, in the Italian-speaking area of Switzerland, is just as beautiful as Montreux in the French-speaking section. This tour required quite a bit of train travel, as we were in Stockholm for the Jazz and Blues Festival, in Oslo for the Kronberg Festival, then in Freiburg, Germany, for a week off. From there, we had to do the North Sea Jazz Festival in the Hague.

It was in Sweden that I met Tara Ollia, the Finnish woman who had come to Freiburg while we were off and who would also be at the North Sea Jazz Festival later. It was at North Sea that Sun Ra made sure my room was next to his so he could watch my comings and goings. In fact, he put Jothan and me together in the suite adjoining his. It was here that he chose to deal with what I'm sure he saw as my recent violation of his regulations regarding white women. No sooner had we checked into our rooms than there was a knock on my door. It was Sun Ra. "Here," he said, handing me a page of music. "I want to hear how this sounds."

I looked at the music and was surprised that it was one of my favorite Sun Ra songs, "Tapestry from an Asteroid," from the first album I had heard of his music, *We Travel the Spaceways*. I had never seen the melody written out before, but I had often talked to him about this song, suggesting we should once again put it into his repertoire as an instrumental. Usually to begin a show, June would sing the melody with no accompaniment, a cappella.

After he left, I got my music stand out of my bag, set it up, and began to go over the song. Just as I had finished playing through the bridge, the middle eight measures, Sun Ra came back into the room.

"You gotta attack the first note of that phrase on the bridge," he said, and hummed what he wanted, emphasizing the first note followed by the rest of the phrase. He then went back to his room, obviously listening. It was a beautiful melody, but something else was happening here. Sun Ra was pulling rank, using music to put me in my place, as only he could.

I understood what he was doing and knew I had to be on the alert. Tara was scheduled to come to the Netherlands and showed up at the hotel looking for me. The thing about the North Sea Jazz Festival is that no one ever sleeps during festival time. There is a bar downstairs at the nearby Bel Air Hotel that stays open all night. With hundreds of musicians all around, some of whom haven't seen one another in years, sleep is rarely a viable option. Tara and I hung out and made it back to the room with time enough to get a few winks.

Later that morning I was up and ducking Sunny until he caught up to me in the hotel restaurant and gave me a piece of his mind.

"I'm not trying to run your life or anything, but I just want to tell you: If you don't stop messin' round with these white women, you gonna end up having a baby by one of 'em, and that'll be just like me having a baby, and I don't sleep with none of 'em."

He was making the point that I knew he'd wanted to make since he had seen Philippa the month before. The importance of his statement was not so much about the issue of white women but about the way he defined our relationship. The idea that if I had a baby it would be like his having a baby was real food for thought, especially with my understanding then of how much of a mentor he was to me. And though he chose the issue of white women as the catalyst for his reprimand, what was startling to me was that he was articulating how he had been seeing our relationship. And here, I had been feeling it, too.

The frequency of our tours, both domestically and internationally, meant we were on the road together quite a bit. The whole sense of family the Arkestra provided, temporarily replacing my blood relatives, was definitely inside Sunny's statement. With such natural ease, he had assumed the role of parent, and I that of the ever-rebellious son, challenging the rules of the house with as much gall as I had done with my own father. And here, with Ra, as with my own father, I indeed had to bear witness to the wisdom of an elder.

In the case of my father, the issue was personal responsibility. As I turned eighteen and began working, my father gently but firmly explained that I had to start contributing to the household budget. My mother also wanted me to come home at what she thought was a reasonable hour. I, on the other hand, felt that if I had to give up my "hard-earned" money and be curfewed, I might as well get a place of my own. And so I did. The lesson of taking personal responsibility, of giving back to the people who have given me so much, was one I had missed back then. I would now miss the Sun Ra lesson on personal responsibility that was tied to the question of the social responsibility of the artist. At the time he uttered it, I rejected it, so thoroughly polarized I had become inside my own world, doing my own thing. Who the hell did he think he was, telling me what to do?

It took a few years, but what I remember him saying in that uncharacteristic statement was that he represented a continuum, and that he saw this as being sustained through me and several others in the Arkestra after he was gone. Most important to me was his feeling of kinship. I had felt it to some extent all along. But it wasn't until he said it that I knew he felt it too.

Later that July, we went to Milan, where we recorded for Giovanni Bonandrini on the twenty-fourth and twenty-fifth of the month. There was a lot of drama surrounding this recording. Sun Ra had circulated a rumor that we weren't going to be paid for this date until September. After hearing this from a couple of people, even though nothing was said directly to me, I decided to see what was happening, so I went to Sun Ra and asked him.

"Sunny? What's this I hear about we can't be paid until September?"

"That's right! We not gonna get paid 'til then," he said in a blunt and matter-of-fact tone.

With a few recordings under my name, my ego thought I deserved better treatment, and neither of us was going to go for this. Sun Ra had a way of abruptly ending a honeymoon, which left you constantly having to renegotiate your position. Most people would get worn out or lose the inclination to challenge it. All of that would merely give him more strength.

"I can't make this, then, Sunny. I have to get paid when I finish the recording," I said.

"Well, you don't have to make it. You can just stay right here at the hotel," he said, looking straight into my eyes.

The implication was as clear as the choices I had. I could toe or not toe the line, but that wouldn't stop the record date. He had tossed the ball back into my court without even addressing my demand. Now I had to measure what it would be like to stay in the hotel after traveling 3,000 miles with the band while they went into the studio to record. There was no choice. Sun Ra had the upper hand.

There's a phrase in Buddhist culture, something about "turning poison into medicine," which is totally empowering. It means that in any situation there is a possibility of winning and allowing others to win as well, if we are mindful of the two parties. There are always winning options available. I was going to go into the studio and be a member of a team that was going to make the best possible Sun Ra recording ever. There were a couple of reasons why this needed to be so. Sunny was doing fine now, but in the past few months, his health had become more unstable. Who knew how long he was going to be around?

To top it off, there was this other issue that concerned me. The last recording we had done, *Purple Nights*, was great in the studio but bad news on disc. The poor mixing left a lot to be desired.

Intuition told me that this upcoming recording session, *Mayan Temples*, would be Sunny's swan song. He had all the elements assembled. John, Marshall, Noël Scott, and Jack Jacson on reeds were in great form as usual. The other sections in the band were now following their lead and working better together. Michael, Tyrone, and I had developed into a completely intuitive power-house brass section. Michael was already a good vocalist, and Tyrone and I were becoming capable background and foreground vocalists as well. June Tyson, whose presence always added a distinctive style and taste to every gig, was there for this one, too. The percussionists had been jelling for a while now, with Buster Smith, Clifford Barbaro, Ron McBee, Jorge Silva, and Elson Nascimento, plus Jothan Callins playing bass. We were ready.

And so I opted to be a team player on this one and backed off. I did mostly ensemble work, taking a brief solo on "I'll Never Be the Same." The lion's share of the solo space went to John Gilmore and Michael Ray, both at the top of their games. John played extraordinary tenor on the Sun Ra classic "Opus in Springtime." The rhythm drove him to the top on "I'll Never Be the Same," and he was appropriately full and breathy on "Time After Time." In a comment after the date, John said, "I knew it was gonna be something else when Sunny started playing like we were in a club somewhere."

That was the secret of the date. Sunny did it like it was live! He introduced the songs on the piano, as was his way, more loosely, forcing us to listen more and thus creating a fuller feeling. Sun Ra, by the way, played some incredible keyboard both in accompaniment and solo. It was all relaxed, and yet the edge of spontaneity was present. In a studio, you generally do more than one take. But the element of surprise is often in the first take and that's what really lends excitement to a date. I'm sure that's one of the artistic reasons the Sun Ra discography is filled with live recordings.

Sun Ra had managed to integrate musicians from four decades into this recording. A swan song indeed! And some of the songs were done in one take. It's the closest thing to being representative of a live performance under ideal conditions.

When we finished the date, Sunny got up from the piano and began to walk out of the studio and back to the hotel. Knowing that we were off to another gig in a few days, Bonandrini wanted to know, "Who's gonna mix the date?"

That was the least of Sunny's concerns. His job was to create music, not to tamper with dials and adjust sound levels. As far as he was concerned, he was finished. Michael Ray and I made eye contact. We stayed. This time, this date was indeed going to be properly mixed.

The mixing ate up almost twelve hours. When Bonandrini took us back to the hotel, Sun Ra was still up. Even though he hadn't wanted to stay for the mixing, he did want to hear the results. Michael and I played the mix and saw the sun rise on Sunny's face and in his room as he showed how pleased he was with what he was hearing.

I went to bed about daybreak only to be awakened by June Tyson knocking on my door, asking me to sign for the money she had in hand. It appeared that Sun Ra had decided to pay me now after all. Most of the other guys in the band who didn't protest didn't get paid, at least not right then. That was Sun Ra's way: If you don't ask, you don't get it.

The album, released as *Mayan Temples*, is probably one of the greatest of Sun Ra's recordings, covering a wide range of material. And, I have to immodestly add, this was directly due to the mixing Michael Ray and I had done. That made it one of the better sounding of Sun Ra's releases.

When we returned to the UK later that August, it was to play at the Brecon Jazz Festival in Wales and the Edinburgh Jazz Festival in Scotland. These two festivals made for some other interesting occurrences.

On our way to Brecon, we stopped in Cardiff for the night. I had never been to this city, which seemed so quiet and proper. I decided to go hang out, but without anyone in the band to accompany me, I was really on an adventure. I was fearless, however, because when we arrived at the hotel I noticed that a meeting of a Buddhist group had taken place in one of the conference rooms earlier that day. A good sign! So I felt right at home in Cardiff, and since the hotel we stayed at was a little stuffy anyway, I left to find the life in the city.

I found a pub and a good-natured group of folks to hang out with for what turned out to be most of that night. We exchanged ideas, songs, beers, and jokes. Among the people was one of Cardiff's most special creatures, who wanted me to know what the inside of her flat looked like. So we walked there in a downpour. Being the curious person that I was, I spent what was left of the night in her abode. At daybreak, a cab ride to the hotel got me there just before the bus was ready to pull out.

Slim Gaillard, a Jazz legend, was emceeing the Brecon Festival. Slim, a contemporary of Sun Ra's, born January 4, 1916, once had a solo act in which he played the guitar while tap dancing. With "talking" bassist Slam Stewart, they created the team Slim and Slam. Their song "Flat Foot Floogie" was a hit in the late 1930s and early 1940s. The date that always caught my ear was the track Slim did with Charlie Parker and Dizzy Gillespie back in 1945, "Slim's Jam." His creative use of language on that date placed him in the continuum, predating rap or hip-hop as we know them by some thirty-five years.

While my Buddhist practice was having a profound effect on my desire to engage in any form of drug intake, after less than a year's practice, I had not completely healed inwardly. So there was still some outward expression of inner turmoil. Every now and then I would still sniff coke or smoke marijuana. I hadn't done a lot to change the company I kept because my inner conflict hadn't been resolved.

If we look at drug abuse as partly an identity crisis, then we might be able to understand that drug rehabilitation (which I never took part in) can only be effective if there is a shift in consciousness. Through the ritual of chanting Nam-myoho-renge-kyo, I was able to bring forth my true identity, Buddhahood, which led me to an understanding of the omnipotent, omnipresent, omniscient reality in which all needs are met, all desires fulfilled.

While we were at Brecon, a fellow who knew my music from the recordings issued under my name offered me psychedelics. I, in turn, shared them with my brass-section mates. We played Sun Ra's music at that festival in the most unusual condition I had ever experienced. Every song was like a magical excursion. That evening, I saw Sun Ra's music in a completely different light. From today's position of total abstinence, I could hardly recommend such an experience to anyone, but then again, without Sun Ra's presence, it wouldn't be possible anyway.

The festival in Edinburgh had become so popular that there were no hotel vacancies in the town. We had to stay about twenty-five miles from the concert grounds, out in the country at a place called the Black Barony Hotel. The area around the hotel itself was said to have been haunted. We had lots of fun with Noël Scott around that one.

Noël, nicknamed Christmas, one of the two alto saxophonists and occasionally an inspired dancer, had been with the Arkestra off and on since 1980. At the Black Barony, he had been given a room that was said to be particularly haunted. After our first night at the Barony, the sleeplessness that Noël described the next morning, as well as the screams that were overheard coming from his room, led us to believe that he had slept with one fine ghost.

One of the workers at the hotel was so taken with the camaraderie of the Arkestra that he decided to come to our concert in Edinburgh. Anyone who saw the band perform on that night would be hooked. Sun Ra was totally in his element as we played this concert with the Jivin' Lindy Hoppers, the group of dancers with whom we had rehearsed at London's Mean Fiddler back in June.

The Lindy Hoppers were dancing on the ceiling on this incredible night, and Sun Ra was back in Chicago playing a floor show at the Club DeLisa with Fletcher Henderson. All of us took each other to unbelievable heights. The concert was truly inspiring, and our friend from the hotel was so excited that when we got back, he began taking food out of the refrigerator and preparing it for us. With these guys, however, he didn't know what he was in for. He became a short-order cook for the entire band, preparing meals at two in the morning according to individual demands, with everyone taking it and him to the max. Even Sun Ra got his own specially prepared meal brought to his room, while the rest of us hung out in the kitchen and ate. It was a wonderful gesture on the part of our newly found friend that may not have been appreciated by the management of the hotel; nevertheless, it made for a memorable occasion, though after we left town, he lost his job.

The idea of playing for dancers was the theme of our first Stateside gig after Edinburgh. On September 9, 1990, we were at the Cat Club on East Thirteenth Street, playing for the New York Swing Dance Society. This group usually chose far more traditional and conservative musicians than Sun Ra for their affairs. Someone must have gotten the idea that since we did songs from the swing era the Arkestra would work well here.

There was always a high point in the course of the society's evenings in which Frankie Manning, a master swing dancer, would lead the crowd of dancers in a rendition of the popular Shim Sham Shimmy. Mr. Manning, at that time in his seventies and in great shape, had danced at the Savoy way back when. Even though they were about the same age, Sun Ra's version of swing was not what Frankie Manning was used to, and the Shim Sham Shimmy demonstration was supposed to be Frankie's moment. Unfortunately, there had been no thought given to a rehearsal with Mr. Manning and Sun Ra like that done with the Jivin' Lindy Hoppers in the UK. So while this particular event did not go over well, the rest of the evening was delightful.

The three women in my life, each of whom had a Gohonzon, were also at this affair. I was surprised to see Amber Taylor in the audience, but not as surprised to see Mickey and Philippa. Mickey had been studying swing dance for several years and often partnered with Frankie Manning. Philippa generally knew my whereabouts because she was still managing the Solomonic Unit. Amber and I had been in and out of touch with each other. We had spoken on the phone several times, but the last time I had seen her was just prior to our California trip back in April. It was at that time when she told me, "You are without a doubt the most selfish person I have ever met!"

Her words had reverberated in my mind for a long time. I talked to her after the gig only to find out that she was leaving New York and moving to Amsterdam.

Since the earlier part of that year, in between gigs with Sun Ra, I had started working for Carnegie Hall on their shelter concert series. It was a special outreach program designed to bring music to people who were homeless and unable to attend paid concerts. The program allowed me to work out arrangements and compositions before a discerning audience. Since they had not paid anything to hear this music, my audiences in these arenas were not obligated to stay unless the music was compelling. The series proved to be a great training ground, allowing me to expand my group from a quintet to a sextet that included my old buddy Billy Bang.

We had in fact gone into the studio back in June to record an extended work of mine, "Suite Songs for the Planet Earth." While on tour with the Arkestra, I let Sunny hear the tape from the session and I realized, after he had commented on it negatively, that I was still like the son seeking approbation from his disapproving father. His statement, however, helped to release me from my own delusion and reinforced the fact that I had to be my own critic. A September gig would help me understand how complicated my new relationship with Sun Ra was, and how difficult it must have been for him to maintain his sense of control. My group, the Solomonic Sextet, was due to play in Washington, DC, as part of the District Curators' Multi-Kulti performance season. Since I had been booked for September 15, and Sun Ra was to play on October 6, my name was larger than his and at the top of the poster. Since his performing date was on the bill right along with those of three other artists from Philadelphia—Rufus Harley, Jamaaladeen Tacuma, and Odean Pope, all billed together as part of the American Discoveries Festival—and my group was the only one hitting on our date, it was easy for Sunny or anyone else to see that poster and misinterpret the type sizes used. The thing that one might miss, looking at the poster, was that I was playing at DC Space, a small room that held about one hundred people, but Sun Ra and the Arkestra were performing at Freedom Plaza, an outdoor venue that thousands could attend. But perception is everything, and he clearly did not like the way the poster was laid out, with his photograph under my name.

The Solomonic Sextet was well received by an enthusiastic Washington audience. We had just come from doing a gig at the University of Virginia at Charlottesville the night before, so we were tight and we were on. The sextet had a strong lineup, with Carlos Ward, Billy Bang, Fred Hopkins, Masujaa, and Charles Moffett. In spite of the applause and the encores, we got one of the worst reviews in the *Washington Post* that I have ever received anywhere. I was once told that when you get negative reviews, it means that you have arrived. Well, if that's how it goes, so be it. Needless to say, it was about time.

Later, in the middle of October, Art Blakey died barely a year past his seventieth birthday. He was eulogized in Harlem at the Abyssinian Baptist Church. I went to the service to pay my respects and give thanks for getting that brief moment to play with him the year before in Soviet Georgia.

After the funeral, many of those folks from downtown found themselves at Bradley's, one of Blakey's regular hangouts. It was at Bradley's later that night that I met Martha Sammaciccia. I had seen her before around the music, but even so, there was something else about her that was attractively familiar. Martha was a thin woman with prematurely graying hair. Very Italian, with a strong Brooklyn accent. Her lovely brown eyes, great sense of humor, and interest in the occult, especially tarot, allowed us to establish an immediate rapport.

Martha had been in a relationship with Blakey during his last years, which accounted for her presence at his funeral. With her Italian background, she was different from any woman I'd ever met before. Her passion ran hot and cold and so quickly that I didn't know which one of the Gemini twins was present on a given day. Her mood swings were largely due to the fact that she was a one-man woman, and I was still not ready to be in anything like a committed relationship.

The idea of dealing with one woman at a time was the farthest thing from my mind; I was having too much fun as a single man. By then, I had been dealing with a number of white women, not only because I was running from who I was, but also because it was primarily white women who peopled the Jazz clubs that I generally found myself in. But more than that, for me, each of these relationships, regardless of culture or color, made me see more of myself. And that was because the practice of Buddhism, if dealt with properly, allows one to turn back into oneself. I had to look at the person in the mirror. The principle of esho funi says clearly that you and your environment are one, that everything around you, in essence, is but a reflection, a picture of your inner-life condition, telling on yourself.

My relationship with Martha began during a time when other interesting things were happening. Tara Ollia, the Finnish woman I had met in Sweden, had come to New York to stay for a couple of weeks. She came with a friend, and I offered the two of them the space to stay at my apartment.

I had a gig at a new club in the Village on Waverly Place. A fellow I'd met through Sirone years before, a tall and slender dark man, had opened a huge room for live music and dancing. We worked out a deal in which I was to play there with the Solomonic Sextet. Our gig happened the same weekend Sunny was to play in DC; consequently, the Arkestra gig was one of the few I missed during this period. The agreement was for a guaranteed salary regardless of the gate. I therefore had to come back a few days after the gig to get paid.

I brought my newly arrived Finnish friends along with me after the show. The man entertained us with drinks and stories. Tara's friend was apparently attracted to him as he charmed her and showed her around the club. They were out of our sight for a considerable period of time and I never received the money.

Later that week, Tara and her friend moved into a hotel in Manhattan. A few days after that, I got a call from Tara. She told me her friend had been raped by the man. I immediately went to the hotel to try to piece together what had happened. I was told that Tara's friend had gone back to the club and had been asked to stay after closing. Once he got her drunk, I was told, the owner then demanded that she have sex with other workers in the club. When she refused, he allegedly beat and raped her.

I couldn't believe what my ears were hearing; it sounded like a nightmare. The man had welched on his deal with me, but I didn't think he was capable of this depraved act. On the other hand, I didn't know any of the involved parties well enough to trust the veracity of their story. It was as if I'd been thrust into a drama I had nothing to do with. Yet I felt responsible because I was the one who had introduced them to him. I believed that another woman would better know what to do in this situation, so I contacted Philippa, who, upon hearing the story, suggested the women go to the police. She volunteered to go with them. After they filed the report, the police were obligated to contact the Finnish embassy.

With the potential for a major international incident brewing and the pressure applied to the local precinct by the Finnish embassy, the police were made to conduct a thorough investigation. A Black man was being charged with the rape of a white woman in a Greenwich Village Jazz club. I could see the sensational headlines coming in the tabloids.

Ironically, the thing that prevented him from being charged with rape was the interview I had with a detective who had been trying to contact me. I called the detective one morning from Martha's apartment and told him about the first time I had taken Tara and her friend to the club. The detective was quite interested in the fact that Tara's friend had left our sight with the man for close to half an hour while Tara and I sat at the bar. Tara's friend had not included that detail in her narrative. So the detective, armed with that information, requisitioned Tara's friend only to find out that she had willingly engaged in sex with the man in one of his offices at the club during that half hour on the first day they had met.

Neither Tara nor her friend understood why that particular bit of information invalidated her claim that the man had raped her the next time she was with him. Moreover, they didn't think he should have been excused from forcing her to have sex with other people. Nor did they understand how a white woman who would willingly have sex with a Black man was perceived as unworthy of the protection of American law. The police told her that she should forget the incident and later explained to the Finnish Embassy why no action would be taken.

After finding out that his ass would not be on the auction block in one of the state penitentiaries and that he had my attention to detail to thank for it, the man quickly paid me my money, and I was thankful never to have to see him again.

Sun Ra's workload for 1990 was tremendous. Although he was older than Art Blakey, it was in the latter part of his life that he, like Blakey, was getting full recognition and regular employment. The touring that Sunny did in 1990 would easily have worn out a younger man, and the fact that he now had chronic high blood pressure didn't help. The event that took him over the top was preparation for the chamber orchestra collaboration with the Arkestra that was held in late October in Orleáns, France. I missed the performance because of prior commitments, but I heard that even with Jothan Callins aiding in organizing the music and conducting the orchestra, the task was still too much for the Captain of the Spaceship. Sun Ra was hospitalized in November after suffering a stroke. Around Thanksgiving, I gave him a call and reminded him of the wonderful time we had the year before on that day in Columbus, Ohio, as we celebrated him and the day.

During this time, Martha was filling me with stories about Art Blakey's last year. Over the next two years, I would hear similar stories, but with Sun Ra as the main character. Sunny always talked about how the glory came first and then came the shame. Interestingly, he didn't mention fortune: Despite all the high-profile work we had done that year, it hadn't translated into enough of a windfall to cover his medical costs. On December 1, several folks in New York organized a benefit for him at the Village Gate. A number of musicians, including Junior Cook, Charles Davis, and Dewey Redman, donated their time and music. And the Arkestra performed for the first time under John Gilmore's leadership to a packed house.

I did a set with the stringed Solomonic Unit as a septet that included Billy Bang, the guitars of Anthony Michael Peterson and Masujaa, the Moffett family—namely bassist Charnett and drummers Codaryl and, of course, Charles Moffett. Charles Davis had Michael Weiss with him on piano, and they played a couple of Sun Ra songs inside of their quartet set.

Another benefit, at Sweetwater's on Amsterdam Avenue in Manhattan, took place in early 1991. This time trumpeter Eddie Gale was in town with his own quartet, and he played a set for us. John Gilmore once again led the Arkestra. These couple of gigs, while garnering much-needed cash, demonstrated once again the lack of preparation for the inevitable, as the Arkestra's performances under John failed to generate the excitement of the previous year. John's choice of material was different, much more conservative than Sun Ra's.

The one thing that I was determined to do, and probably even more so now that Sun Ra was ill, was to work totally from music. I had already been working as a teaching artist for Carnegie Hall and Young Audiences New York; it was now time to fully develop those areas of music-related work: writing, recording, teaching, performing, and arranging. Nothing but music. This meant, among other things, that I also had to stop driving a cab. No time for that. And no sooner had I put the thought out to the universe than it came back in the form of a gig with Ed Blackwell.

This really wonderful drummer had put something together he called the Ed Blackwell Project. My first gig with the group, according to Kunle Mwanga, who was working with Blackwell, was going to be at the New Orleans Jazz and Heritage Festival the following spring.

By February 1991, Sun Ra was also ready to work again. The site was Toronto, at the Bermuda Onion. Fortunately, Charles Davis was on hand, and he had solid ideas regarding the way things should be handled. Because of his longtime relationship with key band members, he also had the ear of John and Marshall. Now that Sun Ra was not in a position to tell folks what to do, even the little things undone or omitted from consideration caused much confusion. And the lack of preparation necessary for anything to get done at all made it painfully apparent. Had Charles not been there to suggest that Sunny should have a limo pick him up from the club and return him to the hotel, even such a basic common-sense thing would have gone undone.

Listening to Sun Ra on our first night in Toronto made me remember how thankful I was Michael Ray and I had been diligent with the *Mayan Temples* recording. We would never again hear Sunny as he'd been on that date less than a year ago. He would always be able to play, but now he seemed like he was playing out in space, as if he were already gone.

The room at the Bermuda Onion was packed. When we had played the Toronto Jazz Festival nearly two years earlier, the band had been smoking. Much of the audience this time consisted of people who were there because of the band's past glory. It felt like people were waiting in anticipation of things that would not happen. Sun Ra's playing and persona were too subdued; you would hardly know it was the same person. His piano playing, while always different, now had a tentative and unsteady quality to it. His speech was slightly impaired by the stroke he had been recuperating from, so he rarely said anything now. No longer was he singing or dancing. While onstage, he wore a set of dark glasses so no one could see his eyes. One had the eerie sense there was no Sun Ra. But there was, and it was Sun Ra seated behind an acoustic piano.

Just the year before, we had watched him combat difficult conditions on a number of occasions, so there was no reason not to believe that this too would pass. But we had never seen it go this far before.

A few months later, in April 1990, Sun Ra received a grant from the New York State Council on the Arts that allowed for a tour of different venues in the New York area. We worked in Long Island, up in Utica, at Hamilton College in Clifton, and in Binghamton. Martha Sammaciccia accompanied me on some of these gigs, which were as exciting as the springtime romance we were having. A good indication of Sun Ra's condition was that he took no notice of Martha's presence on these gigs and said nothing to me.

◖◗

In New Orleans, I worked with another musician who was ill, but Ed Blackwell had been on a dialysis machine for years and had made a pretty good adjustment. His playing had never been sharper or more focused. Blackwell was being honored at the New Orleans Jazz and Heritage Festival in April 1991. He had played there only once before since he had left in 1960; it was after he had been arrested for miscegenation, a law regarding which was still on the books in New Orleans at that time. His crime was marrying Frances, the woman who, thirty years later, was still his wife and with whom he had had several children.

Blackwell's good sense of humor showed as he recalled an event that had occurred during his first trip back to his native New Orleans with Old and New Dreams. At that time, he had come back as a favorite son. "Yeah, man, when the mayor gave me the key to the city," he said, "I told him he'd better make sure there wasn't no outstanding bench warrants on me."

Blackwell obviously had a love-hate relationship with the fabled city of his birth, also the birthplace of Jazz. He could be blunt and incisive with his criticism, as when I asked him about a habit I had noticed of trumpeters playing in the streets with one hand. "That's 'cause they ain't playin' shit," was his answer. One could never say that about Blackwell's drumming. In fact, Geraldine Wyckoff's commentary on our performance in a September 1991 article of *JazzTimes* had this to say:

> Blackwell, who left New Orleans in 1960 after being thrown in jail for miscegenation and being called to New York by Ornette Coleman, had not performed in his hometown since 1983, when he appeared with Old and New Dreams. For his two Jazz Fest appearances—an evening concert at the Riverboat Hallelujah and daytime at the Fair Grounds— Blackwell brought his own group, the Blackwell Project, with altoist/flutist Carlos Ward, bassist Mark Helias and trumpeter Ahmed Abdullah.

There was no "formula" Jazz to be heard on these sets. No one introduced the titles of the group's original tunes. There was no "head, a solo from each musician, back to the head" regimentation, which seems to be all too familiar these days. Instead, there was an uncalculated freshness stemming from Blackwell's light and exuberant rhythms. Indeed, the tap dancing that Blackwell says goes on in his head was heard by the audience as well as by his fellow musicians, who eagerly took up the call. Even the alto and trumpet at times took on percussive roles, reminiscent of New Orleans brass bands—Jazz ready for dancing. The Ed Blackwell Project emphatically proved that melodically and rhythmically free Jazz can swing like crazy and can be heralded by a wide audience even in these musically conservative times. Granted, the nighttime concert crowd was filled with ready-for-Blackwell musicians. But those at the Fair Grounds set—including many unsuspecting listeners—went wild for Blackwell's conceptual approach to the music as well.

An interesting reason for the effect we had was the combination of Venusian ones and tens. Blackwell was born on October 10; I was born on May 10; Mark was born on October 1, and Carlos was born on May 1. Though we might have represented a combination of earth and air signs, the dominant element represented by number-one people is fire characterized by energy and force.

Over the coming months, Blackwell asked me to play other gigs with his project, including the North Sea Jazz Festival, the Montreal International Jazz Festival, and at the Village Vanguard. Of those, Montreal was the only place I hadn't played with Sun Ra. The amount of money I was making with Blackwell, however, was ten times what I earned with Sun Ra.

After the North Sea gig, I arranged to spend a week in Amsterdam with Amber. She had moved into a lovely place. After catching up on old times and doing Gongyo with her, I returned to New York that August to do the Vanguard gig with the Project, which was a full week's booking.

The week with Blackwell at the Vanguard was one of the greatest small-band musical experiences I'd ever had. The gift of being able to work on music night after night in one setting with musicians of the caliber of Carlos, Mark, and Blackwell was a tremendous and unique opportunity for me. It was quite different from my own ensembles because I didn't have to be concerned about everything, and it was also different from the Arkestra sets because I was on the front line, playing throughout.

On the last day of August, a still-ailing Sun Ra took the Arkestra back to the UK. We arrived on a Saturday, and our first gig was that Sunday in Manchester, allowing us to open on Monday for a fateful weeklong run at Ronnie Scott's in London.

We were to be featured on a double bill opposite local pianist Julian Joseph, who had recently had a release issued on Atlantic Records. Julian, like saxophonist Courtney Pine, represented a new breed of Black Brits singing their own songs. Many of these musicians had been seen in a documentary that had recently aired on American television, featuring the late Art Blakey performing with a group known as the Jazz Warriors. As part of his group for the week at the club, Julian would have the tremendously talented drummer Mark Mondesir and saxophonist Jean Toussaint, a former Jazz Messenger who had made London his home.

The owner of this room, himself a saxophone player out of the hard-bop school, had as a young man emulated Hank Mobley, so I'm sure he dug John Gilmore. The club was a much larger British equivalent of the Village Vanguard. It was a well-established Jazz club in its own right that would generally not have hired Sun Ra. Near the end of Sunny's life, he had for the first time become accepted enough to work in such places. The tragedy is that patrons were witnessing only a fraction of his greatness.

We stayed at the Grafton Hotel on Tottenham Court Road. For me, it was a déjà vu experience from the moment I had arrived in London. As I walked around the town during the daytime, I kept feeling that this trip was going to have some significance. On the first day of our weeklong stay, Tyrone Hill and I met these two women, one Black, one white. A few days before I had left to go on this trip, Mickey Davidson had questioned what she was seeing as my new exclusive interest in white women. "Damn, man, all I see you with lately is white women. You can't find no sisters to hang out with?"

"Listen, I don't be lookin' for nobody!" I remember retorting. "The only women I deal with are those I find in a club. I don't have no time to be chasin'."

"So don't no Black women come to the clubs?" she came back.

"That's exactly what I'm saying. If they do, I ain't see none."

As if to make me eat my words right before my eyes, here in a London club was a pretty brown woman whose name was Monique Ngozi Nri. Immediately, we started up a conversation. It turned out that she had come to the club with Sarah Daniels, a friend of hers from the university they attended. It was Sarah who was hip to Sun Ra and who had brought Monique along. The immediate thing that signaled something happening here was that, in the course of our conversation, I started asking Monique for her birthday and sign. When she reversed the question on me, I learned that Monique's father and I had been born on the same day. My interest in astrology made me pursue that connection further.

During our stay at the Grafton Hotel, I was following a routine of rising early and doing my morning prayers. Tyrone, who had his own Gohonzon, had let me know that he was also interested in the practice. So when I'd start chanting in the morning I would call him to my room.

That Tuesday afternoon and every other day, for that matter, I was on the phone with Monique. It seemed so easy for me to converse with her about a wide range of subjects. As it turned out, Monique was a writer, and she had gotten permission from the editor of the publication she wrote for, *Art Rage*, to do an article on me. Our conversations led to my asking her out to dinner for that following Friday. Our rather innocent encounter was developing into something. Exactly what, I didn't know.

Monique truly had a diasporic background, with a mother born in Barbados, Celeste Veronica Nri, and a father, Cyril Onuora Nri, coming from Nigeria. Her parents met and married in England, where she was born. Monique wasn't quite Bajan, nor was she exactly Nigerian. Her younger siblings, two sisters and a brother, were all born in Nigeria proper, and had come up with the term *Bajerian* to describe their cultural mix.

The audience at Ronnie Scott's was different from those we had encountered in our other UK experiences. The band had been learning to work around Sun Ra's condition, and while we were not at last year's level, it was still an exciting ensemble. Throughout the week, however, we seemed to attract a staid and stuffy bunch of folks. By Friday, when Monique came back to hear the band, Michael Ray and I had decided to interject a little humor with an improvised barb directed at the folks there. We broke into one of Sun Ra's chants, *"I could have enjoyed myself on this planet, if the people had been alive."* Monique got a kick out of that, but most of the other audience members missed it.

Our gig at Ronnie Scott's ended that Saturday night. Earlier, Monique and I had spent the entire day together. Once I got back to the States, we kept in touch by phone and through the mail. It was amazing to me that I had enough interest in her to actually compose a letter. I hadn't written a letter in years; it took too long.

Later that month, Miles Davis passed, and Monique and I talked about his passing on the phone. Fortunately, I had just got through seeing him, still in top form, at the North Sea Jazz Festival when we both played there that past July. I'd been with Ed Blackwell. Notwithstanding our encounter in Japan, I had tremendous respect for Miles. So I wrote to Monique:

10/2/91

I did spend some time thinking, after talking to you yesterday, about the phenomenal coincidental fact that your father and I share an arrival date. Yes, you see, because we all do come from "somewhere there to nowhere here." There is more to this common arrival date than we know and I'm sure we will find out soon enough. The Mysteries of Life make it all worthwhile.

Miles Davis was the king of the trumpet. He was, however, the king because of an amount of creativity possessed by him that was unmatched by his peers or by musicians who came after him. The King is Dead! Long Live the King! Freddie Hubbard is now the trumpet king. Any record by Miles Davis from the period of 1955 to 1969, I feel is representative of his peak creative period. People like Miles and Duke Ellington, Max Roach, Ornette Coleman, John Coltrane, Sun Ra, are the people who made me proud to be an African born in America. They were and are people who approached their craft and their very existence with such dignity that one could only consider them royalty. . . .

Love, Ahmed

○

The other thing catching my attention during this time was the Senate confirmation hearings on the appointment of Judge Clarence Thomas to a lifetime position on the Supreme Court. For me, Clarence Thomas was symbolic of what had happened to quite a few Black people after the special lobotomy performed on us during eight years of Ronald Reagan and three years of George H. W. Bush. Thomas was a Black man with no soul. Black only in color. George Bush had cynically nominated a man with few to no qualifications, rewarding him for being the anti–affirmative action poster boy. Thomas had been given the job of dismantling the Equal Employment Opportunity Commission after he himself had been a recipient of affirmative-action benefits. As I was watching the hearings, I called Monique in London.

"I can't believe this guy! Where did they get him from? We don't have Black folks like that in America," I said heatedly, and immediately we got past the pleasantries and into current events.

Clarence Thomas had a white wife, but it had never occurred to me that the anger I felt toward him, a man I had never met, was really directed at myself, a man I knew only too well. I was projecting my anger, watching him be rewarded for taking the easy way out. I subconsciously knew that was exactly my present situation.

A few weeks before these hearings, I had received a distress call from Iyabode concerning my son Rashid. He had been arrested, she told me, for shoplifting while on a school trip during a Columbus Day bus excursion. Since he had been arrested at a Pennsylvania mall, he was in jail in Philadelphia. While trying to reach me, she had also called Mickey. Iyabode, however, was resigned to leaving him in jail, possibly to teach him a lesson. Fortunately, Mickey was as upset as I was and ready to drive to Philadelphia immediately to help me bring Rashid home.

Because he was a minor, there was no problem releasing him to us. In fact, all that was needed was an adult to come to the stationhouse to pick him up. We got him out that night.

On the way back to New York, both of us questioned him about what had happened. His story didn't make any sense, and when we dropped him off in Brooklyn at his mother's and her husband's place, it occurred to me that something else didn't make sense.

The Iyabode I knew had been a concerned and loving parent. I thought it odd that she was asleep when we returned and that she hadn't even bothered to get up to say anything to either Rashid or myself and Mickey. The whole incident lent more urgency to Mickey's annoying insistence and repeated admonition, "You better get your sons!"

I was feeling guilty enough without hearing someone else who knew me throw my irresponsibility back into my face. I thought I had been close enough to my sons when they were younger to know that this act on Rashid's part was an unconscious attempt to get my attention. Inside, I knew I had neglected him and his brother, but at that time, I also knew I wasn't ready for them to be around me. Not right then.

All the anger I felt toward myself, I could justifiably project outward at this Black Republican, Clarence Thomas. Yes, he was a piece of work, but in reality he was not that different from a number of other politicians, political appointees, or far too many Black men (myself included) in general. He was just ridiculously callous and in his own state of self-denial, emboldened by the Republican (and sometimes Democrat) philosophy that Black folks have no rights that anyone else need honor.

In our short time together, Monique had made it clear that she was an avowed feminist. When Anita Hill came forward with accusations that threatened the Thomas nomination, I was a happy person. At the time, I thought I was happy because this man was at last going to be exposed for what I could see he was and for what I didn't want to fess up to in myself. In retrospect, I realize that the controversy stirred by Anita Hill around sexual harassment was the beginning of another learning process for me.

Prior to that trial, I had no idea what sexual harassment was. People of my generation had been conditioned to accept it as a fact of life. I suspect that most men didn't really know what it was, including the senators on the panel, considering their own personal histories.

Having Monique as a guide in this instance, I was able to understand something about the common mistreatment of women, of which I was obviously guilty. As head of the Office of Equal Employment Opportunity, Clarence Thomas had already declared his opposition to the marginalized masses by nullifying the effectiveness of an arm of government constructed to ensure fair employment and respectful conditions in the workplace. Given this information, which came up in the course of the hearings, would it have been a great leap forward to assume that someone who abused power in one arena could do so in another?

Interestingly, folks in the Black community were torn over whether to support Thomas or Hill. Little information had been made available about Hill except that she was attempting to stop a Black man from getting ahead. Yet the information available on Thomas indicated he was an opportunist, totally willing to sell out his people in exchange for a comfortable position.

The debate that raged in America regarding Thomas and Hill took on another dimension in the Solomonic Sextet's tour of Eastern Europe during October 1991. We were traveling throughout Europe at a compelling time. Skirmishes had broken out, and the United States Information Agency warned us and our sponsors that we would not be protected if we went into Yugoslavia. The government probably already knew of the potential threat of a more serious outbreak of war to come.

Our tour started in Sofia, Bulgaria, with a gig at the National Palace of Culture, and 5,000 people in attendance. Prior to our concert, we were given a guided tour of the city with an interpreter who gave us some of the fascinating history of his country. The Turks, he informed us, had occupied Bulgaria for many years as part of the Ottoman Empire. We found out that most of the stops on this tour were in places that at one time had been part of that empire. He spoke of the alliance Bulgaria formed with the Russians in an effort to rid their country of Turkish domination. As well, he mentioned the Bulgarian alliance with Germany during

World War II, ostensibly for the same purpose, as they traded one strong-arm country for another.

The food in Sofia at our hotel was awful, and the reception to us as individuals when we weren't onstage was lukewarm. In performance, however, we got a tremendous response from the audience.

After Sofia, our next stop was Skopje, Yugoslavia. It was on the road from Sofia to Skopje that a debate broke out among the members of the Solomonic Sextet. Carlos Ward, Billy Bang, Masujaa, John Ore, and Charles Moffett were the top-flight musicians I had chosen for this tour. Philippa traveled with us, acting as road manager. She was careful to stay out of the debate.

I was surprised to find Carlos and Charles, two musicians I respected, in completely different political camps from Masujaa, Billy, and me, around the issues related to Clarence and Anita. It was like a microcosm of what was raging in Black communities across America. Billy and I both had political problems with Judge Thomas. Charles and Carlos were supportive of him because he was a Black man. George H. W. Bush had struck a major political victory against clarity by appointing a Black man who, according to the information presented, was less than qualified for the position, and was an activist against the interests of his own people. The debates between us, needless to say, were hot and spurred a standoff.

On the road to Skopje, we also came upon vocalist Leon Thomas. It happens that we had stopped on the road to stretch our legs somewhere in the middle of a highway between Sofia and Skopje. Just then, Leon, who was traveling in another van in the same direction, had spotted me and asked his driver to stop. Next thing I knew, someone hollered out, "Look out, Double-A! What's happenin'?" just as if I had last seen him only yesterday. In fact, I hadn't seen him in about seven years.

"Hey!" I answered, as did all the other guys in the midst of a round of warm embraces. Leon was especially glad to see us. Apparently, he knew we were scheduled to perform before his gig on that same night. He explained that he had band trouble. His regular group couldn't make it, and the Jimmy Dawkins Blues Band, which he had been paired with, had some serious problems as well. He asked if he could work out a deal with us as a backup band. At first, I said, "I don't know," given that the trip from Sofia was a long one. We were also scheduled to be filmed for television and would probably arrive in Skopje with just enough time to take care of our own business, without the added responsibility of rehearsing someone else's music. But this was Leon Thomas, and we all knew him and he was in a dilemma. Fortunately for us and him, it turned out that his people did show up by the time we arrived at our hotel.

Our audience in Skopje was a smaller yet more enthusiastic crowd of about 1,200 people. Oliver Belopeta, producer of the festival, which was magnificently filmed for Yugoslavian TV, was a gracious host, wining and dining us after we had arrived, almost making us forget our road fatigue. I had met Oliver the previous year in Stuttgart. This current tour, in fact, put together by Philippa, had occurred as a result of connections I'd made traveling the Spaceways with Sun Ra. As well, Philippa had previously arranged a tour for saxophonist Oliver Lake through USIA and was knowledgeable about that organization. She had worked diligently to put this whole thing together.

From Skopje, we went to Thessaloniki, only to encounter disorder at the border. The Greeks did not appreciate the choice the people of Skopje had made when they changed the name of their country back to Macedonia. The historical significance to the Greeks was that Macedonia was the home of Alexander the Great. Under King Philip II, the Macedonians, led by the young Prince Alexander III, had conquered and dominated the city-states that made up the Greek peninsula. Eventually, Greek culture became dominant, with Macedonia receding into the background. For Alexander's ethnic descendants to reclaim their original name proved discomfiting, even to today's Greeks. They therefore demonstrated their disapproval by holding us for hours at the border because we dared to enter Greece after performing in Macedonia. We almost missed our flight to Athens. Eventually, we flew from Thessaloniki to Athens to perform at the Orpheus Theater, where we had to match wits with a local promoter who seemed intent on recording us without our permission. He had provided alcohol at our sound check, resulting in at least one of our members being so drunk that he was unable to play. With my attention focused on a serious case of intoxication prior to our Athens debut, I was fortunate that Philippa was there picking up on how the promoter was preparing to document us without our permission—and with high-tech equipment, mind you. Our only recourse was to threaten not to go on unless we got the tape. Our bargaining power was considerably enhanced by the large audience that was demanding that we play.

Our agreement with the USIA, ironically, had probably encouraged this exploitive move. This promoter wasn't paying us. We had no contractual agreement with him. Our dealings were completely with the USIA, which might have led him to believe he could do whatever he wanted. We had signed no agreement that he was obligated to honor. But he was aware of our power as a group; otherwise I'm sure he wouldn't have gone through the trouble. In any event, we won the day, and the tape was handed over to us after the concert.

After the event, we attended a reception at which we encountered Kostas Yiannoulopoulos, the promoter and producer of Sun Ra's *Live at Praxis* recordings of 1984. When the slick local promoter saw how Kostas received us, he was thereafter suitably humble and apologetic. When he took us to the airport that next morning, he must have apologized to me at least ten times. From Athens, we flew to Thessaloniki for our last concert on Greek soil.

The value of Charles Moffett on this tour cannot be overstated. He was the person I turned to whenever I needed to talk to someone. Our relationship had developed into a healthy one, and even though I was the designated bandleader, I often found myself calling on his wisdom and experience. This tour served to solidify our relationship.

To add to the international intrigue, in Thessaloniki, a young person was directed to my dressing room by a USIA government official. The young man professed his awareness of the condition of Black people in America, informing me of similar oppressive conditions for a minority population in Greece. He wanted to know if I'd be willing to make a statement during our performance about the condition of these people. I knew this had to be a setup; even if it wasn't, I wasn't going to make a statement about something I knew nothing about. Despite this cloak-and-dagger operation, the concert went well. We were the only Jazz group on the European classical and folk music series, and the mayor of the city came out to take pictures with us. Our final stop on this tour was in Istanbul. We entered Turkey from Thessaloniki in a wonderful modern bus that the seven of us had to ourselves. Positif Vibrations, which had brought Sun Ra and the Arkestra to their country the year before, was now presenting our Solomonic Sextet. We stayed in Istanbul for a week, during which time we performed in several concerts and at the opening of a new club.

Our first concert in Turkey was opposite the great Max Roach, whose group included trumpeter Cecil Bridgewater, saxophonist Odean Pope, and bassist Tyrone Brown. The greatness of Mr. Roach was on display at all times, and for me, it was most especially evident when I approached him after our set. "It was truly an honor to open the concert for you, Mr. Roach," I said.

"No, man, you didn't open for us. This is a double bill," he responded, in his usual and genuinely gentlemanly fashion.

As the Arkestra had, we stayed at the Pera Palas in Istanbul, an elegant historic hotel. At the club that the Solomonic Sextet helped open, we had the added honor of playing for four of the five members of the Art Ensemble of Chicago. The AEC—consisting of Lester Bowie, Roscoe Mitchell, Joseph Jarman, Malachi Favors, and Don Moye—had also been featured at Positif Festival.

For us, this Eastern European tour was a huge success. To be able to play my own music on tour was one of my desires, and here it was fully realized and definitely appreciated. It was for me actual proof that the practice of Buddhism worked. By now, my only desire was to have my vocation and my familial relationships fully integrated.

When I came back to New York, my pockets had the mumps. I called Iyabode and asked if I could come visit Rashid and Shahid. I had brought gifts for them and their little sister, Merakhu, along with some money for their mother. I wanted to spend a few hours with them, and it was all lovely except for a real subdued attitude from Iyabode. I detected something different about her, but I couldn't quite put my finger on what it was.

I had already committed myself to being a better father to my sons, but I had no idea how I was going to do that, or of the amount of karma I would need to change in the process. For now, it was all internal.

# X
# IS THERE LIFE AFTER RA?

> When men are brothers,
> They are brothers because they
> know they are.
> They walk the initiate bridge
> degree of pointlessness. . . .
> Friends of pointless . . .
> Intuition companionship.
> Sincere understandingness . . .
> of/on angelic planes of being.
> That is why I have said they are not my brothers
> if they are not brothers.
> —Sun Ra, "Cosmos Evolution"

In late October, I got a call from Kunle Mwanga shortly after I had returned from our Solomonic tour. He said he was calling to tell me that Blackwell was not going to be using me on the next series of gigs. He made it sound like I was being fired. I thought the call was a little odd, since I had been given those gigs only for the period of April to August, with no expectation or discussion of more work after. But before I had left for Europe, two months after the Vanguard gig, I had been invited to a surprise birthday party for Blackwell on October 10. I thought everything had gone well on the gigs we did, and what with the invitation to his party, I was a little confused by Kunle's call.

Weeks later, I was still ruminating about that call. It was a Monday morning in November, just before Thanksgiving. Mickey was driving us to do a lecture demonstration at a local school in East New York. Mickey had known Blackwell since they had both joined the faculty at Wesleyan back in the 1980s. For some reason, she was strongly opinioned (not unusual for her) about my gig with Blackwell. We got into an intense exchange about my confusion, but I couldn't understand why Mickey was so upset about it.

Before I could find out, I looked to my right in just enough time to brace myself for a car that had run a stop sign and was headed straight toward the passenger side of Mickey's car, exactly where I was seated. The car missed our side by seconds and inches but hit our rear so hard that we spun around completely, right into a fire hydrant. Both vehicles were totaled. Consequently, our gig was lost but our lives were spared.

When the ambulance came, I was put into traction. I felt some back pain, so I agreed to go to the hospital to determine what damage had been done. Mickey was all right and left for another appointment.

While in Jamaica Hospital, lying there and unable to move, I did some deep thinking about what I was doing. Monique had come to America in early November and had stayed for a couple of weeks. During her last weekend in New York, just before this accident, I had begun to wake up out of the fog I had created and to appreciate her and the potential she represented. In spite of my growing desire for her, outwardly, I was trying not to take our relationship too seriously. I was still into the lifestyle I had been in for the past three years. This car accident, the second one I'd been in with Mickey, was the last of two jolts of lightning sent to awaken me.

The first had occurred at the New Music Cafe, a club on Canal Street. I had a gig there on November 16, which Monique accompanied me to. The Solomonic, initially a sextet but—without Billy Bang—now a quintet, had another change from the tour, with Fred Hopkins replacing John Ore on bass. Since Philippa was still representing me (but didn't know about Monique) and since we still had a relationship that I hadn't told Monique about, I was skating on thin ice. I had gotten away with this sort of thing so much in the past that I hadn't even tried to consider the current ramifications. Monique was determined not to let me get away with it anymore, even though I had just met her two months before. Not that anything happened, but Monique was making it clear that from her point of view I was her man now. As for me, I hadn't gotten there yet. When Monique saw me paying too much attention to Philippa, she became quite angry. She did not appreciate me placing her to the side, once she was seated. In short, Monique picked up on the vibes between Philippa and me and understood what they meant. Meanwhile, Fred picked up on Monique's anger and moved in for me to calm her down. At the end of the evening, the choice facing me was which one of the two I'd be leaving with and leaving behind. I chose Monique, leaving Philippa hurt and infuriated.

As if that wasn't enough, Monique and I cut everyone else loose and went to Bradley's after the gig. Bradley's was an open space for both the general public and musicians. It was friendly and relaxing, most especially for Black men and their white women. Having walked through the door, I steered Monique toward the back, where after-gig musicians habitually congregated. And among the first people there to embrace me, rather closely, was Martha. My relationship with her had been on and off for the past year, and that night her body language and her eyes clearly glinted that she wanted it on. My own body language was obviously indicating that I too wanted it on, past habits being what they had been.

Monique, still sizzling from what she had picked up on at the New Music Cafe, had become extremely sensitive to the slightest signs. We had joined a group of musicians and writers at one of the tables, and after a while, Martha came over to engage in conversation. Monique, reading it all, decided that the time was now. She actually went against her usual composure and lashed out at Martha, something to the effect that this was her man here, clearly insisting, "Hands off."

That night, I realized I was going to have to make definitive changes, to separate business from love and love from wandering. I could see my life changing before me, so much so that between the day after Monique left and the day before the car accident, I wrote her this letter:

11/21/91

My Dear Monique,

I have to take the position that because things have worked out as if you are now a part of me, then this must have always been so, even if we didn't know it before. You have the eyes of my sister, and I the birthday of your father. We are both reminded of someone in our distant past, someone close, family. And yet, fortunately, we are not related through blood. Kindred Spirits is what comes to mind. I look at you (can you tell?) with pride. I am happy to have a woman as beautiful as you on my arm. When I met you, I didn't think I would fall in love with you, but I knew you were interesting to me for some unexplained reason. Little did I know that you would be all up in me so quickly. To a certain extent, I feel as if I want to downplay these last couple of weeks. There is a part of my nature that strongly resists change and there is another part that craves it. The significance of what we've just experienced means some kind of change is inevitable. Human revolution is a natural result of practicing Buddhism. What I enjoyed most about your visit was that we lived through a wide range of emotions and always talked it out. That isn't easy but absolutely essential, I feel, if there is to be any longevity to this beginning relationship. It isn't completely true what I told you about having no expectation in regard to your visit. I spoke to you about a relationship that I had with a woman from Denver approximately three years ago. Well, that kind of disinterested me in long-distance relationships. Upon reflecting, I realized my reluctance (if it can be named) was due to not seeing clearly. I was not a Buddhist in 1988. So, when I made myself to re-understand what I should have already known (the only thing to fear is fear itself), then I was cool. You're probably at this moment saying: "He's so dry!" So be it.

I love you, Ahmed

As I lay there in that hospital in traction, I recalled this letter I had written, realizing that a few hours before, I had been seconds away from possible death or permanent injury. I remembered that before my tour, I had understood the need to reestablish my relationship with my sons and reminded myself that, in order to do this, I needed stability in my life.

What I was thinking when I came out of the hospital after three hours was that I should turn Monique on to the practice of Buddhism. Over the years, I had regretted that I could not offer such a thing to Iyabode and to my sons. While Mickey and I were together I couldn't see the importance of the practice. Philippa had a Gohonzon, but she had stopped practicing. Amber had one too, but she had moved to Amsterdam. My relationship with Martha, though a passionate one, was marred by too many fights. So here I was, getting a fresh start, another opportunity, and I believed I was being jolted into a new awakening. Monique was now the person who had entered my life in a dynamic way, breaking through all my resistance. Now I knew I needed to help her help me through some layers that I couldn't even see. One of the precepts of Buddhism is that we practice for ourselves and we practice for others. I needed a spiritual center, and with Monique, maybe it was all possible.

The other significant thing about the car accident was that it made me more appreciative of life and the things it had to offer. Our Thanksgiving Day dinner, a family tradition, was sometimes difficult for me to attend. It wasn't that I didn't love my family—in fact, quite the contrary. I loved them so much it hurt sometimes, even to the point where I would stay away rather than deal with the pain. This time, however, I wanted to be there.

That Thanksgiving 1991, in my parents' home at 118 Avenue D, turned out to be a day that truly deserved the name. It looked as if everyone in my family had the same idea. My oldest sister, Lorraine, was there with her son and daughter, Pepe and Angela. Angela's son, Stephen, was also there. My sister Helen showed up with her son and daughter, Derrick and Lisa. Lisa brought her three children—Eric and her pair of two-year old twins, Jason and

Jocellyne—whom I was seeing for the first time. I was grateful that Iyabode let me bring along Rashid and Shahid. The only people missing were Lorraine's daughter, Michelle, and her sons, Kyle and Scottie, who were all living in California.

It was a great and warm dinner.

When Monique came back to visit me in New York that December, I began to have conversations with her about Buddhism. To my delight, she seemed genuinely interested in the practice. She even expressed a desire to accompany me to a Buddhist meeting, so it wasn't long before she learned how to do Gongyo, the morning and evening prayers. During this visit, I also took her to meet my mother and father. We went to their house and stayed the afternoon, eating and conversing together, and in the midst of this wonderful moment, Monique took pictures of me with them.

Since Monique was going to stay until after the holidays, we were able to bring in the New Year together with Sun Ra during his gig at the New Music Cafe, the same place at which a month and a half before we'd had that intense encounter around Philippa. Our New Year's Eve festivities were marred by the news that Pat Patrick and Kusenaton had left the planet.

Kusenaton, a saxophonist and above all a Chicago bluesman, had worked with Sun Ra here and there since the late 1970s. He was also an illusionist who often combined that talent into his work as a musician. Kusenaton was a wonderfully out-there character, always fun to hang out with. Pat Patrick, one of Sun Ra's original Space Trio (predating the Arkestra), was a great saxophonist, having mastered both baritone and alto. He had also become quite a capable bassist.

Pat was a charter member of the Arkestra (even before Gilmore and Marshall), who had come to New York with Sun Ra back in the early 1960s. He had also worked with a number of other bands, including those of Edward Kennedy Ellington and Thelonious Monk.

One of the Arkestra's inside jokes reflected the respect Sunny had for Patrick. During many a rehearsal, Sunny would want to know if a certain member had put a song to memory. To test that person, Sunny would ask, with that little mischievous smile on his face, "You got it down Pat or you got it down Ahmed?" Which sometimes made me wonder what else he was saying, because if you didn't have it down pat that meant you didn't know it yet. Pat was possessed by such a youthful quality and look that even the word of his death felt like a contradiction.

The gig itself was odd, not unlike the last time I had played this room. Neither gig was well attended. I don't believe it was well advertised either; however, loyal Sun Ra supporters always showed up and knew where and when we were playing. By now, Sun Ra was the same quiet person he had gradually become. The unfortunate thing is that the cats in the Arkestra were getting used to this new persona. He would be left alone and away from everyone else for long periods of time. There were occasions when his soiled clothes and body would give off such a stench that folks would avoid him altogether. Being around men, and in this case fellow musicians—who weren't inclined, much less trained, in the art of caring for others—was not the most helpful situation.

During a break between sets, Monique asked me to take her over and introduce her to Sun Ra. Sitting in his wheelchair, off to the side of the stage, he acknowledged her while I was telling him how we had met when the band had played at Ronnie Scott's that September.

June Tyson, who also made the gig that night, and Monique got on very well. In fact, in a half-joking manner, we asked June to sing at our wedding, which we said was going to occur later in the year. Emphatically, she said, "Yes!"

Something was obviously changing in me, and the letter I wrote to Monique on her return to England indicated my inner thoughts. I had no idea how powerful words were, much less the forces I was setting into motion. I wrote to her in 1992:

I am pretty sure now that you are my destiny woman, which is the equivalent of *soulmate*, only not so overused. What does that mean? It means I agree with you that we have work to do together, a family to build, experiences to share, and a lot of love in store. As a result of your presence in my life I have rethought many concepts and the amazing thing is the effortless way new ideas are manifesting. For a relationship to endure there has to be mutual influence and mutual growth and development, and there is. I have a plan that in the end involves the success of our relationship. For me, it involves spending more time with my sons, my father and mother and sisters. The idea here is that we can use this practice of Buddhism to change karma in our immediate families. When it comes time to create our own family, all of our ancestors will aid us in the success of our union. I love you very much in a very special way.

At the time, I didn't really know what power those words would have. By the beginning of March I was on my way to the UK to meet Monique's family. I spent a week at her apartment in Balham, London, and had a wonderful time with her family. Her brother, Cyril, and his mate, Diana, had just had a little boy, Chigozie, and Di was now pregnant again. I also met Monique's charming mother, Celeste Veronica Nri, and her sisters, Mary and Debbie.

On the first night we went out, we crossed paths with Debbie. We had just finished eating at a Thai restaurant and were on our way to Monique's car, heading to Ronnie Scott's, and Debbie suddenly appeared in her car. We thought it odd but a good omen, because Monique was close to her little sister.

Monique had developed the pictures she had taken of me with my parents. She gave them to me, insisting that I take them to my parents to let them see the results. Our time together was warm, but what impressed me the most was Monique's family, the harmony, the way they got along together, the obvious bond and feelings they had for one another, and the close relationship between Monique and her mother. Their ritual Sunday dinners reflected their togetherness. When you have a family working together, you have the foundation for a nation. Something that was probably missing in my own life back then was evident in Monique's.

She was the oldest of her siblings, and perhaps that helped to account for that sense of togetherness. In my case, when my oldest sister, Marilyn, had died, her death seemed to mark the beginning of a separation in my family. The bond was gone. With Monique, it appeared to me that her presence as the oldest was the focal point, the unifying element that made it work.

Back in the States, I was in New York only a week before I was set to go out again, this time with Sun Ra. We left for yet another European tour on March 17, St. Patrick's Day, which was also the day I dropped by to visit my parents with Monique's photographs in hand, procrastinator that I am. Significantly, the seventeenth was also Marilyn's birthday. My parents loved the pictures and were very happy I had brought them. When my mother saw a picture of Monique, she asked, "Who's that?" When I told her that the person in the photo was probably going to be her daughter-in-law, she smiled.

The tour, booked by Gabby Kleinschmidt, was extensive, and for a man who was bound to a wheelchair, it was strenuous. Sun Ra was also without John Gilmore, who at the time was too ill to tour. We were scheduled to play in some places I had never been. In Sweden, for example, we played in Malmö and Lund. In Denmark, we were at the Pumpehuset in Copenhagen. This Danish gig was marked by an unexpected meeting with Charles Blass of Columbia's WKCR. Charles had spearheaded the group of three students who had previously set up a 114-hour broadcast of Sun Ra's music back in 1987. Here in Denmark, in March, Charles managed to do what turned out to be the last taped interview with Sun Ra.

One of the highlights in Copenhagen was a music workshop. Apparently, Sun Ra had been booked to do it, but he was in no shape and hadn't been up to it for quite some time. I really don't know who had conceived of the workshop idea. All I know is that I had gone to Sunny's room on the afternoon after we had checked into the hotel only to be asked by Spencer Weston and Sun Ra to go participate in it. When I got to the club where it was being held, I saw and heard Jothan Callins and Michael Ray improvising their way through a workshop peopled with some discerning music students who didn't seem too satisfied with the way it was being conducted.

I had the advantage of listening to them and having time to size up the situation. Quickly, I realized that I should approach the workshop with a series of anecdotes. I interjected myself into the situation and began with my relationship to Sun Ra. In effect, it was my story, one that only I had lived. And since it came from my heart, I was able to turn the situation around, telling them about the human Sun Ra as opposed to the technics of his music.

After the workshop, Pierre Dørge, the Danish guitarist and bandleader, came up to me and handed me the money for the workshop. He told me that in his opinion I had saved the day. Since it had been included in the overall fee for the band, I turned the money over to Spencer Weston.

Something about that workshop and the conditions under which it had been rendered prompted me to understand that there was a need for each of us to generally take more responsibility. It's odd how Buddhism changes your perceptions of reality, but the fact was that we needed a serious paradigm shift in the face of Sun Ra's physical deterioration.

We should have known about that workshop the moment it had been booked. Apparently, Sunny's habit of not passing along that kind of information was no longer a working model. At least some of us had to be more aware, more responsible.

Many of the guys in the band had long tried to stay away from Sunny lest they be lectured. Now there was another reason—what his soiled clothes were now speaking to. One would have been hard put to say something to Sun Ra about it. But the musicians living and/or working so many years with Sun Ra should have understood that something had to be done to help keep him both presentable and clean, now that it was obvious he couldn't do so himself. Drummer Buster Smith, it must be said, was the most diligent of us in that regard, but Buster didn't live in Philadelphia.

While on this tour, and in the absence of Gilmore, I was given to preaching to the guys. I spoke about how we needed to come together to deal with the Arkestra's business and not allow Sun Ra to be left with all of the responsibility on his shoulders in his condition and most especially at this time.

These not-too-successful attempts came to an end on March 29, Monique's birthday, when we reached Aarburg, Switzerland, and I found out from her that my mother had died.

*Destination Unknown*, recorded that day, is one album I will never forget. Though some say it was not one of Sun Ra's better recordings, for me it was actual proof of the power we are capable of summoning, even during the most difficult days of our lives. I treasure that recording because it brought my mother and Monique together in a most unusual way. It was Monique's arrival date on this planet as well as the day I heard about my mother's departure. And both of those events had a tremendous impact on me that day, though neither of the two were present in the flesh.

Our next stop was Munich. It was there I could feel another kind of psychic power coming over me. Maybe it was my mother's spirit guiding me already. While on the streets of Munich, several of us were standing outside our hotel and I happened to mention that Leonard Jones lived there. Leonard had played bass with me many years before at Ali's Alley. I hadn't seen him since the last time I was in Munich. And here he was walking down the street with his son by his side.

After doing our gig that night, I left Sun Ra and the Arkestra to return home. I had been reading Isabel Allende's novel *The House of the Spirits*, a magical tale that rivaled the life I felt I was then living.

Monique also flew into New York to be at my side by April 1, when I was scheduled to arrive back in the city. It would not be an easy thing to see my mother in her coffin. Not an easy thing to face alone at all. Mickey Davidson, who had initially been contacted by my sister with news of my mother's death, called to encourage me to go to the funeral home. I had such a fear of death that it was difficult for me to make this one. Fortunately for me, Monique intuitively knew this and was also very supportive. That night, however, I got so drunk that I could hardly awaken in the morning to get to the funeral on time. I had to wear dark glasses to cover my red and shameful eyes. I almost had to be carried to the funeral home.

Both my mother and father were eighty-nine. Her arthritic condition, coupled with high blood pressure and compounded by old age, was what ended her life. My mother's death was pretty devastating for my father as well. I really came to understand that he must have loved my mother a great deal. In fact, our relationship after my mother's death grew closer to what it had been in the early days when I was growing up.

My father had been getting treatment for colon cancer for years. We all knew that he had been seriously impaired by it for the past few years. We were really concerned that his illness would result in his leaving first, and that in her invalid condition we would have had to rally to aid her. Ironically, it was our father who needed comforting.

Then, after my mother's death, he stopped getting chemotherapy. This meant he was going to be in more pain, so the three of us decided, along with our older children, to set up a schedule so we would all spend a day or evening with him. During the time I spent with him, we talked about politics and sports but stayed away from in-depth conversations of an emotional nature. I never did get to ask him what had happened to my brother, Harry. But even without asking that kind of penetrating question, it was good to be around him and to share long stretches of time together. Monique stayed with me during these nights, which amounted to the first time I had slept at my parents' since leaving at eighteen. On one of those nights, I heard myself ask her to marry me.

Monique stayed in New York for three weeks, and we were married on April 17 at city hall. My sister Lorraine was one of the only people we had told, and we asked her to be our witness. After our brief ceremony, we went to the Odeon, on West Broadway, to have lunch. I was still in a state of shock, but a couple of things happened to let me know that I was "on the right road going in the right direction." At the Odeon, we sat next to a large luncheon party made up of people who had been filming a television commercial in the vicinity. The director of the date, Mr. Levine, was a person I had done a commercial with a couple of years before. Recognizing him, I made conversation, letting him know we had just been married. Immediately upon hearing that, in a wonderful gesture, he ordered us a bottle of Dom Pérignon, the most expensive champagne listed, and proposed a toast to us from his table. Later that day, when Monique and I told my father about our marriage, he told us that we would be together for fifty-four years because my mother and he had shared that much time.

We spent the day after our wedding at Birdland, by then situated at 105th Street and Broadway, a new club that used the old name. Some fascinating poets and musicians of New York came together in what was an amazing day of celebration and fund-raising for the poet Fatisha, whom I had worked with and who was also suffering with cancer. I had been asked to do a duet with Mickey Davidson, and we did Paul Laurence Dunbar's "Negro Love Song." Monique and I found ourselves anointed by this fantastic world of spoken-word artists we had not been aware of. In the mix of poets was a little guy with a long beard and cane who delivered a remarkable poem with such profundity that I would remember him for many years. His name was Louis Reyes Rivera.

Soon after that event, Monique had to go back to London to put her affairs in order. She had a job, an apartment, friends and family, all of which would be affected by her move to New York. We had gotten married so quickly that Monique had not even told her mother, with whom she was so close. She had come to New

York to support me, and would go back home a married woman. We had virtually eloped, and because of the peculiar timing of our marriage, we had both been low-key about it. Some might have thought it odd that we got married days after my mother's death. But I could hear my mother's voice repeating what I often heard her say to the women in my life who had problems with me: "He'll be all right once he gets married." So in my gut, I knew it was the right thing to do.

More gigs with Sun Ra were scheduled for May in the Midwest. I made them all and continued preaching. The tour included stops in Milwaukee and Columbus, and one memorable night in Minneapolis at a place called Glam Slam. This marvelous room, owned by the popular artist Prince, reminded me of First Avenue, another Minneapolis club where he often played. On this occasion, trumpet great Clark Terry and saxophonist Red Holloway, who were also in town performing, came backstage between shows to pay their respects to Sun Ra. I was impressed. I found out that Red Holloway had actually played with Sun Ra years before John Gilmore had joined the Arkestra.

Respect to Sun Ra while he was living was a constant. I was concerned, however, with the fact that the leadership potential within the Arkestra was not being acknowledged.

It's an interesting fact that the bands of Art Blakey and Count Basie, closely followed by those of Miles Davis, have produced the largest number of leaders within the music. From Blakey, we get Clifford Brown, Donald Byrd, Hank Mobley, Kenny Dorham, Lee Morgan, Benny Golson, Bobby Timmons, Freddie Hubbard, Wayne Shorter, Cedar Walton, Reggie Workman, Curtis Fuller, Gary Bartz, Carlos Garnett, Olu Dara, Donald Harrison, Terence Blanchard, Wynton and Branford Marsalis, Frank Lacy, etc. From Basie, we get Lester Young, "Papa" Jo Jones, Billie Holiday, Buck Clayton, Harry "Sweets" Edison, Eddie "Lockjaw" Davis, Dickie Wells, Jimmy Rushing, Illinois Jacquet, Buddy Tate,

Lucky Thompson, Don Byas, Joe Newman, Joe Williams, Thad Jones, Frank Foster, Al Grey, Benny Powell, Oran "Hot Lips" Page, Jimmy Forrest, and Eddie Durham—and the list goes on. From Miles, we get John Coltrane, Cannonball Adderley, Herbie Hancock, Sam Rivers, Ron Carter, Tony Williams, Chick Corea, Kenny Garrett, "Philly Joe" Jones, Bill Evans, Wynton Kelly, Paul Chambers, Dave Holland, etc.

It could be said of Blakey and Basie that they were not necessarily composers in the classical sense. Thus, they turned their bands into workshops for young composers who would then write for these ensembles of crack musicians. Access to such high-profile forums allowed younger musicians coming through a Basie, a Blakey, to be later recognized in their own right.

With Miles, it was also because of his visibility and the mystique he had created. The best-known musician to come out of a Miles Davis band was, of course, John Coltrane. People might not have known who Trane was had it not been for Miles. But once the phenomenon that would become Trane had manifested itself, the fact that he had come through Miles made Mr. Davis the person folks understood to be a major talent scout.

Duke Ellington took another approach. He encouraged loyalty through independence, producing a slew of dates aimed at featuring the stars in his bands. So that even while musicians like Harry Carney, Johnny Hodges, Clark Terry, and Ben Webster, etc. stayed with him, they developed their reputations as Ellington's men—that is, they remained closely identified with his orchestra.

In Sun Ra's band, things were different. Few musicians who had worked with Sun Ra were known to have gone off to work as leaders. This fact, I believe, lessened the regard in which Sun Ra was held. Given the standards set by Count Basie, Art Blakey, Duke Ellington, and Miles Davis, I felt that if the Jazz public knew the individual greatness of the cats in the band, respect for Sun Ra would only heighten. He too would have been known as a leader of leaders. The Buddhist precept, to do something for oneself and for others, is what guided me here to this comparison.

The fact that John Gilmore and Marshall Allen had never seriously entertained the thought of leading their own bands had now become quite troubling to me. I was once asked by Keith Knox, of Silkheart Records, if I could persuade John to do a date on that label. This was back in 1988, and Silkheart was offering good money, several thousand dollars. When I approached John, his response was, "I better not do it, 'cause Sun Ra might want to rehearse."

He missed the point. To my way of thinking, if they had been charged with the responsibility of getting a band together, organizing music and all, those musicians who hadn't done any work as leaders would be encouraged to do so. They would also have had people around them who had worked with Sun Ra over the years and who had demonstrated leadership ability.

I was pushing what I called the Satellites of the Sun project. The idea was to show that Sun Ra had people in the Arkestra with leadership abilities. We could demonstrate this inside the safe environment of the Arkestra by designating leaders to lead bands partially made up of current members. The concept was borrowed from a gig Sam Rivers had included me in on back in 1977.

The idea took root around the Fourth of July, during a Central Park gig that we did beside another group, Sonic Youth. It was to be one of Sunny's last public performances. Michael Ray and Gloria Powers worked with Philippa Jordan and me to try to get this project off the ground. Originally, Satellites was a tribute to Sun Ra. I had asked Sunny about doing it and he gave his approval.

Monique returned to the States on July 19. Having gotten her affairs somewhat in order, she came back to stay this time.

We had made some contact with people at Lincoln Center, believing it would be a fitting place to honor Sun Ra. Rob Gibson, who at the time had an administrative role at that institution, used to produce shows with Sun Ra and many other adventurous musicians when he worked in Atlanta. Stanley Crouch, who in his earlier New York incarnation had been supportive of Ra, now had an influential role at Lincoln Center and consequently had also been contacted. Though Stanley wasn't necessarily overflowing with enthusiasm for the project, he did give it a hearing. The major problem in realizing what could have been a marvelous celebration was not the external resistance, but rather our own internal discord.

It was becoming increasingly obvious that it was going to be difficult to pull this project off, primarily because of our inability to work together without Sun Ra. What we had envisioned as a cooperative effort was constantly being undermined by subtle inaccuracies and inappropriate information generated through cover letters sent out by Gloria Powers. We had agreed upon a Satellites of the Sun letterhead that listed both Gloria and Michael's New Orleans address and our New York address as places of contact. Yet when we received copies of letters that had been sent out to major institutions across the worldwide Jazz community, we noticed several printed on Gloria and Michael's own "Rhythm and Muse" letterhead. We also found that ideas we agreed upon in conference calls would later be changed without consensus. A conflict of interest—which was already becoming apparent with Gloria's need to push Michael—became further confused with the arrival of a benefactor who had other notions and goals regarding the project. Gloria wanted to make Satellites the Mike Ray Show. And though I have a great deal of love for Mike and appreciated the fact that Gloria was in his corner, the paradigm they were embracing was antithetical to a collective and cohesive Satellites of the Sun.

I proposed Rivers's model—an idea through which we could all win, an approach quite different from that even created by Sun Ra. But, the only configuration they would support was one in which there was one winner, Michael Ray, which was essentially no different from that already created by Sunny.

In September 1992, Monique and I left New York to go to London to plan our second wedding. This one would be a Buddhist ceremony at the Soka Gakkai Center at Taplow Court in

Maidenhead, near London. It was going to be a proper wedding, and it had to be preceded by a long conversation with Monique's mother. I had to beg her forgiveness for our haste in marrying in April while seeking her approval for our September 27 nuptials.

○

While we were gone, my father's condition had grown worse, and he had to be placed in hospice. We also learned that a wealthy friend of Sun Ra's music had donated some money to help move the Satellites of the Sun project forward. Our friends in New Orleans, however, used the entire sum for their own purposes, obviously with no thought as to the work input or expenses incurred and absorbed by others. Most important, they apparently decided to play off the fact that the idea itself had come from someone other than themselves. That ended the possibility of celebrating Sun Ra through the Satellites of the Sun.

When Monique and I returned from London, I learned that the cancer had already spread to my father's brain. He was no longer able to recognize any of us. He died on October 16, 1992, a few weeks shy of his ninetieth birthday and close to six months after my mother's death. In planning his funeral, my sisters and I decided I would do the eulogy. I had learned a lot from him throughout my life and most especially during those last six months when I was afforded the opportunity to spend more time around him as an adult. His most powerful message to us concerned the importance of family, a fact that was at the heart of the eulogy I delivered.

During the funeral, which took place October 20, I recalled in my eulogy how on that last Thanksgiving we'd enjoyed together, my mother and father had had almost all of their children and grandchildren together in one place. The eulogy was well received.

I give much credit to Sun Ra for helping me to see the power of those Southern/African roots that were so much a part of who my father was and so much a part of who I couldn't help but be. We buried him at Frederick Douglass Memorial Park in Staten Island, right next to my mother.

One of the better paying gigs I had gotten for the Solomonic Sextet had been negotiated by Philippa with the Leverkusener Jazztage in Germany for October 22, 1992. So the day after we had buried my father, I was on a plane headed for a major festival that was to be filmed for German television.

Once again, Charles Moffett proved to be a truly supportive person who seemed to totally understand what I was faced with. Charles was the father of musicians, and like a true coach he sensed what I was going through. He was there when I needed someone to talk to. He, too, was a mentor for me, so in a sense I didn't feel so alone. Charles always seemed to know how to say the right thing to ease the tension in a situation. The rest of the group included Billy Bang, Masujaa, Fred Hopkins, and Douglas Ewart on alto, flute, and bass clarinet. Originally from Jamaica, Douglas was the newest addition to the band. I had him flying in from Minneapolis, where he had made his home, to work with the Solomonic. Douglas and I had done the date *Namesake* together a few years before for the Silkheart label under the leadership of multi-instrumentalist Dennis Gonzalez. I liked Douglas's playing because of its cutting-edge quality. But it was the rapport we had in subsequent meetings that prompted me to reach out to him halfway across the country for this gig.

During my last trip to Minneapolis with Ra, Douglas had as usual come to the venue—this time the Glam Slam—to hang out and listen to the music. After the gig, he had come by the hotel, and we hung out through the wee hours. The handful of times we would get together, we always had lots of things to talk about. So when I thought of who should take Carlos Ward's place on the front line, Douglas came to mind with no hesitation.

The circumstances were rough for me. But I had been there before with my mother's death, and I knew how to get through the situation. When we got to Germany, I learned we were sharing the same bill with other groups, one led by Archie Shepp and featuring Yusef Lateef, another led by Andrew Cyrille with

Reggie Workman and Oliver Lake, and one led by saxophonist Teddy Edwards. In this company, I had to get over my remorse and hit hard, because none of these groups were taking any prisoners. There was some wonderful playing by all the groups. But Charles Moffett must have really been inspired, because on our set, during a drum solo, he asked for the microphone and began to sing. It was just enough of a surprise to push us all to another place and to bring the audience around to ask for more.

We had another gig the next day at a local club, which was great, because the three sets we did there allowed us to really bring out the sound of the unit. Our return home was marred by the sad news that June Tyson had been diagnosed with cancer, and because it had been detected so late she wasn't expected to live long.

The spiritualists say October is the window of the future. Events occurring in that month are supposed to indicate what will happen in the year to come. The death of loved ones was obviously the experience that lay ahead for me.

Toward the end of November, we received the news that June had passed. We were informed that she had been placed in hospice right around Thanksgiving. But I just couldn't bring myself to visit her. There had already been too much death, far too close, for me. June had only found out that she had cancer a few months before, when she returned from a vacation with Judith "Wisteria" Holton. Less than six months later, that angelic voice from outer space had been silenced.

Many of the members of the Arkestra, including myself, found themselves in Harlem at a church on 131st Street on the morning of December 1, singing the Hobart Dotson–Sun Ra song "Enlightenment" to give June a send-off. For years, whenever the band had gone on tour, Sun Ra always had us meet at June and Richard's, even after Richard was no longer serving as manager of the band. It was therefore appropriate that June would be funeralized right down the street from where she had been living and from where the Arkestra used to meet, two blocks from where I grew up.

Sun Ra had done his last gig with the Arkestra that prior August. After that, his health grew increasingly worse. There was no one at the house in Philly who could give him the kind of care he needed. Fall turned to winter, and Sunny was sent to the warmer climate of Birmingham, with Jothan Callins accompanying him. By the time June Tyson passed, Sunny had been hospitalized for a couple of weeks. No one wanted to tell him she had died.

That New Year's Eve, the Arkestra played in Portland, Maine, under John Gilmore's leadership. Monique and I rode to and from the gig with Billy Bang and his lady, I Ting, and their little son, Jay. John, still a bit leery of his new role, was getting more comfortable leading the band. However, there was a still a lot to be desired.

The months rolled by into the spring and my several families were being wrecked with death within months of each other. On March 29, 1993, Monique's birthday once again, I received a call from my son, Shahid. "Daddy. Mommy's dead. She was HIV positive."

These sentences hit me at once. *Iyabode dead? Iyabode had AIDS?* I'd noticed her loss of weight over the past few years. I had noticed that her attitude had changed remarkably the last few times I had seen her. She seemed so serene and accepting. I'd heard about the number of times she had been in and out of the hospital. And I had never gone to visit her, either. I was devastated.

I later found out that she had been infected with that illness since her daughter, Merakhu, had been born. It was even more horrendous and frightening to find out that not only was Iyabode HIV positive but her husband, Mumim, and their daughter were as well. It turned out that Iyabode had been carrying the illness for almost five years, and unfortunately she had learned of it during the time I had withdrawn from my sons. The issues in my own life had seemed more important to me, and I'd had no idea what they were facing.

It turned out as well that the boys had not known about their mother's illness until a year and a half before her passing. They had been asked not to tell me anything. Considering the immense stigma that was attached to AIDS, to have had to live with that information and to have been sworn to keep this secret from their father must have been a tremendous burden.

With Iyabode's death, I knew I had to rebuild love and trust with my sons. To begin with, I had to go into another man's house, where they were living. I had to muster up the courage to enter the house of a grieving and dying man who had lost his wife, would lose a child, and was trying to raise my teenage sons, whom I had practically abandoned.

It was a daunting task. When Mumin opened the door, I could feel his anger. By now, however, I was used to the anger people expressed during the loss of loved ones. I was aware that often-times anger—even when it is directed at you under those circum-stances—may not all be about you. Even so, it was difficult to take, because I, too, was angry. Angry that I had not been told directly that Iyabode was dying. Angry that she had died. Angry that my sons were not with me. Angry that I was in such a power-less position.

Most of my anger masked the fear I truly felt about death. There were just too many people I had known for years who were now dying. Even with the few times a year I saw my mother and father, there was still comfort in knowing they were alive. I had known Iyabode for more than twenty years, and she had given me two wonderful sons. I might not have been the best mate for her, but I know that, even in the ignorant way I demonstrated it, I loved her deeply. And certainly my sons had been born out of love.

That following May, I was asked to play a concert that was to serve as a tribute to Sun Ra. Vocalist Kitty Brazelton, wife of Jazz critic and author Howard Mandel, had organized some music for Sun Ra. I declined to do the gig because it was Memorial Day, and my family had made plans to be together on that day. I asked Robert Rutledge to do the gig in my stead. He agreed. With Monique in my life, I was getting my priorities in order.

It was shocking but appropriate that the day and date chosen to honor him would be the day Sun Ra would leave the planet. It was also a time for me to immerse myself in family concerns that further impressed upon me the fact that Sun Ra was indeed family.

At the time he left the planet, I had not been in contact with him except through Jothan Callins, my former roommate within the Arkestra, who was there in Birmingham. Jothan kept me abreast of Sun Ra's condition, which was certainly serious, as it had been for years. It was amazing that Sunny had been able to hold on as long as he did. He chose the time of his leaving the planet to be the time when it would have maximum impact, Memorial Day.

Plans were made to have a memorial tribute in New York at the Bottom Line, but there needed to be folks in Birmingham who would represent the Arkestra at the actual funeral as well. We needed money to make the trip. Elson and I had taken on the responsibility, independent of each other, to try to get some of the guys down to Birmingham. I had called everyone I could think of, even vibraphonist Jay Hoggard, who had made *Life's Force* with me. Jay was then Mayor David Dinkins's son-in-law. I thought there might be some emergency funding available to deal with such a situation as the death of a person as notable as Sun Ra. David Dinkins was a Jazz lover. And yet still, no luck.

It was now that I wished a Satellites of the Sun tribute had been launched, because it would have heightened the awareness of Sun Ra's importance and would probably have facilitated the task we had before us.

I remembered the donation made to Satellites of the Sun by the wealthy Sun Ra supporter and gave her a call. Folks had claimed she had some money, and she was getting public mileage out of her association with Sun Ra based on the one performance she'd done with the band while Sunny was alive. Her response, however, was negative. She told me that "those people down there" were not Sun Ra's family. His "real" family, she went on to tell me, were the people in the Arkestra. Since I hadn't called her for the purpose of tracing Sunny's genealogy, I realized there was no need to continue our conversation. What we needed was to attend a funeral, not argue about who should preside over it.

Three days into our respective efforts, Elson and I communicated to exchange notes. By the time we had filled each other in, I found out that some money had been given to Alton Abraham by Evidence Records to aid in Sun Ra's funeral and burial. Elson had also been in touch with Jack Reich in Rhode Island, who was ready to help out in some way.

Evidence reissues were flooding the market; however, only a minuscule portion of that money was actually going to the members of the Arkestra. The only one who could profit from them was Abe, as we called him. I thought that the cost of flying a few members of the Arkestra down to help send off Sun Ra would be a mere pittance. When I telephoned Alton, he gave me a long monologue on Sun Ra's sexuality. Sun Ra was nothing but a homosexual, he said, as if that possibility could justify ripping off Sunny's music and taking all the profits.

I was surprised at Abe. This was the first time in all our dealings that he verbally expressed any kind of disdain for Sunny. After his long monologue, he agreed to send money the next day. Elson and I had decided that five of us were going, and we'd learned that it would cost $2,000 to get five people to Birmingham and back.

When the money from Abe was not forthcoming and he became unavailable, we turned to Jack Reich, who put up his credit card after I personally gave my word that he would be repaid when we got the money Alton had promised. With that, Marshall Allen, Jack Jacson, Tyrone Hill, Elson, and I left New York on June 4, to arrive in Birmingham in time to attend the memorial wake. Jothan Callins, a native of the city and a cofounder of the Alabama Hall of Fame, to which Sun Ra had been previously inducted, had gotten hotel rooms courtesy of that institution. Jothan had been keeping in touch with Elson and myself, encouraging us to make this whole event happen while working closely with Sun Ra's family in planning the memorial.

John Gilmore voiced much objection to our going. But John was a sick man and, great saxophonist though he was, there were certain things he just didn't understand. What we were doing was spiritually correct, and the fact that seven of us finally showed up despite all obstacles proved it. Seven is a mystic number totally befitting the mysterious Mr. Ra. The seventh person was drummer Samarai Celestial, who had driven in from Knoxville.

At the memorial, I got a glimpse of the full musical life Sun Ra had lived in Birmingham prior to going to Chicago. There were people still alive who had worked in his earliest bands. There was a vocalist, for example, who spoke about Sunny's unique instructions to him that he remembered from fifty years before, "When you want to sing high, think low, and when you want to sing low, think high."

Another band member spoke of Sun Ra's uncanny ability to cop the latest arrangements from big bands all over the country through the use of wire recordings. Sunny, the man recounted, had highly developed ears combined with the notational ability to make his band the most popular and advanced in the city of Birmingham. John Szwed's *Space Is the Place* is most effective in the research done around that aspect of Sun Ra's life. A good portion of Szwed's biography deals with Sunny's life before he left the Magic City and re-created himself in Chicago.

Jothan did a great job of organizing the memorial program. The seven of us played with a local bassist, and with Jothan at the piano and on flugelhorn, we had a full ensemble. We played "Discipline 27"; "Enlightenment," a blues by Jothan; and "Space Is the Place." Besides the two people mentioned, many others came up to the podium in between musical selections and gave praises or read the poems of Sun Ra. Jothan gave me some time to speak on behalf of the Arkestra, and I expressed my feelings about the spiritual family we represented under Sunny's leadership. To emphasize the point, I ended by reading "Cosmic Evolution," a poem that highlights Sun Ra's take on the question.

The next day we rode to the cemetery for a graveside funeral. We were driven there in two white limousines, courtesy, I was told later, of Alton Abraham, whom I was shocked to see at the funeral. I was sure he was just as shocked to see us, as he had done nothing to help us get there. As if to play things off, Alton dealt with the proceedings in his usual authoritative and demeaning manner. He was going to try to instruct us on what to play, when to play it, and where we should stand, until he understood, by the way we ignored him, that his services were neither desired nor needed. We had already decided what we were going to play and how we were going to conduct things. As the coffin was closed, to begin the services, we played Sun Ra's "Interstellar Low Ways." And after the reading from the Scriptures and the sermon, we marched around the coffin singing, "*They'll come back, in shining ships of gold, with wisdom never told, a touch of myth-world splendor. And they'll take back, the others who are not; of Earth's dimension one. The others who are ready. Melody, harmonic rhythmic planes. Chromatic magic is, eternal outward on. Pleasant spheres. Nothing is, yet everything is all, a pleasant neverness. Mythic worlds, lightning, darkness.*" Sun Ra frequently chose that song for encores, and we chose it to send the Captain of the Spaceship home.

It was an emotionally full moment for all of us, so we congregated to collect ourselves and to console one another. When Abe came over to patronize us with his hollow compliments, I could barely contain my anger, so I walked as far away from him and the graveside as possible. I needed to get myself together, alone. Alton must have sensed something, because later on he walked over to me again and volunteered to send the money.

Our stay in Birmingham was short because we had a flight to catch back to LaGuardia Airport in New York. There was yet another memorial that John Gilmore was leading at the Bottom Line with an enlarged Arkestra. This event, which had been well advertised, was the most public statement of the assumption of leadership by John. Our flight arrived in New York in time for us to get to the Bottom Line just at showtime. Fortunately, Amiri Baraka and some other folks had been asked to speak before the Arkestra played, which gave me a moment to reflect on the seemingly impossible feat we had just accomplished.

To his credit, Alton did finally send me a $1,000 check. I promptly made a copy of the check and sent it to John Gilmore while sending the actual money to Jack Reich. John had apparently told Alton that Jack had fronted the money, and for whatever reason, Alton did not appreciate Jack's involvement. It was obvious that Alton didn't want us to get to Birmingham. So his conscience allowed him to give up only $1,000. Gilmore's relationship with Alton went back to their early days in Chicago. He felt a sense of loyalty to Abe that most of the other guys didn't feel. John was in many ways an innocent pure and beautiful spirit who didn't see ugliness in people. With Abe, that was a problem.

Alton Abraham had a plan for the Sun Ra Arkestra. He had already tasted the profits coming from the reissuance of Saturn Records on Evidence. There was some question as to whether he could continue supplying recordings to Evidence with Sun Ra no longer alive. It was rumored that Abe had somehow coerced Sunny into signing the contract for those recordings that had already been released, but after Sun Ra left the planet Abe would have to deal with Sunny's estate. To build a case for his claim on the estate, Abe was attempting to control the Arkestra. He had created stories that cast himself as the teacher and originator of the entire persona of Sun Ra: name, philosophy, dress, and all. Abe intended for John to aid him in his exploitation of the Sun Ra legacy.

Considering that John did not want the responsibility of leading the band, he was more than willing to turn over control to Abe. After all, he had done the same with Sun Ra throughout his life, and Sun Ra had always taken care of him.

The problem here was that Sun Ra had not left a will, and because of that, his entire estate legally went to his family in Birmingham. It is important to remember that Sun Ra spent more time in Birmingham than he had spent in any other place on this planet. He was in his thirties when he left the Magic City. It seemed right that his family in Birmingham should inherit his estate, given the fact that he hadn't provided for any other stipulation, though he had plenty of opportunity to do so.

John Gilmore's poor choice of Abraham over Sun Ra's family was broadcast in a *DownBeat* article written by John Corbett. The writer quoted John extensively and suggested that the situation might be a common one, in which a family has no relationship to the artist, yet wants to claim all of the artist's royalties. In Sun Ra's case, this was a fabrication. Contrary to what anybody in the music world wrote or said, it wasn't the family who were scheming on Sun Ra's estate. Without a will specifying who should get what, everything goes to his legally recognized kinfolk, period. Alton was manipulating John. John was in turn allowing his reputation and credibility to be used to bolster the counter claim that Alton Abraham was about to make against the estate. The only thing Sun Ra's family might be accused of was ignorance of the celebrity status of their illustrious relative. We were already quite familiar with Sunny's sister, Mary Jenkins, having spent moments with her on several occasions when the band visited Birmingham to perform. I had also met and spoken with his niece, Marie Holsten, at Sunny's memorial. Both of them came off as highly principled, upstanding Christian women. Old-school Southern Baptist, straight up.

The problem with Abraham was serious simply because the need at that time was to forge an effective alliance with Sun Ra's family in order to continue his work and to prevent the vultures from looking for ways to put out bootlegged material and otherwise pimp his legacy. John's inability to see this was to prove costly. But then again, he had his hands full.

Those who knew some of this inside information did not believe in the ability of the Arkestra to carry on after Sun Ra had passed. I often wondered if even John thought it possible. Coupled with his sense of self-doubt was the proliferation of tributes to Sun Ra that many people in the Arkestra were asked to make. This only added to the confusion. Many questions came up: Who should lead the Arkestra in the wake of Sun Ra's death? Was there going to be an Arkestra? Who should be the one to contact?

To add to it all, in his willingness to abdicate certain responsibilities, John had given charge of the Arkestra's bookings to Gloria Powers, Michael Ray's partner. As a result, people were getting mixed signals as to the state of things. Gloria wasn't booking the Arkestra. She was booking Michael. After years of struggling with Sun Ra, John now decided he wanted the Arkestra to work for top dollar only. Between these two points, Gloria ended up offering venues a cheapened version of the Arkestra with Michael at the helm. In turn, Michael would form various tribute bands that featured Sun Ra's music, along with garish costumes, and make use of a few Arkestra members. But it wasn't the Arkestra. It was Gloria and Michael building a reputation for the Cosmic Krewe. John and I were the only Arkestra members who refused to participate in this mess. Through a contact that Philippa had in Brad Simon's office, I found out that the confusion as to who was leading the Arkestra was affecting the possibility of work for the band. When I explained what I had heard to John and warned him of the consequences, his reply was, "I can't stop anybody from doing what they're gonna do."

"But of course you can," I countered. "You gave them permission!"

We had a Philadelphia gig in the fall of 1993 that was recorded by the Voice of America—Alton Abraham dealt with the contract. After my recent business dealings with Abe, I was not going to allow him to have control of a performance I was to be a part of. I protested to John and he acquiesced and assigned Jack Jacson and me to handle the negotiations in order to procure the master tape from that concert.

At first we were welcomed by the Voice of America people, who, we came to find out, were old friends of Abe's. After a while, however, they stopped returning our phone calls. What was happening became clear when I received a call from Abe, who told me in no uncertain terms to back off, to leave the business alone; he was handling it, he said. He also once again told me how Sun Ra was nothing but a homosexual anyway, as if that justified his exploitation of and control over us. But it was John's call. He was leading the Arkestra. When John later told Jacson and me to leave the matter alone and let Abe deal with it, we did. That, however, was a wake-up call for me in understanding the hopelessness of the situation, the difficulty of overcoming what was clearly weak leadership. Between what Abe, Gloria, and Michael were doing,

I began to conclude that all of this was really a waste of my time. And it was also part and parcel of Sun Ra's legacy.

With all the recent deaths in my life combined with the stress from being in this weird limbo land, I too was growing extremely ill. I first noticed my illness at my sons' Brooklyn Tech graduation ceremony. Sitting in the balcony of the school's auditorium, watching my sons graduate from my own alma mater, I was overcome with emotion.

Thoughts raced through my mind. With all that I had done in my life, I was here to be at my sons' graduation. Iyabode had been like an angel, and yet I was here to celebrate with them and she wasn't. I felt so unworthy and guilty. Somehow this manifested in problems with my stomach. Sitting in that auditorium, I began breaking out in a cold sweat. I didn't know what it was, psychological or physical, but the pain in my stomach would subside and arise and continue for a long time.

Monique and I were also struggling. She had come to America to live but she had left her support system, her family and friends, in England. She expected me to be her support, but I was too busy being angry, guilty, and frustrated. My belief system was going through its own overhaul. All of it had been building up into emotional stress and physical ailments. I was expecting her to be my support system, not myself to be hers.

Monique had been doing quite well in England, having carved out a middle-class existence for herself. She had graduated with honors from the prestigious University of Bristol, and had been employed in government administration. Back home, she had her own car and apartment and was quite independent. Something about America, perhaps her lack of psychological support, completely turned her around. At first, here, she wasn't working at all or looking for work. Finally she got a job at a driving school for six dollars an hour. Her job reflected the level to which her self-esteem had sunk since her arrival here.

I was going through my own deep changes. The year before, it had looked as if I would never have to drive a cab again. Music was happening for me. For the past four years, I had been on a roll. My band was working, Sun Ra was working, arts in education projects were happening. Now, with my marriage to Monique, Philippa no longer wanted to book the Solomonic Sextet. It was also obvious by now that nothing was happening with the Sun Ra Arkestra, and the educational work I was doing only made up a fraction of my income. I was feeling like Monique had become so dependent that I couldn't leave town even if I had a gig. But the fact was that I didn't have a gig. So I went back to the thing I knew I could always earn money doing—driving a cab. This time I went back on a full-time basis. We needed full-time money. In the middle of this downside-up existence hitting us from everywhere, I received a call in December from Columbia University's WKCR. A young woman, Jennifer McNeely, and a young man, Ben Young, had become familiar with my music through the Solomonic Unit, and in researching WKCR's rich archives had become familiar with some of my history. They explained that they were planning a marathon special, 117 hours, similar to that which had been done on Sun Ra's music back in 1987. This time, however, they wanted to focus on a specific era, the Loft Movement. I was told they wanted to do a five-hour focus on my work alone. They also wanted my band and Bluiett's group to close out the marathon with a live concert at one of the theaters at Columbia. A glimmer of hope was rising for me. Something that I had been a part of was being given some solid attention, and Bluiett and I were being singled out. Perhaps I was not wrong, after all.

While I was planning for the show, Monique's aunt Gwen, one of her favorite people, passed away. Consequently, she had to go back to London and was not in New York for either the marathon or the concert.

During my five hours on live radio I played tapes that had rarely been heard as well as some of my recorded pieces. It was an exciting day for me, providing just the kind of uplift I needed to encourage me to do more.

The day of the concert was the coldest day I could remember. Yet we had an excellent house. The Solomonic Sextet was once again a quintet, as bassist John Ore had difficulty making the gig because of the extreme cold. Carlos Ward, Billy Bang, Masujaa, and Charles Moffett came to play, despite the arctic blast outside. My sons, Rashid and Shahid, also came to the gig. They were enrolled now as undergrads at the University of Maryland. Our relationship had improved somewhat, as Rashid had come to stay with us during the summer before attending college.

In February 1994, just a few weeks after the event at Columbia and Aunt Gwen's death, we received a call at two in the morning from my sister Helen. She was distressed because her daughter, Lisa, had been taken to the hospital in serious condition. At twenty-six, Lisa had been asthmatic most of her life, but this attack proved fatal. She had three children, Eric, Jason, and Jocellyne, who were left in my sister's care. Monique and I had been taking the three little ones to the annual Thanksgiving Day Parade, and so we had developed a real rapport with them. As my sister took on the responsibility of raising her grandchildren, Monique and I tried to help out by including them in our lives as much as possible.

The mounting emotional pressure I was still feeling began to take bizarre effect on my physical body. By now, my Buddhist practice had allowed me to leave all forms of drug abuse cold turkey. My body, however, seemed to be reacting to the combination of years of abuse and all these recent emotional strains. Driving a cab full time as Monique continued to make adjustments to New York's reality added more stress.

Whatever my illness was, it began to manifest in all kinds of different ways throughout my body. Stuff started oozing out of me, from my head, from my skin. I was getting rashes that itched. My penis was swelling up to the point that I had to sit on the toilet to urinate because I couldn't be sure I would aim straight. Stuff was oozing out of that part of my anatomy as well. My life was bordering on hell, but I had to continue driving a cab through all of this because of our financial state.

My condition remained this way for several weeks. When it got too intense, I would go to the emergency room, sometimes with Monique at my side, seeking relief. I was treated as if I were a freak. They had never before seen anyone in my condition. Doctors were called in to look at the size of my penis as if I were a laboratory specimen. The one thing I needed from them was a diagnosis, and that was one thing I didn't receive. They gave me several prescriptions of antibiotics, some of which I took, most of which I didn't.

The one useful piece of advice I was given at the emergency room was in reference to my clothing. They explained that I needed to wear loose-fitting clothes because whatever this thing was, it was leaking through my underwear, and it was further aggravated by tight underwear or anything that wasn't appropriately roomy.

Obviously, by now it was clear to me that Western medicine wasn't cutting it. I really needed an alternative medical cure. Philippa had recommended a naturopath who dealt with cell salt and other cures that encouraged the body to cleanse itself. Monique and I went to visit this woman in the fall of 1994. She recommended a combination of homeopathic remedies that eventually gave me a positive result. My physical illness could not be diagnosed as such because I was actually suffering a spiritual and mental illness. My body was letting me know that I was in need of intense therapy.

Later, on one of the few gigs we had under John Gilmore's leadership, Arkestra drummer Buster Smith told me that Local 802 had been apprised of the condition of all the band members and that I could go there and get financial help, if I needed it. He told me I should contact a fellow by the name of Mike Cipressi. It turned out that Mike worked for a benevolent and much-needed Musicians' Assistance Program that had been created to deal with just the condition I was in. MAP had been designed for musicians who'd been around for a while and had fallen on hard times. Besides getting me a couple of thousand dollars from MAP that I wasn't required to pay back, Mike Cipressi was a counselor in the program who understood the problems musicians encountered in life. He was someone who would listen to me, someone whom I could speak to on a regular basis. He helped me recognize that what I truly needed was a regular therapist. My problems were too deep-seated. So he referred me to a place in the Village, on Thirteenth Street, that would set me up with a regular therapist. Mike also told me that he could talk with the other guys in the Arkestra if I could arrange to bring them together. I didn't think I could do that then, as so many of the cats were based in Philly.

Lee Phillips was the therapist I was placed with. Lee, like Mike, was white. And though I'd known this before going to his office—having discussed it with the woman who had referred me—I still felt some initial discomfort. I was willing to try a white man because Monique and I had tried marriage counseling with an African American male during our first year, when our relationship was climbing on shaky ground. I found that experience to be a disaster, and it made me feel hopeless. The major problem we had was that we were both needy and vying for the attention of the therapist. Because of the enormity of our demands, what we both needed was individual treatment.

My physical illness might have even resulted from that aborted attempt at therapy. It didn't help our home life, which was a constant battle zone between two frustrated people working beneath our capacities and wondering, I guess, if either of us had made the right decision about our marriage. There had been lots of good times, but the string of deaths we had experienced from the beginning, along with what had been happening with me, created a lot of doubt.

In all of the turmoil that we'd encountered as a married couple, we were fortunate to have married as Buddhists. The instructions we had been given on our wedding day by Kazuo Fuji, the man who married us, correctly predicted the hell we were experiencing. It has been said that 50 percent of all marriages end in divorce after the first five years. If those people were married, as we were originally, by the state, it is understandable why, without any ceremony or ritual, their unions could have easily ended in divorce. But we were fortunate to have been married differently. Our Buddhist wedding address began like this:

> Marriage is without doubt the most important ceremony of life because, although it may seem paradoxical, the success of this partnership depends upon the ability of both husband and wife to give to this world their full creative value as individual human beings. Through their united resolve before the Gohonzon to create a wonderfully harmonious yet essentially progressive unit of society, founded upon the rock of their deep respect for each other's lives, they draw out from each other the Three Poisons of anger, greed, and stupidity, which might otherwise afflict their family life with misery for their lifetime. At the same time, through their victory in this struggle they are able to send out waves of peace and friendship, not only to the community that immediately surrounds them but the whole country and the whole world.
>
> The relationship between husband and wife is the foundation of society because not only do they have it in their power to bring fresh new lives into this world but also their home and family should be, in the words of our Buddhist teacher, "an open fortress of faith" that is invincible to attack from the outside yet is open to all who approach in friendship or with seeking minds. It establishes a firm base of faith anchored to the great Middle Way of the Gohonzon and founded upon trust, from which the family can go forth daily into society, shining with the vital energy, wisdom, and compassion that arises from the universal life-force flowing through their lives. Nichiren Daishonin explained it in the Gosho this way: "The hiyoku is a bird with one body and two heads. Both of its mouths nourish the same body. Hiboku are fish with only one eye each, so the male and female remain together for life. A husband and wife should be like them."

We were instructed to stay together first five years, then ten years, then twenty, and then forever. It was an important instruction because it was something that we could refer back to in troubled times.

From the fall of 1994 until February 1997, I went to Lee Phillips's office on Christopher Street to talk through the challenges that had been with me all of my life without my ever understanding them to be that. Initially, I was totally resistant to Lee's whiteness, and that reality would manifest itself in various ways. On some occasions, I would arrive late; on others, I wouldn't explore issues in detail with him. Most times I would find current political issues as topics of discussion that would have little specific relation to my life. At other times, when I spoke of things closer to home, it would usually be about Monique and what she was or wasn't doing. I was going through issues with John Gilmore as the leader of the Sun Ra Arkestra and that, too, was explored. As well, my relationship with Sun Ra was looked at.

My resistance to therapy also took on many forms. I went from fierce arguments with Monique to hours of television watching, or listening to talk radio and getting upset. Generally, I got really angry about things I had no control over.

The fact that Lee Phillips was white allowed me to vent my anger directly at what I saw as the political ideology of whiteness. And after all that energy was spent, what was left was me and the issue of my own identity. It was at the point that he told me he was Jewish that some rapport between us arose.

In my understanding of American reality, this multitiered society we exist in is very complex. There are a number of issues we have to confront to get to the truth of our own individual beings. One reality relates to how other ethnic groups are presented with the option of being "white" in relationship to Black folks, whose only option is to be humane. What I mean by that is that when an immigrant comes to this country as Jewish, Italian, Irish, Greek, Polish, after a generation or less in America he or she becomes "white" or "American," the two words oftentimes meaning the same thing. With that whiteness comes privileges that allow enough self-justification, a sense of superiority over the permanent Black underbelly of this society, to encourage conditions to remain the

same. That becomes the reality as those ethnicities become angli-
fied/white and move into positions of authority (quicker than
Africans who have been here for centuries) as policemen, teachers,
lawyers, judges, and politicians, doing the bidding of a wealthy
corporate elite that never really has to do the dirty work. As
Africans in this society, we are asked to be understanding of this
confused reality. But for some Africans, the politics of "whiteness" becomes attractive enough that we distance ourselves from
our roots and cultures.

Therapy is an interesting calling. Ultimately, if one is true to
that vocation, one has to thoroughly scrutinize the position of
privilege in this society and its resultant effect. I believe America
is desperately in need of healing. But for me the place to begin is
with the man in the mirror. Once I was able to open up to Lee
Phillips, the subject he kept bringing me back to was the loss of
my sister Marilyn. He was able to convince me that the recent
rash of deaths had brought that particular unresolved grief to the
surface for me. The physical illness that had brought me to therapy, the smell and the ooze, was a reenactment, Lee felt, of my
sister's condition prior to her death.

As much as I wanted to resist this theory and the insistence
with which Lee kept bringing me back to this incident from
thirty-some years before, my Buddhist practice made me aware
that the deepest karma we have is with our family. So, in an odd
way, I was beginning to understand that just as it was Marilyn's
death that had brought me to music—in an effort to express the
deep emotion I felt—it was the Arkestra and Sun Ra who had
provided the family I so needed. It was this sense of family that
served to explain why I continued to go back to the Arkestra again
and again. Then Charles Moffett came into my life and gave me a
chance to examine the great benefit of family. Of course, doing so
requires a great deal of courage, because it often isn't easy to live
with the hand you've been dealt.

# XI
# ADIOS, JOHN

It's always interesting and moving; it would have
to be [for me] to have stayed for thirty years. Never
a dull moment. Every day there's always something
happening and there's always fresh music. So what
other situation could you ask for that would be any
better if you're a musician and really love music for
music's sake, not for money and all that? You would
look for an ideal situation where you could satisfy
your musical hunger.
—John Gilmore, on staying with Sun Ra

With Sun Ra gone, the Arkestra family had become more overtly
dysfunctional and extremely difficult to deal with—especially in
my newly awakening state. For years I had played with the band
and, like everyone else, hadn't concerned myself with many of
the responsibilities that make a band possible: organizing musical
arrangements, rehearsals, and travel accommodations; negotiating contracts; establishing contacts, etc. For the most part, all we
did was show up to play. Now to work with this group required
assuming those responsibilities while others were still abandoning theirs. The state of the Arkestra was in reality a reflection of
the condition each of us had been in for years. I was only now
looking at things through a different lens. In this regard, both the
practice of Buddhism and my therapy sessions with Lee were of
great help to me.

Since Sunny's death, the Arkestra had been inching along,
doing a gig every two months. In performances, the band relied
on tunes that had been played so much that there was no need for
rehearsal. And the norm had become an endless string of solos.
The leader of the Arkestra, John Gilmore, was seriously in bad
shape. He had been smoking Sherman cigarettes for years and did

A STRANGE
CELESTIAL ROAD

Ahmed Abdullah
with Louis Reyes Rivera

little exercising. As a result, he was suffering with emphysema, looking unhealthily thin.

Our last gig under John's leadership was at Princeton University on a cold, wet day in the early spring of 1995. On that occasion, John was so weak that he couldn't make it up to the bandstand. His heart had never been in leading the band, and with all the vultures preying on whatever wasn't nailed down or hidden, by May 1995 he was ready to turn the reins over to Marshall Allen.

Marshall, though older than John, was a lot healthier and a much more social being. John roomed by himself and hardly ever hung out when we were on the road, even in his healthier years. Marshall, on the other hand, could always be found at the bar hanging out with the fellas, and he and Michael Ray roomed together throughout the later years. John inspired respect for his tremendous musical ability while Marshall inspired respect for both his persona and his musical ability. So when John turned the group over to Marshall, new life flowed through the Arkestra. Marshall knew he didn't know much about leading the band, and to his credit, he was open to people who did know helping him.

○

During this transitional period between John and Marshall, a few of the guys had moved into position as John's advisors. These were among the weaker individuals in the Arkestra who had been sucking up to John in his deteriorating state to the point where he relied on them to the exclusion of most everyone else.

As Marshall began taking over, he inherited many of these characters. I had a rapport with him that grew out of the couple of gigs we had done under his leadership since Sunny's passing. These were occasions when John could not make it. On those gigs, Marshall had relied on me to pick the songs for the band to play. Our relationship had strengthened to the point where I could once again attempt to assert more input regarding the band's direction.

That July there was talk of a California tour. The Arkestra had not done any touring in three years, and if truth be told, by then,

450

there was barely an Arkestra left to speak of. I wondered to myself why I had even bothered to make some of the gigs that had come up. Too often they were only exercises in frustration. The pathetic jockeying for position done by individuals whom Sun Ra had long since gotten rid of, but who saw new opportunity with John and Marshall, completely turned me off.

An example of these "political maneuverings" became glaringly obvious during a gig that July 30 at Tuxedo Junction, a club in Danbury, Connecticut. Marshall and John had turned the business dealings for the California tour over to a drummer who, though a cool enough individual, had never been permitted by Sunny to be the only drummer in the Arkestra.

On any important occasion, Sunny would use one of three drummers: Buster Smith, Samarai Celestial, or Clifford Barbaro. These were the ones Sunny relied on to be the main drummers in the band, at least since 1988. Anybody else playing drums would work only in tandem with one of these three. While any one of them could be the only ones featured on drums, no one else at the time knew Sunny's music well enough to be the only drummer. Since this particular individual was taking care of the California deal and since we were working with a limited budget, he made sure that this time he would be the only drummer on the tour. Considering that the Arkestra had been presumed dead, the tour itself presented us with our biggest opportunity to date to show that we could carry on without Sunny. And the all-important role of the drummer was crucial to our success.

After watching what I felt was the inept way this fellow was taking care of business when we finished the gig in Connecticut, I got fed up with his posturing and lost it. Aside from the way he had placed himself within the California gig, what pissed me off in Connecticut was the way he played us off when it came time to dole out the money. He had us all waiting around to get paid while he was somewhere else with a pocket full of cash. When he finally made it back to pay me, I let go.

"What the fuck you think you doin'? You supposed to be handling this tour to California?"

"Yeah. I'm takin' care of it," he replied.

"Well, let me tell you something," I said, now all up in his face. "If you handle that like you handlin' this, you better get your shit together. And quick, goddamn it! Because I'm not goin' no three thousand miles to California with some bullshit. Some mother-fucker like you frontin' like he's in charge of some shit and don't know his ass from his elbow."

I was pissed off and angry and so out of character that I surprised everyone who saw what had gone down. But I felt that enough was enough. Someone had to take a stand. And so I did. In the process, I said what I wanted and got it out of my system.

I had another problem with our new leadership: the exclusion of Elson. Others might not have considered Elson an essential musician, but he had played a critical role in getting a group of us to Birmingham a couple of years before. The individuals who had curried favor with John had sought to completely remove Elson from the picture.

I gave Elson a call and expressed my concern about his being left out. Elson was one of the few Sun Ra had trusted to deal with the fine details that come with transporting a band from one place to another. As Sunny's secondary point man, Elson had the most experience in covering details while keeping costs to a bare mini-mum. And here our new center drummer had not only become the shot caller, but also helped to exclude the one person I knew could be trusted to get things done. I could tell by Elson's voice that he was extremely disappointed. He thanked me for calling and we hung up.

The Arkestra was in such a transitional period, it was hard to determine who was making decisions or why.

When we got to California, I learned that a woman named Sue Pearlstine had booked the gig and that the drummer I had cursed out was working with her, along with Jacson and Tyrone Hill. We were scheduled to record some of the gigs to be performed at Kimball's East in Emeryville. Our first gig, however, was in Santa Cruz. I was excited about being in a brass section with Michael and Tyrone again, and every chance we had, we'd rehearse by ourselves. Just as Sun Ra had always insisted on the discipline of rehearsing, we took it upon ourselves to rework the material.

While we were rehearsing in the hotel room on our first day in California, the television's cable box rather mysteriously fell to the floor. A few hours later, while we were standing outside Kuumbwa Jazz, where our performance was, a limb from the tree above us fell to the ground. Still later, in the dressing room, a six-pack fell to the floor, several bottles breaking. In none of these instances was any one of us close enough to have caused the incidents.

I didn't know what to make of these things, but I knew that when things happen in threes there is something of importance about to occur.

Another occurrence during the California trip revolved around my sons' sister, Merakhu, who was living close to our hotel in Oakland. Her father, Mumin, had driven her 3,000 miles across country and then died, leaving her with the woman who was the mother of some of his other children. Iyabode's friends in New York, along with Rashid and Shahid, were concerned about Merakhu. It was more than coincidental that Maisha Ali, the woman taking care of their sister, lived less than a mile from the hotel we stayed at. I made a point of visiting her while out there and was fortunate that my friend Mary Vivian, who lived in Oakland, had a car and knew how to find the house Merakhu was living in.

When we arrived at the house, Merakhu was standing at the door. I was surprised to see her looking so much like her mother in every way. Her complexion, her eyes, her neck—it was as if I was looking at a miniature version of the woman who was the mother of my sons. Even though she was not my daughter, somehow I felt that Iyabode would have wanted me to make this visit. I'm glad I did.

Though sparsely attended, the gigs we had in California went well, except that no one seemed to appreciate the drummer. No one, that is, except me. I had already spent my fury and made my apologies, because at that point, there was nothing that could be done. I fully understood how and why he was on this gig. It had everything to do with this transitional phase the Arkestra was going through. I thought the music actually sounded pretty damn good. There were a number of people in the audience who had expressed the same feelings as well. Edsel Matthews, for instance, of Koncepts Cultural Gallery, who had heard the band on many occasions, thought this was one of our better gigs.

Unusual for me, I roomed with Jack Jacson while we were in California. As it turned out, this was a good thing because it gave us an opportunity to engage in some in-depth conversations about where the band was going and how we each envisioned its future. Jacson and I had collaborated on an attempt to get a tape of a live Arkestra performance from Alton Abraham. In the process, we had formed a sort of a bond, even though we were unsuccessful in getting the tape. As well, Jacson had been working on establishing a Sun Ra Arkestra foundation, which (he thought) would have created an independent entity that would allow the band to continue unhampered by any legal wrangling.

One night after a gig we were in the room talking, and Jacson suggested that it would be great if the band, sounding as good as it did, could find a steady situation on New York's Lower East Side like Sunny had done in the mid-1960s. I thought it was a good idea and filed it away for further consideration.

A few days into our Emeryville engagement, on August 19, we got word that John Gilmore was in critical condition and wasn't expected to live. Those three objects that had fallen three days earlier suddenly began making sense. We performed that night a little on the uneasy side, but out loud we dedicated the music to John's swift recovery.

On the next day, Judith "Wisteria" Holton, who danced and sang with us on these gigs, invited the band to her house for brunch. The invitation had been offered several days before; no one knew or expected that the occasion would fall on the day John Gilmore would leave the planet. That news had come to us the first thing that morning. It seemed quite appropriate that we should all be together to break bread, somehow easing the pain. Noël Scott shared a poignant statement with the group, an excerpt from *On*

*This Day*, a daily meditation guide, that completely expressed the deep feelings most of us felt.

Marshall was obviously moved, but his expression of things intensely emotional would have to wait until we got onstage.

The news of John's death had been broadcast on the Oaktown radio. For our last night at Kimball's, we had a full house in that fairly large room. The music that night was the most exciting the band had created in the past three years. Marshall was playing with a passion that was uncontainable, and he influenced us all to rise to the occasion. After all, this was the Sun Ra Arkestra.

When we arrived back in New York on August 22, I found out from my therapist that the *New York Times* had done an obituary on John. Over the next couple of days, WKCR played sixteen hours of music in which John was featured. With me as her contact person, Philippa Jordan had booked her first gig for the Arkestra at Sounds of Brazil (SOB's), a nightspot in downtown Manhattan. Now, with Gilmore's death, the gig was turned into a memorial.

I stayed in New York for a couple of days and then Monique and I went out of town for a mini-vacation. Rashid and Shahid were still down at the University of Maryland at College Park, so we went to visit them on campus. They were both involved in relationships with young women at the school, and we all went out to eat and socialize. I related the incident about seeing their sister in California, which they naturally found incredible.

We returned to New York on Thursday in enough time for the SOB's gig. The media coverage that had been given to the event, both in the *Times* and on the WKCR broadcasts, brought a good-size audience to the club. In spite of the fact that no one from Philadelphia showed up for the 3 p.m. sound check and that Tyrone and Michael, who had both played California, were unable to attend this event, it was a huge success. There were plenty of brass players, such as Virgil Jones, Dick Griffin, Al Evans, and Earle Davis, and some reed players, including Marshall, Charles Davis, Noël Scott, and Jacson, to make it all good. Violinist Billy Bang showed up, as did guitarist Bruce Edwards, and drummers

Buster Smith, C. Scoby Stroman, Craig Haynes, and Elson Nascimento helped to round it all out.

An incident occurred on this gig between Billy Bang, who was basically sitting in, and Noël Scott and Bruce Edwards that gave an indication of the coming conceptual battle that was rarely articulated but existed under the surface and would no doubt have serious impact on my relationship with the Arkestra.

Bruce and Noël were musicians who were exploring paths in music that had been etched out respectively by Wes Montgomery and Charlie Parker. They had a good grounding in the fundamentals of music, but one would hardly think of their music as adventurous, avant-garde, or spacey in any sense of those terms. Sun Ra, as the leader of the band, had managed to employ people with a wide variety of musical styles and keep them all under one umbrella. After all, his musical understanding covered the total history and future of the music. John Gilmore didn't work the band enough to have to deal with our stylistic differences, but under Marshall's leadership, we were heading into new territory.

When Billy began to play in the adventurous way that he does, asking Noël and Bruce for information regarding the changes and key signatures of a particular number, they reacted in a hostile manner. Billy became really irate; he actually stopped playing, packed up his violin, and left the stage. After all, he was Billy Bang. And who were these keepers of the flame who had no name recognition anywhere outside the Sun Ra Arkestra? And didn't the Arkestra have a reputation and audience based on the idea of pushing the envelope? Fortunately, Monique checked out what was happening and went to the dressing room to talk to Billy. He told her he would return to the stage only because of the friendship he and I had, and that basically "those cats could go fuck themselves."

I acted as emcee that night and took care of paying the musicians for the gig. I was assuming responsibility and doing what I had been saying I'd do for the past couple of years. So often within the Arkestra, folks would complain about situations but rarely would initiate actions necessary to amend things. That was always somebody else's job. The choices I saw available to me were to be a force in influencing direction, continue being victimized through non-action, or leave.

Therapy had helped me to get back on track with my Solomonic band. I was ready to begin self-producing again, and I had found the place to do it. In September, I produced a gig at Context, a combination rehearsal studio/performance space on Avenue A between Second and Third. In preparing for this gig, I used a fellow named Kojo Ade as a publicist/audience development person to help me attract an audience. Context, though situated in one of the hottest areas in New York, had not developed the kind of reputation to attract crowds. While it had a performance space, Context was not yet known as a venue for regular entertainment.

In addition to the therapy sessions I was still involved in, I had recently met a young fellow who had a good effect on my effort to begin work with my own band once again. Tom Sibley, a young filmmaker, and writer Steve Cannon, who had been in the Village for ages, got into my cab one night on their way to see David Murray at Sweet Basil. Tom would later tell me that the conversation we had impressed him enough to follow up with a phone call. He and I soon began working on a project that involved my telling him about my life in music. It was a motivating and empowering experience. Similar to the five-hour show I had done on WKCR the previous year, it made me see that I had something unique to offer.

Though the turnout was lower than expected, the Solomonic Sextet's gig went well, musically speaking. I used Carlos Ward, John Ore, Masujaa, and Charles Moffett, essentially the same group I had taken to Europe a few years before, but with the addition of cellist Kash Killion. This talented musician had worked with Sun Ra on a couple of occasions in both Emeryville and Europe. Most recently, he had been hired by Sue Pearlstine to work with the Arkestra under Marshall's leadership on our gig at Kimball's. He added a wonderful dimension to the band, keeping the music exciting.

It occurred to me that the problem of audience development I was experiencing at Context was no different than the problem experienced by the Arkestra as witnessed in California that previous August at Kimball's. On that gig, the only well-attended performance had been on the last day, with all the publicity surrounding John Gilmore's death. The lack of attendance for the other gigs we had done there was probably due as much to the irregularity of our performances as it was to a public lack of confidence in the Arkestra without Sun Ra. If the Arkestra could perform somewhere regularly, audience development could be better realized. Once Context established itself as a regular performance venue, it, too, would garner a solid base of patrons. And these were related issues.

I recalled having a conversation with Jacson about the need for a spot in New York where the band could work on a regular basis. For me, this was a way of addressing both problems. I needed a place to work with my group and the Arkestra needed a steady performance venue in New York. Context had the potential to be that place. Once again the Buddhist precept of doing something for self and doing something for others was bearing itself out to yield a win-win result.

Saxophonist Ed Montgomery, the proprietor of Context, was totally open to the idea of the Arkestra working there on a regular basis. After confirming arrangements and dates with him I contacted Philadelphia to test the reaction.

Marshall and Jacson had been friends for years. Besides playing music together, they did odd carpentry, plumbing, and house-painting jobs to generate income. Marshall had given Jacson the nickname Buffeye, and we know that if Marshall names you, it sticks. Jacson and Marshall's relationship had strengthened since John's death and Marshall's ascension as leader. Marshall, although getting a little more comfortable commanding the band, wanted nothing to do with business. He was beginning to rely on Jacson to take over that department. I was envisioning a three-way leadership structure for several reasons. I was in New York, where much of the action was, and I had strong desire to see the band succeed. I also had a certain understanding of business I was willing to share with the two of them. It was the camaraderie of the Arkestra, that sense of brotherhood I imagined others felt, that made this band something I was willing to fight for.

The Arkestra had to completely re-create itself. Since Sun Ra's departure, public confidence in the group had waned under Gilmore's leadership. Under Marshall, our stature had to be reestablished. There were a few loyal fans, but there were many who thought the band was finished without Sun Ra, and two years under John's control was enough to convince anyone of that. We had a really difficult job before us.

I had gotten a positive response from Jacson and Marshall regarding the Context performances. I explained up front that my intention was to build a place that would act as a base of operation for both the Arkestra and the Solomonic Sextet. Our first series of concerts were set for the end of November 1995. They were billed as The Sun Ra Arkestra under the Direction of Marshall Allen returns to the Lower East Side. Monique and I called our company Melchizedek Music Productions, referencing the name of power I'd been given by the seeress back in 1986. With this name, in keeping with the spiritual nature of Sun Ra's music, we would summon the angelic forces of brotherhood to protect us. And protect us they did.

I worked out a deal with Ed Montgomery that allowed the band an opportunity to rehearse in the space prior to the concert so we could effectively tighten up our repertoire while adding new pieces. Rehearsing in New York would also allow other musicians to join in and get familiar with Sun Ra's music. A successful big band has to have a number of players available at any given time. Things were set up so that after each rehearsal there would be enough time to take a break and prepare for the gig.

While we'd been in California, Wisteria had made some new gold lamé outfits for us that were quite stunning. We had also taken a group shot that I had gotten a copy of from Sue Pearlstine and placed on the flyer. All the work I had done in producing my own concerts during the loft years and the work I had done with the Group was now being replicated and revised at Context. The major help I got was from Ed, who provided the space and a low-priced ad, and Monique, who made flyers and press releases and sat in the drafty doorway and collected money. Of course, we were helping to build Ed's place, which gave him a vested interest in having us. But I believed we shared a common goal; after all, it wasn't as if people were begging the Sun Ra Arkestra or the Solomonic Sextet to work anywhere in the fall of 1995.

Marshall and Jacson proceeded to organize the guys in the band for the first gig. To their credit, many of the band members did show up for the rehearsal and the gig. Some of the box-office money was used for transportation from Philly to New York. But it was important for Marshall, as the leader, to have an understanding of the need to invest in the future of the Arkestra. Monique and I were putting out far more than we could ever get back in terms of time, money, and effort to produce these concerts. If they worked, we would benefit just as Context and the Arkestra would benefit. But Marshall had the most to gain from our endeavors. It was therefore his job to inspire the musicians to come out for these gigs as Sun Ra had done in the past. But this wasn't something he always understood. The major complaint heard from members of the band was in regard to the low pay for the work at Context. The reality, however, was that the Sun Ra Arkestra was no longer a marketable commodity. The money coming in at the door was a real indication of how low the drawing power of the band had sunk.

Context could easily hold up to 150 people. It was a good place to rebuild the impaired reputation of the Arkestra while allowing us to work in an environment we could control and to monitor our drawing power. We were the ones producing these gigs, and we knew exactly what was coming in at the door; therefore, we could offer a reasonable asking price to someone looking to book us.

Sun Ra had done a similar thing with Saturn Records for years, and his efforts at Slugs' in the mid-1960s were designed to build an audience. Most important for us was that a big band has to work

460

regularly, as there is always a need to familiarize new musicians with the music.

As well, the idea of the Arkestra continuing depended on our ability to attract younger skilled musicians into the band. Marshall was seventy-two; Jacson was in his sixties; I was in my late forties. Tyrone was getting up there in age, as were John Ore and Buster Smith. During this period Noël Scott, though younger, was in and out of the band; sometimes he would show and sometimes he wouldn't. Bruce Edwards was about the youngest individual who consistently made gigs, but he had his own set of issues and attitudes.

We did our first gigs on a Friday and Saturday in November at Context and got good results. The music was exciting, people showed up, and we were on our way. Monique and I tried to encourage Marshall to get more involved on the business side, i.e., to learn how much money was collected, how much the expenses were, and how much each performer received, etc. But he still wasn't completely comfortable hooking up the music and wasn't about to venture into the business. So basically the job fell to Monique and me. And to get anything else done, I had to talk to Jacson, the only one in Philly who understood what I was doing and who kept Marshall's ear.

The possibility of doing more concerts in December arose. We decided to do another just three days before Christmas to catch the college students and others who might be in New York for the holidays. The problem we encountered on this occasion, different from that first series, was housing. We weren't earning enough to pay for hotels. Once again, we went back to what Sun Ra had done before. We had some of the musicians stay with people who lived here. When I had first joined the band, it was common practice to have many of the guys stay at June Tyson and Richard Wilkinson's Harlem apartment.

Monique and I made room in our apartment for the new tenor player, Ya Ya Abdul-Majid. And though he was new to the Arkestra, I remembered him from the days when we first went to Washington, back in 1976.

Philippa had been attending the concerts at Context and was told of our problem. She offered to house Marshall and Jacson. The rest of the guys found various places on their own. Monique's mother and sister had come to America to stay with us for the holidays, so we didn't have enough room to accommodate other band members. But once again, our three concerts were successful.

With these five performances in November and December, the Arkestra had worked more consistently in New York than we had worked in the past four years. And the music was coming together.

After the concerts, I approached Marshall and Jacson with an idea that had come up while we were in Oakland. Edsel Matthews, of Koncepts Cultural Gallery, had suggested that the Arkestra do a performance of Disney songs at some time in the future. The idea was a great hit when Sunny first presented it in 1989. Songs from Disney movies tapped into a universal consciousness that had a certain mass appeal. It was one of the ideas that propelled Sunny forward during the earlier part of the 1990s.

We'd been agonizing over the many bootlegged releases that had come out since Sunny's death. One recently released CD, on Leo Records, featured a live Arkestra performance in Austria of an all-Disney program. Here was an opportunity to capitalize on the exploitation while taking another page out of Sun Ra's book.

The bootlegged recordings that flooded the market were something we had no control over. The Sun Ra Arkestra had no legal rights regarding the issue of those releases, even when our names appeared on the recordings. When Sun Ra passed in 1993, I went to a lawyer, Jerold Couture, to see if we could get paid when our names appeared on those illegal releases. Mr. Couture explained that because we were not legal heirs, the only thing we could do was get everyone who appeared on a release to claim they had never been paid for a particular recording. Only then might we be able to proceed. While John Gilmore was leading the band and working so closely with Alton Abraham, who was responsible for some of those illegal releases, I saw that as pretty hopeless.

The one thing Jacson and I did when we began working at Context was seek to prevent people from recording our music without our permission. I drafted a letter and got Jacson's approval. Philippa Jordan used her access to the internet to put it on the Sun Ra Listserv with the hope that in some way we could minimize future rip-offs.

The Sun Ra Listserv was a way of connecting people throughout the world, via cyberspace, who were interested in Sun Ra and his music. A couple of contributors to the list had or would write books on Sun Ra. Robert Campbell of Clemson University in South Carolina, a professor of psychology, had published *The Earthly Recordings of Sun Ra.* Chris Trent of the UK had assisted him. Chris also published *Another Shade of Blue*, a collection of his reviews of some of Sun Ra's recordings. The Listserv became a great way to communicate with people who have a common love for Sun Ra's music. It truly gave new meaning to his theme song, "Space Is the Place."

Doing songs from Disney movies was an attempt to turn the tables on the exploiters, a way to find victory in the face of what could have easily been characterized as a hopeless situation. Monique and I proposed a series of five Sunday afternoon concerts to be titled Disney for the Entire Family, and scheduled throughout the month of January 1996.

After the success of the November and December gigs we couldn't understand why we were suddenly being met with such resistance to the idea. But we were. While Marshall and Jacson did after a time finally agree, their lack of commitment to the idea manifested itself in various ways. There was opposition to rehearsing the material, to doing the concerts at all, and to everything else coming out of my mouth. Yet the demand was there, as public interest yielded increasing attendance for each of the five Sunday events. We were earning more money each week. One of the people who became interested in our Sunday afternoon shows was director Tom O'Horgan, of *Hair, Jesus Christ Superstar*, and a number of other successful Broadway productions. Tom had known Philippa for many years, and they had recently gotten excited about doing a play on Sun Ra, *Ra's Journey*, with the Arkestra performing onstage. I was asked to coordinate the music and had worked with Philippa on the treatment she was writing. We thought Tom, having been involved in Broadway extravaganzas, was an excellent choice as director. He was also a musician and a visionary with Southern roots (albeit white roots, making them slightly different from Sunny's).

The day Tom O'Horgan came to Context, however, it seemed that everything went wrong. We had a full house and a band that was less than rehearsed, with key personnel missing. Throughout the Context gig, I more or less called the tunes we would play. This happened for a couple of reasons, one of which was that I kept a list of new songs we had rehearsed and for which I had complete charts. Since we had been playing old Sun Ra arrangements for the past few years, we could only play songs for which there was enough music available. With the Disney material, we had created "head arrangements." Once again, we were doing songs that Sun Ra had already done, but without the arrangements for them. Most of these songs were played spontaneously, and the lack of rehearsal and missing personnel showed; we improvised our way through some of this material with a tentativeness that exposed our condition. There were real leadership issues surfacing here.

Monique and I had worked out a deal with Ed Montgomery to book the Arkestra on a month-to-month basis. We required only a couple of weeks lead time to get the word out. We had been building up a mailing list that was up to date and we had received good notices in the *Village Voice* and in a local Brooklyn weekly, the *City Sun.*

February arrived and I was waiting to hear from Jacson as for what to do next. In keeping with the idea of creating themes, Monique and I thought the month of February was rich with possibilities. Here we could at least celebrate the historical legacy of the Arkestra through another concert. When we got no response from Jacson to keep both the flow and commitment going, at the last minute I ended up booking the gig for the Solomonic Sextet. Since it was done in tandem with my Carnegie Hall performances in homeless shelters, it worked out economically for me. I was already subsidized to a certain extent, but without adequate time to publicize my band, prospects for attracting an audience were nil. We really needed a little more time to get the word out.

March was Women's History Month. June Tyson had never been fully celebrated as the first woman to travel the Spaceways, and Monique suggested we should do that for the month of March. I presented the idea to Jacson, who once again put up a great deal of resistance. Jacson never did come out and say what was bothering him, so I couldn't understand why (when we had been doing so well) there was so much opposition to the gigs I was trying to produce. Didn't anybody in Philly understand regular work? It wasn't as if there was any other work being offered the Arkestra. We had begun the job of increasing the visibility of the band, but it was nowhere near on its way to being finished.

After much back and forth, Jacson finally agreed to do the gig. I wasted no time in contacting Richard Wilkinson, who gave me some special pictures of June. I had been in contact with Charles Blass of WKCR, who provided me with taped excerpts from recordings in which June was the featured vocalist. Those tapes, along with other similar albums and CDs that I owned, became the material we played prior to the concert and during intermission.

At the rehearsal I had noticed a change in Marshall. For years Sun Ra had used rehearsals as a time to discipline musicians. With his superior musical knowledge he could easily pull that off. Marshall, however, was completely out of character when he sought to reprimand me for phrasing a song a particular way. Interestingly enough, the song he chose to do that with was Sun Ra's "Tapestry from an Asteroid," the song Sun Ra had used to do a similar thing several years before. I mentioned the event to co-trumpeter Robert Rutledge, who was now playing with the band and had observed the entire scene. Not knowing the complete history, Robert thought the encounter simply odd and couldn't understand why Marshall was making such an issue of the phrasing. The incident let me know that something was going on that I needed to be aware of.

The lesson that came out of this small incident spoke to another dynamic. I was perceived as becoming too influential, too much in charge. There were people within the Arkestra with whom this didn't sit right, and Marshall had to show them that he could "handle" me.

After rehearsal, I was feeling some unvoiced tension from Marshall. First he indicated to me that he had not known anything about a tribute to June, and he seemed disturbed that things were going down without his knowledge. For my part, I knew I'd had a conversation with Jacson, and I had assumed Jacson had conveyed the information to Marshall. There was some intrigue going on here. And I wasn't sure if it was because of Marshall's insistence about not involving himself in business matters or because somehow he thought I was trying to push him out of the way.

The concert celebrating June Tyson was the eleventh performance of the Arkestra at Context in less than a year. June's family came, along with Richard, and made the event worthwhile. The loss of momentum we'd experienced in not having the Arkestra in the space since the end of January meant that our audience had fallen off somewhat. Nevertheless, after three years, it suddenly seemed as if things were changing. There was renewed interest in the band. People were talking about the performances; there was a buzz in the air. Folks who were connected to recording companies were frequenting Context. The work there was filling in the void so that the other gigs that drifted in really gave the appearance that the band was on the move.

The next gig the Arkestra had was in DC on Monique's birthday, March 29. We rented a car and drove down so that we could hang out with Rashid and Shahid as well. Robert Rutledge, a Birmingham native and my good buddy, had been playing trumpet in the Arkestra since December, when it looked as if trumpeter Virgil Jones—a good friend of Robert's who had made several of the earlier Context gigs—was no longer interested. Robert rode down with us and returned with the band.

Monique and I were to spend the night in DC, as it had become one of her favorite cities and we were still engaged in her birthday celebration. As a result of the previous tragedies on her birthday, we decided to do a weeklong acknowledgment of her arrival day.

There is a wonderful aquatic garden in Washington, DC, an oasis Monique and I had happened upon on one of our trips to the district. Now that we knew where the garden was, we went there directly.

Little did I know that the Kenilworth Park and Aquatic Gardens was situated on the street where Jimmy Gray owned a home. As we drove down the block, he stepped out onto his front porch just as we were passing his house. The moment I caught a glimpse of him, I stopped and put the car in reverse. We were both surprised. He had heard about the concert and knew the Arkestra was in town, but he hadn't gone to check it out. A record producer, armchair historian, DJ, and record collector, Jimmy always knew what was happening in DC. He was one of the most knowledgeable people I knew who was involved in the music. When he invited us into his house, I understood why. Jimmy had an entire room, a library, stacked with shelves of records all labeled and in order. He had a section for each artist. He was someone who loved the music and took it seriously. Monique and I were blessed to spend a memorable few hours as guests in his home, reminiscing and sharing a bright moment with him. Jimmy Gray left the planet in 1999.

During the rehearsal for our March gig for June Tyson, we had gotten word that drummer, dancer, poet, and historian C. Scoby Stroman was hospitalized and in serious condition. I had visited him at the hospital before we went to DC, but he had already lost consciousness by that point and I never got to see him again. The day before Monique's birthday, the day before our trip, we found out that Scoby had died. This did shake me up a little, even though I was a lot stronger than I had been as far as my ability to deal with death. Scoby was a good friend and a walking history book. He and I had done many gigs together with him as a drummer and as a dancer. As a drummer, he was on one of the first gigs I did with Sun Ra, back in 1975. Later, he would work with my band Abdullah.

As a dancer, in recent years, he had worked regularly doing lecture demonstrations with Mickey Davidson. On those occasions, Scoby would often pick me up and we would ride together to the gigs. Scoby always had lots of anecdotes about the music. He would share these on our way to gigs, during intermissions, and after.

Scoby was given a royal Brooklyn send-off complete with brass band and African drum accompaniment. The site was the Reverend Herbert Daughtry's House of the Lord Church on Atlantic Avenue. An interesting connection here is that the reverend is married to the sister of Sun Ra drummer Buster Smith. I was asked to be one of four trumpeters who would lead the coffin in. It was a beautiful day in Brooklyn as folks came out in amazing numbers for an early morning event in the middle of the week. Many folks gave deserving praise to Scoby, and after all was done inside the church, musicians spilled out onto Atlantic Avenue and jammed.

But no sooner was Scoby's funeral over than we found out that Rashid and Shahid's sister, Merakhu, had also passed. Sadly, she died of the same illness that had taken her mother and father.

◖

Meanwhile, the Arkestra was looking like a contender. We had already done an extraordinary concert at Philadelphia's newly opened Clef Club on October 27 the year before with Pharoah Sanders, and it was great. Vibraphonist Damon Choice and I kept in touch with Pharoah by phone during the months after the gig. By the following spring, we'd heard that Pharoah had recently signed with Verve, his first major label in some twenty years. So Philippa and I made contact with a person from the Verve organization to see if we could persuade them to do a collaboration of sorts. The potential for the combination of Pharoah doing a recording with the Sun Ra Arkestra under Marshall's leadership was tremendous.

I had talked to the guys in Philly about a meeting that Philippa and I had planned for April 9 with the person from Verve. It was to be at one of Manhattan's posh hotels, and we had agreed upon a place and time to meet.

I got to the hotel and couldn't find Philippa anywhere. I called the fellow's room, but got no answer. I checked at the front desk, but Philippa had left no message. I called her at home; no message. After hanging around for a half hour or so, positioning myself in a place where I could see the comings and goings in the hotel, I went home.

I found out later that Philippa had met with the person from Verve without me. In and of itself, that was a serious move, but the other part was even more shocking. I called Philadelphia and was told by Tyrone that he had heard from Sue Pearlstine that I hadn't made the meeting.

That was most amazing to me, especially since I knew the actual sequence of events. I smelled a rat, but it was hard to figure out where the smell was coming from. As much as things felt as if changes were afoot, there were fundamental life conditions that had become frozen in time.

A few days after that incident, we were scheduled to play a college in  Reading, Pennsylvania, on Saturday, April 13. The cassette tapes from our August gig at Kimball's had just come out. To my knowledge, there had never been any real agreement made regarding those tapes, and there was no indication of a contract forthcoming. It was a strange way to do business. But Jacson and Marshall, along with Sue Pearlstine, were principally responsible for this transaction. Personally, I felt it was good that there'd be something on the market to represent the Arkestra in its present incarnation. But I was never asked how I felt or what I thought should be done, nor was I privy to the business dealings. Yet the use of my name and music automatically made me a partner, or so I thought. One thing was sure, the tapes were going to be put on the open market and for a substantial price. Since there must have been little overhead, I assumed some of that money would go to Marshall and Jacson to facilitate their ability to make the gigs in New York.

The business regarding the tapes, just like the business of getting paid for the gig in Reading, was basically in the hands of Jack Jacson. Jacson had an interesting way of convincing you in a heartbeat that he knew exactly what he was doing in any situation. The fact that in some areas, such as carpentry and music, he was highly skilled and highly articulate led many of us to believe he knew what he was talking about, regardless of the subject.

As it turns out, allowing him to handle business was a serious mistake. The question I asked myself several times was, if not Jacson, then who? And the answer always came back: There was no one else in Philly. The Reading gig was the fourth one handled by Jacson in which there was a problem with money. In this case, we had been repeatedly promised that cash would be made available. After the gig, however, Jacson received a check and thus was unable to pay folks on the spot. That wouldn't have been taken so seriously were it not for the issue of the newly released tape that needed to be dealt with.

At least one other musician in the band had a serious problem with both the tapes and the money, as well as with the handling of business in general. Having done the Reading gig, we all gathered around the van waiting to get paid. When we were told that we'd have to wait until the check was deposited and cleared, the three issues came together and erupted in an after-gig explosion of misdirected energy. All hell broke loose. Accusations and recriminations abounded. It took a lot to calm things down so that we could get back on the road and head for home with no pay. But we managed.

A few days later, Jacson had to come to New York to pay us. One of the important events that came out of that concert had occurred at Damon Choice's apartment, which is where we were to meet to get paid. That someone had selected Damon's space was notable because on the three other occasions when there had been a problem with late payment, Jacson had chosen me as the contact person. My senses were up. Another shift was happening.

While waiting for Jacson to show up at Damon's, Dick Griffin, longtime trombonist in the Arkestra, suggested that at one of the rehearsals we should put down our instruments and have a business meeting. I thought it a good suggestion but felt we should meet expressly for the purpose of business. The combination took hold and we agreed to a date, place, and time, and to contact folks who were not present. For the Sun Ra Arkestra, this was an innovative idea, and we had it down for April 25.

Our historic meeting took place at Damon's apartment. Seven people—Jack Jacson, Charles Davis, Dick Griffin, Elson Nascimento, Robert Rutledge, Damon Choice, and I—sat around for two hours and talked about what was troubling us. I thought this would be the most effective way to figure out what the resistance to me was all about. Interestingly, a couple of people spoke on the problems they had with performing at Context.

"I think we should be at a different place, man. A place that sells food. How about that place uptown by Columbia?" Dick proposed. Silently I asked, How about it?

It was curious to me that here the band had been subsisting for the past four years with no plans and no intention of doing anything but going from gig to gig, as if shows just came along by themselves. These criticisms about what was currently happening weren't necessarily designed to make anything better, because no one had investigated a new location where any of the suggestions could be realized.

To me, the idea of changing venues was a red herring raised because I had spoken out on another issue. It concerned what I felt was a contradiction. The leader of the Sun Ra Arkestra, Marshall Allen, was also working with the group Phish, as were several other ensemble members—Michael Ray, Dick Griffin, and Damon Choice. Phish had a loyal following, and its leader had expressed how influenced he had been by the Grateful Dead and Sun Ra.

While I didn't have any problem with the guys in the Arkestra making their own paydays, I felt that the Arkestra was just beginning to regain some form of respect and that we were not well served by having the leader of the band work under somebody else. Jacson agreed with me on this issue. We both felt that a sign of true respect would have been a double bill, with advertisement for the Arkestra. There was no command for respect when the leader of the Arkestra, along with others in the band, was playing in Phish. It gave the appearance of co-option by a group playing in a style and a genre that were at best derivative.

I also kept emphasizing the fact that we were just beginning to crawl on our own. We were developing a mailing list and a following we didn't have a few months earlier. We were producing our own concerts, which meant that we, and we alone, knew our earning power. We didn't have to turn that information over to someone else prematurely, and we wouldn't be subjected to being paid a fraction of what we deserved. I argued that we should always negotiate from a place of strength. No one can offer you less than you deserve, I said, if you know what you deserve. It was time, I contended, to move away from the prevalent plantation mentality.

In any event, we came out of the meeting with an agreement to continue the concerts at Context until we could find a better home base. The other issues were put on the back burner for now, as we had business to take care of and would need more meetings to clarify everything.

We had gigs coming up over the next couple of days at Context, on April 26 and 27. The meeting seemed to have left us with a positive vibe. Charles Davis suggested that we start off the evening performance with a private moment of silence. It was effective in bringing the band together and getting folks to focus and concentrate. Another positive addition to these gigs was bassist Jaribu Shahid, a Detroit musician who had played quite a few gigs with the Arkestra over the years.

The Saturday gig on the twenty-seventh turned out to be the best gig we had ever done at Context—musically, financially, and spiritually. People came out and filled the house. The music was excellent, especially behind two drummers, Buster Smith's brother, Marvin "Boogaloo" Smith, and Clifford Barbaro. I had made plans to do something special at Context for my upcoming birthday. The weekend of May 10 and May 11 had been available for quite a while and so I wanted to book those dates. Jacson, with his customary reluctance to commit, had waited almost until the last minute before I could decide to take Friday, the tenth, and leave Saturday, traditionally the more well-attended day, for the Arkestra.

I was still driving a cab, using some of that money to help with the production costs. On the Monday before the gig, I was driving through the city listening to WKCR. Ben Young was hosting the 6-to-9 p.m. *Jazz Alternatives* show. I had tried to fax a flyer announcing the concerts at Context for May 10 and 11, but the fax machine didn't work. So I made a trip to the station studio. Ben, supportive person that he was, actually put me on the air and plugged the concert. He announced that I was celebrating my forty-ninth birthday by premiering a new group and a new approach I called Diaspora. The group, he told his audience, would include Arthur Blythe, Masujaa, Charnett Moffett, and Charles Moffett. He went on to say that this was to be the first time Arthur would work with one of my bands in two decades. Ben also announced that my birthday celebration would continue into the next night, when I would appear with the Arkestra.

Little did I know that all the intrigue that had been building for months, all the larceny that had been lurking in the hearts of men and women, would come to a head as people sought to use to use that announcement in an attempt to destroy what we had been trying to build. Within the next couple of days, I received calls from Dick Griffin and Damon Choice informing me that they weren't going to make the gig on the eleventh. I got a call from Philly that the Arkestra wasn't going to make the gig either. The reason given was that someone in New York had heard me on the radio and claimed I had announced that I was leading the Sun Ra Arkestra. I was told by Jacson that he had also heard about an ad in the *Village Voice* advertising me as leader of the Arkestra.

If the accusation hadn't been serious, it would have been hilarious. The only thing I would have done with the Sun Ra Arkestra was fire half the people in it. I had no interest in leading it anywhere. But the fact that this accusation presented itself let me know what was going on. It gave me more information as to who was behind it. If the issue were really about me leading my own band, it would have been easy to explain. Out of all the concerts we'd produced at Context since November, this was only the second one I was headlining.

The false claims about the *Voice* ad could also be disproven. Fortunately, Philippa had bought a fax machine for the guys in Philly, both as a symbol of her investment in the band and because they needed one. I was then able to fax them copies of both the press release and the ad. After I sent them, I called Marshall and he said he couldn't understand what all the fuss was about. So the Arkestra gig was set for May 11. The band would come up from Philly but without Jack Jacson, who had prior commitments around his daughter's graduation.

On May 10, 1996, I celebrated my forty-ninth birthday at Context with a concert that was both well attended and musically gratifying. Performing with Arthur Blythe was wonderful. His huge and beautiful alto-sax sound had no trouble filling the room. Interestingly, someone had come to the concert and actually refused to come in simply because Charnett was playing electric bass; had he heard Charnett play, however, he and his crew would have changed their minds. Charles and Charnett played so wonderfully together, too. At times, I actually wanted to stop playing, take a seat in the audience, and just listen in on this father-and-son team. Trumpeter Dave Gordon, who had also played with Sun Ra, was there, and sat in on one of our numbers. Masujaa, as always, was the reliable component who colored and helped to shape the texture of the ensemble. After the gig, Monique surprised me with a real-life party, bringing the evening to a great and joyous close.

One of the main people spreading complaints and gossipmongering, Damon Choice, had also come to the concert. I'd had a phone conversation with him a few days before, at which time it became clearer to me that he, Dick Griffin, and Bruce Edwards were initiating most of the negativity. But had it just been the three of them, it probably wouldn't have amounted to much. I was beginning to understand more clearly that a spirit of negativity had permeated the Arkestra and had been given ample reinforcement by the fact that Marshall Allen, while developing his skills as a leader of music, was also developing his skills as a leader of people. This fact had led to others assuming that role, like Jack Jacson who felt threatened by his own lack of ability as a leader and was unprepared to deal with business. Or was it me whose own limited success as a leader of my own bands had appeared as some kind of threat to them both?

Fortunately for me, at the time of all this turmoil I was still in therapy. In this healing place, I was able to work out some of the distressing problems that had been arising. Lee Phillips, the therapist I continued to see alone, had correctly analyzed my situation with the members of the Arkestra as a case of sibling rivalry. Really, just out and out jealousy. After I became more fully aware of the severity of the problem, my only recourse was to purge myself of my own negativity and that which I kept seeing in others. One lesson I learned is that what you see in others is often a reflection and/or a projection of yourself. As I began concentrating on eliminating jealousy of others from my own person, I'd find myself around fewer people who acted that way.

The May 11 performance at Context turned out to be a good one, if not as well attended as the night before. Jacson was absent for the first time, but as his musical role was not an essential one, the show did go on. It could well have been that his fear of being expendable as a musician, coupled with his lack of business acumen, spurred the the events that would follow. I believe it was Jacson's general inability to inspire folks coupled with Marshall's acquiescence of the role of leader that brought about an odd sequence of events that to this day has affected my relationship with the Sun Ra Arkestra.

On May 23, we had scheduled another business meeting at Damon's. It was supposed to start at 5 p.m., but actually got started around seven thirty, after waiting for Jacson to show. It turns out that, unknown to us, Jacson had gone to Philippa Jordan's apartment to sign an agreement that made her representative of the Arkestra.

Weeks before this second meeting, I had begun to confront the contradictions that had been culminating after years of working within the Sun Ra culture. Part of our legacy was the psychological damage that resulted from our total dependence on Sunny, who called all the shots and worked out all the details. And now, without Sunny as the focal point, our ambivalence toward each other—which sometimes was manifested in downright hatred—had left its scars. Here we had been trying to rebuild the Arkestra's capacity to pull, and Jacson, obviously with Marshall's consent, was ready to give control away to Philippa. Even without specifically knowing what Jacson had just done, I had suggested we bring someone to our meeting who might help us with expert advice. I had been thinking of Mike Cipressi of the Musicians' Assistance Program, and the offer he had made almost two years before. Jacson, however, nixed this idea, so it wasn't going to happen.

What was most interesting about the agreement between Jacson and Philippa was that the impetus for it, as far as Philippa was concerned, was that a friend of mine, a practicing Buddhist named Sal Clemente, had just returned from Amsterdam, where he had made contact with the owner of the Paradiso. The man had expressed interest in bringing the Arkestra to the Netherlands. Sal had come to Context on May 11, at which time I introduced him to Philippa. She had been thinking about a trip to England, and now she was going to the Netherlands as well. All of this interest in the Arkestra had everything to do with the fact that the band had been working regularly in New York City.

At our business meeting, we talked around many other issues save that one. People again expressed their discomfort with working at Context, and once again, no one but me offered an alternative site. I had been talking to Sal and another acquaintance, the novelist Ed Vega, who had come to Context. They were interested in booking the band at the Clemente Soto Vélez Cultural and Educational Center, a school building that had been converted into an artists' commune on Rivington Street. In later years, this center would be the home of the Vision Festival, organized by Patricia Nicholson and William Parker of Arts for Art. We had been making plans for a three-day celebration there for July 4 through 6. There were several theaters at the center and there was tremendous potential for growth. Monique and I had met with Ed and Sal and had discussed the possibility of showing the movie *Space Is the Place* on the same day the Arkestra would have its opening night, the Fourth of July.

At the Arkestra meeting, we all agreed to end our commitment with Context with a series of Sunday concerts throughout June, traditionally the time of New York's Jazz festival. Scheduled to begin on June 9, these concerts would be a repeat of the January show that had done so well this past winter. However, it was agreed that the four planned concerts would not include the Disney element that marked our January concerts.

Monique and I, working with Ed Montgomery, did our usual mailing of flyers and press releases and took an ad out in the *Voice*. Between May 23 and June 8, I had attempted to meet with Marshall and Jacson about the July Fourth celebration. It never occurred to me, even with the failed meetings, that I should suspect anything regarding the June performances. In dealing with Marshall and Jacson, I had learned how prone they were to leave things until the last minute. So, late that Saturday night, June 8, when I called Philadelphia to see what time to expect the guys for the Sunday concert, I was shocked to hear what Jacson had to say.

"We're not gonna make it."

"What you mean you ain't gonna make it?"

"Marshall's got another gig he can't get out of. And I can't find the other cats, so we ain't gonna make it."

"Jacson, this is Saturday, a few hours before the concert. When were you gonna tell me this shit?" I asked, my rage rising. There was only silence on the other end. Then he mumbled something. I angrily slammed down the phone. Fortunately for me, Monique was home, which allowed me to vent some of the tremendous hurt and anger I was feeling.

As it turned out, Robert Campbell, one of the people who regularly contributed to the internet's Sun Ra Listserv, reported on June 9 that he had recently visited the House of Ra on Morton Street and had been graciously received by Marshall and Jacson. Campbell noted that the Arkestra was trying to line up a tour in Europe (with the help of Philippa Jordan). Absolutely no mention was made of the concert at Context.

Later that Sunday, I left my house to go to Context early enough to have everything arranged for those musicians who were going to show. There had been plenty of advertisement, and people in the band had been informed of the concert, so even if the Philadelphia contingent was a no-show, the New York crew would still be there. I had talked to Damon that morning. He told me he had been in touch with Jacson and that Marshall had told him he didn't have any money to come to New York. A different tale than what I'd gotten from Jacson.

On my way to Context, I met bassist Juni Booth, who was living in the neighborhood. He accompanied me into the building and we sat down together and I talked through my feelings about what I expected. It was a good thing, because it allowed me to salvage some dignity from what could have turned out to be a debacle. Using Juni as a sounding board, I came up with a plan B to put into operation. I was intent on making this work with or without the Philly crowd.

When the musicians arrived, I learned that of all the Arkestra members in New York who were supposed to be available, only Elson and Jaribu Shahid came to Context that day. Whoever was behind this obviously hadn't thought the two of them important enough to contact. As for myself, I had been down many roads with all these guys and would never have expected them, regardless of our differences, to leave me holding the bag like this.

When Monique showed up, we decided to put up a sign informing people that the Arkestra would not perform and that we would instead do a workshop presentation around Sun Ra's music. That was a liberating idea. Given those conditions, we also decided to reduce the cost of admission. After rehearsing and talking through the music with Jaribu and Elson, I knew that even with just the three of us, we could pull this off.

When hit time came, we had an audience of just under twenty people. I introduced us and informed the audience about what we were going to do. I had done something similar in Denmark, back in 1992, but without playing the trumpet. On this occasion, I talked between songs about my relationship with Sun Ra, using the lecture-demonstration format I had been gradually developing. The audience seemed to appreciate our efforts to make the show go on, and this more intimate and informal format allowed them access to information they wouldn't normally have gotten.

I was still in therapy, so I could talk this out with Lee Phillips. By now, Monique and I were regularly sitting with Carletta Joy Walker. It was important and timely that our sessions with Carletta began just as all of this turmoil started. While the situation with the members of the Arkestra was a serious one, the impact it could have had on my relationship with my wife was even more serious. But due to the therapeutic work I'd been doing, I was able to avoid bottling up the tension that had been building inside me—something that had had a disastrous effect on my relationships in the past.

A major scar had developed on my relationship with Marshall and Jacson. The fact that they had conspired against a performance that could only benefit the Arkestra was devastating. Wouldn't it have been simpler to just say, "No, we don't want to do it?" Given what had transpired the previous month around my birthday concert, this whole thing appeared definitely directed at me. It wasn't about money or a gig or Context or Clemente Soto Vélez. It was about me. And the attack was carried out in such a cowardly covert way that I'd never really know who was to blame. But I was protected. And they didn't understand the powerful force they were obstructing; all they saw was that they were doing something to me.

After a long conversation with the tenorman Ya Ya Abdul-Majid the day after the event, I decided that my life from this period on would not include the Arkestra. Even though Ya Ya and I talked and I let out much of my anger, I knew it would be difficult to play music with these guys again. To help heal from this slap in the face, I wrote a letter informing the guys of the effects of their actions and chronicling the events that had led up to the June 9 incident. The letter was twenty-two-pages long (Sun Ra's number). I felt the words were being channeled through me from a higher source and that I was compelled to finish it. I mailed a copy to the guys in Philadelphia, another copy to Marie Holsten in Birmingham, and one to Elson. I called it "The Demise of the Sun Ra Arkestra."

Hoping this would act as a wake-up call, I laid out the causes, as I saw them, of the impending destruction of the Arkestra. I pointed out how the interference we had allowed had taken us off track. Our lack of business understanding, as characterized by Sue Pearlstine's non-accountability regarding tapes and sales, was covered in detail. Another point related to how the mere signing of a contract with Philippa was reason to abandon all efforts at self-determination. I pointed out that our inability to believe in ourselves and to work together in good faith was a major problem. Sun Ra's decision to work with the Brad Simon agency and Jack Reich had arisen from a situation different from this current one because Sun Ra could negotiate from a position of strength. The Sun Ra Arkestra, at this point, was powerless. Negotiating from a position of powerlessness only leads to more powerlessness.

I wrote about the Arkestra's diminished impact, which I felt was due to other bands playing Sun Ra's music. I stated that the Arkestra's ineffectiveness was also due to our inability to stick together. As a result of our own lack of unity, other bands with no direct connection to Sun Ra seemed to fare better playing Sunny's music than the group of musicians who had struggled with him throughout his years. Like Langston Hughes wrote in one of his poems, "They done took my blues / And gone."

I also outlined a plan as to how the current situation could be rectified, including through the establishment of leadership by committee. Such a proposal, if realized, would shift the paradigm of divine-right inheritance—a thing I saw as a major factor in our confusion—into a more pragmatic and efficient force. My suggestion was that Charles Davis, Dick Griffin, and Marshall should act as a committee so that decisions were not placed on the shoulders of one person who was unprepared or had no real desire to lead. I suggested that Elson oversee business matters. Sun Ra had trusted him enough to let him use his credit card to rent vans during the last few years of his life. Elson was still fuming over the treatment he'd received the previous year around the Oakland gig, when he'd been left out, but he still knew how to take care of business and was still game.

I also suggested that I could help out working with the estate. No one else had thought it important to contact and work out arrangements with Sun Ra's family. Folks had been relying on Jacson's attempt to create a Sun Ra Arkestra foundation, which turned out to be a joke without legal substance.

The letter was finished and mailed sometime in July. I subtitled it "Where Is the Love?" I never talked to the crew in Philly about it, although I understood that they did get it and that some of them read it. The disappointment, anger, and hurt I felt would not allow me to play music with the Arkestra and, though it was never stated, I assumed by the lack of correspondence (never having received an explanation from Jacson or Marshall) that they didn't want me to play with them, either.

Despite Philippa's trip to Europe and the Philly duo's rejection of Context, the Arkestra didn't work in New York from May 11 until September 18. It didn't work in Europe until the following year. Damon Choice, the sometimes vibraphone player in the Arkestra, found the band a spot in Manhattan's Meatpacking District at the Cooler. It amazed me that they were going to trade the work we did at Context for a guaranteed salary that was still a pittance. As long as we produced our own concerts at Context, people on the outside could speculate, but none of them knew for sure what our drawing power was. Our advantage in a deal like that lay in our ability to profit from our own gate. We could demand a price at other venues and if we didn't get it, we had the option of going back to Context. But after almost a half year without doing anything in New York, it was like starting all over again, minus a few changes. The main difference was that Jacson was now calling the shots and Damon was acting as liaison with the club's management.

It had been rumored that Jacson had worked in espionage during the Korean War; perhaps as a result of that experience, he took on a sort of covert mentality, making it difficult for me to find out what was going on. During this period, I was acting like an investigative reporter, attempting to determine who the main conspirators were. After months of reflection and investigation, asking questions here, making comments there, I concluded that it was the Sun Ra culture itself that had caused the mess, with a few anti-Ahmed conspirators thrown in to sour the pot.

Sun Ra had set the Arkestra up as a support system for himself. His need to be at the core of it all meant one had to give up autonomy in order to be totally involved in the Arkestra. Gilmore did it, Marshall did it, and to lesser extent, many other guys who worked in the Arkestra did it.

Conversely, groups such as those led by Art Blakey, Count Basie, Miles Davis, and Duke Ellington could all boast of being training centers for upcoming leaders in Jazz. Sun Ra's bands couldn't claim that, because it was never his intention to create anything other than a vehicle for his own self-expression. Sun Ra rarely referred to Arkestra members in interviews, hardly ever announced specific musicians from the stage, and, by keeping everyone in costumes, always promoted the invisibility of everyone in his Arkestra. To leave Sun Ra's Arkestra with any kind of name recognition required the person in question to have had a strong sense of individual will. In retrospect, one might say that the fact that Sun Ra chose people who were supportive of his music and philosophy can be looked at as his special strength which is why his music still remains vital in the twenty-first century. Unlike the aforementioned musicians, Sun Ra was only interested in propagating his own brand of Music of the Spirit!

One had to be almost a nonperson in the Arkestra—except, of course, when one was called on to deliver improvisational episodes that spoke to one's individuality. This momentary visibility proved a major contradiction. That brilliance, revealed from time to time, was vigorously suppressed by Sun Ra in most other situations. The phrase used most often was, "follow the leader," which in itself was a good idea if there was a leader who knew where he was going, as Sun Ra did. Without Sunny, however, and with no one to replace him, there wasn't a snowball's hope in hell of really delivering the message of Sun Ra's music or moving to a higher level of organization.

The other significant thing about the culture involved our loyalty to Sun Ra, which was incredibly strong. That was real. And I was among those who felt it. But I had also been laboring under the illusion that we shared a brotherhood and a sense of loyalty, which had already been crushed by the betrayal I felt around the Satellites of the Sun project. I really didn't want to believe that the brotherhood I had been seeking since childhood was there only in its most superficial form. It would take one more difficult lesson for me to really understand this.

On June 18, a life-changing event occurred. Daisaku Ikeda, leader of the Soka Gakkai, an organization committed to spreading Buddhism throughout the world, was to be the focus of a celebration at Carnegie Hall. I was still working there as a teaching artist. My old friend Robert Rutledge was playing in the orchestra assembled for the event and had seen to it, a month before, that I would also be one of the musicians chosen to perform for President Ikeda. We had been rehearsing several weeks for this day.

It was a great honor for me to play at this extraordinary event. In total contrast to the lack of cooperation and effort I had just experienced with the Arkestra, this presentation was a model of harmony. On the day of the concert, as an added bonus, my connection as a teaching artist at Carnegie allowed Monique access to a box seat, where she viewed the event next to President Ikeda.

In addition to a full orchestra of eighty musicians, there was also a smaller ensemble consisting of prominent Buddhist musicians—Wayne Shorter, Herbie Hancock, Buster Williams, Steve Turre, Robin Eubanks, Shunzo Ohno, Kenwood Dennard, Néstor Torres, and Frank Colón—all making beautiful music together. In the midst of a muddied experience, I was being presented with a beautiful lotus flower, pointing the way to enlightenment. I was being shown a different way to find a musical community through my Buddhist practice.

Meanwhile, there were dates available at Context in June. I got back to work with my own ensemble, Diaspora. We worked there on June 21 and 22. Earlier that year, I had already begun changing the way I was thinking about music. Here and there over the past several years, I had brought in poet Atiba J. D. Wilson (now Atiba Kwabena) to recite with the Solomonic for our Carnegie shelter performances. I had also begun using Monique as a poet inside the ensemble, as once again I felt the need to have words along with the music.

Atiba is a talented artist who also plays percussion and flute and sings. I had met him at one of the Arkestra concerts at the Knitting Factory when John Gilmore was still leading the band. Owing to his musical ability, Atiba added another dimension to the Solomonic performances as a poet and multi-instrumentalist. Monique also had a good ear for music, and I would soon use her as a poet and vocalist. During the May and June gigs at Context, I interspersed reading proverbs from the African diaspora between the songs we played. The group included Chico Freeman, Alex Blake, Masujaa, and Charles Moffett.

Charles was ill at the time, suffering from cancer. After these last two gigs, his wife, Shirley, felt it would be better if I didn't book any more gigs with him, because Charles always came ready to give 120 percent. Shirley felt he needed to preserve his strength and I respected her wishes. I would have done whatever she asked if it in any way helped keep him alive. Charles was really important in my life, even more so in light of my disappointment with the Arkestra. I'd miss talking, playing music, and hanging out with this special human being who was like a father/brother/friend/mentor to me. Shirley, however, was fighting for the actual life of her husband of thirty years.

Chico Freeman's presence on this gig was also significant. For the past nine years, each time we played, a new reality would manifest in my own musicianship. Back in February 1978, at the beginning of this cycle, Chico had played with me at Ali's Alley. That gig was so well attended and exciting that it received a review by Robert Palmer in the *New York Times* that in part said: "During the past few years he has been developing as a bandleader, and the group he led at Ali's Alley over the weekend—like all his bands, it was called Abdullah—was simply magnificent."

This performance was also released on Cadence Records as *Abdullah Live at Ali's Alley.* Nine years later, in 1987, Chico worked with me at Carlos 1. I had just formed the Solomonic Quartet with Charles Moffett. That gig was also reviewed by Robert Palmer in the *New York Times*, and the following year a Solomonic Quintet recording was made for Silkheart Records. Now, ironically, here in 1996, yet another new approach was being created, with Chico Freeman as the horn player. And even though we didn't have a good house for either of the two nights, my understanding of this cyclical history let me know I was heading in the right direction.

◖◗

The days after those last gigs at Context were difficult for me. I stopped playing my trumpet for months. I was fortunate to still have a therapist, and Monique and I were still working with Carletta Joy Walker. Writing, too, had become an increasingly promising option for me.

Late one night in August, I was listening to a broadcast on WBAI while driving my cab. Julia Cameron, author of *The Artist's Way*, a book encouraging healing through writing, was speaking.

She kept me enthralled long past my shift. I was late returning the cab and was inspired enough to call Monique to tell her to tune in as well. Cameron suggested something called "morning pages," a sort of stream-of-consciousness technique that enables a writer when awakening in the morning to express the unconscious part of their being. I thought this would be the most effective way to figure out what the resistance to me was all about.

The next day, I bought her book and went to work, immediately doing my morning pages. This single daily act took me to a level of awareness that was just as intense as any I had previously experienced traveling the spaceways with Sun Ra. I was feeling a renewed sense of power, so much so that I didn't feel the need to play music. I could drive a cab and still feel powerful. Besides, right then, I felt that if I had played my horn I might have felt the need to go back into the house of darkness now exemplified, in my life, by the Sun Ra Arkestra. As it was, while I was driving and writing my morning pages, I would go around to the Cooler on Fourteenth Street, just to see if I saw anyone. I then had to admit that I had an addiction to the Sun Ra Arkestra and to the music, or so I thought. I had to struggle against this, but I couldn't lose this struggle. Then an unexpected family tragedy ironically became the catalyst to open another clearer path for me.

That mid-September, Monique and I got calls from her uncle Claude in Barbados and from her mother, Celeste, in the UK. We were informed that Monique's first cousin, Leona Hurley, had been murdered by her husband, Kwele. We had no indication that there had been any history of abuse. There was nothing we knew about them that could have led us to believe that such tragedy could have occurred. *Murder?* Both Leona and Kwele appeared to be culturally grounded. In fact, they were part of the same Ausar Auset community that Iyabode belonged to. As well, Leona was a student at the Pacific College of Oriental Medicine, where Monique was the registrar. At family affairs we might be the only members to wear African dress. Leona had lived in Brooklyn, in Ditmas Park, and we had been to family gatherings at her sisters' houses in Queens and in New Jersey on several occasions. This was such an overwhelming shock. And months later, as we got past the impact, we chose to use this incident as a wake-up call. Monique and I had been trying to work out our problems, and we knew that sometimes we could be very upset with each other—but to lose it like that? We could never let that happen.

The shock of this murder posed many unanswered questions that revolved around the perception of power and powerlessness. Did Kwele feel so disempowered by Leona that he needed to take her life? With a weapon?

Using my cab as a laboratory I went about exploring this question of power. I began interviewing my passengers, asking them to define power or to give me their most striking metaphor or image thereof. I was sincerely seeking answers to this question as a means of understanding myself better. I was able to engage in many thoughtful and provocative discussions with passengers.

Tom Sibley, the filmmaker I had met while driving, was married to a beautiful Black woman, Nikki. In some ways she reminded me of Iyabode. Nikki was pregnant during this period and we had interesting discussions about the topic of power. As a result of those discussions, it occurred to me that one of the most powerful images we have is that of a pregnant woman; but this is rarely considered when we think of power. As we all know, all human life comes through women, yet we live under a patriarchal system that denies the power of women in an effort to falsely elevate the power of men. But if creativity—procreativity, as the word implies—brings one closer to the Creator, who is closer than a woman with child? Aren't we most powerful when we give life, when we procreate, given that our perception of reality is through the lives we live? Of course, by the same token, women need men to aid in the production of life, so real power would mean a balance between male and female, internally and externally. If neither is assumed to be superior, then it would be easier to adopt a win-win paradigm, a real revolutionary concept.

Domestic violence, as I was understanding it, reflected the imbalance within society. The false premise under which we all live suggests there has to be a winner and a loser. This creates unsuspecting victims of people who see physical superiority as a distorted sign of power. I began to understand that to do something simply because you can doesn't make you powerful.

Inspired by reading *The Artist's Way*, I decided the interviewing I did in my cab was going to be a book project, *A Question of Power*. Before I got that far, however, I was empowered through Monique's encouragement to leave the cab industry behind me. I took off from driving after February 14, 1997, the day Charles Moffett left the planet.

Hours before Shirley had informed me of Charles's passing, I had a dream that he had asked me to play "Canto II," our theme song. A couple of days later, she called back to ask me to play at his funeral at St. Peter's Lutheran Church. I hadn't been playing much since our last concert in June, and had done no public performances. But for Charles I would pick up my horn again and play my last gig using the name Solomonic in his honor. I was going to retire the name after that.

Drummers Pheeroan akLaff and Wade Barnes agreed, along with Charnett Moffett and Masujaa, to play "Eternal Spiraling Spirit" with me at the funeral. Over the years, that song had become more meaningful to me, as I had evolved to the place where I now understood the message it delivers. I was also inspired to read William Ernest Henley's "Invictus," that poem I had memorized from my teenage years. Charles's spirit was such a powerful and unconquerable force that I thought Henley's poem appropriate.

His death was another deep jolt for me; he was the last of my mentors. From that day forward, I was in effect on my own. I not only stopped driving a cab but I went to one more therapy session and ended that as well. Once again, I didn't know where I was heading, but I was moving into my fiftieth year on the planet and felt more emotionally prepared to face whatever would come. My Carnegie Hall shelter gigs were coming up again, inadvertently allowing me an opportunity to do a public concert for Charles. Antonio Rodriguez, the coordinator of special events for the homeless, working in conjunction with Carnegie Hall, set up Henry Street Settlement as a concert site. I put together a program of music and poetry to celebrate Mr. Moffett. He had done those gigs with me for almost a decade.

The group I used included Carlos Ward, Masujaa, Alex Blake, Wade Barnes, and Monique Ngozi Nri reading poetry and singing. We were graced with the presence of Charnett Moffett, who came to the concert and played his tail off for his father. The concert was liberating. I was doing something to demonstrate the strong connection I felt with Mr. Charles Moffett.

I taped the gig and sent copies to Bob Rusch of CIMP Records and to a couple of other record companies. I had done CIMP's first recording under the Cadence label, *Abdullah Live at Ali's Alley*, in the early 1980s. Charles had also done several recordings for that label. Bob gave me an almost immediate positive response. He couldn't record the entire band, he said, because his ears weren't attuned to music that included poetry. Nevertheless, we set up a date for June 17 and 18 to record the CD that is titled *Dedication*. On the CD, we played music Charles had helped to develop with the Solomonic over the years but which had never been recorded. In the ten years that we worked together, we made only that one recording on the Silkheart label.

The group for the recording date was Carlos Ward, Alex Blake, Masujaa, and Codaryl Moffett, Charles's son. Everyone had played with Charles. Carlos and Masujaa had been in the Solomonic group from the early days, and Alex had played a couple of gigs as the group was evolving into Diaspora. All the musicians came to play, as can clearly be heard in the product we got from the date. Codaryl Moffett's presence on the recording, playing his father's drum set, was a great asset. It truly helped to give the recording its title. Codaryl had been playing with his father since the age of two. What he brought to that date was not only what he knew of his father's playing, but a wealth of experiences that were his own and which spoke to his own potential greatness.

Between March and May, prior to the recording date and after Charles's death, I was getting plenty of phone calls from Philippa Jordan, who was now organizing a tour for the Arkestra. The tour was to be the group's first European engagement since March and April 1992. The Arkestra would play in Germany, Belgium, and the Netherlands. The reason for the phone calls was that in organizing the tour with Jacson as her contact, she felt completely ineffective in pulling the whole thing off.

I was resistant to working with the Arkestra on any level after the affair at Context. But so many things had happened since then that I actually found myself considering the offer. The loss of my good friend was still unnerving. In addition, I had stopped driving a cab completely and I was determined to realize my dreams on my own terms. Doing those morning pages had helped me in my recovery and made me a great deal stronger.

While I believed I had correctly understood the series of events as they had transpired the year before, I was feeling like letting bygones be. Perhaps I loved Sun Ra's music too much. Maybe I didn't believe the guys I'd known for all those years were capable of such a deep level of skullduggery. Maybe I just enjoyed that sense of security the Arkestra afforded. Maybe it was because music was my destiny.

I listened to Philippa's plea for help in how to deal with the situation. She was determined that she couldn't make the tour happen without my presence. So she would have Jacson call me to work out a financial arrangement. I remembered Miles's warning: "Never turn down a gig; just ask for more money."

The position I was to be in was an interesting one. I was going to give advice to Jacson and Marshall, through Philippa, that would make them more effective, when they had done everything they could to render me ineffective.

I knew my suggestions would allow them to get the job done, so my first move would be to demand extra money for my services. I wouldn't ask for a lot, because I knew they didn't have it, but a symbolic gesture was important just then, since an apology would have been meaningless and was not forthcoming. I also knew I'd be expected to render services, keep a low profile, and let it seem as if Jacson and Philippa were taking care of business for Marshall. That was probably the hardest job I'd ever had. One of the places we were supposed to play, the Paradiso, had also figured significantly in the intrigue that had led to the decision to let Philippa represent the Arkestra. The feeling back then was that a European tour was going to happen and that they could basically dismiss me, since they felt that they no longer had to work at Context.

On a day in April, Philippa called to let me know that Jacson was going to call to make me an offer. I'm sure if it were up to him he wouldn't have bothered. After all, it had been ten months since the Context affair and not even a squeak. But he wasn't running the show; he was only fronting.

"Hey, Ahk," he began.

"What's up, Jacson?" The small talk lasted for a few minutes.

"Did Philippa tell you about this tour we're getting ready to do?"

"Yeah, I heard about it."

"We'd like you to make it with us, Ahk."

"That's cool. I'm down. But let's talk about money." Philippa had already filled me in on how much the gigs were paying. I therefore knew how much to ask without upsetting the budget while also getting my symbolic victory.

"Whatever you're getting, I want three hundred dollars more." There was a long pause on the other end.

And finally: "Okay, Ahk, I'll see what I can do."

As things came up and Philippa called, I would advise her and she would talk to Jacson. One issue involved a replacement for baritone saxophonist Charles Davis. He had been expected to go on this first European tour to aid in bolstering the credibility of the Arkestra. Unfortunately, and typically, until the last minute no one had bothered to check with Charles to see if he was available, by which time he had already made other plans.

Jacson had proposed getting Ronald Wilson, the wonderful tenor saxophonist from Chicago, who was living in Oakland. In the past and most recently during the August 1995 trip to

Emeryville, Ronald had been a valuable addition. The cost of flying him to Philly for rehearsals, then to Europe and back to Oakland, however, was an expense that would have wreaked havoc on the delicate budget we were working with. Jacson was fixed on this choice and Philippa was about to go through the roof. She asked me to try to do something.

It happened that a baritone saxophonist who had come to New York a few years before had been sent to my house by Francisco "Ali" Mora (now Francisco Mora-Catlett), himself a former Arkestra drummer. Alex Harding, like Francisco, was a Buddhist, and so he came to chant with us on his first day in the city, and we established a relationship from that day onward. While the Arkestra was performing at Context the year before, I had run into Alex and had asked him about his interest in playing Sun Ra's music. He, in fact, was supposed to have come down to Context during the June series that never was. I called him to see if he was still interested. He said yes. I then worked on convincing Marshall of the need to mentor a younger musician. Alex, after all, lived in New York. His wouldn't be a one-shot deal, either, and he actually played baritone sax, Charles Davis's instrument, while Ronald played tenor. Marshall agreed and eventually Jacson gave in. Alex is an excellent musician and he and Marshall hit it off well. It was a perfect match; Alex added a lot to the saxophone section.

There were a number of things I did along those lines, but basically with a low profile. My desire was to get the job done. It didn't matter to me who did and didn't know what I was doing. The tour went extremely well. The Moers Festival concert was nothing short of fantastic. Even though the music wasn't all that together, the spirit of togetherness and unity as well as the sense of achievement after five years of working without Sunny was a special moment.

Before we began the gig, we took a page out of Charles Davis's book and advanced it a bit. We made a circle and actually did an invocation to Sun Ra, which was different from what we did at Context. Before we ended the circle we chanted the name "Ra," bringing Sun Ra back into that room. You could feel it! Electricity and excitement were in the air as we went out onto the stage and played to our first large festival audience in years. The audience picked up on this transcendental occurrence and sang, *"Yah dada da dah dah da dah da . . .We travel the Spaceways!"* for several hours after we had finished. The response we got was rare and comparable to the response we'd get when Sun Ra was alive.

The festival producer, Burkhard Hennen, had remarked earlier in the day about a concert Sun Ra had done at Moers years before that had similar magical dimensions. On that occasion, it had apparently been raining all day. Sun Ra—angered that it was going to rain on his performance—commanded the rain to stop. And it did, much to the amazement of all who bore witness.

The other gigs we did on this tour didn't come close to the magic at Moers, but we did raise one up in Tilberg, Netherlands, before we returned home. I left this mini-tour with a renewed sense of warmth and brotherhood. After we returned to Kennedy Airport, I embraced Jacson and Marshall and told them I'd be in touch. That was May 21, 1997.

A couple of weeks later, just as the Arkestra was going south to Birmingham, Alabama's City Stages to perform, I was headed north to Redwood, New York, to record the CD *Dedication* with Ahmed Abdullah's Diaspora.

When I returned home after that successful recording, I got a call from Sue Pearlstine, who asked if I would be available for an Arkestra gig in California from August 22 through 25, inclusive. I had been flying high from the recording date, my first in ten years, playing my own music, and from that tremendous victory at Moers still fresh in my mind. I had all but forgotten and forgiven the debacle of Context in 1996, so I agreed to make myself available for the August weekend. The latter part of that July saw the release of John Szwed's long-awaited book *Space Is the Place*, on the Pantheon Books imprint. I picked up a half-price copy from the Strand, the bookstore on Broadway and East Twelfth Street in Greenwich Village, as soon as I'd heard it was out. I read it within a couple of days and could see that John had relied heavily on Jack Jacson for certain information. My suspicion was confirmed when I questioned Szwed about his sources, especially in regard to FESTAC. I thought the festival had been disturbingly misrepresented, considering how spectacular that monthlong government-supported affair was.

I understand why Szwed relied on Jacson. After all, Jacson had convinced even me that he knew what he was talking about, and I had known him a lot longer and a lot better, or so I thought. But there was another myth regarding Sun Ra's reality that most people bought into, which was that those who lived in the house on Morton Street were better informed and more knowledgeable about the Sun Ra experience than anyone else. If you didn't know better than to follow that line, you'd be left with two choices: Marshall or Jacson. Marshall put everything into his music and didn't talk as much as Jacson, who gave the impression of having expertise in a number of areas. There were some things in the book that I felt were troublesome to the legacy and history of Sun Ra, yet from a broader point of view I also thought it was a significant achievement to have a major publishing house present his story.

Around the beginning of that August, I started calling Sue Pearlstine to get more details about the trip that was to happen in three weeks. Monique would be going out on job-related business, and we were trying to coordinate our traveling plans. Sue had by then become evasive. Each of the three times I called her, she'd tell me she had another call coming in and promise to get back to me. I then called Jacson who, at the time, happened to be on the phone with his daughter. He too promised to get back to me. I called Jacson at least two other times but got no response.

Then, at about 10 p.m. on Sunday, August 10, I got a call from Tyrone Hill.

"Hey, Ahmed, do you know anybody in Jacson's family?"

"No. What's the matter?"

"Jacson's dead, man."

"Dead? What happened?"

"We found him on the floor in his room. The body's still here. We're trying to find somebody in his family, a next of kin or someone to contact, man. So you don't know nobody in his family, huh?"

"Naw, man, I don't know anybody in his family."

That was one of the strangest calls I had ever received. I asked around here and there and was able to piece together that as of late Jacson had been drinking heavily. Someone at the house heard a thud early in the morning, about 5 a.m. No one checked Jacson's room until around 11 a.m., at which time his body was discovered on the floor. By then he was already dead. The guys at the house were obviously in a state of shock. They had been living with him all these years, yet called me in New York some eleven hours after his body had been discovered to ask if I knew any of his family. Jacson had been taking care of most things pertaining to business and, just as in Sun Ra's case, folks were paralyzed into inaction without him. I was told by Pico that he had been summoned to the house to make the appropriate calls and get things moving. By 1 a.m., fourteen hours after the body had been discovered, Jacson was finally removed.

A few days later, Elson called to tell me that my ticket to California had been canceled and that Jothan Callins would be going in my stead. No one wanted to take responsibility for allowing this to go down. It was Sue who had initially called me. Marshall was the leader of the Arkestra and Jacson was dead, leaving me a raging goddamn bull. Actually, I was angrier at myself for having allowed this crew to do this to me one more time. Sue later claimed Jacson wouldn't let her tell me about the change, all the while saying he would take care of everything. Marshall, of course, never knew anything about anything that was happening. The biggest problem I had with Marshall was that he never had any understanding of reciprocity and he never had my back, no matter what I did for him.

This time the letter I wrote to Marshall was short and to the point. No twenty-two pages, no agonizing, no remorse, no sympathy. Just pure anger: "Don't let another death happen in the House of Ra before you take some responsibility. All the blame for what has happened can't be put on dead Jacson!"

After Jacson's death, Marshall began to rely more heavily on Elson, who two years before had been treated a little better than I had been in relation to a California gig. He, at least, had not expected to go. He hadn't been lied to or avoided; he just hadn't been considered, even after his years of loyalty and investment of time. And I was the only person who had spoken up on his behalf.

Elson, now one of the few Arkestra members with any understanding of business, tried to talk me back into the band, but it would have been impossible for me to work under Marshall. I explained to Elson and Philippa (who was still working with them) that it was the spirit of the Arkestra that needed to be healed, and that I was doing fine healing my own spirit away from them, thank you very much.

Elson suggested that the problem was Philippa and that it was her interference that had caused the upheaval. He also saw Sue Pearlstine as an issue. While I understood that, yes, there could be a problem with people outside of the Arkestra, I felt the major problem stemmed from the lack of understanding of karma and Marshall's sometimes vindictive lack of leadership. It was much easier to blame others for coming in and starting trouble than it would be to search within for the source of it. Elson's efforts to get me to come back clearly weren't going to bear fruit—especially when he suggested I should come back and just basically keep my mouth shut.

○

Little by little, I became convinced I needed to document my experiences with Sun Ra and the Arkestra. I was reminded of what June Tyson had been telling me for years: "No one would believe this; I gotta write a book." I began to see that the struggle within the Arkestra wasn't limited to that entity alone. It was the struggle of African people wherever we found ourselves. It might well have been the struggle of all people. I know with African people, it's our investment in charismatic leaders who take us only as far as the development of our own innate leadership allows. It was a struggle that clearly showed itself in our desire to determine our own destiny without understanding what was needed to accomplish that end. It was significant for me that Jacson would come to the fore as a leader of the Arkestra to aid in a historical distortion of FESTAC, one of the more recent and major diasporic efforts at self-determination. His distortions and contribution to *Space Is the Place* catalyzed my effort. Add to this my relationship to both Sun Ra and his music, my own development as a musician, and what I saw as the disintegration of a wonderful Arkestra, and there was no way I couldn't write it. I had to.

As fall arrived, Philippa began to get more offers for the Arkestra. In November, as a result of Alex Harding doing a gig with the David Murray Big Band and turning the contact person over to Philippa, the Arkestra was able to work a few gigs at a new venue, the Minetta Lane Theater in the Village. The May gig at Moers itself led to another trip to Germany that November. Although I was asked, I refused to participate in that one, except as a behind-the-scenes advisor to Philippa.

As if to show how closely we were connected, despite our disagreements, one morning before the gigs in Germany, I had stepped out of a diner in Brooklyn to hear Michael Ray calling me from a car. Michael was heading to the airport to return to New Orleans after having just returned from a Philly rehearsal with the Arkestra. I was leaving a meeting with a writers' group in which I had just finished reading pages from this book. Michael was apparently preparing another trumpeter for the gig in Germany that he too was not going to make.

According to Philippa, the two nights in Germany provided good money, but had uneven results. Work, however, seemed to be coming in. Elson was handling some of the business, most notably calling musicians. And Philippa was handling other things while also getting the gigs. Elson obviously had been conferring with Marshall on personnel as Philippa had been conferring with him on the work. Without Michael Ray and myself, the band didn't have a good trumpeter on hand. So they decided to use my friend Robert Rutledge once again, along with Dave Gordon.

Between Robert and Philippa, I was kept totally up to date on what was happening with the band.

Philippa knew from the effectiveness of the Context gigs that a regular presence in New York was a basic necessity for a big band. Late into 1997, she entered into negotiations with the Fez. For some eight years, the Fez had been built up both by its owners and the Mingus Big Band into a trendy spot. All of the things the guys complained about not having at Context were present at the Fez. They had food, a bar, a hot space on Lafayette Street, not off the beaten path like Context or the Cooler. And it already had a reputation as the home of a big band playing the music of a charismatic composer: Charlie Mingus. What could be more perfect?

# XII
# MIXED SIGNALS

It's better to be ignorant than to be wise, because it is written that not many wise are chosen. So therefore I just consider myself as ignorant 'cause every day I learn something and if I knew everything, then I couldn't say that, but I learn something every day. So I must be ignorant, if I got to learn something every day.
    —Sun Ra, on the concept that ignorance is bliss

I got a call from Michael Ray late that November. He called to say Samarai Celestial, who had been playing with Sun Ra off and on since 1979, had left the planet. Samarai was a wonderful drummer, always fun to be around. He had that rare quality of being a leader who also knew how to follow. We had done the gig together at Moers back in May. The magic of that gig had everything to do with the presence of all who were a part of it, and Samarai was major in that regard. His death was a great loss. The Moers gig indicated—more than other gigs I had been on since Sun Ra had passed—that there was hope, a chance to take Sun Ra's music to the max.

Oddly enough, on that same day, just after I had talked to Michael, I walked out of the house to get some air and picked up a postcard:

Brother Ahmed, the end is near. I have brain cancer. I'll save a place in heaven's glorious orchestra for you. —Arthur Jones.

He also said he had just heard Carlos Ward and Andrew Cyrille in a Parisian duo performance, which was how he got my address. I had not seen Arthur since 1984, when he played the Sound Unity

Festival coordinated by William Parker, Patricia Nicholson, and company. There had been rumors circulating that he was already dead. But to get this particular correspondence on the same day as I had gotten the news of Samarai's death was overwhelming.

I tried to find a way of contacting Arthur. Reaching Noah Howard via the internet, I was able to get a number for pianist Bobby Few, Arthur's longtime friend. Yes, he knew where Arthur was, and yes he had a number for him.

It was around Thanksgiving when Arthur Jones and I talked. He sounded well, talking about how he had found an African healer who was giving him some oils that he felt were causing the cancer to go into remission. He was in good spirits and quite clear, remembering and recalling with no prompting. When I first had gone to Paris, back in 1976 with Sun Ra, I had gone looking for Arthur but couldn't find him then because he had been committed to a mental institution on the outskirts of the city. Here, now, over twenty years later, we shared a lengthy conversation, reminding me of the fact that, although I had not seen him in years, I had known him since the 1960s. He had been the first serious musician to befriend me.

That following February, during a rehearsal with Diaspora, Carlos Ward broke the news to me that Arthur had left the planet. Arthur and Samarai represented a generation of musicians from a particular era who, though they had made significant contributions to the development of Jazz, were basically invisible, even to most scholars and followers of the music. There were many of us. Quite a few were able to hang in there with some sense of sanity, but many more had fallen along the wayside in their attempts to survive.

During this period, I had gotten fully engrossed in the writing of this book with help from the excellent poet and scholar Louis Reyes Rivera, who had been recommended to me by Amiri Baraka. By now the writing had become an exercise in magic. As soon as I would put something on the page, it would be followed by all sorts of inspirations and visitations.

I was rehearsing with Carlos for another performance through the Carnegie Hall shelter series. I had been doing these gigs now for close to ten years. They were a great opportunity to try new material, and, newly resolved to stay out of the Arkestra despite my love of Sun Ra's music, I wanted to use the shelter series as a way of working Sun Ra's music into Diaspora's repertoire.

I called on Ryan Tucker, a guitarist who had heard my music years before, to join us. We had met in a karmic kind of way, in that his lady, Diana, had once gotten into my cab during the time of my "power" interviews. Our conversation led to her asking my name. She recognized my name from conversations with Ryan. As it turns out, Ryan had been most impressed by my composition "Eternal Spiraling Spirit," which he had heard while still a high school student in Baltimore. Ryan was a seeking spirit, awakening his consciousness to the point where he understood the importance of Sun Ra as a spiritual being and as an advanced composer. Ryan was actually a good musician who had spent time studying music and philosophy with Sun Ra. He would prove to play a vital role in informing our rhythm section for Sun Ra's music.

I used Monique as a vocalist and poet, Louis as a poet, and Ryan and Masujaa on guitar. RaDu, who had worked with Sun Ra, was my choice on bass. On drums, I brought in Codaryl, who had the ears of the universe; he could hear anything and then create exciting drum lines for it. Carlos Ward, with alto and flute in hand, had never spent any time with Sun Ra but was quite excited by the challenge Sunny's music afforded.

We had three gigs with the shelter series. After the first one, I realized I had come upon a fresh approach. The possibilities unfolding here in playing Sun Ra's music were exciting. I wrote on the Sun Ra Listserv that we had accomplished this feat. Excepting "Mystery of Two," which I had recorded years before, I had not included Sun Ra's compositions in my repertoire. Up until that point, I had kept the Sun Ra music within the Sun Ra Arkestra.

This new fusion signaled another level of understanding and possibility.

As it turns out, Philippa had found a way to get the Arkestra a regular working situation at the Fez. She had negotiated a contract between the Fez and the Arkestra under Marshall Allen's leadership. The agreement was for a fee that would decrease over time, with the expectation that attendance would increase with time.

After two successful weeks, Philippa took off to go to Europe to try to find summer touring work for the Arkestra. When she returned, she found that her role had been minimized, as Elson had taken over all of the band's business matters. Prior to her leaving, she had been the one to get the money, make payments to band members, etc. When she returned (not surprisingly to me, but obviously to her), Elson had taken over that responsibility and wasn't about to turn it back over to her. Meanwhile, I was having a good time of it. Through my association with Louis, I had found a new home in Brooklyn, Sistas' Place, in the heart of Bedford-Stuyvesant. The music of Diaspora, which now included the music of Sun Ra, was being well received in that environment. It was, in a sense, coming full circle with Sun Ra's music, in that Sistas' Place was down the street from the East, which used to be two blocks away, on Jefferson Avenue. The East was where, in 1975, I played my first gig with Sun Ra. Sistas' Place and the East had in common the fact that Leon Thomas was the first musician to inaugurate both venues.

Sistas' Place is run by some committed sisters and brothers whose case I had been attracted to back in 1986, when they had won against a 101-count indictment of a trumped-up conspiracy case brought against them by the federal government.

Around this time, late February 1998, the Arkestra was slated to be filmed at the Fez by a small European company. At Philippa's suggestion, the young German film director had asked me to do an interview. I agreed, but wanted to arrive and leave early because I didn't particularly want to hear the music or see the cats.

As it turned out, the film crew was late, a series of technical problems slowed things down even further, and band members began to arrive, set up, and prepare to warm up. It was now time for me to leave, so the interview never took place.

Other problems, centered mostly around compensation for filming and a general lack of trust of anyone involved in the production, plagued the project. The whole affair ended up serving as a good enough reason for Elson to politic against Philippa. Since the director had initially come to her, the project was viewed as Philippa's idea. The fact that it was falling apart was also blamed on her. With all this happening, the problem of the band's drawing power became another issue. At the last minute, the club's manager had been forced to change the time of the show. With the poor turnout they had been having, the club owners wanted to cut the band down to one set and have another act come in to do the later set. Elson then tried to renegotiate a contract that he had never originally negotiated. That added more gas to the flames.

A few weeks later, in March, I got a distressed call from Philippa about what was happening at the Fez. The club manager had called her and told her about Elson's demanding to see the contract. She felt she had put too much time and effort into the Arkestra's development to be sidestepped like that. Working against Elson's attempt was the Arkestra's not-quite-convincing reputation, coupled with the subtle racism of the music industry. This meant the people at the Fez (who were already dealing with Sue Mingus, a white woman) preferred to accept an Arkestra represented by Philippa than one represented by a Black man. Unfortunately, Elson's manner, coupled with his locks and thick accent, could not convince them otherwise. Marshall, as leader of the Arkestra, again opted not to take a stand, which resulted in the band being pulled from the Fez prior to a Sunday gig on March 15.

It was at this point, on the ides of March, that Philippa called to ask me to intervene in the affairs of the Arkestra. There were several major festival gigs pending, and she expected the band was going to get rid of her. One festival producer, Jim Dulzo from Detroit, came to the Fez and expressed concern that the Arkestra wouldn't stay together until his September festival. He was concerned that if the band couldn't handle the scrutiny of the downtown New York music scene it was unlikely to handle the scrutiny of a major festival. His question to Philippa was, "Who's leading the band? Who do you go to when you want something done?" That question became the impetus for her to call me.

Bret Primack, a longtime writer for several Jazz publications who had also attended the Fez and heard about the problems Philippa had, suggested she might have the wrong person leading the band. Of course, it wasn't her call, but she was managing the group. Whom did she represent, if not the person leading it? Who was the liaison between manager and band?

The Fez gig was transitional and premature. The Arkestra hadn't yet found its new footing without Jacson, a kick-ass martial artist who therefore commanded respect for his physical prowess alone. And Jacson had also functioned as a flutist, bassoonist, and percussionist, which meant he also earned respect as a musician. Elson, a percussionist, didn't possess the same level of musicianship, nor Jacson's physical ability. He was slow in getting respect and working into his role as "straw boss." He might have been more effective without Philippa, a white woman, handling business. The Sun Ra Arkestra was not an easy crew. Discipline was low (Marshall could never be considered a disciplinarian), and as a matter of style there was too much indecision.

When Philippa called, I told her straight out I wasn't interested in rejoining the Arkestra in any capacity. I was too busy working on incorporating Sun Ra's music into Diaspora. Right then, I told her, I couldn't even consider talking about it until the end of the month, after my last shelter gig on March 23 at the Hudson Guild Theater and one at Sistas' Place on March 28.

A few days later, I was awakened by a dream that was so real I actually expected to see Sun Ra sitting right there in my bedroom. In the dream, he told me that *Diaspora* stood for "Dispersions of the Spirit of Ra" and that I had to play his music. His statement was emphatic and final.

I had been doing this already, so it took me some time to decode this message from the other side. I had never in my life dreamed of directing a big band, but I had been leading ensembles of six or more pieces since 1972. What more could it take to add ten or more musicians?

I called Philippa and presented her with an idea. I would create a new entity, an all-star project, and bring together as many of the excellent musicians who had come through Sun Ra as I could get hold of—people like James Spaulding, Charles Davis, Vincent Chancey, Craig Harris, Dick Griffin, etc. As well, we'd feature several of the current Arkestra members, Michael Ray, Tyrone Hill, and Elson. Marshall would cover the reeds, we had the brass, and I already had a rhythm section. I would bring in other people outside of the Arkestra who had serious reputations and respect for Sun Ra's music. They could even be people who had never played Sunny's music before but who long had a desire to do so. We could also include ex-Arkestra members who had gone on to establish their own niches while still retaining their love for Sunny's music.

Philippa was reluctant at first, and I was too busy with my own gigs, but right then I told her she had to own the idea. There could be no wavering. She had to present it with authority and conviction to whoever she talked to, including Marshall and Elson.

I explained that this would be the only way I could work with that group. While I was willing to support Marshall, I was equally convinced he wouldn't know how to support me. Nevertheless, I had to be the one to make personnel and other artistic decisions. This project could be the way to mend fences and push the music.

Philippa took stock of the fact that after Elson had intervened and asked to draw up a new agreement with the Fez—without Marshall backing her in any way—she had been dismissed. Fired.

They had been foolish enough to disrespect her without finding out the details of the other gigs she had been working on. At that point, she said she could not represent a group that demonstrated no confidence in her. But, by the last days of March, she became more convinced that the All-Star Project was the only way to go—that is, unless she wanted to give up everything relating to Sun Ra's music. There was no way she could change her relationship with Marshall, and Elson in effect had Marshall working for him.

I asked her to make the initial call to Marshall and to at least present the idea. If he was interested, I told her, I'd follow up with a fuller explanation. After talking to Marshall, I could then talk to Tyrone, Michael, and Elson, in that order. She agreed.

On April 1, I got on the phone and spoke with each of them individually for the first time in several months. Each, in turn, agreed to do a gig with me in New York on June 6, followed by a tour in Europe and a possible Midwest tour, all under the auspices of this new entity, with Marshall Allen at the center.

I explained to each of them the long- and short-term advantages of this new concept. We would be creating something that Sun Ra had done once, in 1983, so even while this would be different, I offered, we already had a precedent. The All-Star Project would be a gigantic experimental workshop that would include Sun Ra's poetry, his lyrics, and dancers, too. This would in no way be a permanent group with fixed personnel, but an ever-evolving entity that would jump-start an obviously failing Arkestra, using key members for this purpose. The great thing was that it would allow people who had been playing the music for years an opportunity to work with others and share those years of experience. We had further impetus with the recent release of a first recording by Tyrone Hill, featuring Marshall Allen and coming out on the CIMP label, just as my own recording had.

Philippa and I were now working together on this. Once we got verbal agreements from the guys in the Arkestra, we had to convince the booking people to change the billing to the Sun Ra All-Star Project, directed by me and featuring Marshall Allen. This configuration reflected the one that had been in place all along, at

Context, at the Cooler, and at the Fez: Marshall was at the center of the presentation on stage but wasn't the actual leader off stage.

The producers at the Knitting Factory and at the festivals in Europe and Detroit all agreed. The person whom Philippa dealt with at the Knitting Factory, Glenn Max, got so excited as he riffed off our planned personnel that they offered us a larger venue and more money.

On the ides of April, after not hearing from anyone for a few days, I decided to give Elson a call. Just as I was doing so, Philippa called me to say that sabotage was brewing. She had Glenn Max on the phone telling her that all the names we had submitted under the All-Star Project were now touted as part of a super Arkestra under Marshall's leadership. The Knitting Factory was about to renege on its agreement and gave us an ultimatum. According to Philippa, we had until 7 p.m. that day to straighten things out; it was already five. We needed far more time. I immediately called Elson.

"I been tryin' to reach you for a couple of days now. What's going on?"

"Oh, Ahmed, I don't think this a good idea," he said with his thick Brazilian accent. "This gonna destroy the Arkestra."

"Elson, the Arkestra is already destroying itself. Can't you see that? You guys couldn't even keep that gig at the Fez, man, and that was a dream situation."

"No, but that's okay, Ahmed. This would really be it."

"Well, Elson, how's that gonna be it? It's not what I'm intending to do."

"What about the other guys, Ahmed? You know Sunny wouldn't do anything like this, man."

"The hell he wouldn't! In 1983, when he had the All-Stars, he only used Marshall, John, and Clifford Jarvis. And Clifford wasn't even playing in the band at the time. It ain't like these damn gigs are gonna make anybody rich, and they damn sure ain't makin' no money playin' in the Arkestra, anyway. Besides, they can always do something else while we're doin' these gigs."

"I don't know, Ahmed. It's not good idea."

"Listen, Marshall already agreed and so did Michael and Tyrone."

"They chang'ah they mind. They not gonna do it no more. Besides, they gotta be outta town on June 6. They gonna be in Syracuse and Cleveland."

"They ain't tell me nothin' about no gig, man."

"No, it just come up, Ahmed."

"Listen, Elson, I'm gonna do this project whether you're in it or not. The reason I asked you to be in it was because of all the hard work you've been doing. But that's okay, if you don't want to be in it, guess what? It can't be stopped! So you can do whatever the fuck you want. You can't stop this. You hear?"

I hung up on Elson and immediately called Marshall. I was boiling now.

"Hello," Marshall answered.

"Marshall, I just finished talking to Elson. He said something about y'all pulling out of the gig."

"I told you I could make it if nothin' came up. Well, somethin' came up."

"Something came up? Since I talked to you two weeks ago?"

"Yup."

I found every word I could think of to call him that was both insulting and demeaning and then I invented some. Got real creative.

"Hey, you can't talk to me like that."

"I just did, you sorry excuse for a muthafucker, and furthermore—"

"Hey, you watch your mouth!"

That was Thursday. Philippa had assumed she had a relationship with the Knitting Factory that would have allowed them to give us time to work things out. She didn't and they wouldn't. Unfortunately, we didn't know that a contract had been given to Marshall after a verbal commitment had been given to us. Glenn Max, the young person at the Knitting Factory, had reneged on his offer, justifying it by saying he wanted the same group that had been there the previous December, led by Marshall Allen. This, of course, was the opposite of what he had expressed to us.

We wouldn't know for at least a month that the Knitting Factory had already reneged on the deal, but we found out exactly a week later that lawyerly pressure had been applied by a person whom Elson's friend and partner, Jack Reich, had hired to do the job. The lawyer had threatened the Knitting Factory, claiming we had no right to use the name of Sun Ra either as an Arkestra (which was not our intention) or as a Project. The letter sent to both Philippa and myself from a Rhode Island firm gave away the connection to Jack, who lives in Rhode Island, and to Elson, who works with him. The letter, dated April 23, claimed to represent Marshall Allen and further stated that Michael Ray, Tyrone Hill, and Elson weren't going to play in the Sun Ra All-Star Project.

We found out that Jim Dulzo in Detroit had also been sent this ridiculous nonsense. Jim did what anyone with intelligence would have done: He called us to warn about it and to say that it changed nothing in his mind. In fact, he said, the letter was further proof of the lack of professionalism that had led him to encourage us with the project from the start.

The inability to see the larger picture and the perception that there wasn't enough money to go around played into all of this. These two factors were further influenced by the fact that for years Elson and Jack Reich had been selling Sun Ra T-shirts, which were generally more popular than recordings, especially at festivals. Between them these two were just counting the money.

The problem that the letter portended was a serious one and had to be addressed. Our credibility was being attacked, but we couldn't back out now even if we wanted to. This crew was trying to make sure no one would ever see the All-Star Project come to fruition.

At the time, Philippa was also working as legal secretary to an entertainment lawyer whose take on all this, particularly with a Rhode Island lawyer sending a letter to New York, was unappreciative, to put it mildly. He sent a sharp letter on our behalf to the Knitting Factory, stating that we had a tape proving that an offer and a verbal agreement had been made to the All-Star Project. Our lawyer further suggested that the Knitting Factory bring both parties to the table and work out the details. He then warned us that we should get written commitments from all of the musicians we said we could deliver.

By this time, we had found out that Elson had gone to several of the musicians whose names we had submitted and attempted to persuade them to play in the Arkestra under Marshall instead of in the All-Stars. An undeclared and uncalled-for war was now in motion.

Meanwhile, my old friend Pico had come back into the picture. On his way from Texas to Philly, he had been stranded in New Orleans and called me from Michael Ray's house, requesting a loan. With an advance that had come in from the Detroit gig, I wired a MoneyGram to bail him out of his difficulty.

When he got back to Philly, I called him in an attempt to cash in on his longtime relationship with Marshall, hoping that Pico could help us strike up a proper dialogue. I explained to Pico all that had gone down in as much detail as I could. After hearing me out, Pico explained that Marshall would probably rather be the codirector. I had no problem with that at all.

The first thing I had to do, of course, was apologize to Marshall for having been so insulting. That wasn't difficult. After all, he and I had shared some special experiences over the years. I could overlook the incidents of the past couple of years, as my eyes were on the bigger picture. If we were to play the music together, we had to clear the air. After I spoke with Marshall, he once again agreed that the project was a good idea and that he would consider being a part of it. I offered him codirectorship, as Pico had suggested, and I read him a quote from Sun Ra that we wanted to use, taken from Valerie Wilmer's *As Serious as Your Life*:

While in high school, I never missed a band, whether a known or unknown unit, I loved music beyond the stage of liking it. Some of the bands I heard never got popular and never made hit records, but they were truly natural Black beauty. I want to thank them and I want to give honor to all the sincere musicians who ever were or ever will be. It's wonderful to even think about such people. The music they played was a natural happiness of love, so rare I cannot explain it. It was fresh; and courageous; daring, sincere, unfettered. It was unmanufactured avant-garde, and still is, because there was no place for it in the world, so the world neglected something of value and did not understand. And all along I could not understand why the world could not understand. Was it because the world considers music as only a commercial commodity? I am glad that that is not my code.

Before I had talked to Marshall, for the sake of clarity, I had written out the ideas for the project so there'd be no further misunderstanding. Philippa and I had been asked both by our lawyer and by the festival organizers to describe the project. I read segments of it to Marshall. He once again gave me the impression that he was down with the program.

These conversations went on for several days, and I actually thought we were working something out. Conversations with my brass buddies, Michael and Tyrone, also gave me reason to believe we could solve all of this amicably.

Marshall said he'd give me an answer in a few days. I kept pressing Pico as to what was happening, and he finally asked if I knew that Marshall had already signed the contract for the Knitting Factory gig. The plot thickened. More flimflam! We now understood why they'd felt emboldened enough to call Detroit. The Knitting Factory had done a complete flip without even doing us the courtesy of informing us.

By then it was mid-May, and the gig was to go down on June 6 (my sons' birthday); we couldn't fail. We contacted Jerold Couture, the lawyer I had spoken to when Sun Ra passed in 1993 about the plethora of CDs being illegally released. Jerry Couture was not coming into the situation cold; he understood the magnitude of the problem. But I had stopped consulting with him after 1993, as there wasn't enough unity in the Arkestra then to allow us to get what was rightfully ours. What Monique, Philippa, and I were now facing was a logically illogical extension of that same issue.

When the lawyer who represented Marshall, Michael, Tyrone, and Elson attacked our credibility, that bunch made a significant error. It's been said that people in glass houses shouldn't throw rocks. Jerry suggested we get something in writing from the Sun Ra estate, the only legal entity entitled to Sun Ra's intellectual property. Mr. Couture suggested we go for the jugular and get exclusive rights to usage from Sunny's estate. Our initial intention was to get something to cover the period when our gigs would take place. Since the issue of credibility had been raised, he felt permission was necessary in order to do the gigs. Jerry also suggested that we ask to use both names, "Sun Ra" and "Arkestra." He felt that by now there could be no good-faith negotiation; the Philly crew had already proved as much. Accordingly, we had to take them out of commission in order to launch our project. I agreed with his logic even while I had no real interest in the Arkestra name. On June 5, we got written permission to proceed. I faxed a copy to Philadelphia, then called and faxed another to the Knitting Factory. The musicians I had gathered together had been rehearsing and had every intention of making the gig. On the evening of June 5, there appeared on the Sun Ra Listserv a long letter written by Gloria Powers, Michael Ray's lady.

She had posted under the subject heading "Marshall Needs Help" that I had taken over the Arkestra from Marshall. She claimed that I had stripped Marshall of his right to lead the Arkestra via some legal chicanery. This became the most public account of our situation to date, and it now took on international significance. The false account she posted on the Listserv distorted everything. It had to be answered, but the fact was that people who were getting the story on the internet for the first time had no way of knowing what had transpired over the past two months. They wouldn't understand the complexity of issues that had characterized the situation for the past five years.

Gloria's involvement also brought up issues relative to Satellites of the Sun and the sabotaging of that project. Now here she was again taking the offensive in a veiled way, so that those unaware of the history would not fully understand the subtle dynamics.

With that in mind, I attempted to give some historical background and understood that somehow I had to take the high ground. Monique and I had overextended ourselves so much in getting this project off the ground that we had run out of money, had no backup and, on top of that, had been removed from America Online right in the middle of a word war.

Consequently, we had to fax Philippa our response, which she then sent out on the Listserv. Philippa insisted on adding some legal threats into the mix. I didn't necessarily agree with her. But nevertheless, considering the attack, I was willing to back her up.

Most of the people who emailed the Sun Ra Listserv about this affair came out sympathetic to Marshall and the Arkestra, which ended up making me the heavy in it all. The picture that Gloria painted of Marshall—and even the title of the posting, "Marshall Needs Help"—gave the impression of a long-suffering dedicated musician being robbed of his birthright through underhanded means. She was pulling at heartstrings to the point of suggesting that she feared this sordid affair could cause Marshall to become seriously ill. There was no question about it: We were the bad guys. Since she also painted herself as a disinterested neutral party relaying vital information, who wouldn't believe her story?

The way the issue was framed, we were the ones who had taken these gigs from the deserving members of the Arkestra. For years they had eked out a meager existence in order to be totally available at the behest of Sun Ra. I was the usurper intent on disinheriting them and taking leadership away from its only rightful possessor, Marshall Allen. Gloria further implied in her posting that she knew my true intentions, despite my disingenuous comments to the contrary.

There were, however, quite a few people who knew better. They could see through the maze, enough to come out in support of what I was really trying to do. In truth, I believed and still believe that Marshall had been taken advantage of. I believed he needed help, and that the people who were now stepping forward were manipulating the situation for their own ends wanted to benefit from the Sun Ra legacy at the expense of the rest of us. Where were the Jack Reichs, Michael Rays, and Gloria Powers when we were struggling to recast the Sun Ra Arkestra as a viable institution?

Elson, who lived in New York and had been around throughout the earlier struggles, was now refusing to answer my phone calls. And, after a point, whenever I called the house in Philly and Noël Scott (who had only occasionally been around) answered the phone, he would hang up. Apparently they were both insisting on ending dialogue between Marshall and me. Meanwhile, the conversations I had with Michael and Tyrone were supposed to make me believe they were still considering their participation in the All-Star Project, right up until Gloria Powers began her distortions online. I received permission from the estate to move forward. With that in hand, I no longer needed any of them. I was truly able to say goodbye to rubbish.

In a sense, I was fortunate not to have had internet access, as I didn't have to see the attacks on a daily basis. One of the most curious facts about human nature I discovered through this ordeal was how ready individuals are to cast judgment with limited information.

We had to rely on Philippa to answer some of the accusations, which were pretty spiteful and hurtful to me, considering my original intent. Gloria and company were partially successful in their propaganda blitz, for even with the estate backing me up, we didn't do the gig on June 6 at the Knitting Factory; the people there gave the gig to the Arkestra and backed off on having the All-Stars at all. Behind all of the online attacks and controversy, no one in New York got to hear or see what the project was all about.

The All-Star Project represented a conceptual divide that had been around since the SOB's gig that memorialized John Gilmore. Sun Ra's music had always been multifaceted and on the cutting edge, which is what principally brought people to it. Marshall Allen, in his desire to work something out, relied heavily on people already in the band. By 1998, he had been leading the band for three years. He had to change from being a central sideman without a conceptual framework to the leader of one of the most conceptual ensembles in the history of the music. To his credit, he was doing this in his seventies. The declining audience at the Fez had everything to do with the conceptual choices Marshall had made. As well, ever since our involvement at Context, neither he nor anyone else with the Arkestra understood the need to focus on audience development.

The one thing that Marshall had in addition to his tremendous musical ability was a personality that made people want to work for him despite everything else. I certainly did. In that department, with his Gemini ways, he was closer to Sun Ra than anyone else. They arrived on the planet three days apart, Sun Ra May 22, Marshall May 25. Quite frankly, it would have been a great thing if we could have worked together to make this All-Star Project a reality, but unfortunately, things had moved to a point of no return. I couldn't turn back because of the damage that would be done to my reputation. It would have been brilliant if someone had stepped in to arbitrate the situation, as our lawyer had suggested, but nobody seemed interested in that. Folks seemed more interested in choosing sides. Whose side are you on?

I had seen this problem coming several years before. It was a reason why the Satellites of the Sun approach was so important: It would have allowed all of us to work together, developing individual concepts and approaches while also paying tribute to Sun Ra. Most musicians are only interested in getting the next gig, paying the bills, getting name recognition, etc. Rarely is the musical concept thought about. That falls on the shoulders of the leader, composer, arranger. Tell me what to play and in which key and I'll play it, you dig?

The All-Star Project was going to take another approach, using the fact that people had already gone through the hurdle of name recognition to take us to the next level—which is to say, okay, you have a recording out under your name, now what? In other words, everything missing from Marshall's Arkestra would be included. The element of spontaneity that came from having strong individuals in an ensemble would be our hallmark. Sunny's music would be our core.

Even after June 6, we'd learned that Elson Nascimento had been calling Detroit and the North Sea Jazz Festival countless times, telling people that certain members of the Arkestra weren't coming. He had called so many times that the festival person we talked to in the Hague told us he didn't care who *wasn't* making it; his only concern was who *was* going to make it. With the written permission from the estate, we could prove we were exclusively authorized by the only legal entity, Sun Ra's family, to use his name. The person we talked to at the festival thought that in view of this document, we should use the name Arkestra. I was absolutely adamant, however, that I wanted nothing to do with the Arkestra name. And this was one gig that Gloria, Michael, Elson, and Jack Reich couldn't stop.

For our debut at the North Sea Jazz Festival, we rehearsed an ensemble in New York that included baritone saxophonist Alex Harding and tenors Arthur Doyle and Roland Alexander. Altoist Noah Howard met us in Europe. Robert Rutledge and I played trumpet, with Eddie Gale also meeting us in the Netherlands. The two-guitar idea worked well with Ryan Tucker and Masujaa. Ryan, however, was not able to make the North Sea gig because of some personal business he had to tend to, so I got Kelvyn Bell in his stead. With Kelvyn and Masujaa both using synthesizers, the chordal component promised to be exciting. Billy Bang and his incredible violin would also meet us in the Netherlands. The rest of the rhythm section would include bassist RaDu ben Judah, along with drummers Codaryl Moffett and Roger Blank. Miles Griffith, Monique, and I would handle the vocals, with Louis reworking Sun Ra's poetry for the occasion. Initially, we opted for two dancers, but our budget allowed only Maria Mitchell to work alone. To round it all out, Philippa sewed seventeen costumes in black with gigantic Sun symbols around the heart.

There'd been so many musicians I knew, talented and unrecognized, who had died too soon that I began seeing the All-Star Project as an opportunity to bring people together under the Sun

Ra banner. This project was natural for our more adventurous spirits. We had fought for the right to present this concept all the way up to July 11, when we marched up on that stage at the Jazz festival, brass and reeds playing and others chanting "We Travel the Spaceways," victorious against many odds. Standing room only and standing ovations. It was great!

We made an even more impressive showing on September 6, in Detroit, when we added powerful tenor saxophonist John Stubblefield along with Roland Alexander. We exchanged Roger Blank for Andrei Strobert and replaced Eddie Gale with Vincent Chancey, and it worked. We couldn't afford to fly Noah Howard or Billy Bang from their homes in Europe, but all the other people with us at the Hague were the same as those at the Montreux-Detroit Jazz Festival. We were able to make a demo CD from our performance in Detroit and thus had officially launched the Sun Ra All-Star Project.

Through it all, I finally learned not to deal with people who give lip service to brotherhood while simultaneously attempting to destroy what I need to do. My greatest lesson is that we always have choice. For years, I had chosen to be around people who would do things contrary to my own interests. But they were also a reflection of me, no better and no worse. I too had been struggling to learn to truly love myself among people who didn't know what love was. As I began to grow and change, I no longer needed them in my life. But when you've been around some other mode for so long, it takes a lot to first realize it and then to break away.

That year, on Sun Ra's arrival day, May 22, I went to hear and see Marshall and the Sun Ra Arkestra perform at the Vision Festival in New York. I don't know if the events had affected them as they did me. By then, I'd become the musical director of Sistas' Place, booking as many adventurous musicians as I could back into the community from which they had rooted and sprung. Now, there was no real contact between the Arkestra and me, but it was joyful to hear Sun Ra's music mixed in with Marshall's. The music sounded as if they had been jolted into a new awareness. Perhaps it was necessary for them to have united against me in order to do what they had to do. When they saw me in the audience, they gave me mixed reviews—I was treated warmly by some and given the cold shoulder by others. Marshall, however, made a point of acknowledging my presence by playing some fierce alto saxophone as he walked around the room and came right past me.

Whether or not the others wanted to understand it, we were all Children of the Sun. And with all the turmoil behind us, there now existed two different ensembles honoring the legacy of Sun Ra.

# XIII AFTERWORD

We arrived in Barbados on July 16, 2022. We came here to acknowledge the second arrival date of Celeste Veronica Nri, OBE, since she left the planet on May 9, 2021. The *we* who traveled here are Monique, our daughter, Tara, and myself. In a most incredible connection, Mum Celeste, who was with her second-born daughter, Mary Nri, came online from Barbados to wish me a happy birthday while I was teaching a class called the Unsung Heroes of the Sun Ra Arkestra. The next day, Mother's Day, she left the planet.

We began this memoir with Monique informing me about my own mother leaving the planet. Thirty years later, I had the opportunity to celebrate my mother-in-law, who had been an adoptive mother to me for the last twenty-nine years. In Barbados, we are staying in the house she left her family on the west coast of this beautiful island country.

*A Strange Celestial Road* was completed by 2000. In the twenty-two ensuing years, more than enough has happened to create a sequel. One of the most significant things was the attack on the World Trade Center on September 11, 2001. That event profoundly affected things in my life. The most remarkable thing for Monique and me was that we were blessed with the birth of our daughter, Tara Abdullah-Nri, on the next day, September 12, 2001.

Tara came onto the planet two months prematurely. At four pounds, she had to stay in an incubator for a month. She brought great joy to our lives because of her presence, and as well, great apprehension due to her size. It was good that I had documented my existence before she came on the planet, because the life we were going to embark on was a totally different one.

Working on a memoir requires a good amount of self-reflection. It was great for me because I came to realize, with all of the time I had logged as an educator, that my mission in life was exactly that. I was in my fifties and had completed my phase as a traveling musician with one of the most peculiar and special ensembles in the world. But being a working musician had meant that I could not spend time with my children, and missed out on many important events in their lives. With Tara, I was given a second chance.

The events of September 11 changed my ability to earn a living as a teaching artist. I was working as a teaching artist for Carnegie Hall and also as music director of Sistas' Place. Carnegie Hall was income producing and Sistas' Place was a labor of love. With Tara only a year old, I was offered an appointment to teach a course on Sun Ra at the New School for Jazz and Contemporary Music. In 2002, I became an adjunct professor and a member of the faculty there.

Meanwhile, my work as music director of Sistas' Place had taken on a new life. We partnered with the developing organization known as the Central Brooklyn Jazz Consortium, which was created to support the many Jazz venues in the area and produced an annual Jazz festival during April. Originating in 1999, the CBJC had as its chairman Jitu Weusi, who was one of the founders of Uhuru Sasa Shule, aka the East. Of course, Weusi was an accomplished educator as well, and was still an assistant principal at a local elementary school. Music education was a major component of the CBJC's mission. And I was appointed chair of the education committee.

With support from the folks at Sistas' Place, I was able to initiate an annual African American tribute to Brooklyn greats honoring Max Roach, Eubie Blake, Kenny Dorham, Chief Bey, Randy Weston, and Gigi Gryce.

We partnered with musician educators including trumpeter Cyril Greene, who was teaching at an elementary school in Coney Island, and pianist Harry Constant, who was music teacher at a middle school in Brownsville. I had known them for years, and they were at the top of their game. We brought them together for a tribute to Max Roach with trumpeter Cecil Bridgewater—who had spent three decades working with Roach—to create a horn arrangement of "Lonesome Lover," the Abbey Lincoln (Aminata Moseka) composition. Harry Constant's students provided the band, and Cyril Greene's students provided the chorus. We also enlisted Max's group M'Boom to perform. We produced this event at the church that Max Roach was raised in, Concord Baptist Church of Christ, in February 2002. Watching Harry Constant and Cyril Greene work with their students got me interested in the possibility of teaching music, not as a teaching artist, but for the Department of Education.

In 2003, I submitted an application for the Teaching Fellows program of the NYC DOE and was accepted. By 2004, I was a music instructor in a public school. One of the people who knew of my work as a teaching artist contacted me about doing a recording of Sun Ra's music. The only problem was that this memoir had not been published. Tom Bellino, founder of Planet Arts Records, and also the major force behind the Vanguard Jazz Orchestra—which was also a band without both of its leaders, Thad Jones and Mel Lewis—knew how difficult it was to re-create a band without a charismatic leader. By 2004, however, I had really moved on from the Sun Ra Arkestra. But as a result of the second dream Sun Ra had presented me with, I knew it was important to record his music under the banner of Diaspora (Dispersions of the Spirit of Ra).

Tom had received a grant to do the recording. My job was to create a magnificent band, an all-star band, as I had at the North Sea Jazz Festival and the Montreux-Detroit Jazz Festival. Tom happened to have been at the North Sea Jazz Festival working with the Village Vanguard Orchestra when we performed in 1998. The recording was called *Ahmed Abdullah's Diaspora: Traveling the Spaceways*. The original name of this memoir was exactly that: *Traveling the Spaceways*. When we could not find a publisher in those early days, we decided to change the name to what it has become. This recording project sealed the deal for me. I was able to record something on my own terms using people I wanted, to honor one of my mentors. And besides that, I was in a full-time teaching position both on the elementary-school level teaching general music and at the college level teaching the compositions and philosophy of Sun Ra.

The activities at Sistas' Place and the CBJC attracted international attention. A promoter from Milan, Gianni Morelenbaum Gualberto, wanted to include us in his series of concerts at the marvelous Teatro Manzoni. We decided we wanted to go into Italy hitting hard, so we identified two places we could work before we played Milan. One was New York's Sweet Rhythm, run by James Browne; the other one was a venue in Newark run by an activist named Slim Washington (no relation to Salim). The brother was a real supporter of Sistas' Place and ran an organization called Black Telephone Workers for Justice. Our mission was to have musicians work at those three Black-owned venues. We were able to make some of those projects work.

○

The next project Monique and I conspired on involved education. In our effort to secure our daughter, Tara, the best education possible, we had enrolled her at the East Village Community School on the Lower East Side. The school had an advanced curriculum. It was important that it had a relationship with Third Street Music School Settlement. Her brothers had studied violin there and Mickey Davidson's Malcolm had really flourished as a musician at Third Street. We were excited to get Tara enrolled because she could begin violin in the first grade, learning the Suzuki method. By the time Tara was in second grade, we were not so thrilled with the results we were learning about at parent-teacher conferences. While the school was integrated and on the artistic Lower East Side, a neighborhood I knew well, things were changing in that community, as they were around New York. Gentrification— the thing that happens when people with the most money get to move into a neighborhood and change things to work for them— was now in effect on the Lower East Side. We are talking about roughly from 2008 to 2010. We realized in conference with her second-grade teachers that Tara was invisible in the classroom. Monique was very active at the school, so we completely understood the problem and our options.

The school where I was teaching, PS 3, in Brooklyn, was not integrated as of 2005. It was a school made up of African children from the continent, African children from the Caribbean, and African American children. And the leader of the school, Kristina Beecher, was also of African Caribbean heritage—and she was a former student of the school. Tara started there in the third grade, and we could see immediate results. Monique became president of the PTA when Tara began at the school, and we were able to really make some gains for our children.

By 2013, Monique and I had moved out of 17 North Elliott Place, where we had lived since she came to the US in July 1992 and found a home in Flatlands, Brooklyn. On the October day we were planning to move in, I found out that the Sun Ra Arkestra was performing at Jazz at Lincoln Center. This was a preview of what was to happen with the Arkestra as a result of staying together under Marshall Allen's leadership, with Elson Nascimento taking care of business. I called the house in Philadelphia and told them I wanted to perform with the band. My request was heeded, and in October 2013, I made it to a rehearsal and donned a space plate to travel the spaceways once again. It was a great experience and the first time I had performed with the band in fifteen years.

The centennial of Sun Ra's arrival was in 2014, so the Arkestra under Marshall's leadership found themselves working more than they had at the height of Sun Ra's popularity in the 1990s. This would be the way things would go right up until 2022, when the band was nominated for a Grammy. Although they didn't win, their nomination was extraordinary. Sun Ra had found a way to give up his death and ensure his spirit was alive.

In 2019, just before the pandemic hit, Melchizedek Music Productions created its first independently produced CD, which combined the spiritual energies of two bands whose leaders were influenced by Sun Ra, myself and multi-percussionist Francisco

Mora-Catlett. The groups are presented together as Diaspora Meets AfroHORN and the album is called *Jazz: A Music of the Spirit, Out of Sistas' Place*. We thought we had to get out in front and put out what it is that we believe will provide light and hope in these harrowing times, and so we did.

In 2020 the world was shut down due to Covid-19. In the midst of all that, an unknown person named George Floyd was brutally murdered in Minneapolis on Marshall Allen's ninety-sixth arrival day. The filming of his murder by a twenty-first-century Ida B. Wells named Darnella Frazier, using a cell phone, and the fact that there was a grassroots organization known as Black Lives Matter already in place helped to amplify the outrage against his modern-day lynching. A worldwide uprising ensued, signaling a Third Reconstruction in America, much as the outrage against Emmett Till in 1955 ignited the Second Reconstruction. The difference between 2020 and other periods of uprising was wrapped around the fact that never in recent times had there been such a collective feeling of hopelessness, a collective depression brought on by the unnatural separation of human beings during the pandemic. I believe the level of empathy that brought people out to protest in record numbers as they did for George Floyd was a spirited and spiritual outpouring of the Third Reconstruction. It will require a spiritual resolution. Art forms of the spirit are needed, and artists are needed, because art is about truth telling. As Sun Ra said, "You got to face the music, you got to listen to Cosmos song!"

The practical usage of the teachings of Sun Ra and those other progenitors of the Music of the Spirit is absolutely a necessity in this twenty-first century. The education needed to cope with the world we are living in certainly requires attention to spiritual practices. This Third Reconstruction has to be approached from that higher sphere. My hope and belief is that this life I have lived can be an aid in that regard.

# ACKNOWLEDG-MENTS

I would first like to acknowledge Blank Forms and specifically Lawrence Kumpf and Ciarán Finlayson, who have worked tirelessly to make this manuscript the kind of book it's supposed to be. I thank them for providing me with the editor, Leopold Froehlich, who has been essential in guiding me toward a book that is representative of who I am. I would also like to thank Louis Reyes Rivera for the years of work he did in helping me complete this manuscript. And, as well, I would like to thank Dr. Salim Washington, who wrote the brilliant foreword and who has been a friend as well as a musician and arranger of music I have used for the last quarter of a century.

My mother and father, Anna and Lubia Bland, created the environment I wanted to incarnate into. It was in Harlem during that period of time where I could hear this phenomenal music called Jazz: A Music of the Spirit. It was in Harlem in the 1950s and '60s where I could hear it in our apartment on 131st Street because my sister Marilyn played it. It was in Harlem where I could hear it because my sister Lorraine had a husband who played it. It was in Harlem after Malcolm X's assassination, where Leroi Jones established the Black Arts Repertory Theater/School, at 108 West 130th Street, where the people of the neighborhood could hear it. It was in Harlem where I could hear it 'cause John Coltrane played it! I thank my mother and father and the Bland family; my sisters Helen and Lorraine; my sons, Rashid and Shahid; our daughter, Tara; my nephew, Derrick; and all of our many cousins who are so much a part of our life.

My wife, Monique Ngozi Nri, has been my partner for thirty years as of this writing. I salute her for the joy, fulfillment, and love she has brought to my life. We always say that when we are together, magic happens, and it does! The most amazing thing is that we were able to bring a child onto the planet—Tara Abdullah-Nri—and she is exactly who we wanted her to be! In this book I often talk about how I have learned through the women who have been in my life. All of them have helped me to be a better human being, and because I have a loving wife who has embraced them, I can truly say I still love them all.

One of the amazing things Monique and I did in the summer of 2022 was spend some time with Mickey Davidson and Carol Bourne. We also spent time with Philippa Jordan. I would like to acknowledge how much I learned from each of these women. Monique has also embraced my sons, Rashid and Shahid, as if they were her own. All of my children have been a source of learning for me and I want to thank them for being in my life. I have said that Iyabode was like an angel and certainly I would not have had the experience of FESTAC, one of the greatest in my life, and one of the inspirations for this book, without her.

My elementary school teacher Willis A. Williams provided a model of what a proactive educator should be all about. Similarly, H. W. Brindel provided an opportunity for me to hear a trumpet player close up and personal in a classroom at Frederick Douglass Junior High School. That experience changed my life. Also, from my Harlem days I have to thank the Clark family that Diane was a member of, she and all her siblings and her mother, father, and aunt Bebe who used to sing at the same church my mother attended, Greater Central Baptist Church. I would like to thank my younger brother James "Butch" Brown and his family, Bertha, Jessie, and Bobby for providing a much-needed sanctuary when my sister Marilyn left the planet.

The friends I had on the Lower East Side—especially Arturo Algarin and Donald Tilner—helped me navigate a transitional period of my life. Rene McLean, who is still my friend today, I met when we moved downtown. I have to thank Pat Mallory for giving me my first education in the politics of liberation. I'm grateful and thankful for the sanctuary Marty Koenig provided in his Friday night folk dance classes. Ellen Coaxum was the first person, outside of my own family, to offer a glimpse of what it would mean to create a family of my own. I'm eternally grateful that she brought her son Oba Henry Coaxum into my life.

My longtime friend Ramsey Ameen and I shared bright and beautiful moments together over the fifty years of our friendship. I do miss the fact that I can't pick up the phone and have those two-hour conversations with him. Another friend, whom I didn't know quite as long as Ramsey but whom I would have extended conversations with, is Louis Reyes Rivera. Through working on this manuscript, we became even closer. I'm very fortunate to have his grandchildren Rahjahn and Rayna as my music students at PS 3. They give me great joy!

I probably would never have thought to become a full-time educator without the experience of working at 1310 Atlantic Avenue. Rupert Vaughn was the person who brought me into that institution at another critical stage in my life. It was through my work at 1310 that I met Cal Massey, who became one of my first musical mentors. The late great trumpeter Arthur Williams was one of my college buddies from 1965 to 1967 at Queens College, along with Faruq Lamon Fenner who is still on this planet. Faruq used to play trumpet; now he plays CDs at City College of New York's WHCR on *Lamon's Jazz Break* on Sunday nights at eight. We share the same 1947 year of arrival on this planet.

I want to thank Reggie Workman and Jimmy Owens for cofounding the Collective Black Artists, an organization that has had a profound influence on my relationships in this music, namely those with Charles Brackeen and Hamiet Bluiett. Charles was influential in my working with the Melodic Art-Tet and Roger Blank as well as Ronnie Boykins, which of course led me to a long relationship with Sun Ra. Charles also introduced me to Ed Blackwell, the master drummer whom I had the opportunity to work with in three different periods of my life.

I will always feel a debt of gratitude to Sam and Beatrice Rivers for providing a forum where I could develop as an improviser and bandleader. Likewise, Rashied Ali presented opportunities for me and many other musicians to develop our abilities. Producers like Alan Douglas, Alan Ringel, and Larry Shengold gave me opportunities to record early on in my musical life, as did James DuBoise, Ali Abuwi, and Juma Sultan who created the recording studio at We. Saxophonist Kappo Umezu also provided me with one of my early recording dates, with Seikatsu Kojyo Iinkai.

For my career as a music educator, as a driver, and as a developing parent, I owe a great deal of thanks to Mickey Davidson. She gave me a gig working lecture demonstrations through Young Audiences, which eventually led to my working at Carnegie Hall. That in turn led to my working with the NYC Department of Education. I want to acknowledge Noal Cohen and Michael Fitzgerald for writing the book *Rat Race Blues: The Musical Life of Gigi Gryce*, which informed me about that artist and allowed me to find an option available to me as a music teacher in the public school system. I want to thank my sister Helen Salters for providing me the loan that allowed me to go back to school to earn my master's degree in education, and I must thank principal Beecher for hiring me at PS 3, and in fact rescuing me, when my future as an educator in the DOE was in jeopardy after my first year of teaching.

Carol Bourne, who was instrumental in providing me significant work at an important period of my life, must be acknowledged. I want to also acknowledge the work that Philippa Jordan did on the Silkheart recordings *Liquid Magic* and *Ahmed Abdullah and the Solomonic Quintet, featuring Charles Moffett*. She was responsible for two European tours. And as well, her work with the Sun Ra Arkestra, post–Sun Ra, was of significant importance. Viola Plummer and the December 12th Movement must be acknowledged for providing a home in Bedford-Stuyvesant where I could do the kind of creative booking that allowed Sistas' Place to develop an international reputation and become a historic landmark institution. Furthermore, I want to thank Viola Plummer for allowing me to be the Sistas' Place representative at the Central Brooklyn Jazz Consortium meetings in their critical developmental stages. I want to thank Bob Myers, formerly of Up Over Jazz Cafe, for many nights of hanging out and conversations that were so necessary in moving the music forward in Brooklyn.

Sistas' Place is connected to my experience of seeing John Coltrane's last New York concert in 1967 in Harlem. We begin our season every year around John Coltrane's Arrival Day and are located in the African American community of Bedford-Stuyvesant. That concert at Olatunji's Cultural Center began my query into how this music should be named. Calling it merely Jazz or avant-garde was insufficient. John Coltrane touched the spiritual essence of one's being. It was the epitome of Jazz: A Music of the Spirit!

In 2021, Ed Rhodes, the brilliant and recently deceased music scholar, informed me that in May 1967 the John Coltrane Quintet had also performed a concert at Baltimore's Left Bank Jazz Society. That was such valuable information because the intentionality evident in moving the music to where it could do the most service to humanity, most especially to the people who were most needy, the people of African descent, was obviously paramount in John Coltrane's last statements. I want to acknowledge Ed Rhodes for his genius in uncovering that bit of information, which I lived my whole life without knowing.

John Coltrane, Amiri Baraka, Louis Reyes Rivera, Monique Ngozi Nri, and Viola Plummer deserve great credit in my becoming a music director, thereby being able to formulate the thesis "Jazz: A Music of the Spirit." After the Teatro Manzoni concerts of 2005 and 2006 in Milan, Louis and I talked about how we could name and claim the phenomenon we saw evolving at Sistas' Place. Louis had a weekly show on WBAI called *Perspectives*, which ran during the afternoon for a couple of hours. After the Milan concerts, we began to have forums with people like Larry Ridley, Robin D.G. Kelley, Farah Jasmine Griffin, Akua Dixon, Monique, Salim, and others to come up with a workable thesis.

We were able to identify three male progenitors right off the bat—Duke Ellington, Sun Ra, and John Coltrane. Feminist that my wife is, she would not allow us to stay there. So, we also found three female progenitors who were no longer living and whose life's works exemplified the Music of the Spirit—Mary Lou Williams, Nina Simone, and Betty Carter. Each of these artists, through their work, represented principles we wanted younger musicians to develop in our effort to establish an art of liberation. As other artists left the planet, those we felt had made significant contributions were included. With the addition of Abbey Lincoln (Aminata Moseka), Jackie McLean, and Yusef Lateef, there are now nine progenitors

The founding racial order of the United States, which justified the enslavement of Africans by defining us as three-fifths of a human being, is challenged by the thesis Jazz: A Music of the Spirit, because creating a culture requires full human beings. The progenitors have nine things in common: (1) a transformative event has taken place in their lives, (2) they have an advanced understanding of improvisation, (3) they understand the concepts of leadership and originality, (4) they are dedicated and devoted to a higher power or higher cause beyond themselves, (5) they understand music as a vocation, and the need to teach it with passion, (6) they are activists on behalf of the communities from which they come, (7) they understand the principle of self-determination and ownership of the music they create, (8) they understand the need to build institutions supportive of artists who create Music of the Spirit, and (9) they understand the need to tie back to the African source of our art forms.

I must acknowledge Amiri Baraka again for making me aware that Louis Reyes Rivera was exactly the man for the job. When Amiri left the planet before he could write the foreword, I had asked Greg Tate, who had written the liner notes for the Diaspora Meets AfroHORN record. Greg also left the planet before he could write the foreword. With reluctance, because I had hoped the task was not jinxed, I asked Salim Washington. I want to acknowledge the years of friendship we have enjoyed since 1998.

**ACKNOWLEDGMENTS**

Francisco Mora-Catlett and I met through Sun Ra and we have been friends since 1975, when I joined the Sun Ra organization. Our collaborative work on the project we did in 2019 must be acknowledged.

There are two authors whose books I recently read and believe are vital reading for the times we are living in. One is Eddie S. Glaude Jr., who wrote *Begin Again: James Baldwin's America and Its Urgent Lessons for Our Own*. The other is Peniel E. Joseph, who wrote *The Third Reconstruction*. In the volumes named, these scholars, I believe, correctly analyze the times we are living in and the dangers we face.

Finally, I want to thank Marshall Allen, Elson Nascimento, Noël Scott, and all the musicians of the Sun Ra Arkestra for keeping the Spirit of the Music alive.

I have had many mentors in this Jazz: A Music of the Spirit but none as influential as Sun Ra. This book is certainly a dedication to his genius and the generosity of his time, musicianship, wisdom, and knowledge about the sacredness of our art form.

AHMED ABDULLAH joined the Sun Ra Arkestra as a trumpeter in 1974 and remained a member for more than twenty years. Born in Harlem in 1947, he became an important figure in the New York loft jazz movement, forming the group Abdullah in 1972, and going on to found the Melodic Art-Tet with Charles Brackeen, Ronnie Boykins, and Roger Blank in the early 1970s and The Group with Marion Brown, Billy Bang, Sirone, Fred Hopkins and Andrew Cyrille in 1986. Abdullah is a cofounder of the Central Brooklyn Jazz Consortium, has been the music director of Dianne McIntyre's Sounds in Motion Dance Company, and is currently music director at the historic venue Sistas' Place in Bedford-Stuyvesant, Brooklyn. He has been a music instructor at Carnegie Hall and Brooklyn Philharmonic Orchestra, and teaches at the New School for Social Research in Manhattan and an elementary school in central Brooklyn.

LOUIS REYES RIVERA (1945–2012) was a Puerto Rican poet from Brooklyn. Known as the "Dean of Nuyorican Poetics," he led creative writing workshops in community centers and prisons across New York; lectured on Latin and Black diasporic history and literature at New York colleges including Hunter, Boricua, Pratt, and Stony Brook; and was a leader in the 1969 student movement at CUNY, leading to the founding of its department of ethnic studies. Rivera was also a prolific editor, working on books such as John Oliver Killens's *Great Black Russian: A Novel on the Life and Times of Alexander Pushkin*, and a translator of works by Puerto Rican poets Clemente Soto Velez and Otto Rene Castillo. His own poetry collections include *Who Pays the Cost* (1977), *This One for You* (1983), and *Scattered Scripture* (1996), which received an award from the Latin American Writers Institute.

SALIM WASHINGTON is a saxophonist, composer, and scholar based in Durban, South Africa, where he is a professor at University of KwaZulu-Natal. He is a cofounder, with Farah Jasmine Griffin, of *Clawing at the Limits of Cool: Miles Davis, John Coltrane, and the Greatest Jazz Collaboration Ever* (2009) and a contributor to *Yellow Power, Yellow Soul: The Radical Art of Fred Ho* (2013).

A Strange Celestial Road:
My Time in the Sun Ra Arkestra
by Ahmed Abdullah
with Louis Reyes Rivera

Published by Blank Forms Editions

Artististic Director: Lawrence Kumpf
Managing Editor: Ciarán Finlayson
Editing: Leopold Froehlich
Copyediting: Polly Watson
Proofreading: Lily Bartle
Design: Alec Mapes-Frances
Printing: Oddi

First edition

Printed in Croatia

Blank Forms Editions is produced with
support from Robert Rauschenberg
Foundation, The Andy Warhol
Foundation for the Visual Arts, Agnes
Gund, and the founding Blank Forms
Publisher's Circle including Jane Hait
and Justin Beal, Christian Nyampeta,
Linden Renz, and Charline von Heyl
and Christopher Wool.

Blank Forms would like to thank Donna
Allen, Ed Cardoni, Pierre Crépon, John
Corbett, Fernanda Escalera, Gisela
Gamper, Ed Hazell, Clarice Lee, Evan
Neuhausen and Johan Kugelberg
of Boo-Hooray, Christopher Trent,
and Monique Ngozi Nri for their
generous support and assistance.

Cover: Sun Ra in Germany, 1988.

Front flap: Sun Ra at Philadelphia Jazz
Fest, 1978. Photo: Peter B. Blaikie.

Rear flap: Ahmed Abdullah in
Germany, 1984.

Image credits: Pages 286 and
292 © Desdemone Bardin/Estate
of Desdemone Bardin, courtesy
Sebastian Bardin Greenberg and
Jerome Greenberg; page 271,
courtesy Michael R. Bernstein from the
collection of Benny Kearse with special
thanks to Desiree Collins; page 297
© Christian Him; pages 257–68 © 2023
Marilyn Nance / Artists Rights Society
(ARS), New York; pages 245, 246,
273, 280, and 288 © Raymond Ross
Archives/CTSIMAGES.

ISBN 978-1-953691-18-7 (hardcover)
ISBN 978-1-953691-16-3 (paperback)

Blank Forms Editions
468 Grand St. Unit 3D
Brooklyn, NY, 11238